Keywords for Southern Studies

KEYWORDS FOR
Southern Studies

Edited by Scott Romine & Jennifer Rae Greeson

THE UNIVERSITY OF GEORGIA PRESS   ATHENS

© 2016 by the University of Georgia Press
Athens, Georgia 30602
www.ugapress.org
All rights reserved
Designed by Erin Kirk New
Set in Adobe Garamond Pro
Printed and bound by Sheridan Books, Inc.
The paper in this book meets the guidelines for
permanence and durability of the Committee on
Production Guidelines for Book Longevity of the
Council on Library Resources.

Most University of Georgia Press titles are
available from popular e-book vendors.

Printed in the United States of America
20   19   18   17   16   P   5   4   3   2   1

Library of Congress Cataloging-in-Publication Data

Names: Romine, Scott, editor. | Greeson, Jennifer Rae, editor.
Title: Keywords for southern studies / edited by Scott Romine and
Jennifer Rae Greeson.
Description: Athens : The University of Georgia Press, [2016] | Series: The
new southern studies | Includes bibliographical references and index.
Identifiers: LCCN 2015043948| ISBN 9780820340616 (hardcover : alka-
line paper) | ISBN 9780820349626 (paperback : alkaline paper) | ISBN
9780820349619 (e-book)
Subjects: LCSH: Southern States—Civilization.
Classification: LCC F216.2 .K49 2016 | DDC 975—dc23 LC record available
at http://lccn.loc.gov/2015043948

Contents

Keywords for Southern Studies

Introduction   JENNIFER RAE GREESON AND SCOTT ROMINE

Any collection that aims, as this one does, to represent the upheaval and diversity of a field that is remaking itself must confront at the outset the difficulties posed by that upheaval and diversity. What *is* "southern studies" today, well into the twenty-first century, in the age of the global-superpower United States? Whatever it is, we think it is mimed by the form of this volume, which does not presume to present a canon, a comprehensive account, or a curated catalog that demarcates the contours of a stable, shared field. Instead, this book contains an idiosyncratic collection of essays on keywords that individual scholars have chosen as particularly critical for the project of southern studies as each of them personally understands it. The result is a collection that is contingent and fragmentary, but capacious enough to hold side by side various disciplinary and theoretical approaches, generational affinities, and intellectual perspectives on an arena of inquiry whose boundaries are constantly being renegotiated.

It is in this very indeterminacy and flexibility that southern studies is becoming an important model for other interdisciplinary intellectual enterprises, perhaps particularly American studies writ large. We realize only too well that just a generation ago southern studies marched obstinately in the rearguard of American studies both politically and methodologically; while we are not prepared to claim that it has leapfrogged fully to the vanguard—indeed the unevenness of the shift is evidenced across this volume—we do believe that its ongoing radical reconfiguration demands broadening notice and broadening participation. At this moment, in this volume, "southern studies" emerges through a process of scholarly definition from the bottom up rather than from the top down. Contributors approach the field through the lens of assumptions and possibilities afforded by single critical terms, rather than by making or subscribing to broad pronouncements about the object or method of the field of study.[1]

Indeed, it is the almost universally agreed-upon impossibility of making such broad pronouncements that is the hallmark of southern studies today, for it has been reconfigured as an enterprise whose object has become irrevocably obscure. What is southern studies *studying*? The self-evident answer would seem to be the U.S. South, the self-evident corollary of which is that the U.S. South is neither solid nor exceptional. It lacks an essence (and therefore cannot be known in essentialist terms), a polity, and clearly defined boundaries. Such, at least, are some of the echoing premises of contemporary studies of what has proven to be a slippery object of interrogation.

In a parable told by the Buddha, blind men are brought together to examine an elephant. The results are well known: each grabs a different part and reports a different result. The Buddha then offers his lesson: scholars (the less-remembered subject of the parable) are quarrelsome and disputatious, not to be trusted for an accurate depiction of reality. Whatever its value as an assessment of scholarly temperaments, the parable makes the commonsensical assumption that there's an elephant at the other end of scholarly inquiry: a thing to be known—ideally, at any rate—in ways that are comprehensive and accurate.

The field of southern studies, however, seems uncertain of the existence of the elephant, and in some instances actively interested in its demise. In a 2008 review, for example, Leigh Anne Duck calls for a "Southern studies without 'The South'" as a potentially "enlightening" mode of "exiting the realm of our most basic assumptions."[2] For scholars such as Duck, the problem with "the South" is precisely the assumptions that have accumulated around it, the conceptual baggage generated by earlier generations of scholarship and popular belief that, arguably, has served to obscure as much as to clarify. As Michael O'Brien has observed in his influential *Idea of the American South* (1979), the South itself can be viewed in one of two ways: either as a "solid and integrated social reality about which there have been disparate ideas" or "as an idea, used to organize and comprehend disparate facts of social reality." Opting against the elephant, O'Brien approaches the South as "centrally an intellectual perception . . . which has served to comprehend and weld an unintegrated social reality," observing that the idea of the South "has secured such a hold on the American mind that it is a postulate, to which the facts of American society must be bent, and no longer a deduction."[3] Although not entirely unprecedented, O'Brien's wedge between the idea of the South and the social reality it purported to represent would prove enabling to later scholars interested in the production, maintenance, and usage of the South as, variously, an invention, an imagined geography, a geographic fantasy, or (in Duck's terminology) "the nation's region."

For many contemporary scholars, the present slipperiness of the U.S. South constitutes a hard-won triumph over the positivist certainties of an early generation of scholarship that, for reasons both historical and institutional, tended to position the South as "Uncle Sam's other province." As Matthew D. Lassiter and Joseph Crespino observe in *The Myth of Southern*

Exceptionalism, "Liberal historians in the postwar decades called for a distinctive southern history based not on a set of empirical differences between region and nation but, rather, on the presumed divergence of a collective southern *identity* from national *myths* and American *ideals*."[4] For other fields as well, presumptions of southern exceptionalism served as methodological anchors. In a postwar academy flush with resources, southern literary studies coalesced around a set of ostensibly southern senses (of place, community, family, "the concrete") and Faulknerian formulas ("You would have to be born there," "I don't hate it!" "The past is never dead. It's not even past"). Sociological studies of the U.S. South, meanwhile, became institutionalized in the decade in which Franklin Delano Roosevelt identified the region as the nation's "No. 1 economic problem."

Indeed, one solution to any "southern problem"—of which there have been many, from the founding to the present—is to declare it a *southern* problem, not a national one. Imagined Souths have been used to *contain* problems ranging from poverty and racial oppression to cultural backwardness and religious fanaticism. But if some monolithic fantasies of the U.S. South have trended toward abjection, others have headed in a romantic direction, imagining the South as a land not of poverty but of resistance to materialism; not of racial oppression but of benign paternalism and noblesse oblige; not of cultural backwardness but of tradition, piety, and bucolic agrarianism. Although scholarly methodologies have tempered their extremes, it is probably fair to say that such fantasies have exerted a persistent force on the study of the U.S. South that, until recent years, has been predicated on difference, especially difference within the nation.

As the solid object of study has receded from us—indeed, as scholars have pushed away from it—its conceptual underpinning has come into focus. "The South" exists only as one side of an implicit binary ("North"/"South") and thus exists always in implied relation—usually antithesis—to what is outside it. Many of the essays collected in this volume seek to disrupt this binary conceptual structure, though contributors use a variety of tactics. Some expose the structure itself and ask how it works and what it is good for; others pursue the multivalent lines of relation between "the South" and terms other than its opposite. The keywords in this volume, then, represent not merely ways to think *about* the U.S. South but also ways of thinking *into* and *through* and *beyond* it. The question at issue has evolved from "what is southern studies studying?" to "what does southern studies *do*?"

As the essayists in this volume strip away the mystifying assumption of difference or otherness, they show us what southern studies can do. They train our attention on regimes of white supremacy, labor discipline, and what Colin Dayan has resonantly termed "servile law"—American regimes exemplified by, though never confined to, the southern United States. They illuminate the residues and persistences of interacting peoples and places, markets and material cultures.[5] They interrogate new approaches that have broadened the archive and conceptual scope of southern (and American) studies. They investigate the structures of feeling that continue to consolidate and dissolve various Souths, remapping the gap between "real place" and space as it is configured affectively.

As the contributors to this volume exceed the binaristic relation that underpins "southernness," they uncover multiplying, interconnecting webs of relation. They show us that to do southern studies is almost always to work interdisciplinarily: to work in and across a field of intersections and sutures between a geographic, social, economic designation and the products of culture that engage it or something within it. They also show us that to do southern studies is to work transnationally, for beginning from a construct that is defined geographically but not politically invites or requires troubling traditional geopolitical borders by thinking across, within, and between them.

This geopolitical frame brings us to a final critical consonance among the essays in this volume. Many of them share a note of urgency, an urgency directed not toward the loss of the object of study or the ambiguous state of the field but rather toward the present moment. Americans today stand as citizens of a unilateral global superpower without—from the perspectives of many involved in this work—possessing an honest or realistic sense of what the United States is, what it has been, and thus what it could become. This ignorance, whether willful or not, is underwritten by the persistence of monolithic fantasies of the U.S. South—fantasies that continue to inflect the cultural production of space in the United States in this era of global unilateralism, producing feedback loops that exceed (as they always have) the borders of the nation. Doing southern studies is undoing the monolith by—in the words of one essayist in this volume, Shirley Elizabeth Thompson—"pursu[ing] a radical interdisciplinarity" forged from "critical and contingent methods and theories" and "more precisely articulating the disruptive knowledge of subalterns." Doing southern studies is unmasking and refusing the binary thinking—"North"/"South," nation/South, First World/Third World, self/other—that postcolonial studies has taught us is the most damaging rhetorical structure of empire.[6] Doing southern studies is thinking geographically, thinking historically, thinking relationally, thinking about power, thinking about justice, thinking back.

NOTES

1. The organization of this collection follows this logic. Although our section headings describe broad family resemblances between terms, neither they nor the "keywords" themselves are intended to approach taxonomic precision. For similar reasons, we have avoided—although some contributors have not—the term "New Southern Studies," which carries, at least implicitly, the promise of a coherent and distinctive effort but whose constitutive features remain contested.

2. Duck, "Southern Nonidentity," 329.

3. O'Brien, *Idea of the American South*, xxi, xxii.

4. Lassiter and Crespino, introduction to *Myth of Southern Exceptionalism*, 8.

5. See C. Dayan, "Servile Law" and *Law Is a White Dog*.

6. Particularly Said, *Orientalism*, and Suleri, *Rhetoric of English India*.

PART I   Regimes

HOUSTON A. BAKER JR.

Incarceration

There is a United States northern narrative of incarceration. It is a story highlighted by expressive traditions that foreground legacies of Puritan and Quaker spirituality. Puritans migrating to the New World envisioned themselves as architects of a "City on the Hill" that would serve as a beacon and moral compass for Old World redemption. They conceived themselves as anchoritic "sinners in the hands of an angry God," a God who, if provoked, would launch a fierce "Quarrel with New England." The Jeremiadic Puritan imaginary features perilous ocean voyages and vigorous holy assaults by Puritans on "savage" Native Americans. There are also holy errands into the wilderness to hear God's voice and receive his deliverance. From the first third to the middle of the nineteenth century, such fervid theocratic visions of mission, conquest, and salvation yielded to—or perhaps more aptly, "morphed" into—secular analogues. Religion, transcendentalism, urban industrialism, and bureaucratic state apparatuses converged in new formations.

Monastic solitude transformed into Ralph Waldo Emerson's and Henry David Thoreau's transcendental and Walden Pond wisdom on the Over-Soul. Protestant gospels of faith and work, sin and penitence, were casuistically transformed into a carceral system that created, and then punished, social pariahs. Gallows and whipping posts were moved indoors, ending theocratic state-sanctioned spectacles of punishment in the public square. Demographics that had been civilly excluded from the republic's founding were officially criminalized and incarcerated. The criminalized were stripped of personhood and cast into tight spaces of labor and confinement. Almshouses, orphanages, madhouses, poorhouses (as Thomas Jefferson's *Notes on the State of Virginia* make clear) were all historically parts of America's colonizing polity. But like the instrumentalities of punishment such as public whipping posts and pillories, those criminalized for "difference" such as madness or *insufficiency* were hauled inside. They were banished from the sight and rights of civil society. No institution was more iconic with respect to the plight of what might be called the "republican damned" than the penitentiary.

Deemed "penitents" by Quaker protocols of punishment and rehabilitation, penitentiary inmates were deprived of all human contact. Absolute solitude was the prescription from their warders. Secular solitary confinement would lead the condemned on a journey of regret, remorse, and redemption. It was assumed that the journey also required profitable penitent labor. The profit from such labor would not, however, go to the penitent but would be confiscated to enhance the coffers of the state. Pennsylvania's—the "Quaker State's"—legislature approved architectural plans and financing for the Eastern State Penitentiary in 1831. The penitentiary was constructed during succeeding years on eleven acres located just outside Philadelphia. Hence, what might be termed "northern, republican incarceration" was established less than a morning's walk from Independence Hall, birthplace of the Declaration of Independence and the Constitution of the United States of America.

With its symmetrical, radiating, glass-roofed cellblocks and central guard tower, Eastern State Penitentiary was a model Panopticon. The eighteenth-century philosopher Jeremy Bentham first conceived of an architectural space that featured a way of viewing all inmates from a central guardhouse or tower. The panoptically incarcerated would always be under surveillance. The first prisoner to enter Eastern State Penitentiary was a black man convicted of burglary and sentenced to two years of "confinement in solitude with labor." Eastern State, as its name denotes, was part of the state apparatus of punishment. Its operation demanded taxonomies of belonging and exclusion that served state interests. A phenomenology of inside and outside was indispensable to its project.

The French philosopher Michel Foucault persuasively analyzes in *Discipline and Punish* and *Madness and Civilization* how the birth and effective management of the modern state demands sites of incarceration. Asylums, jails, and prisons are placeholders—negations of the civil habitus meant to separate *in*-mates from the sociality of life outside. Such sites are meant visibly—in the eye of the law—to differentiate the *in*-sane and criminal from the prudent and rational man of the law. Foucault's wisdom might translate in the idiom of everyday life as the following hypothetical statement: "We know we are innocent, law-abiding, sane, and blessed *citizens* at a glance. We have only to note that we are not restricted by: narrow cells, forbidding stone walls, razor-wire barricades, psychiatric-ward invisibility, and maximum-security isolation. We are not 'in-mates.'"

Nineteenth-century French commissioners such as Gustave de Beaumont and Alexis de Tocqueville traveled to America to observe the marvels of the northern carceral regime at Eastern State Penitentiary. English novelist Charles Dickens did the same; he left with a dim view of what discipline and punishment—U.S. northern urban style—augured for man's humanity to man. Tocqueville pondered what "republican carcerality" portended for the fate of the penitent and the larger society. He wrote: "It is well known that most individuals on whom the criminal law inflicts punishment have been unfortunate before they become guilty."[1] Structural conditions, in short, breed insufficiency, harmful associations, and criminal behavior. Still, the complete-solitary regimen of Eastern State Penitentiary seemed calculated to drive inmates mad. Tocqueville felt that New York's Auburn State Penitentiary (1819) offered a model of incarceration that was more conducive to rehabilitation leading to a restored citizenship. Inmates at Auburn State dined and labored in congregation, though also in silence. Its cells were tiny spaces intended principally for detention and sleeping. Like Eastern State, Auburn was a profit-accruing venture with no significant returns to the inmates who produced the profit.

Tocqueville's sense of the structures and implications of the carceral are analogous to Foucault's observations. Those "marked" by signs of a reputed religious condemnation (e.g., born "black" like the scriptural Ham) or burdened by economic misfortune (e.g., conceived in poverty) are the socially damned who are criminalized into incarceration. To maintain civil society and the content of its privileged rulers, staff, and administration, it is deemed necessary to create a damned caste that is "convicted in the womb."

There is a construction and account of U.S. history that makes clear the inalienable conjunction between the Constitution of the United States of America and the proximate architectures of American incarceration. The Constitution is rife with taxonomic exclusions and anatomical chimeras (e.g., "three-fifths" of a person). It has been remarked that when Tocqueville toured the United States, the only fully franchised citizens were white men. The most privileged of that white male demographic were rich by financial account and pseudoaristocratic by self-proclamation.

Perhaps none were more "pseudo" in their aristocratic protestations and wealthy in their accounts than large plantation owners of the American South. Hence, the Constitution had to be hammered out in terms that would satisfy both a northern narrative of *nationhood* and the tale of an immensely wealthy and irrepressible southern sphere. That southern sphere's immense profits derived from the labor-in-bondage that was American chattel slavery. Statesman James Madison observed that southern slavery—the incarceration of black laborers by the millions in abject plantation servitude—formed the "line of distinction" between northern and southern delegates at Independence Hall. The Constitutional Congress that convened at Independence Hall—well in advance of Tocqueville's tour—was, not surprisingly, constituted by an all-white, male-bonding exercise in compromise and exclusion. The convention arrived at common cause not so much by a fierce commitment to liberty "for all" as through a mutual northern and southern devotion to a plutocratic autonomy and ideological cohesion predicated on racial and gender exclusion.

We know the success of the Independence Hall constitutional project from its boundless and continuing legacy. It guaranteed untold inherited wealth and privilege for countless white American generations. Madison's "line of distinction" was, ultimately, a demarcation between the privileged white male rich and the populous and punished damned "other." Ultimately Madison's line was the economic *bottom line* of plutocratic self-interest. The final draft of the Constitution approved by the convention is marked by the delegates' self-interested fictions and denials. Women are granted no suffrage. Native Americans are designated beyond the pale of settled civilization. Black slaves are legally fictionalized as creatures never seen: three-fifths of a man. Specifically, Articles I and IV of the Constitution and their clauses mandate the following: continuation of the African slave trade to the United States until 1808; apportionment of representation among the several states on the basis of a definition of black slaves as "three-fifths of all other persons" (three-fifths clause). There is also the "fugitive slave" provision mandating that escaped slaves must, by law, be returned to their owners.

Calculated deletion of the word "slavery" from the Constitution by the delegates in no way compromises the truth and the historically verifiable record that slavery was written into the founding legal document of the United States. The national legal "bright line" was constituted and conditioned by an order of incarceration complementary to the state apparatus of penitence and penitentiaries. Chattel slavery, through constitutional compromise, exclusion, and fiction, became a template for American incarceration. Such slavery was the very engine of plantation production in the Middle and Deep South of the republic. Commerce, labor, social stigmatization, expropriation of revenue, and punishment on a grand scale are foundational in the U.S. southern narrative of incarceration.

In *The Nation's Region: Southern Modernism, Segregation, and U.S. Nationalism*, scholar Leigh Anne Duck astutely analyzes how the South's imputed backwardness and refusal to "modernize" have served to reinforce a dubious "regionalist" definition of the nation. The telos of "regionalization" is to differentiate—putatively in the "national interest"—the abject, backward id formations of the South from the supposed rational and progressive modernization of the North. Economically grounded in plantation slavery, the South's colossal wealth produced by servile labor and brutal punishment is something on the order of an "outside embarrassment" to northern religious protestations and boasts of "liberty for all." The North's penitentiaries hide punishment out of sight.

13

A myth of *regionalism* is not, of course, sustained and maintained solely by those who deploy it negatively and by projection to boost their positive image of the nation. Once crafted, as Duck and others have demonstrated, those who are vilified by myth may very well take up at least the *exceptionalism* of the myth as a point of pride. The South, that is to say, in both memory and present articulation, can proclaim its most redolently abject formations such as plantation chattel slavery a proud and defining institution, ordained by God and sanctioned by the laws of man. However, any memorial romance of the South's "old plantations" bathed in southern charm would seem immediately to fade before the term "prison farm."

The historical backstory of the South's agricultural economies of labor and profit forms a *longue durée* commencing with the "gang production" of sugar as a cash crop in the Mediterranean. With European navigational successes such as the fifteenth-century voyages past the Cape of Bojodar financed by Portugal's Prince Henry the Navigator, the West Coast of Africa became accessible for trade, expropriation of gold, and the securing of African bodies for labor. Sugar and other forms of plantation production (tobacco, rice, cotton) demanded monumental numbers of laborers in order to turn their greatest profits. The African slave trade produced such labor.

In minimalist description, one might say that in the transatlantic African slave trade, European and American trade goods and firearms were bartered in Africa for human bodies to be carried to African coastal barracoons or prisons. After the captives were factored or brokered to slave-ship captains for trade goods, they were packed into the dark holds of ships to endure the Middle Passage to New World plantations. From *The Interesting Narrative of the Life of Olaudah Equiano, or, Gustavus Vassa, The African* (1745) comes the following description of the "hold":

> The closeness of the place, and the heat of the climate, added to the number in the ship, which was so crouded [sic] that each had scarcely room to turn himself, almost suffocated us. This produced copious perspiration, so that the air soon became unfit for respiration, from a variety of loathsome smells, and brought sickness amongst the slaves, of which many died, thus falling victims to the improvident avarice, as I may call it, of their purchasers. This wretched situation was again aggravated by the galling chains, now become

insupportable, and the filth of the necessary tubs, into which the children fell, and were almost suffocated.[2]

The Middle Passage could last as long as four months. Ships' captains used "tight packing" methods—taking on hundreds of shackled African bodies, each allotted no more space than the length and breadth of a body on its side in a fetal position—to maximize profits. If there can ever be such a situation as "normal incarceration," the Middle Passage certainly constitutes "X" or "Extreme Incarceration." In *The Slave Ship: A Human History*, Marcus Rediker describes the overwhelming violence and constraints of the slave ships to which the "hold" was privy:

> The slave ship was a strange and potent combination of war machine, mobile prison, and factory. Loaded with cannon and possessed of extraordinary destructive power, the ship's war-making capacity could be turned against other European vessels. . . . The slave ship also contained a war within, as the crew (now prison guards) battled slaves (prisoners), the one training its guns on the others, who plotted escape and insurrection. Sailors also "produced" slaves within the ship as factory, doubling their economic value as they moved them from a market on the eastern Atlantic to one on the west. . . . The ship-factory also produced "race." At the beginning of the voyage, captains hired a motley crew . . . who would on the coast of West Africa, become "white men." At the beginning of the Middle Passage, captains loaded on board the vessel a multi-ethnic collection of Africans, who would, in the American port, become "black people" or a "negro race."[3]

The carceral economics of slave ships were driven by global mercantile capitalism and informed at every turn by a dehumanizing regime of racial terror. Such economics were forebears and models for the southern prison farms romanticized as "plantations" of chivalric courtesy and manners. Degraded by captivity and the abjection of the ship's "hold" and above-deck terror, Africans shackled into circuits of Atlantic slavery suffered a mortality rate in the millions. They were lost to fire, storm, disease, sadism, suicide, and murder. The transport of the prison ship and its discipline were exemplars of the dehumanization that the Martiniquan statesman and poet Aimé Césaire calls "thingification." In *Discourse on Colonialism*, Césaire writes: "No human contact, but relations of domination and submission which turn the colonizing man into a classroom monitor, an army sergeant, a prison guard, a slave driver, and the indigenous man into an instrument of production. . . . My turn to state an equation: colonization = 'thingification.'"[4] Enslaved Africans in the American South were deemed "chattel"—movable *property*. What comes together not *in* southern incarceration but *as* southern incarceration is chattel slavery in plantation economies of racial terror.

In such economies, the forlorn jail is little more than an allied instrument of the plantocracy's power. In some accounts, such as Jonathan Walker's *Trial and Imprisonment of Jonathan Walker, at Pensacola, Florida, for Aiding Slaves to Escape from Bondage* (1845), the jail is a surrogate structure, designed as a secondary terror station for the paddling, whipping, and derogation of slaves accused of behavior insubordinate to the planter class. Slave owners' power and authority were deemed absolute. Their physicians, ministers, lawyers, judges, overseers—the entire administrative cast of apparatchiks in the world that the slaveholders made—were bent fully to the will of the masters. They invented diseases, sculpted slaveholding homiletics and apologetics, and, most importantly, crafted a body of law designed to make the enslaved stand in fear.

One outcome of the *state* dominance and subjugation of the plantocracy was the accumulation of untold southern slaves and the production of almost inconceivable wealth. More than 40 percent of African captives who entered the economic arrangements of the British mainland colonies arrived at the port of Charleston. Savannah's wharfs came to set the global value of cotton. For Frederick Douglass, such accumulation and power amounted to fiduciary piracy writ large and at the price of carceral horror. Douglass has but one name for the nation's constitutional endorsement of southern economics: "The Prison House of Slavery." The South constructed itself as a carceral state, one predicated on the "thingification" of race. But not without northern complicity designed to move white wealth and privilege meters upward. The conjugation and conjuring of the law (especially constitutional law) required to make the U.S. South a "prison house of slavery" was written *as law* at the Constitutional Convention. The Constitution and its additions and evacuations through the years—especially as they pertain to race—have been vastly determinate in the U.S. dynamics of law, criminal justice, and incarceration. In *The Law Is a White Dog: How Legal Rituals Make and Unmake Persons*, scholar Colin Dayan writes:

> If we turn for a moment to the definition of the slave as a *person in law*, we realize just how strange legal logic had to be in order to birth this being. For this piece of property became a person only in committing a crime. The crime proved consciousness, mind, and will. No longer disabled in law, the slave could be recognized as a thinking thing. He was treated as a person, capable of committing acts for which he might be punished as a criminal. It is quite possible if we push this reasoning further, that all definitions of personhood, whether applying to a free citizen or a slave, rest ultimately on the ability to blame oneself.[5]

Dayan compellingly analyzes how legal fiction, magical thinking, and tortured logic serve the carceral ends of power in one instance through a discussion of *Ruffin v. Commonwealth of Virginia* (1871). Woody Ruffin, an incarcerated black felon, murdered a white man while working in chains on the Chesapeake and Ohio Railroad. He was sentenced to hang but entered an appeal. His counsel based the appeal on the fact that Ruffin had been denied his Sixth Amendment rights of an impartial jury and a speedy trial. Justice J. Christian ruled for the court that since Ruffin was a convict and had been so at the time of the murder, he was in fact "civilly dead" and thus possessed no rights guaranteed by the Constitution to freemen and citizens. Ruffin, as a slave of the state, was civilly dead. Dayan writes: "The prison walls circumscribe the prisoner in a [legal] fiction that, in extending the bounds of servitude, became the basis for the negation of rights, thus reconciling constitutional strictures with slavery."[6]

At the end of the Civil War, there was great jubilation as more than four million slaves in the South were freed. Their new freedom was putatively guaranteed by the Thirteenth, Fourteenth, and Fifteenth Amendments to the Constitution. The amendments respectively mandated: abolition of slavery and involuntary servitude; the guarantee of citizenship, due process, and equal protection under the law; and the right to vote. In any analysis of U.S. incarceration, it is the Thirteenth Amendment that provides firsthand evidence of the coextensiveness of the law and American incarceration. The Thirteenth Amendment reads: "Neither slavery nor involuntary servitude, *except as a punishment for crime whereof the party shall have been duly convicted*, shall exist within the United States, or any place subject to their jurisdiction" (my emphases). One might say the phrase "except as a punishment for crime" is veritably the *hold* of the law. It provides a gaping maw, a semantic "open hole" that is not unlike the opinion of Justice Christian in *Ruffin v. Commonwealth*. For what constitutes "crime," "conviction," or "punishment" in the United States but the bizarre hermeneutics of America's always already racialized justice and its magistrates?

The South's white supremacists and vigilante factions at the end of the Civil War believed that a great crime had been committed against their regional interests and peculiar institutions by a "War of Northern Aggression." They meant to take back their southern way of life at the end of smoking gun barrels or by gruesome spectacle lynchings on landscapes where black men's mutilated bodies swayed at the end of a rope. Violent white terrorists specialized in burning crosses and torching black dwellings. Their acts were seldom deemed "crimes" by either North or South. There was no unified call, that is to say, across "regions" for a national or executive offensive to restore "law and order" to black American life.

The wave of violence that beset black freedom was, of course, not without parallel. The entire South in its dimensions of plantation power and endorsement of a carceral black slavery was the essence of unloosed white violence against the black body. Rather than a residual violence, the unleashed white vigilantism of the postbellum era was merely an avatar, indeed an arriviste doppelgänger of the normal state of southern society.

Establishment of the Federal Bureau of Freedmen, Refugees, and Abandoned Lands was meant to institute Reconstruction. Reconstruction was supposed to carry the force of law into territories of white supremacist violence. Only the presence of federal troops on the ground in the South, however, gave Reconstruction a glimmer of a chance at success. When federal troops were withdrawn from the South as a condition of a national presidential election compromise (Hayes-Tilden, 1877), white violence reigned unchecked, and white supremacy was the über-law of the South.

One might say that on the day after the surrender at Appomattox in April 1865, the legal and carceral agents of the South commenced to create a set of regulations transparent in their intent, which was to criminalize and thrust back into virtual slavery the black southern millions just granted freedom by the war amendments. There were "pig laws," "Black Codes," "antiloitering laws," and other laws targeting black "surliness" and black petty larceny. But there were no Eastern State Penitentiary emulations in the South. The South had relied on plantation protocols of violence and terror for disciplining blacks. The absence of southern prisons was due, at least in part, to the South's aversion to the federal state supervision that marked, say, the Quaker State's penitentiary organization and operation. The South's postbellum substitute for the carceral prison house of slavery was a system of convict leasing.

Blacks convicted of a *criminal offense* (e.g., stealing a pig, being without money, whistling at a white woman) were not to be housed or warehoused "inside." They were, instead, hired out by the law to public and private industries to "work off" their fines and sentences. Scholar David Oshinsky's striking monograph *Worse than Slavery: Parchman Farm and the Ordeal of Jim Crow Justice* offers a persuasive account of the ways in which the South conspired to dragoon black bodies into the project of rebuilding the infrastructure of a war-torn land. Contractors "leased" black prisoners from the states in partial payment of the *convicteds'* assigned fines. The contractors could work their leased property brutally for the duration of their sentences.

Black chain gangs building roads and laying railroad tracks. Prison farm black convicts generating enough revenue to pay an entire state's education budget. Black convicts transported in barred cars designed for animals to clear southern swamps. Black convicts laboring in turpentine camps and logging camps providing profitable revenues for their white "lessors." All of these were the "incarcerated." They were chained to a system of convict lease labor no less draconian in its deprivations and terror than the transatlantic slave trade that ensnared Olaudah Equiano.

Convict leasing was worse than slavery because it was cheaper and nearly maintenance free. To lease black labor, the lessor paid a pittance and had no vested protective interest in the welfare of the laborers. By contrast, a slave from the Charleston auction blocks might cost a master as much as eleven thousand dollars. By rational choice, the purchaser would be at least minimally cautious about the health and welfare of his purchase. By contrast, working leased convicts to death and punishing them brutally to accrue greater profits was economic pragmatism in the convict lease system of southern incarceration. Then came *Plessy v. Ferguson* (1896) as a further southern instantiation of racialized and procrustean offices of U.S. law.

In 1892, a light-complexioned man of creole descent by the name of Homer Plessy boarded the East Louisiana Railroad and took a seat in the white car. Plessy was a participant in a black civil rights organization's plan to test and contest the Louisiana Separate Car Act, which segregated blacks from whites on public carriers (not unlike Rosa Parks half a century later in Montgomery, Alabama). Plessy sat in the white section, identified himself as black, and was arrested. His case eventually made its way to the Supreme Court of the United States, where his lawyers (like Willie Ruffin's counsel) argued that Plessy's arrest was a violation of rights granted by constitutional amendments. In the Supreme Court's ruling in *Plessy*, the sophistic point of legal reach was the distinction *not* between a "felon" civilly dead and a free man but rather between "legal equality" as stated by the Fourteenth Amendment and "equality based upon color," that is, "social equality." Supreme Court justice John Harlan dissented from this majority reading of matters because he knew the resultant doctrine of "separate but equal" would constitute a disastrous legal fiction. For the court's majority ruled that as long as there are "equal facilities" for blacks, it is proper to keep everyday southern life safe from a "commingling of the races." This was the infamous birth of "separate but equal" as an acceptable legal standard. *Plessy* marks the birth of Jim Crow and, in sad retrospect, the Supreme Court's and highest law of the land's endorsement of white supremacy and black subjugation as the national legal norm.

It is not without merit to argue that the horrors of the "Scottsboro Boys" case and its iterated trials of the 1930s could have happened nowhere other than amid the white supremacist venues and legal protocols of Jim Crow and its carceral imperatives. The Scottsboro case involved nine black boys who hopped a freight train from Chattanooga to Memphis, Tennessee, in 1931. They were pulled off the train in Scottsboro, Alabama, and two young white women who had also hopped the freight accused the boys of gang rape. There were eight trials, only one of which resulted in exoneration, and then only of the four youngest boys on the condition that they leave the state of Alabama forever. Scholar Dan Carter in *Scottsboro: A Tragedy of the American South* brilliantly analyzes all facets of the Scottsboro proceedings and demonstrates that the boys were known to be innocent from the outset. There was no physical or forensic evidence of rape. Though their plight became a cause célèbre for an international community of activists (especially those rallied by the Communist Party of the United States), the unexonerated Scottsboro boys languished in jail for decades. It was known that no rape occurred. But the law guaranteed that *all* the Scottsboro boys lived torturously and died tragically.

Michelle Alexander's comprehensive and perfectly crafted book *The New Jim Crow: Mass Incarceration in the Age of Colorblindness* (2010) provides the brilliant grid of connections that add detail and fullness to the foregoing account of incarceration. Alexander takes pains to demonstrate how, ironically, southern jails and even the prison enclave Parchman Farm became sites of black nonviolent resistance during the Civil Rights Movement. She analyzes the effects of the prison rights reform efforts of the 1960s and 1970s and fully explicates how U.S. politics have always been and continue to be utterly contingent upon race, depersonalization, and economic profit. Her felicitously argued condemnation of the politics of "law and order," the "war on crime," the "war on drugs," and "get tough on crime" from the deregulating 1980s to the present day establishes unequivocally causal links between caste, law, and mass incarnation in America.

The essence of Jim Crow is the legal creation of a black underclass—a separate and indisputably unequal caste. When *Brown v. Board of Education* overturned *Plessy*, there was jubilation akin to post-Appomattox jubilee. The ensuing years, however, brought little legal "remedy" and, in fact, bled into the cataclysmic white violence of southern resistance to civil rights. Civil rights and voting rights acts became law, but enforcement was often tepid. By the end of the 1960s, "law and order" had become the rallying cry of the White House and its chief executive, Richard Nixon. Postindustrialism and the export of the U.S. manufacturing sector overseas for corporate profit were legalized by the courts and supported by the corporate plutocracy—northern and southern. A post-Fordist world had no civil or economic space or tolerance for those who were not skilled or educated enough to join a U.S. service economy. A prison-industrial complex to remove the excess and residue of past industrial good times was welcomed.

The United States today holds under the surveillance and discipline of its prisons, jails, Immigration and Nationality Act "holding" facilities, and parole and probation offices more than seven million people at any given hour of any given day. The largest prison populations and the highest incidence of executions nationally are in the southern states of the United States, leading some to talk of "prison slavery," echoing Frederick Douglass's "Prison House of Slavery." Michelle Alexander's cause and call is for a social movement to abolish the offices of mass incarceration in the United States. If a raison d'être is demanded, one might call to mind Colin Dayan's caution that "penal incapacitation in its many forms is accompanied by fabulous taxonomies that reword distinctions between human and inhuman, predator and victim, virtue and vice, even flesh and spirit. . . . Law words and legal fictions work wonders on the commonsense world of experience outside the courtroom. In the process of defining harm, assessing damages, or assessing blame, legal reasoning sometimes deforms the individual in its purview, or gives them a negative status in the civil order."[7] In a sense far more than metaphorical, the law may be not only a white dog but also a ghost ship of the transatlantic slave trade.

NOTES

1. Tocqueville and Beaumont, *On the Penitentiary System*, 164.
2. Equiano, *Interesting Narrative of Olaudah Equiano*, 37–38.
3. Rediker, *Slave Ship*, 9–10.
4. Césaire, *Discourse on Colonialism*, 42.
5. C. Dayan, *Law Is a White Dog*, 89.
6. Ibid., 61.
7. Ibid., 112, 205.

SUGGESTIONS FOR FURTHER READING

Alexander, Michelle. *The New Jim Crow: Mass Incarceration in the Age of Colorblindness.* New York: New Press, 2010.

Baker, Houston A., Jr. *Turning South Again: Re-Thinking Modernism/Re-Reading Booker T.* Durham, N.C.: Duke University Press, 2001.

Blackmon, Douglas A. *Slavery by Another Name: The Re-enslavement of Black Americans from the Civil War to World War II*. New York: Anchor, 2009.

Foucault, Michel. *Discipline and Punish: The Birth of the Prison*. New York: Vintage, 1995.

———. *Madness and Civilization: A History of Insanity in the Age of Reason*. New York: Vintage, 1988.

Oshinsky, David M. *Worse than Slavery: Parchman Farm and the Ordeal of Jim Crow*. New York: Free Press, 1997.

Smith, Caleb. *The Prison and the American Imagination*. New Haven, Conn.: Yale University Press, 2011.

Tarter, Michele Lise, and Richard Bell, eds. *Buried Lives: Incarcerated in Early America*. Athens: University of Georgia Press, 2012.

Plantation

MATTHEW PRATT GUTERL

In the simplest of terms, we usually imagine that a plantation is a uniquely southern thing: a big, antiquated farm, set in the land of moonlight and magnolias, peopled by large numbers of poor, dark-skinned workers, and presided over by a small white minority. Its complex social structure echoes a certain stylized European feudalism, with both the farm and the social structure dependent on the abundant labor and service of African slaves and the proper functioning of race. We understand this representation of the plantation to be fixed in time, as an expression of the slaveholding South, from the settlement of the colonies until the Civil War's conclusion. And we understand the plantation to be defined by its scale so that a small farm with one or two slaves does not, we presume, make a plantation; only something much bigger, more sprawling, fits the term.

Subjecting this familiar idea to critical scrutiny is important, because this too-simplified representation is itself an argument—it is somewhat accurate but also too narrowly drawn, and narrowly drawn with a purpose, I think. The labor regime of the slaveholding South has a long racial history, but it was re-created in the wake of the Civil War as part of an effort to domesticate the region, to transform it from the forward base of a hemispheric empire into a well-bordered region of a well-defined republic. After the war, describing the plantation as a medieval thing made it easier to imagine its supposed opposites as modern and democratic. So, then, to be critical of "the plantation," one has to set it in a larger context, loosen it a little from its historic relationship to the stylized Old South, and rethink the question of scale and purpose. This requires reading and thinking broadly.

We might start this effort to regain critical scrutiny in the 1930s, a decade renowned for its fascination with the slaveholding past. In William Faulkner's *Absalom, Absalom!*, published in 1936, a young man with fevered dreams of wealth, racial domination, and brute power journeys to the West Indies to gain knowledge and then to the Mississippi frontier, where he hopes to bring that knowledge to real life. Newly settled there, he uses his captured French architect and his Haitian slaves to carve a realm of one hundred acres out of the wilderness. What Thomas Sutpen creates in Yoknapatawpha

County—his settlement is soon known simply as "the Plantation"—is a powerful beachhead for slavery. As time moves on in Faulkner's world, the site is surrounded by other parallel manifestations of white settlement and slaveholding practice and then fades into local legend as a reminder of the antebellum past, but Sutpen's original idea—his rough-hewn settlement in the vanguard of the slaveholding world—clings to the bones of the place.

We learn many things from reading Faulkner's story closely. We learn that plantations are everywhere—everywhere because they were conceived as stabilizing agents in a world marked by diffusion and movement. If we look up from the pages of *Absalom, Absalom!*, we see them still around us. The state of Rhode Island has the term "Plantation" in its official name, a reminder that its initial settlement was, like Sutpen's, ambitious. Plimoth Plantation is a living-history museum, located in New England. The Parchman prison in Mississippi is described as a plantation. There are cities and towns, companies and furniture styles all named after plantations. If we think about this dispersion, we might note that a "plantation" seems to refer to any aspiring settlement, any outpost at the edge of civilization, any penal colony, or to the population established in any of these locations. Metaphorically, for Sutpen and for many others, "plantation" suggests implantation, often in rocky soil; growth dependent on luck and skill; cultivation; and perhaps most importantly, will. Affectively, the term is nostalgic, gesturing backward—and, strangely, with affection—to the original, to the thing transplanted in new terrain. "Sutpen's Hundred" wasn't just an outpost of slaveholding; it was also a transplanted idea, taken from the center of the slaveholding world to what was, in the timeline of Faulkner's fictional narrative, a distant borderlands.

One can see this history—the growth and spread of plantations to match the expansion of the South and of colonialism more broadly—in the old maps of the antebellum Mississippi River, where the shoreline is inscribed with the names of the families who own the great (that is, large and productive) plantations. There is a history of empire to be found in the names of those plantations, with Creole owners living closest to New Orleans and Anglo surnames found upriver, where settlements came later. Like a DNA strand, the map captures the decline of old empires, the rise of new nations, and the rapid expansion of chattel bondage. One sees the way in which this institution reproduced itself—socially, politically, economically—as it climbed northward.

More than a big white house on a broad stretch of land with a handful of slaves, the plantation is thus a place, a practice, and a politics. As such, it is tied to histories of colonialism and slavery but also fixed on the land, in the way that a lighthouse marks the establishment of waterways. Imagined this way, the plantation has history, though not usually in the way we imagine such things, and not as a fixture of one particular moment in time. With roots, as Patricia Seed reminds us, in colonial settlement in the New World, the plantation endures as a symbol of race and power. Studying such a thing is a challenge.[1] To focus on the plantation, one needs to keep that long history in mind and to remember as well the varied meanings of the concept that make it possible for things as different as "plantation shutters" and "plantation politics" to resonate right up to the present day.

Breaking down the generally understood notion of "the plantation" forces us to ask some important questions: If the institution is a global expression of colonial settlement, what is the unique connection between the South and the plantation? How does a global object, joined to the history of imperial settlement, reproduced in many different contexts, become confused with the history of one specific region in one specific nation? What are the politics of that specific memory? These questions are important because they trouble our certainties that the plantation is fixed in time and space and ask us to look for it outside the Old South.

In the summer of 1937, for instance, the photojournalist Dorothea Lange toured the state of Mississippi. Hired—along with several other documentary photographers—by the Farm Security Administration to document the grim circumstances of rural life across the depressed, desolate South, Lange found herself at the Sunflower Plantation Project, a modernization effort in the Delta, aimed at reeducating African American tenant sharecroppers and turning them into productive wage laborers, and at replacing nineteenth-century technologies with modern machines, all in the midst of a big, productive cotton-growing complex. Here, we see the plantation reestablished as something that does the hard work of economic modernization, a philosophy of development at the very core of the emergent American century. Bewitched by the beauty of the region, Lange created photos of the plantation "project" that reproduced with stylized perfection a centuries-old representation: the aesthetic of the slaveholding southern plantation. But they also capture the dominant ideology of American empire, an emphasis on uplift through the improvement of economic infrastructure and related social systems that connects the Sunflower Plantation Project with the occupation of Haiti, the Marshall Plan, Cold War efforts in the Global South, and Iraq and Afghanistan.

Lange's photos capture the idealized plantation in action. In one, a small child, wearing just a denim short-john and a hat, speaks to the master, who leans in, hands on his knees, bent over patronizingly. A white mechanic stands in the background, a bemused half smile on his face. The encounter is staged on a floor of dirt, creased and crisscrossed with tire tracks. A large barn with corrugated-tin siding sits in the background. Such an image was, for Lange, part of a series, not just a stand-alone shot. In another, thirty black workers—a small subset of a group numbering two hundred, brought "to hoe cotton for a dollar a day"—fan out across a carpet floor of the cash crop. There, in another, is a black woman cradling a hoe, her premodern figuration in juxtaposition to another image, this time of a black man astride a great, powerful tractor. There is a vast field, with rows upon rows of cotton, and here, in contrast, is a group of resting laborers, sitting on the stoop of the nearby grocery store, quietly attending to their boss, who seems oblivious to their presence. And another of the planter's manse, positioned as the dominant, dramatic expression of power and privilege on the vast, flat terrain of the Mississippi Delta.[2]

Lange's composite portrait of the plantation reminds us that it was—and is—a complex, a network of interlaced institutions, and not merely a big farm. It reveals the plantation to be an instrument of political economy, a beachhead of a certain civilizing mission. Here, through Lange's eyes, we see the South imaged as a backward region in need of modernization—a central motif in American culture—but we also see that backwardness racialized, expressed as "the Negro problem," with a simple solution (the reestablishment of the plantation) that dates back to slavery. Lange's photos thus remind us that our vision of the plantation as a complex was drawn once more—in bright colors and bold lines—in the decade of the 1930s, at a moment when aristocracy was under direct assault, when social structures were called into question, and when the racial patterns set a century or so earlier were remade for a new, modern world.

This was the decade, after all, of *Absalom, Absalom!*, published a year before Lange's photographs, a novel that, as mentioned earlier, featured a vicious and ambitious archetype who carved his one-hundred-square-mile plantation out of the wilderness, and whose notion of the plantation was shaped by his own hemispheric sojourns. Other points of connection are more disturbing. In the same year as Lange's sojourn at the Sunflower Plantation Project, planters in Florida were under investigation for labor practices that bordered on slavery, evidenced in their systems of debt peonage and brutal regimes of discipline punishment. Popular novelist Margaret Mitchell published *Gone with the Wind* in 1936—the same year as Faulkner's text—and the novel was replete with images of heroic rascals with heart-melting grins and damsels wrapped in colorful fabric, all attended to by a vast, and generally contented, black population. The decade marked by the Great Depression, then, witnessed the reemergence of the plantation as something worth remembering and, strangely, restoring—as something that did critical economic and cultural work in American life.

Tara, the archetypal plantation of Margaret Mitchell's novel, is perhaps the most memorable—that is, durable—Old South icon created in this period. As visualized in the 1939 film, it is built at the top of a long, rolling hill, with a gently winding road leading up to it. Gerald O'Hara's plantation house is a broad, whitewashed structure with four massive pillars, signifying strength and power, holding up a vast roofline. Everything about the house is big, from the staircase inside so large that human figures are miniaturized when they walk up and down, to the various bedrooms and libraries, so vast it can hardly be supposed that all these spaces and peoples can fit under one roof. The landscape is big. The rooms are big. The personalities are big, too.

As a place, Mitchell's version of the plantation is familiar to almost everyone who has thought about—or carefully studied—the slaveholding past. Invoking the word brings to mind clichéd images of tree-lined promenades, vast homes with sprawling porches centered on equally vast agricultural plots of land. Every plantation requires a master and a mistress, paired representatives of white supremacy and representations of the peculiarly feudal affect of the entire complex. And everywhere, the cliché dictates, there must be slaves or servants or peons—small and large, male and female, old and young. Populated by a small stratum of white overseers and masters and a dense layer of black slaves, the plantation is neither a farm nor a factory, but rather some deeply, disturbingly racialized combination of the two. Tara invokes the generally recognized representation noted at the beginning of this essay: the familiar idyll, fixed in one region and one time.

In this imagining, the plantation is marked as much by scale as it is by location. It signifies a complex, an intricate network of social and economic relations, an unequal, hierarchical prefiguration of the company towns of the Fordist economy, with their standardized production lines and citizen-consumers. Relations between masters and slaves—or, as Lange's photographs suggest, between boss and field hand—appear amicable and not merely productive. The plantation, the myth of Tara proposes, provides everything necessary for everyone who lives there, so long as they keep to their respective stations.

This is an enduring myth, this idea of the plantation as an organic domestic space, with its various peoples arranged together in something like More's utopia. Established after the Civil War as a feature of the Lost Cause mythology, this image flourished during the 1930s, was given new meaning during the massive resistance to the Civil Rights Movement, and survives to the present day as a touchstone for southern identity. It is at the root of the idea that the South is more courtly, more polite, more family oriented than the cold, hard North. It also supports the notion that rural plantations were, in their own way, the antithesis of the modern capitalist factory of the urban, northern city.

And yet Tara is also a productive homestead, a capitalist pied-à-terre, groomed and cultivated by the elder O'Hara, himself an immigrant eager to climb the social ladder, to join the ranks of great planters. For Gerald O'Hara, Tara isn't just a set piece for the performance of race and class or a single site in a wide-ranging economic system—a node in a network. It is also a machine that produces great wealth and concentrates that wealth for a single person or family in the master's house. O'Hara's eager establishment of Tara—the fields, the slaves, the manse, and the affective and material relations that bind all of these things together—is no less a reflection of ambition than Thomas Sutpen's more transparently, more brutally cruel establishment of his hundred acres. The plantation is supposed to make both men rich *and* perpetuate the institution of slavery. Plantations, we now know, courtesy of a generation of scholars from James Oakes to Ed Baptist, were fundamentally capitalist institutions seeking to wring profit from brutal, efficient labor regimes.

Critically studying the plantation, then, means refusing to prioritize that idealized, domestic comity. To understand the larger, global significance of the plantation, one needs to have a longer narrative in mind, to recognize that the movement of that complex institution across time and space is the story of the modern age, of slavery and exploration and domination; that one can trace the establishment of plantations in settler societies and extractive colonies and see the history of the modern world unfold, with the proliferation of such things—implantings, again, of Western domination—at the razor's edge of empire and expansion; that plantations, in Philip Curtin's history of the concept, originate as forward operating bases for ever-expanding empires and then become—as time moves on—critical bulwarks in the now-settled homeland for that continued, relentless expansion; that, by explicit design, the plantation makes some people rich and puts others in chains—literally or, as Lange's photos unwittingly suggest, metaphorically.

As the plotlines of Faulkner and Mitchell suggest, the plantation of the Old South was also a sort of aspirational, if unachievable, ideal for many southerners, at odds with the much-celebrated, small-scale Jeffersonian yeoman thought to be the foundation stone of American democracy. Capitalist to its core, the plantation required—for growth—expansion across the open ground through the acquisition of more land and slaves. But it also demanded, as time went on, a certain degree of theatrical performance, as a landscape of small farmers might become, if the circumstances were right, a world dominated by great planters. That performance—so perfectly mythologized in *Gone with the Wind* and so routinely misunderstood by many as chivalric and courtly—was rooted in the stratification of the planter class and the slaveholding South in general, a class stratification built on a broad, thoroughly antidemocratic foundation of captured and enslaved labor. So deeply ingrained was this linkage between place, practice, and politics that the post–Civil War plantation, David Oshinsky reminds us, quickly became the model for an emerging penal system geared toward the enforcement of debt peonage and white supremacy.[3]

Given this gruesome history, one would imagine that the material remains of the plantation complex would be a source of shame, with commemorations that match—in emotional tone—the deeply contemplative, melancholic ruins of the concentration camps of Europe. One would think that the hoopskirts and big white houses and accented mannerisms of the great planter class would be subject to ridicule and consigned to the dustbin of history.

Perversely, though, the plantation has endured instead as a symbol of an Old South deemed worthy of restoration and visitation, a likely site for family reunions, weddings, and getaway weekends. The long line of old plantation homes along the banks of the Mississippi prospers as a site of visitation but only haphazardly communicates a full history of the institutions and networks that fostered the creation of these massive structures. These sites along what is known as the Old River Road seem more closely connected to the world of Dorothea Lange and William Faulkner and Margaret Mitchell than to the actual nineteenth-century history of chattel slavery. Open the website for the Old River Road Plantation Adventure, for instance, and the theme music from the film version of *Gone with the Wind* plays.

One answer to this question—why does the plantation continue to endure as something *worth* restoring and even celebrating?—would depend on the intersection of race and nation. After decades of work as a war correspondent, for instance, journalist Tony Horwitz returned to a childhood interest in the South and heard echoes of the defeated nationalisms of the world in the nostalgia of Confederate reenactors. "Bosnia," he indexed for his readers in the opening pages of *Confederates in the Attic*, ticking off the analogies, "Iraq, Northern Ireland."[4] Horwitz's clever observation—that the language of the Lost Cause sounds a lot like the lamentations of the Irish for the lost counties of Ulster or the bitter complaints of Serbs about their vicious defeat at the hands of the Croats—reminds us that such nostalgia has a political history, and that the contemporary renovation of the plantation as an artifact suitable for weddings and family reunions cannot be separated from the geopolitics of modern America, from, that is, the racial realignment of the political party system; the massive battles over structural segregation, desegregation, and resegregation; and from the post-civil-rights-era emergence of "the South" as a political "battleground" once more.

29

There is, then, no such thing as an innocent nostalgia for the plantation, no veneration for the grand old houses and ruffled shirts and promenades and teas on the front porch that can be stripped clean of the complex's bone-breaking, race-making past. More than anything else, thinking critically about the plantation requires us to remember *that* and to acknowledge the historically and politically significant role of these homesteads in the global history of slavery and empire.

NOTES

1. See Seed, *Ceremonies of Possession.*
2. The photos can easily be found on the website of the Prints and Photographs Division of the Library of Congress.
3. See Oshinsky, *Worse than Slavery.*
4. Tony Horwitz, *Confederates in the Attic,* 6.

SUGGESTIONS FOR FURTHER READING

Baptist, Edward E. *The Half Has Never Been Told: Slavery and the Making of American Capitalism.* New York: Basic Books, 2014.

Curtin, Philip D. *The Rise and Fall of the Plantation Complex: Essays in Atlantic History.* Cambridge: Cambridge University Press, 1998.

McPherson, Tara. *Reconstructing Dixie: Race, Gender, and Nostalgia in the Imagined South.* Durham, N.C.: Duke University Press, 2003.

Oakes, James. *The Ruling Race: A History of American Slaveholders.* New York: W. W. Norton, 1998.

Oshinsky, David M. *Worse than Slavery: Parchman Farm and the Ordeal of Jim Crow.* New York: Free Press, 1997.

Seed, Patricia. *Ceremonies of Possession in Europe's Conquest of the New World, 1492–1640.* Cambridge: Cambridge University Press, 1995.

Nation

JENNIFER RAE GREESON

State is a thing
Nation is a concept

Scholars of nationalism generally agree that "the nation" is a modern invention that came into being in the late eighteenth and early nineteenth centuries. The concept has been theorized ever since. For more than two hundred years, political thinkers have pondered the extent to which "nation" is a constructed category resting on "invented traditions" and myths of origin.[1] At the same time, they note the paradox that "nation" is a powerful and deeply lived idea, so powerful indeed that individuals have consented to fight and die in its name again and again across the modern era.

To isolate what it is we have in mind when we talk about "nation," it is useful to consider how political theorists differentiate between the concept of nation and the concept of "the state." The state is a political entity, the nation a cultural one. The state is a locus of legal, juridical, and military power, while the nation is a site of slipperier forces such as "belonging" and "identity." The relationship of an individual to the state is defined as citizenship; the relationship of an individual to a nation is defined as a feeling—patriotism, or a sense of "nation-ness."

Despite some claims from Americanists—misguided, in my opinion—that we have entered a "post-national" age, "nation" remains an exceptionally critical term for studies of both the United States and "the South."[2] This is most generally the case because the category "nation" organizes a conceptual relationship between places and people, territory and population; and both American studies and southern studies entail a constant negotiation between geographic locales and cultural production as organizing terms. But the history of the American hemisphere gives more-specific relevance to "nation" as a category of analysis for our work. In the second edition of *Imagined Communities*—the book on nationalism with arguably the greatest impact on cultural studies in the United States in the past two decades—Benedict Anderson proposed that the "creole pioneers" of the American hemisphere invented modern nationalism.[3] In the later eighteenth century, he argued, settler colonists born in the New World felt themselves entitled to the global stature of denizens of their Old World countries of origin; frustrated by their peripheral status in the imperial system, they created "free and independent"

New World nations out of whole cloth—not only the United States but also Haiti and the republics of Latin America.

In the case of the U.S. South, Confederate partisans attempted a similar, if short-lived, invention of a new nation in the 1860s, and they leaned heavily on the rhetoric of New World national independence movements to do so, as Drew Gilpin Faust has shown.[4] Perhaps unsurprisingly, then, most work on nationalism in American studies that considers the situation of the U.S. South has focused on the "sectionalism"—or competing North/South nationalisms—surrounding the Civil War.[5] More interesting for southern studies, though, is not the blip of sectionalism and Confederate nationalism—though it did lead to dying aplenty—but rather the enduring asymmetry of "nation" and "state" throughout the rest of the existence of "the South" as a concept. The category of "nation" normally ties the feelings of belonging or homeland to a legitimate state; when the two categories do not precisely converge, the constructedness of "nation" is thrown into even greater relief. We might define "the South" here as either the *subnational* U.S. South or the *transnational* hemispheric or Global South (and for the purposes of this essay I largely use the former definition). Either way, the odd case of "the South" stands to illuminate many dimensions of U.S. nationalism that might otherwise strike us as natural or unworthy of note.

Indeed, much of the political theory of nationalism in recent decades has focused on the intersections between the idea of the nation and other sorts of geographic constructs. After the widespread decolonization and nationalization of the former Third World at midcentury, political and cultural theorists began to explore the intersections of nation and empire, nation and metropole, nation and colony, positing nationalism as a fundamentally comparative or relational ideological category.[6] Their work did not consider the role of the subnational region—the ostensibly distinct region contained perpetually within the political borders of the larger nation-state—as such a comparative imperial construct against which ideas of nation might be maintained or troubled. Nor could it do so, for the geographic relationship between an enduring subnational region such as the U.S. South and the larger nation within which it is contained cannot be conceptualized within the rubrics of empire. In the case of territories added to a nation-state over time through imperial acquisition—for instance, in the case of the U.S. West—some geographic and historical distinction between the ostensibly divergent internal territory and the "nation proper" may be maintained. But when did the United States exist without Virginia?

Nevertheless, the notion of a subnational region like the U.S. South cuts against the grain of the most basic assumptions of nationalism quite as much as any other geographic construct. In Johann Gottlieb Fichte's formulation, "the nation" is the conceptual structure by which the external political borders of the state are transposed into the internal borders of consciousness for its inhabitants.[7] This means that nationalism must create two principles simultaneously: a principle of internal coherence ("what is inside these political borders is alike and harmonious") and a principle of external exclusion ("what is outside these political borders is alien and irrelevant"). To locate difference within the borders of the nation-state is to explode both of these nationalist principles.

Some contemporary scholarship on nationalism has identified such a disruptive difference within the nation-state in terms of population rather than place; this work seems more directly relevant to exploring the interaction between the idea of the "United States" and the idea of its "South." In an influential 1991 collection of essays, *Race, Nation, Class: Ambiguous Identities*, Étienne Balibar and Immanuel Wallerstein proposed that competing forms of group identity within a nation-state create uneven relationships to "the nation" among its inhabitants—whether those competing identities are chosen as affiliations or, as is more often the case, imposed on segments of the national population from above. Following Balibar and Wallerstein, a goodly number of works published in American studies in the 1990s considered how the operations of U.S. state power toward groups of the nation's own inhabitants might be considered more imperial than national. These works explored how plural "cultures of U.S. imperialism" may be directed internally as well as externally to the borders of the nation-state.[8]

This work in American studies rubs up against the idea of "internal colonialism"—a concept that has been developed most extensively in studies of the relationship of Ireland, Scotland, and/or Wales to Britain.[9] The concept of internal colonialism posits an "oppressed nation"—culturally, historically, ethnically distinct—held within the political borders of a dominating, recognized nation-state. This idea has sometimes proven seductive to scholars in southern studies thinking through the relationship of the United States to its "South," but it simply does not apply to the actual situation of the actual southern United States—at least, not in any way other than as a metaphor so broad it becomes nonsensical.

But an "internal colonialism" model that focuses on *population* rather than *place*, again, seems more compelling when applied to the situation of the U.S. South. Indeed, the idea that African Americans in the southern United States are colonial subjects of the nation-state has been put forth quite consistently across the twentieth century by those thinking about the operations of Western nationalism. As early as 1928, the Communist International declared the "Black Belt" of the United States to be, quite explicitly, an "oppressed nation."[10] In the Comintern's view, the majority of residents of this "district" of the United States had their wills and interests countermanded by the laws and practices of the recognized nation-state, and thus a revolutionary movement was as justified among the people of the Black Belt as among any other colonized or occupied group on the globe. In the 1950s, intellectuals in the decolonizing Caribbean took up a related line of thought; among others, Frantz Fanon wrote of the parallels between colonialist pathologies in the French Caribbean, in French Africa, and in the southern United States.[11] More recently, historian Stephen Hahn has argued in a Pulitzer Prize–winning book that the twentieth-century movement we call "black nationalism" had its origin among rural African Americans in the former Confederate states in the decades just after the Civil War.[12]

So long as we follow contemporary political theorists in understanding "nation" to be a relational concept—predicated always on a principle of exclusion or juxtaposition to an "Other"—we see that southern studies challenges American studies to recognize that some of the primary terms of difference against which "the United States" has been defined reside *within* the body politic and the state borders, rather than outside them. This is the case whether we think primarily in terms of population or geography, or consider "the South" a subnational or a transnational region. Southern studies thus also should challenge American studies to think seriously about *centralization* within the national borders and its effects. Particularly at issue, from the perspective of scholarship on nationalism, is the centralization of cultural production in the United States, for contemporary political theorists hold the nation to be a cultural construct produced in media from newspapers and novels to scholarship and pedagogy. A southern studies approach highlights the fact that the various geographic areas within the United States have had uneven access to its centers of cultural production, and thus that various internal geographic areas have had uneven influence in the production of national "reality."

Raymond Williams has provided what is still the most clarifying theoretical statement of the interaction between the subnational region—an ostensibly distinct region distanced from the centers of national cultural production—and the broader idea of "nation." He first reminds us that the word "region" initially denoted an administrative subdivision of a larger state, such that every part of the larger state carried a regional subdenomination.

> And then what is striking, in matters of cultural description, is the steady discrimination of certain regions as in this limited sense "regional," which can only hold if certain other regions are not seen in this way. This is in its turn a function of cultural centralization. . . . It is closely connected with the distinction between "metropolitan" and "provincial" culture. . . . Yet this is no longer a distinction of areas and kinds of life; it is what is politely called a value-judgment but more accurately an expression of centralized cultural dominance.[13]

The paradox here is that *to represent the subnational region*—as a place or population differentiated from an implied national norm—is, tacitly, *to produce the national norm itself* through an ideological juxtaposition. Williams observes: "[Regional] can, like dialect, be used to indicate a subordinate or inferior form, as in 'regional accent' *which implies that there is somewhere . . . a 'national accent.'*"[14]

"Nation" is a critical term for southern studies not because we should be looking for analogies or approximations to nationalism or colonialism in the situation of "the South." Rather, it is a critical term because southern studies has much to reveal to American studies about how the idea of "the United States" has been and continues to be both constructed internally and projected externally onto the larger world. Southern studies must make American studies conscious of the fact that every time the U.S. South is depicted as unique, perverse, divergent, or exceptional within the United States, a dimension of "the United States" itself is being defined. And "the United States" is not defined in simple opposition to its "South"; instead, the structure of the juxtaposition with an *internal* Other means that "southness" is simultaneously held apart from, and acknowledged as a part of, the national idea.

The internal Other of its "South" has proved essential to the creation and maintenance of U.S. nationalism from independence forward and has provided a bedrock conceptual structure on which Americans have learned to think about the place of their nation on the globe in terms of geography, race, and projection of power. As an *internal* term of opposition, though, "the South" has always provided a vantage for disrupting ostensible national norms, upsetting national pieties, and exposing the constructedness of the U.S. national idea. (Nationalism, of course, holds the nation to be real, natural, and inevitable.) In my own book, *Our South: Geographic Fantasy and the Rise of National Literature*, I have sketched some of this complicated ideological dynamic between "nation" and "South" as I see it at work in the formation of U.S. national literature between the Revolutionary War and the turn of the twentieth century. Leigh Anne Duck, as well, has parsed the imaginative relationship between "nation" and "South" in the modernist era in *The Nation's Region: Southern Modernism, Segregation, and U.S. Nationalism.*

To close this essay, I will suggest (drawing from my book) some examples of how representing "the South" is symbiotically bound up with representing the nation, across the history of the existence of the United States. Differentiating its "South" may bolster or trouble the U.S. national idea. Most often, it does both.

To begin at the beginning: How did early nationalists distinguish their suddenly independent nation from the rest of the colonized American hemisphere? The first U.S. nationalist writers defined "the South" in terms generally assigned to the colonized Americas as a whole: tropicality, plantation production, racial heterogeneity. These writers then held "the United States" apart from its deviant "South" and thereby proved their nation to be new and independent on the scene of the American hemisphere. Yet these early U.S. notions of southern distinctiveness, formed as they were within established colonialist vocabularies, easily shaded into analogizing the southern United States to extranational underdeveloped and still-colonial sites, such as the West Indies and the Spanish American colonies—thus emphasizing the porousness of the southern national borders and the (largely) still-colonial economic function of the United States.

This potentially disruptive alignment of "the South" with what we would today call the "global South" then quickly came to serve as a way to naturalize and domesticate U.S. imperial ambitions. During and after the Mexican War, Americans often (and not unjustly) styled westward expansion as a "slave power" conspiracy; as federal troops occupied the former Confederacy during Reconstruction, they conceptualized the U.S. South as a "domestic Africa." And as Americans pursued colonial acquisitions overseas at the end of the nineteenth century, they looked to their domestic South to reassure themselves that they had always subjugated, domesticated, and civilized "barbaric" and "colored" peoples within their own borders. Turning westward across the Pacific and toward the southern American hemisphere, both pro- and anti-imperialist Americans asserted that they had done this "empire for liberty" bit (in Jefferson's pithy phrase) since the founding of the nation.[15]

Indeed, many of the most enduring uses of "the South" in the production of U.S. nationalism have concerned maintaining the signal idea of American innocence—the exceptionalist notion fundamental to U.S. nationalism, which holds that the United States is not implicated in the power grabs and exploitations of the modern Western imperial world. For instance, consider how the legacy of slavery is (or is not) understood to impact the United States as a whole. As early as the late eighteenth century, slavery was defined as an anomalous subnational system "peculiar" to the U.S. South. This quarantine of slavery to a specific subnational region not only obscured the obvious fact that slavery was legal throughout the vast majority of the United States in the late eighteenth century. More important, the equation of slavery with the "peculiar" U.S. South veiled the fact that the rapid development and industrialization of the entire United States—which enabled U.S. nationalization in the first place and enabled the United States to compete against Europe as a manufacturing and trade center by the mid-nineteenth century—was built on enslaved labor. ("Without slavery you have no cotton, without cotton you cannot have modern industry," Marx observed offhandedly in 1847. "Cause slavery to disappear, and you will have effaced America from the map of nations.")[16] The deep indebtedness of the United States—the whole nation-state—to enslaved labor is a fundamental historical reality that American studies has yet to fully confront, thanks to the compartmentalization afforded to the idea of "the United States" by its differentiated "South."[17]

These few observations should suggest to the reader many more interactions of "nation" and "South" in U.S. culture. Fundamentally, using "nation" as a category of analysis reveals to what extent southern studies may be disruptive to American studies—and thus, to what extent southern studies is essential for a clear-eyed and self-aware investigation of the United States.

NOTES

1. One of the hallmarks of contemporary scholarship on nationalism as a category, exemplified by Eric J. Hobsbawm and Terence O. Ranger's *The Invention of Tradition* and Benedict Anderson's *Imagined Communities*, is its cognizance of related nineteenth-century inquiries, particularly Fichte's 1808 "Reden an die deutsche Nation" and Renan's 1882 "Qu'est-que-c'est une Nation?"

2. Even the group-authored introduction to John Carlos Rowe's edited collection *Post-Nationalist American Studies*, the flagship volume of this approach, concedes that "none of us believes that the nation-form has been or will any time in the near future be superseded"; see "Introduction," *Post-Nationalist American Studies*, 1.

3. B. Anderson, *Imagined Communities*, 49–68.

4. Faust, *Creation of Confederate Nationalism*.

5. Historian William R. Taylor's *Cavalier and Yankee* is the most influential study in this vein; more recently, see works by Peter J. Parish and especially Susan-Mary Grant, *North over South*.

6. Especially Eagleton, Jameson, and Said, *Nationalism, Colonialism, and Literature*; Deane, "Imperialism/Nationalism"; and Bhabha, *Nation and Narration*.

7. Fichte, "Reden an die deutsche Nation," 539–788.

8. Kaplan and Pease, *Cultures of United States Imperialism*; Moon and Davidson, *Subjects and Citizens*. This work on state power and differentiated populations within the U.S. borders culminates in studies of enslavement and incarceration by scholars such as Colin Dayan, Saidiya Hartman, and Michelle Alexander, although this work is not focused on nationalism per se.

9. See, for instance, Hechter, *Internal Colonialism*.

10. *1928 and 1930 Comintern Resolutions*, 22.

11. Fanon, *Black Skin, White Masks*, 80.

12. Hahn, *Nation under Our Feet*.

13. R. Williams, *Writing in Society*, 229–30.

14. R. Williams, *Keywords*, 265–66, emphasis added.

15. Jefferson's phrase is from an 1809 letter to Madison, his successor as president; for an excellent discussion of its import, see Dimock, *Empire for Liberty*, 3–9 and 38–39.

16. Marx, *Poverty of Philosophy*, 121, 122.

17. This is becoming an important new nexus between southern and American studies; see especially Edward Baptist's *The Half Has Never Been Told* (2014) and Greg Grandin's *Empire of Necessity* (2014).

SUGGESTIONS FOR FURTHER READING

Anderson, Benedict. *Imagined Communities: Reflections on the Origin and Spread of Nationalism*. Rev. ed. London: Verso, 1991.

Balibar, Étienne, and Immanuel Wallerstein. *Race, Nation, Class: Ambiguous Identities*. London: Verso, 1991.

Greeson, Jennifer Rae. *Our South: Geographic Fantasy and the Rise of National Literature*. Cambridge, Mass.: Harvard University Press, 2010.

Hahn, Stephen. *A Nation under Our Feet: Black Political Struggles in the Rural South*. Cambridge, Mass.: Harvard University Press, 2003.

Taylor, William R. *Cavalier and Yankee: The Old South and American National Character*. New York: George Braziller, 1961.

Empire

HARILAOS STECOPOULOS

Over the past twenty years, the urge to reframe American studies as transnational has led scholars to discover "empire" as a keyword and heuristic. Whether defined as "a relationship, formal or informal, in which one state controls the effective political sovereignty of another political society" or as "a large, composite, multi-ethnic or multinational political unit, usually created by conquest, and divided between a dominant center and subordinate, sometimes far distant, peripheries," the study of empire has become integral to scholarly analyses of U.S. culture and society.[1] What Susan Gillman dubs "U.S. empire studies" is now a recognized subcategory of American studies, generating important articles and books on topics as varied as the literary origins of the Monroe Doctrine, pedagogic practices in the U.S.-occupied Philippines, and African American anti-imperialist activism.[2] Furthermore, the current interest in U.S. empire has inspired a fair amount of Americanist soul-searching with leading scholars pointing out that American studies not only emerged from imperial contexts in the 1930s and 1940s—witness Perry Miller "discovering" America on the banks of the Congo River—but also frequently reinscribed American exceptionalism in its attempt to define and explicate national character.[3] Thanks in part to the imperial turn, the self-conscious, even agonistic, transformation of American studies that began during the 1960s has persisted beyond the heyday of identity politics and into the new millennium.

That said, the emergence of empire studies, while in many ways a salutary development for the field, has also raised certain methodological and political problems. Those problems come with the territory, so to speak; as Edward Said famously argued over twenty years ago, imperialism is "a word and an idea today so controversial, so fraught with all sorts of questions, doubts, polemics, and ideological premises as nearly to resist use altogether."[4] For many Americanists interested in empire, two concerns have emerged as paramount. First, scholars worry that even as empire studies undertakes a radical critique of the United States' hegemonic project from within, it also tends at times to ignore or silence important voices from without—voices that offer distinctive and autochthonous engagements with U.S. imperialism. That neglect of the subaltern perspective has inspired Latin American scholars in particular to charge that transnational American studies paradoxically authorizes complacency among U.S.-based scholars. Second, the new interest in overseas empire has generated problems on the subnational level by encouraging the neglect of communities that may manifest distinctive and often overlooked engagements with—and protests of— empire. The steady interest in Native, African American, and Latino/Latina cultures has not ensured a concomitant focus on other communities and geographies.

The latter problem is of particular relevance to southern studies scholars who focus on what is typically understood to be a subnational geographic formation. Insofar as empire is often defined as, to borrow from William Appleman Williams, "the forcible subjugation of formerly independent peoples by a wholly external power," the term seems to assume a political geography that stands in vexed relation to the U.S. South.[5] In certain ways, of course, Williams's definition seems wholly applicable to the southern situation. For many (neo-) Confederates, not to say white supremacists, the North's defeat and attempted reconstruction of the South and the post-Reconstruction control of the South by northern finance and federal regulation render empire an appropriate term with which to understand the southern predicament. From Senator Ben Tillman of South Carolina to Agrarian Donald Davidson to Texas sheriff (and fierce anti-Obama partisan) Parnell McNamara, myriad white southern politicians and intellectuals have argued that, as "Uncle Sam's other province," the South constitutes a colony dominated and exploited by an imperial metropole. The quotidian effect of those arguments has emerged in the fetishization of southern insurrection and separatism, often epitomized by the urge to fly the Stars and Bars on state buildings in defiance of federal-cum-imperial Washington. At the same time, we should recognize that the white southern impulse to understand the North as an imperial metropole also has inspired other types of politics. It is worth noting, for example, how the virulently racist Tillman rejected calls for an American empire at the turn of the century because he feared that expansion into overseas communities of color would weaken white authority in the United States. In this case, concern over the maintenance of domestic white supremacy leads to an anti-imperial stance—a stance eagerly welcomed by the mainly white northern members of the Anti-Imperialist League. Or, to take another case, we might remember that Agrarians Donald Davidson and Robert Penn Warren found in the tragic defeat of Native Americans the perfect analogy for the suffering of the white South. Even as those antimodern intellectuals celebrated a Jeffersonian image of the rural South largely dependent on the elimination of native peoples, their critique of white northern capital also inspired sympathy for those very communities. Such unusual sentiments don't so much demand new valuation of white southern ressentiment as constitute an important reminder that hegemonic politics can generate significant social and cultural contradictions to which we should attend.

While the southern indictment of northern imperialism remains important to our understanding of the region's culture, past and present, that indictment has little purchase among today's southern studies scholars. On the contrary, sensitive to the implication of Native American, postcolonial, and other forms of subaltern studies, contemporary academics tend to find in problems of imperialism and colonialism a new way of understanding the region's many disturbing inequities. Scholars now recognize, for example, that the white oppression of African Americans in the turn-of-the-century South might be profitably understood in tandem with the nation's conquest and occupation of the Philippines (1898–1904). The contemporary historical record supports such homological analysis with U.S. newspaper cartoonists portraying Filipinos in racist imagery usually assigned to African Americans and African Americans such as southern-born David Fagen deserting the U.S. forces to join the Filipinos and fight the perceived common enemy of white America. Eager to exploit the potential political import of such parallels, Archibald Grimke and a group of Massachusetts African Americans argued to President McKinley that his imperial policies upheld, tacitly or otherwise, white supremacist violence in the Southeast. "We, sir, at this crisis and extremity in the life of our race in the South, and in this crisis and extremity of the republic as well, in the presence of the civilized world," they wrote in an open letter, "cry to you to pause, if but for an hour, in pursuit of your national policy of 'criminal aggression' abroad to consider the 'criminal aggression' at home against humanity and American citizenship, which is in the full tide of successful conquest at the South."[6] For those activists, as for North Carolina writer Charles Chesnutt and Massachusetts intellectual W. E. B. Du Bois, U.S. expansion in the Philippines was inseparable from the beatings, lynchings, economic privation, political dispossession, and other forms of racist terror prevalent in the former Confederate states.

Such political arguments depended in significant ways on a remapping of the South with respect to both the nation and the world at large. To locate American "criminal aggression" in "the South" and "abroad," as Grimke and his confreres did, suggested that those sprawling spaces manifest connections and affinities that challenge normative national notions of geography. Drawing largely on such anti-imperialist and antiracist remappings of the U.S. South, contemporary scholars have redefined the space of the South as an object of study. If the old southern studies typically found in regional ressentiment ample reason to validate a metropole-periphery spatial form that depended on a traditional geographic understanding of national region, the New Southern Studies tends to argue that the white South was itself part of the imperial center and thus complicit with the oppression of other communities, particularly communities of color. Some of the more influential new geographic visions of the South link the usual vision of the region— basically, the thirteen states of the Confederacy—to other national and hemispheric zones. Robert Brinkmeyer has demonstrated that traditionally insular conceptions of the South ignore the region's important connections to the U.S. Southwest and West, connections that demand more of intellectuals than an idle nod toward the idea of the Sunbelt. Working in a different historical mode, Melanie Benson Taylor has reminded us of the Native conceptions of the Southeast, conceptions that predate European settler colonialism. Finally, Jon Smith and Deborah Cohn have helped pioneer what is arguably the most compelling new approach to the scholarly remapping of the region through their insistence that the so-called domestic South must be understood as part of a hemispheric American South.[7] Those alternate and overlapping redefinitions of the U.S. South have emerged from the study of imperialism and have, in turn, helped license new examinations of expansion that challenge disciplinary limits and regional and national borders.

 41

The New Southern Studies engagement with imperialism has also contributed to a broadening and diversification of the southern literary canon. If a post-civil-rights conception of southern studies has finally recognized that African American writers are, in certain cases, southern writers—and vice versa—the willingness to take empire seriously has legitimated the study of Central American, Caribbean, and Vietnamese American texts within a newly variegated and expansive southern frame. Thus in the case of the Vietnam War, scholars have grown more attentive to black and white representations of that conflict—for example, Louisiana-born Yusef Komunyakaa's poem "Tu Do Street"—and that sensitivity to what we might call a global southern literary map also has generated interest in such Vietnamese American texts as Monique Truong's *Bitter in the Mouth*, a novel set in North Carolina.

The imperial turn that stands at the center of much of the New Southern Studies has also helped inspire radical rereadings of important southern texts. While critics have generated imperial, better, anti-imperial, interpretations of works by Sutton Griggs (Caroline Levander on *Imperium in Imperio*), Joel Chandler Harris (Jeremy Wells on *Uncle Remus: His Songs and His Sayings*), and Flannery O'Connor (Patricia Yaeger on "Parker's Back"), the massive corpus of William Faulkner has received the bulk of the new responses. From John T. Matthews's reading of the Rincon short stories to Richard Godden's essay on *Absalom, Absalom!* to Barbara Ladd's piece on *A Fable*, some of our most acclaimed Faulknerians have succeeded in reframing his works as texts deeply engaged with questions of imperialism and colonialism.[8] Indeed, the West Indian subplot of *Absalom, Absalom!* has become for many scholars one of the best-known portions of his corpus, and Yoknapatawpha County now seems linked in important ways to such distant sites as Haiti, China, and Mexico. The Bard of Oxford is, needless to say, still very much recognized as a *southern* writer, but that label no longer means Faulkner's achievement rests exclusively on chronicles of "a little postage stamp of native soil"; instead, we see him as a novelist whose richly capacious aesthetic is of a piece with a truly global reach.

Of course, one doesn't have to turn to Faulkner to appreciate the deep intertwining of the imperial and the southern in U.S. literary culture; Mark Twain, an older and no less famous regional writer, makes that imbrication abundantly apparent in his own inimitable manner. While Twain hailed from the border state of Missouri, his fiction has long had an important place in the American vision of the South and its racial crisis. His Virginia ancestry and short stint as a Confederate irregular are only two of the many biographical details that speak to his southernness. At the same time, as Amy Kaplan, John Rowe, and other scholars have taught us, Twain was also very much a global writer sensitive to, if sometimes equivocal on, questions of colonialism and imperialism. From his early writing about the Sandwich Islands to his magnum opus *Following the Equator*, from his allegorization of conquest in *A Connecticut Yankee in King Arthur's Court* to his long-overlooked *Tom Sawyer, Abroad*, Mark Twain engaged in a sustained fashion with the problem of European and American empire.

Of all the many Twain texts to which we could turn, perhaps the most useful might be the late works where a concern with global issues stands in dynamic relation to an examination of the South and its racial crisis. Twain's turn-of-the-century texts are in many respects a devastating catalog of man's inhumanity to man, covering the cruelty of anti-Semitism in Austria, King Leopold's brutal reign in the Congo, the atrocities of the Boer Wars, and the horrors of the U.S. campaign in the Philippines. Yet the Jim Crow South tends to be absent from that catalog. Twain devotes precious little overt attention to the notorious problem of lynching and race riots before the turn of the century, despite the fact that he was well aware that white mob murder was on the rise and may have read some of the African American and British journalistic coverage of racist violence in the U.S. Southeast. Twain in fact would turn to the subject in his 1901 essay "The United States of Lyncherdom" and grow so concerned with the epidemic of violence that he planned a book-length study of lynching in America. Yet he soon decided not to publish the piece—it appeared posthumously—and dropped the book project in order to preserve his connection to southern readers. As he noted wryly to his publisher about the proposed book, "I shouldn't have even half a friend left down there [in the South], after it issued from the press." Biographer Justin Kaplan elaborates on this comment by pointing out that Twain's decision to avoid making public statements about lynching had a great deal to do with affective as well as financial rewards. Describing Twain's 1902 trip on the Mississippi, Kaplan writes, "Crowds waited for him, with applause and flowers, and his eyes filled with tears. For such love who can blame him for putting aside, out of a lifetime's work, one book [the projected history of lynching] and one article ["The United States of Lyncherdom"]?"⁹ Kaplan's analysis is in many respects persuasive, yet he never considers how Twain's need to preserve an affective southern connection bears upon his increasingly international art. What is the relationship between Twain's decision to leave his critique of Jim Crow unfinished or unpublished and his increasingly global indictments of prejudice and violence? Does the South have to remain safely sequestered in the past in order for Twain to decry empire overseas? Can one engage empire and region with one voice?

While suppressed during Twain's lifetime, "The United States of Lyncherdom" is a likely text with which to begin such an inquiry, not least because it engages what seems on the face of it such a painfully and quintessentially southern theme. Written in response to news of a 1901 lynching, "The United States of Lyncherdom" doesn't flinch from detailing the horrors of white racist violence. Twain informs his readers that upon discovering a murdered white woman, the white community of Pierce City, Missouri, "lynched three negroes—two of them very aged ones—burned out five negro households, and drove thirty negro families into the woods."¹⁰ More significant still, Twain responds to the likely southern defense of racist violence by emphasizing that the fatal attack on the white woman in no way justifies vigilante action: "I do not dwell upon the provocation which moved the people to these crimes, for that has nothing to do with the matter. . . . The only question is, did the assassin *take the law into his own hands*. . . . If the assassin be proved to have usurped the law's prerogative in righting his wrongs, that ends the matter; a thousand provocations are no defense" (140). The alleged violation of the white woman by an African American cannot license mob violence. That Twain challenges the southern logic of lynching suggests a recognition that, even as lynching began in the colonial spaces of the continental West, it had by the late nineteenth century become a crime largely identified with his native region. As he puts it in a gesture that highlights his own regional complicity, "Are we Southerners all Dr. Lazears, General Lees, Stonewall Jacksons? no, we are all lynchers" (140).

Yet even as this son of Missouri stresses that the South is the epicenter of lynching—in the words of a cited *Chicago Tribune* piece, "four Southern states, Alabama, Georgia, Louisiana and Mississippi are the worst offenders" (141)—he also attends to the infectious spread of white supremacist mob murder. As Twain insists, lynching has become "a fashion which will spread wide and wider, year by year, covering State after State, as with an advancing disease. Lynching has reached Colorado, it has reached California, it has reached Indiana—and now Missouri! I shall live to see a negro burned in Union Square, New York" (141). However regional it may appear, the terror cannot be linked exclusively to—and thus be contained by—the South. Lynching is both a southern and an American crime. Twain's analysis relies on southern exceptionalism and, at the same time, complicates that exceptionalism by emphasizing how racist mob murder can jump from the regional to the national scale.

That sensitivity to the complex spatial logic of lynching, that awareness of how mob violence can defy predictable geographic fantasy, adumbrates Twain's urge to understand white American racist violence in imperial terms. Pursuing a line of argument familiar to readers of the Colonel Sherburn-Boggs episode in *Adventures of Huckleberry Finn*, Twain claims that only resolute and implacable men can confront and challenge the epidemic of mob murder sweeping the South and the nation. Yet such figures are hard to find at home, and he suggests in a bitterly satiric vein that the nation should look instead to those stalwart individuals fervently committed to the civilizing (read: imperial) mission: Christian missionaries working in China. Tongue firmly in cheek, Twain begs for the missionaries' help in civilizing their native land:

> We implore them to come back and help us in our need. Patriotism imposes this duty on them. Our country is worse off than China; they are our country-men, their motherland supplicates their aid in this her hour of deep distress.

They are competent; our people are not; they are used to scoffs, sneers, revilings, danger; our people are not; they have the martyr-spirit, nothing but the martyr-spirit can brave a lynching-mob, and cow it and scatter it; they can save their country, we beseech them to come home and do it. (145)

Twain pursues the argument that those who would convert the so-called savage heathen often ignore the degree to which their own communities are in fact far more backward than the object of the civilizing mission. Such an argument has a long history that dates to Michel de Montaigne's "Of Cannibals" (1580), if not before, but the thesis has special relevance to an important, if hardly uncontested, northern view of the South during the late nineteenth century. As Jennifer Rae Greeson has demonstrated through her brilliant reading of Edward King's travel series *The Great South* (1875), influential Reconstruction-era American writers and publishers sometimes viewed the southeastern states as "a domestic Africa" whose seemingly barbaric ways offered a surfeit of exotic journalistic material.[11] King and other white men of letters had little interest in developing the progressive political implications of that argument, but such African American activists as Ida B. Wells would value that sensational remapping of the South, arguing at home and in Great Britain that the U.S. South desperately required the sort of Christian civilizing mission typically sent to Africa and Asia. Twain works in a similar mode in "The United States of Lyncherdom" by invoking the American dedication to the civilizing mission as absurd and hypocritical in light of the growing phenomenon of American mob murder.

He drives home that point by arguing that seemingly well-intentioned Christian missionaries are remaking China in America's savage image:

The Chinese are universally conceded to be excellent people, honest, honorable, industrious, trustworthy, kindhearted, and all that—leave them alone, they are plenty good enough just as they are; and besides, almost every convert runs a risk of catching our Civilization. We ought to be careful. We ought to think twice before we encourage a risk like that; for, *once civilized, China can never be uncivilized again.* We have not been thinking of that. Very well, we ought to think of it now. (144)

An essay that begins with the lament of a lynching in Missouri shifts to an impassioned claim that the Chinese and other so-called savage peoples are "plenty good enough just as they are" and have no need to be converted and civilized by anyone, least of all Americans. Twain finds in the epidemic of lynching an important reminder that the appeal to civilization is often little more than a cover for violent and inhumane behavior. And in an era when an expansionist United States often sent its soldiers into another country "against the country's will," his reminder resonates on both the national and the international scales.

But as is so often the case in writing that engages both the southern and the imperial questions, Twain does not remain content with a linear movement from one spatial scale to the next and instead organizes his argument through a dialectical movement that recalls the regional crisis with which he began, and then, in turn, remaps it on a massive scale. In his attempt to convince American missionaries to abandon their imperialist venture in China and help the United States "uncivilize" itself, Twain cites a telegram describing an African American hung and then burned alive in Texas—a missive that then inspires him to sketch out a scene worthy of Bosch. Adopting a bitter tone, he urges the missionaries

> to read that telegram again, and yet again, and picture the scene in their minds, and soberly ponder it; then multiply it by 114 [sic], add 88; place the 203 in a row, allowing 650 feet space for each human torch, so that there might be viewing-room around it for 5,000 Christian American men, women and children, youths and maidens; make it night, for grim effect; have the show in a gradually rising plain . . . all being ready, now . . . let all the far stretch of kerosened pyres be touched off simultaneously and the glare and the shrieks and the agonies burst heavenward to the Throne. (145)

Even as Twain urges the missionaries to return repeatedly to the grisly telegram, he feels compelled to paint an even more macabre image for them. And that grisly image depends, tellingly, on a horrible calculus that multiplies the field of racist murder, expanding it beyond one victim and one mob to the state of Texas to the nation and to "the curvature of the earth." According to Twain, the missionaries and, indeed, all prospective readers of both the telegram and his essay should find in this one case reason to multiply the murder of the one man by 115 (the number of African Americans lynched in 1899) and then add 88 (the number of African Americans lynched during the first half of 1900). Those calculations will demand, in turn, a new spatial form, as Twain invites his readers to then situate the 203 victims in a detailed configuration, leaving ample room for spectators to experience the resulting horror. The plotting could not be more precise. That this remapping of the Texas plain renders it at once southern and American, and somehow planetary, emerges with terrible force in the last line of the passage when Twain commands, "Let all the far stretch of kerosened pyres be touched off simultaneously and the glare and the shrieks and the agonies burst heavenward to the

Throne." At once adumbrating and exceeding Hannah Arendt's well-known argument about the banality of evil, Twain finds in the arithmetic of lynching a new way of understanding the South's relationship to the capitalist imperatives underwriting white supremacy in both the United States and its growing overseas dominions. The terror of lynching multiplies and expands into the terrors of empire. In scrutinizing itself, the South does indeed "look away," to the nation, to the world.

47

NOTES

1. Doyle, *Empires*, 45; Howe, *Empire*, 30.
2. Gillman, "New, Newest Thing," 196. See Murphy, *Hemispheric Imaginings*; Wesling, *Empire's Proxy*; Von Eschen, *Race against Empire*.
3. See, for example, A. Kaplan, *Anarchy of Empire*.
4. Said, *Culture and Imperialism*, 3.
5. W. A. Williams, *Empire as a Way of Life*, 6.
6. Archibald Grimke, letter quoted in Gatewood, *Black Americans*, 210.
7. See Brinkmeyer, *Remapping Southern Literature*; M. B. Taylor, *Reconstructing the Native South*; Smith and Cohn, *Look Away!*
8. See Levander, "Sutton Griggs"; Wells, *Romances of the White Man's Burden*; Yaeger, "Southern Orientalism"; Matthews, "Recalling the West Indies"; Godden, "*Absalom, Absalom!*, Haiti and Labor History"; and Ladd, "Faulkner's Paris."
9. J. Kaplan, *Mr. Clemens and Mark Twain*, 366.
10. Twain, "United States of Lyncherdom," 140. The text used (and hereafter cited parenthetically) was established by Terry L. Oggel in "Speaking Out about Race."
11. Greeson, *Our South*, 237.

SUGGESTIONS FOR FURTHER READING

Duck, Leigh Anne. *The Nation's Region: Southern Modernism, Segregation, and U.S. Nationalism*. Athens: University of Georgia Press, 2006.

Greeson, Jennifer Rae. *Our South: Geographic Fantasy and the Rise of National Literature*. Cambridge, Mass.: Harvard University Press, 2010.

Hagood, Taylor. *Faulkner's Imperialism: Space, Place, and the Materiality of Myth*. Baton Rouge: Louisiana State University Press, 2008.

Schmidt, Peter. *Sitting in Darkness: New South Fiction, Education, and the Rise of Jim Crow Colonialism, 1865–1920*. Jackson: University Press of Mississippi, 2008.

Wells, Jeremy. *Romances of the White Man's Burden: Race, Empire, and the Plantation in American Literature, 1880–1936*. Nashville: Vanderbilt University Press, 2011.

Labor

TED ATKINSON

Belaboring Southern Exceptionalism: An Organizing Principle

Defined as people toiling in fields, factories, homes, and elsewhere in the U.S. South, southern labor has an extensive history. Often it calls to mind economic exploitation through various forms of non-wage and wage labor from the past to the present: chattel slavery, sharecropping, prison chain gangs, coal mining, textile manufacturing, domestic servitude, migrant and seasonal harvesting, and poultry processing, among others. Southern labor defined as a subject of academic inquiry has a far less extensive record. The seeds of the discipline were first sown in the early twentieth century by historians, sociologists, and documentarians treating the U.S. South as a marginal or isolated concern. For the most part, accounts of the region were part of broader narratives of labor history and politics in the nation as a whole. When the South took center stage, it was usually held up as a discrete enclave of hidebound customs, social abjection, and economic backwardness, as typified by studies of southern textile workers in the 1920s, projects that blended photography and prose to document the plight of sharecroppers during the Great Depression, and the thoughts on the history and current conditions of southern labor included in W. J. Cash's *The Mind of the South* (1941). Such treatments resonated with the finding that the South was "the nation's No. 1 economic problem" in the *Report on the Economic Conditions in the South* prepared for President Franklin D. Roosevelt by the National Emergency Council in 1938.

Early attempts to study southern labor fed into a master narrative shaped by what has come to be known as "old" southern labor history. In this account, southern workers were by and large a passive lot mired in the depths of poverty, entrenched on opposite sides of a racial divide figured in binary terms as black versus white, and entranced by religious dreams of the afterlife to such a degree that striving to improve conditions in the here and now failed to qualify as a worthy cause. Conventional wisdom held that southern workers could not achieve solidarity to save their lives—sometimes literally. Scholars documented a long history of sporadic and failed attempts at organized labor in agricultural production and industrial manufacturing: suppressed slave revolts in the antebellum South; unsuccessful efforts by the Knights of Labor to gain a foothold in the South in the late nineteenth century; the riots and strikes staged by Piedmont textile workers that peaked from the late 1920s to the mid-1930s but eventually lost steam; and the short-lived rural dissidence of the Sharecroppers Union (SCU) and the Southern Tenant Farmers Union (STFU) during the early years of the Great Depression. The failure of the union organization campaign known as "Operation Dixie," an initiative by the Congress of Industrial Organizations (CIO) to consolidate gains by labor during World War II, became a foundation for the diagnosis of worker docility as the cause of chronic anti-unionism plaguing the South. The consensus view solidified in the context of Cold War historiography downplayed or erased Depression-era labor activism as communist infiltration. It was not until the publication of Robin D. G. Kelley's *Hammer and Hoe: Alabama Communists during the Great Depression* (1990) that scholars began to recover lost history and complicate the received narrative.

The emphasis on weak unionization worked in tandem with assumptions about relations between labor and management. The prevailing view was that powerless southern workers were at the mercy of ruling elites from the plantation paternalism of the Old South to the embrace of industrialization as rightful heir to King Cotton under the auspices of New South boosterism. The clear delineation between agricultural and industrial epochs took a cue from the Southern Agrarians, who decried the dehumanizing effects of industrial capitalism and the erasure of rural folkways in *I'll Take My Stand* (1930), all too conveniently ignoring for rhetorical purposes that agriculture itself had long been an industry with its own practices for extracting labor and natural resources for profit. For the planter class and those aspiring to join its ranks, contra Andrew Lytle's famous aphorism in his contribution to the Southern Agrarian manifesto, a farm really was a place to grow rich. The casting of capitalism as an unwelcome and disruptive latecomer to "the southern way of life," like the correlation between weak unionization and worker docility, had a long run before facing scrutiny. Paul Gilroy, in *The Black Atlantic: Modernity and Double Consciousness* (1993), exemplifies an alternative approach in defining the system of slavery as more than a discrete and distinct mode of labor exploitation and racial domination. Gilroy's definition involves the option of viewing slavery as "the inner essence of capitalism" or as "a vestigial, essentially precapitalist element in a dependent relationship to capitalism proper."[1] Either way, slavery stands not as an antiquated system that eventually gave way to the march of modernity but as one that paved the way for laboring under capitalism. The revised understanding of relations between slavery and capitalism that Gilroy employs in cultural studies is on display in recent work by historians exposing the deep structures of slavery supporting sharecropping and manufacturing (Blackmon) and connecting slave labor in the U.S. South to broader hemispheric and global flows of capital (Johnson).[2]

The willingness to question key assumptions of "old" southern labor history was evident by the late 1960s. Scholars such as Herbert Gutman and E. P. Thompson led a major paradigm shift in labor historiography from institutionalism to social history. In this context, F. Ray Marshall's *Labor in the South* (1967) and George Brown Tindall's *The Emergence of the New South, 1913–1945* (1967) worked to flesh out previously skeletal accounts of labor activism in the U.S. South while following the standard operating procedure of making unions and other advocacy organizations primary focal points for scholarly inquiry and analysis.[3] That the vast majority of southern workers were not affiliated with unions explains how Marshall could make what seems now an egregiously misguided prediction about the future prospects of organized labor in the South. Relying on C. Vann Woodward's claim in "The Search for Southern Identity" that the region was under transformation by a "Bulldozer Revolution," Marshall concluded that the South would become more like the heavily unionized Midwest and Northeast.[4] Marshall was not alone in that prediction—he used recent findings to bolster the same argument about rosy union prospects that V. O. Key had made in *Southern Politics in State and Nation* (1949) on the basis of post–World War II labor movement gains. In retrospect, Marshall was right about the future achievement of greater parity but fundamentally wrong about how it would come to pass. He based his prediction on data showing southern union membership outpacing that in other parts of the country—a short-lived trend that elicited a backlash from management and its political allies in the form of "right-to-work" laws and other anti-union measures. Marshall failed to consider the possibility that organized labor would grow weaker in previous strongholds steadily becoming loops in the Rust Belt, resulting in a convergence of the downward and upward unionization trends somewhere below—or "south"—of the line indicating below-average viability. What Marshall viewed as a progressive form of North-South synergy John Egerton saw as quite the opposite, positing a model succinctly expressed in the title of his often-cited book *The Americanization of Dixie: The Southernization of America* (1974). At the base of Egerton's argument is the familiar ballast of southern exceptionalism: he points to anemic unionization as initially

50

endemic to the region but now assuming epidemic proportions in the nation at large.

By the 1980s, the "new" southern labor history was completing the turn toward social history as the dominant critical paradigm. Crucial to this enterprise was *Like a Family: The Making of a Southern Cotton Mill World* (1982), a project started by a cohort of scholars at the University of North Carolina at Chapel Hill. Taking dead aim at the notion of southern industrial workers immobilized by passivity, the contributors used the tools of the social history trade as they "uncovered an authentic, vibrant, familial culture and a native tradition of militancy and collective action in the South."[5] After *Like a Family*, a proliferation of studies zeroed in on local domains in the South and drew from the personal accounts of workers to illuminate their lived experiences in a host of occupations, ranging from dock workers to tobacco-farm laborers to coal miners to steelworkers. Scholars placed considerable stress on southern exceptionalism as an organizing principle, debunking claims that southern industrial workers were acquiescent to a distinctly regional brand of paternalistic management and that religion was a regionally applied dose of what Marx described as an incapacitating opiate. Instead, revisionist accounts held that workers could mobilize to force "welfare capitalism" onto management or draw on Protestant evangelical traditions to foster a religious type of working-class consciousness and solidarity.[6] One of the most vibrant strains of revisionism, led by Kelley's *Hammer and Hoe*, has involved rethinking the post–World War II labor moment. Jacquelyn Dowd Hall argues that it is possible to see such labor activism as civil rights unionism in a "long civil rights movement" extending beyond the traditional timeline measured as roughly a decade. As such, "Operation Dixie" seems not merely a southern failure ensured by inherent racism and anti-unionism but a missed opportunity that cuts across the North-South divide on the power of fervent Cold War anticommunism.[7]

For scholars aligned with the "new" southern labor history, the "missed opportunities" thesis could apply to numerous historical events. Not surprisingly, this scholarship has attracted criticism—not least the repeated charge of academic wish fulfillment or romanticization leveled by proponents of a resurgent or "new" institutionalism for whom southern exceptionalism, supported as ever by emphasis on anemic unionization, is a matter of course. In *From Cotton Belt to Sunbelt: Federal Policy, Economic Development, and the Transformation of the South* (1991), Bruce J. Schulman rehearses Egerton's claim in contending that the "rise of the South" brought about a "de-unionizing of America." To make the case, Schulman describes southern attitudes toward unionization in a manner bordering on essentialism. "By the end of the 1970s," he writes, "anti-unionism had practically replaced racism as the South's signature prejudice." For Schulman, the southern aversion to unions is part of the "environment" and serves as an indicator of "cultural and economic heritage."[8] In *Fighting against the Odds: A History of Southern Labor since World War II* (2005), Timothy J. Minchin fashions a blend of institutionalism and the social history model, homing in on the southern textile industry and arriving at much the same conclusion as Schulman and other predecessors in both "old" and "new" southern labor history: that resistance to organized labor is a feature as uniquely southern as affinities for fried food, right-wing political ideology, and fundamentalist Christianity.

"The Concern of All": Scoping Out Southern Labor Studies

The Wobblies, also known as members of the Industrial Workers of the World (IWW), have a long-standing motto: "An injury to one is the concern of all." The predicate of the motto might readily apply to the current conditions of the academic field formerly known as southern labor history. It would seem that southern labor, once the focus of relatively few, has become the concern of all—or at least of all the scholars representing the disciplines that have converged in a vastly expanded field now known as southern labor studies. In the formative years, as noted above, it was primarily historians who carried the banner; as it stands now, specialists in literature, film, music, sociology, political science, gender studies, working-class studies, and other areas are bringing the insights of their disciplines to bear on the study of southern labor and drawing on labor as a critical term for examining various cultural products—everything from blues music to FSA photography to William Faulkner's fiction. Since institutionalism has been highly influential *in* the discipline of southern labor history, it stands to reason that it can be instructive with respect *to* the history of the discipline itself. Toward this end, the story of how the field's professional organization has developed over the years is a microcosm of the discipline it promotes. In 2007, during the joint Labor and Working Class Studies Association–Southern Labor Studies Conference convened at Duke University, a group of participants voted to form the Southern Labor Studies Association to ensure that the conference would continue to remain viable in subsequent years. The chosen name was an acknowledgment of the now-expanded scope of an organization with roots tracing back to the mid-1960s, when the Association of Southern Labor Historians (ASLH) took shape and sponsored the then-fledgling Southern Labor History Conference.

In the evolution of southern labor studies, the trace of cultural studies as an engine of interdisciplinary realignment is readily apparent. And the expansive scope forged in large part by interdisciplinary influence is in keeping with a major paradigm shift in scholarship on the U.S. South as a whole—a development evinced by this volume, in which scholars take stock of key critical terms at a pivotal juncture. In recent years, even the most fundamental of concepts, "the South," has faced intense reassessment from those interested in moving beyond monolithic conceptions of the region. Contemplating what "the South" now means raises important questions for southern labor studies, not least the very basic "Why *southern* labor?" Implicit in the question is the persistence of southern exceptionalism as an organizing principle that remains influential even as new scholarship pushes the conceptual bounds of "the South" to new limits.

The fruits of this critical labor are on display in a bevy of recent studies promoting interdisciplinary exchange as a means to subject received critical paradigms and historical narratives of southern labor to what might be called "interrogation by expansion." An exemplary text is *Radicalism in the South since Reconstruction* (2006), which the editors of the collection describe as a contribution to "the emerging body of work devoted to reconsidering the idea of Southern radical exceptionalism." Citing scholarship committed to the "rethinking of indigenous Southern [labor] politics and culture," the editors acknowledge the "necessarily fragmentary nature" of the field because of geographical, historical, institutional, or personal frames of reference for scholarship on special topics. The editors add that this effect "has allowed the overall notion of Southern exceptionalism to stand in many respects." As a corrective, both the form and the content of the collection work to counter fragmentation by placing "historical periods and topics in dialogue with each other so as to get a sense of the range of Southern politics and history." Though the contributors do fulfill the mission to "open the scholarly conversation about Southern radicalism more widely than has been the case," the focus does remain decidedly national.[9]

Other recent scholarship has widened the scope even further to theorize a "Global South"—that is, models of the U.S. South shaped by globalism, globalization, and the transnational turn in literary and cultural studies. In this body of work, scholars examine the South under the framework of a global rather than a national distinction between North and South. As a case in point, *The American South in a Global World* (2005) counters traditional understanding of the South as an isolated region within the United States and, in the process, offers ironic twists on the claims of southern exceptionalism. In his contribution to the collection, James L. Peacock touts the benefits of a global perspective, arguing that "some features of the South that have been regarded as odd from a northern or national standpoint turn out to resemble common patterns around the world, while within a global perspective it is the U.S. North that is odd and exceptional in some ways."[10] Fortunately, merely trading one model of regional exceptionalism for another is not the overarching aim of this enterprise, which makes invaluable contributions to southern labor studies. This volume includes trenchant examinations of labor politics and culture shaped by the influence of globalization on the U.S. South and vice versa—among them the "flexible labor" practices implemented by FedEx in the corporation's Memphis hub; a North Carolina company's uses and abuses of the H-2A visa program allowing foreign nationals entry into the United States for temporary or seasonal agricultural work; and the intersecting, often conflicting global and local currents affecting Appalachian residents and coal workers in the context of mountaintop removal. This study of current conditions is a testament to the profitable critical outcomes acquired by blending institutionalism and the social history model in an interdisciplinary context.

Such a strategy enables binary opposition to give way to racial and ethnic diversity in demographic treatments of southern labor. Fluid models of (uneven) economic development and consequent labor conditions and practices complicate the long-standing rural/urban binary applied within the South and in support of perpetuating the model of division between North and South within the United States. This type of scholarship convincingly counters exceptionalist models such as the "southernization of America," recasting a regional process by which the South forces an inherently progressive U.S. nation to turn back—or, better yet, backward—with regard to economic policies and labor practices as instead a global process by which the South assumes a prime spot, albeit a dubious one, at the cutting edge of advancing neoliberal capitalism. Figuring key components of this system— from "right-to-work" laws to reliance on contingent labor to generous corporate tax incentives—as uniquely "southern," even if many of the historical and material roots are traceable to the region, makes the rapid and intricate flows of capital and labor through multiple registers difficult to detect, much less to comprehend more fully. Rising to this challenge involves tracing activity along multiple vectors that define intersections between the global and the local. At this juncture, this work would seem to involve extending the interdisciplinary path now well established under the auspices of southern labor studies. In this vein, the editors of *Southern Radicalism since Reconstruction* make the provocative claim that engaging more fully with the history and politics of labor in the U.S. South is not possible "without some sense of the intersection of political and cultural work."[11] This claim productively figures cultural production as a mode of aesthetic expression capable of documenting and making meaningful the considerable toil and trouble, dignity and shame, and profits and losses associated with forms of labor that occur *in* the South but are by no means uniquely *of* the South.

55

Affording Agency: James Still's River of Earth *and Southern Labor Geographies*

Recent popular narratives of neoliberal capitalism stress total dominance achieved through a process of scalar multiplication registering from global to local domains. Such narratives figure workers around the world as unable to mobilize in sufficient numbers or strength to challenge the powerful forces unleashed by globalization. Accounts of the failure to organize should come as nothing new to scholars in southern labor studies, perhaps even going so far as to suggest that in prevailing narratives of the globalized economy workers of the world seem exceptionally "southern." But there are always other stories to tell—ones in which "southern" workers are not merely passive victims of economic factors beyond their control but actors who find ways to exercise agency, even under the most dehumanizing circumstances, in striving to improve the conditions of their lives and labors. One such narrative is James Still's *River of Earth*, a novel about the effects of coal mining on Appalachian eastern Kentucky during the Great Depression. It has garnered some critical attention since its publication in 1940, mainly in the context of Appalachian studies, but it is long overdue for rereading as a document of labor struggle at the predawn of globalization, which by some current measures has brought full day and by others a long day's journey into night. There is only space here for a gestural reading that outlines what can be termed the novel's "labor geography." This brief case study is intended to suggest the efficacy of cultural production as a means to rethink received narratives of docility that collude with a residual southern exceptionalism to foreclose more-productive critical strategies in advancing southern labor studies.

Geography is all the rage in cultural studies, and scholars concentrating on the U.S. South have effectively channeled its interdisciplinary currents toward reassessments of traditional regionalism. In *The Postsouthern Sense of Place in Contemporary Fiction* (2005), Martyn Bone employs geography as part of an interdisciplinary approach that seeks in part to move the U.S. South from the margins closer to the center in discussions of uneven economic development under the rise of global capitalism. Bringing the work of David Harvey, Fredric Jameson, and Edward Soja into contact with Southern Agrarian critiques of capitalism, Bone posits "a critical framework through which to approach a post-Agrarian social geography in which agricultural real property has been displaced" by what then-Agrarian Allen Tate called "the abstract property relations of finance-capitalism."[12] This social geography can be refined even further into a "labor geography" useful for mapping the spatial contours of working lives that take shape locally but resonate globally. As Andrew Herod explains in *Labor Geographies: Workers and the Landscapes of Capitalism* (2001), this concept is helpful for "thinking about how the social actions of workers relate to their desire to implement in the physical landscape their own spatial visions of a geography of capitalism that is enabling of their own self-reproduction and social survival." Herod argues that emphasis on what David Harvey calls the "spatial fix"—the mechanism by which capital alters a particular space at a given time for the purposes of adaptation and continued expansion—can lead scholars to neglect the agency of workers. This factor is instrumental in perpetuating narratives of southern labor docility. As a corrective measure, Herod calls for scholarly attention to the ways that "workers attempt to create in their own image what we might call 'labor's spatial fix.'"[13]

River of Earth matters to this critical discussion because it lends itself to a constructive remapping using the coordinates of labor geography. Initial mappings have charted two chief interpretive courses: reading the novel as a lyrical, mournful expression of Still's Appalachian brand of agrarianism or as a case study in how the dominance of the coal industry in Appalachia makes "unrelenting economic necessity" the determining factor in the lives of coal workers and their families.[14] For good reason, both interpretations rely heavily on key structural components of the text. Like John Steinbeck's *The Grapes of Wrath*, which was released a year before *River of Earth* by the same publisher, the narrative centers on a family's displacement from the land and the trials and tribulations that come with ensuing migration. Unlike Steinbeck, Still confines the movements of his characters to a relatively small geographical radius. The Baldridge family at the center of the narrative moves back and forth between agricultural real property and so-called company towns—the latter having become increasingly visible fixtures on the southern landscape at the time of the novel's production. In Still's representational scheme, the mother and father symbolize the contested southern "way of life": Alpha Baldridge embodies residual agrarianism; her husband, Brack, emergent industrialism.

The narrator, Alpha and Brack's young son, whose first name is withheld, is keenly attuned to familial tensions engendered by these starkly contrasting socioeconomic philosophies. Still makes abundantly clear how the economic uncertainties of the Depression and the consequent peaks and valleys of coal production register with destabilizing effects in the lives of the Baldridge family and in their extended network of kin and community. In response, and in keeping with their philosophical principles, Alpha and Brack envision diametrically opposed labor geographies. Alpha's involves transforming space by establishing roots—in literal and figurative terms. "Forever I've wanted to set us down in a lone spot," she says to Brack in touting the benefits of subsistence farming. Punctuating the argument, Alpha says, "To make and provide, it's the only trade I know, and I work willing."[15] She cites the mythical figure of "Walking John Gay," whom she holds up as a model of the unsettling effects of migration in an attempt to convince her husband to accept her plan. But Alpha's plea is to no avail: taking John Gay's walking as a sign of freedom, Brack's geographical preference is for routes that eventually lead underground to coal mining. Brack explains, "I was born to dig coal. . . . Somewheres they's a mine working. Fires still burning the world over, and they got to be fed" (241). This affirmation, delivered in the wake of great hardship, upheaval, and tragedy, reinforces what Brack says in response to Alpha's implicit likening of him to the mythical walker: "I choose mine work, the trade I know. I choose to follow the mines" (52). Granted, Brack's mining claim, as it were, might be read as tragically ironic, especially in contrast to that of the powerful company that mobilizes capital to make the miners a contingent labor force. Alpha's dream of rootedness might be similarly understood, functioning as a pipe dream at best. Both characters, such a reading might contend, exemplify the docility that has made efforts to mobilize southern labor ineffectual. But again, there are other stories to tell.

For all that sets them apart, the labor geographies envisioned by Alpha and Brack Baldridge have in common a fundamental claim to choice as a human right expressed in terms of spatial imagination and transformation. When Brack's relatives descend on the house, having been idled by a downturn in coal production, Alpha responds by envisioning a contraction of space. "We've got to live small," she explains to Brack. "We've got to tie ourselves up in such a knot nobody else can get in" (8, 9). Taking matters into her own hands, Alpha moves her immediate family, some furniture, and the dwindling food supply into the much smaller smokehouse and sets fire to the dilapidated dwelling invaded by Brack's parasitic relatives. In keeping with his penchant for wandering, Brack's spatial transformations are expansive.

Acting out of familial devotion and communal solidarity, Brack imagines the house and garden somehow widening to meet the needs of kin and neighbors. Brack's work ethic inspires him during lulls in coal production to sense that the mines are on the verge of opening up. Brack's capacity for spatial expansion also enables him to comprehend how his labor is part of a vast network connecting the local and the global: he knows that getting work requires "orders down from the big lakes." When pressed by one of his children to explain these distant environs, Brack responds, "There's ships riding the waters, hauling coal to somewhere farther on" (50). The lesson is not lost on the young narrator given that his curiosity about the world beyond the peaks and valleys, both topographical and existential, fuels his desire to avoid working in the mines—or becoming "slave to a pick," as one of the justifiably bitter but insightful veteran miners puts it (200).

River of Earth is not an unacknowledged proletarian novel that documents unremarked southern radicalism equal to the mass and militant movements that have advanced the causes of labor throughout history. But its labor geographies are useful models for mapping what David Harvey calls "spaces of hope." Harvey contends rather forcefully that bodies caught up in the flows of capital "are never to be construed as docile or passive," for their capacity to labor is what produces capital. Even in the most seemingly abject cases in which capital dominates, Harvey argues, "the transformative and creative capacities of the laborer always carry the potentiality . . . to fashion an alternative mode of production, exchange, and consumption."[16] Such spaces can be found in *River of Earth* and in other narratives, whether fictional or factual, that have been mined all too easily and often for evidence of an inherently southern incapacity to alter harsh circumstances caused by unfair labor practices under capitalism. Devoting the necessary scholarly attention to these spaces is crucial for achieving a more balanced approach able to account for the noninstitutional means that workers in many Souths have employed to resist capital injustices.

NOTES

1. Gilroy, *Black Atlantic*, 54–55.
2. See Blackmon, *Slavery by Another Name*, and W. Johnson, *River of Dark Dreams*.
3. See Brattain, "Pursuits of Post-Exceptionalism," 4.
4. See C. Vann Woodward, "The Search for Southern Identity," in *Burden of Southern History*, 3–26; Marshall, *Labor in the South*.
5. Brattain, "Pursuits of Post-Exceptionalism," 5.
6. Ibid., 6.

7. See J. D. Hall, "Long Civil Rights Movement," 1233–63.

8. Schulman, *From Cotton Belt to Sunbelt*, 162.

9. Green, Rubin, and Smethurst, "Radicalism in the South," 4, 5.

10. Peacock, "South and Grounded Globalism," 269.

11. Green, Rubin, and Smethurst, "Radicalism in the South," 5–6.

12. Bone, *Postsouthern Sense of Place*, 50.

13. Herod, *Labor Geographies*, 35.

14. Ross, "Industrialization," 206. For the former point of view, see Stoneback, "Rivers of Earth," 7–20.

15. Still, *River of Earth*, 51, 52. Text hereafter cited parenthetically.

16. Harvey, *Spaces of Hope*, 117.

SUGGESTIONS FOR FURTHER READING

Eskew, Glenn T., ed. *Labor in the Modern South*. Athens: University of Georgia Press, 2001.

Hall, Jacquelyn Dowd, et al., eds. *Like a Family: The Making of a Southern Cotton Mill World*. 1982. Chapel Hill: University of North Carolina Press, 2000.

Kelley, Robin D. G. *Hammer and Hoe: Alabama Communists during the Great Depression*. Chapel Hill: University of North Carolina Press, 1990.

Marshall, F. Ray. *Labor in the South*. Cambridge, Mass.: Harvard University Press, 1967.

Minchin, Timothy J. *Fighting against the Odds: A History of Southern Labor since World War II*. Gainesville: University of Florida Press, 2005.

Peacock, James L., Harry L. Watson, and Carrie R. Matthews, eds. *The American South in a Global World*. Chapel Hill: University of North Carolina Press, 2005.

Tindall, George Brown. *The Emergence of the New South, 1913–1945*. Baton Rouge: Louisiana State University Press, 1967.

LEIGH ANNE DUCK

Segregation

The array of policies and practices commonly known as "Jim Crow" was far more complex than that glib title suggests: it both eviscerated black southerners' citizenship rights and limited their access to public and commercial spaces from the 1890s into the 1960s, and also—in somewhat different ways—restricted the rights and access of people from multiple regions and multiple ethnicities for an even longer period of time. Faced with a complicated political and social phenomenon, historians have responded with vigor, expanding their inquiries to include almost every form and focus of that changing discipline. Thus, for example, one can find comparative histories of southern U.S. and South African segregation, labor and gender histories of political organizing among segregated black southerners, and cultural histories of how various forms of expression bolstered Jim Crow's production of "whiteness."[1] Until quite recently, however, segregation has received little specific attention in literary criticism: in her afterword to Brian Norman and Piper Kendrix Williams's 2010 collection *Representing Segregation*, Cheryl Wall notes that scholars "are just beginning to explore the ways that segregation's legacy informs the work of most twentieth-century black writers" and calls for such attention to white writing as well.[2]

One might posit that the legal and social issues central to Jim Crow are better suited to historical explication than to literary and cultural studies, but recent scholarship defies such a conclusion, productively investigating, for instance, how segregation shaped the aesthetic aims of African American writers and the concerns of modernism more generally, and what we learn about segregation more broadly by examining representations and experiences of Asians and Asian Americans, American Indians, and mestizos.[3] Further, the potential that attention to Jim Crow could benefit our understanding of literature per se was confirmed in 1995, when Kenneth Warren's *Black and White Strangers* demonstrated how the formal and thematic obsessions of U.S. realists reflected broader conversations about racial segregation. Rather than a simple mismatch, the generally—but not absolutely—deferred emergence of "segregation" as a keyword in literary studies indicates long-simmering questions about periodization, terminology, and even scholarly objectives. Fortunately, these are questions that scholars from multiple fields now seem ready to confront directly, leading Thadious Davis to suggest that "just as slavery was the dominant subject of many U.S. historians and literary critics in the last half of the twentieth century, segregation may well be the dominant subject emerging in the first half of the twenty-first century."[4]

To twenty-first-century readers familiar with critiques of how "the official narrative" concerning southern literature once ran, this delayed attention to segregation may seem unremarkable: a criticism seeking to foreground "community (and not contestation)" could hardly afford to admit how thoroughly the region's social structure depended on "coercion," let alone the violence with which many white southerners treated black resistance.[5] But while the most determined and sweeping interventions into pastoral accounts of southern writing began to appear in the late 1990s, concerns had been expressed for some time. The volume *Southern Literary Study: Problems and Possibilities*, for example, emerged from a conference held in 1972, and though all the participants were male, a few were also African American; this somewhat diverse set of voices may have influenced the volume's appendix, "A List of Topics Suggested for Further Study," which includes the representation of slave revolts, "white consciousness of black art," "race, class and party," and black southern writers generally, with particular attention to George Moses Horton, Charles Chesnutt, Sutton Griggs, Jean Toomer, and Sterling Brown.[6] Even Louis D. Rubin, justly proclaimed "the primary architect and developer of southern literary study in [the twentieth] century," took this occasion to complain that "the scholarship expended upon southern writing is . . . too often uncritical" and to call for further consideration of race.[7] One might expect such disciplinary energies to highlight racial segregation as an area for study, not least because the struggle over Jim Crow was still very much alive in critics' memories and, in some respects and areas, still continuing. Instead, the topic was only cited once, and even then as a source of intellectual limitation: Rubin worried that liberal scholars might project their feelings about their era's racial oppression onto the past.[8]

This difficulty in recognizing segregation as a topic relevant to literary studies has not been restricted by region, however, and to understand this broader delay, we might look back at another collection of essays seeking to expand and enrich academic inquiry: *"Race," Writing, and Difference*, which first appeared in 1985 in the journal *Critical Inquiry* with Henry Louis Gates Jr. as guest editor and was published one year later as a book. Credited with helping to "transform the academy," this project explicitly sought to study and defy the process by which language "inscribes" the "trope" of racial difference.[9] Nonetheless, southern U.S. segregation—a largely linguistic set of rules that sought to produce and enforce racial differences—was rarely mobilized as an analytic category in this volume.[10] The brief exceptions to this rule, however, began to suggest the consequence of this concept for contemporary literary study.

Though Kwame Anthony Appiah cited W. E. B. Du Bois's famous formulation from *Dusk of Dawn* (1940) that "the black man is a person who must ride 'Jim Crow' in Georgia," his main concern was to explore the shifting ways in which Du Bois understood and configured race, which was in many instances less formal and legalistic, and more affective and substantial.[11] Such tracings constituted a prominent analytic strategy in the 1980s and 1990s; to say that literary research in this period did not examine U.S. segregation per se is not, of course, to say that it disregarded race, racism, and racial oppression.[12] Though rarely a principal concept of such scholarship, Jim Crow had long shaped and even legally enforced concepts of "race," such that it was almost always present—albeit often only as unreferenced background—in works that sought to understand the meaning of race or the construction of racial identities in the postslavery United States.[13] For Appiah, this approach to "race" raised the question of periodization. Revealing how the institutional (and specifically academic) ideologies of the late nineteenth century—which buttressed segregation in the United States and colonialism globally—led Du Bois to take the concept of race as a given, Appiah noted with regret that the author was "later . . . unable to escape the notion of race he had explicitly rejected."[14]

The resulting methodological debate revealed how trenchant these questions of segregation and periodization could be. Appiah's commitment "to the final repudiation of race as a term of difference" did not align with Gates's claim, in his introduction to the issue, that critics "must turn to the black tradition itself to develop theories of criticism indigenous to our literatures," another prominent analytic strategy of the era.[15] As essays in a subsequent issue of *Critical Inquiry* began to articulate this difference more fully, they did not focus on the history of segregation, but that context shaped their sense of what critics should do. Where some scholars supported Appiah's challenge to the central concept of segregation—"race" itself—others advocated using concepts of racial tradition and identity to study the cultural expressions of those disfranchised by and resisting that institution: in Houston Baker's words, "to explore the ongoing 'poetry' of liberation expressed in the timeless struggle of Afro-Americans for black community empowerment."[16] These two methodologies conflicted inherently, and though the ensuing discussion focused on how to approach texts, participants sometimes confronted each other as if broader segregationist policies were at stake.[17] While Tzvetan Todorov, for example, described the idea of a racially specific literary tradition as "cultural *apartheid* [emphasis added]"—the name for the severe form of South African segregation that was still enforced at that time—Gates responded by describing the rejection of such a tradition as "neocolonial," a term usually applied to European and U.S. impositions in the politics and economies of developing countries. As Farah Jasmine Griffin noted in 2008, this dispute has not subsided.[18]

Elucidating both the prominence of politics and the challenge posed by periodization in this debate, Kenneth Warren has since argued that the category of African American literature was self-consciously created by writers and readers in response to Jim Crow, such that "the ending of legalized segregation, however imperfect it has been in desegregating American society, could not but change" the relationship between text and public. Scholarship, he contends, has not yet parsed this shift, in part because it has prioritized articulating continuity—a long and specifically African American (or, increasingly, black diasporic) literary tradition—over examining historical discontinuities.[19] Almost simultaneously, Thadious Davis has described contemporary black writers' focus on historical narratives as an effort to suggest, if only in fiction, "the possibilities of a communal space, a racial home," at a time when the end of de jure segregation, along with various forms of globalization, disrupted the "common narrative" that had underpinned black racial identity in the United States. In looking at how the South's segregated "black space" continues to be used in creating "racial art," Davis's project differs diametrically from Warren's argument that African American literature no longer constitutes a distinct category; this opposition renders their consensus on the need for further attention to segregation especially noteworthy.[20] More than three decades after "*Race," Writing, and Difference*, scholars from divergent perspectives agree that segregation should be moved from the background to the foreground of literary research.

Concerns about its significance for the category of African American literature are not the only challenge in exploring the periodization of Jim Crow, however; as Warren notes, that institution's ending has been acutely ambiguous because "the civil rights gains of the 1950s and 1960s did not end racial disparity, particularly at the bottom end of the economic scale."[21] This shift from the absolute constraint of Jim Crow to "disparity" has not been meaningless: residential restrictions, once enforced by residential contracts and other overt forms of discrimination, have decreased at the aggregate level since the passage of the Fair Housing Act in 1968, and an increasing percentage of students—again, at the aggregate level—attends schools with significantly diverse populations.[22] More fine-grained observations, however, reveal discouraging developments. Both schools and residential patterns have become increasingly segregated by economic status, a pattern particularly constraining for the disproportionately large percentage of poor African Americans and Latinos; schoolchildren in these demographic groups are experiencing "deepening segregation" into schools typically deprived of adequate resources.[23]

Given that aspects of Jim Crow continue in certain forms and spaces, some writers use terms from a previous era to characterize this one as well. For example, describing the millions of African Americans arrested and sentenced through disproportionate application of antidrug laws, which restrict voting and other rights even after a term has been served, Michelle Alexander uses the term "the New Jim Crow." This phrase is explicitly motivated by the desire to muster a coherent group of activists, as Alexander appeals to the "civil rights community" that fought de jure segregation in the past.[24] Such usage, however, obscures the crucial difference between practices that oppress all African Americans and those that are influenced also by class and are not so restrictive with regard to race.[25] As oppressive practices change, it seems likely that strategies for resistance may need to change also, a crucial problem in contemporary efforts to conceptualize the relationship between the present moment and that of de jure segregation. Scholarly research in the humanities, which is well situated to explore how the institutions and concepts specific to racial segregation have interacted—synchronically and diachronically—with other ways of understanding and enacting culture, could prove helpful in this regard.

While the chronological concerns that Appiah noted in *"Race," Writing, and Difference* have recently developed into a pressing argument that scholars consider how segregation per se influences the production and circulation of literary texts, Hazel Carby's essay from that volume implicitly explored Jim Crow's spatial parameters, a question that has attracted interest more gradually. Describing how southern African American women writers of the 1890s configured their social position as resulting from "internal colonization," Carby highlighted literary interest in the link between U.S. segregation and global forms of oppression.[26] This connection became increasingly important to African American writers and activists throughout the twentieth century, and in recent decades, scholarship has also focused on the diaspora created by the slave trade and on efforts to form pan-African and transnational anticolonial movements. As Sandra Gunning notes, however, this work has tended to emphasize continuity, threatening "to elide the very real impact of color, status, region, and gendered experience as sites of intra-racial difference within the context of black diaspora."[27]

Though paradigms emphasizing commonality have not tended to encourage interest in the specificities of Jim Crow, transnational research has become a multifaceted field, with increasing impetus to articulate relationships between the local and the global. As Carl H. Nightingale has recently argued, though policies enforcing racial segregation characterized much of the colonized and even postcolonial world in certain forms, they also varied, leading him to coin the term "archsegregationism" for the cases of the United States and South Africa.[28] At the end of the twentieth century, such differences provided material for comparative research, but more-recent critical paradigms mitigate against such scholarship, which tends to naturalize the borders of the nation-state as the predominant or even most meaningful demarcation of human grouping.[29] Meanwhile, however, transnational research on the United States and South Africa has been gaining momentum. Relatively early examples include Rob Nixon's examination of cross-cultural influences emerging from the transnational anti-apartheid movement and James Campbell's analysis of how the African Methodist Episcopal Church operated in each context; since 1999, the field has had its own journal, *Safundi: The Journal of South African and American Studies*.[30] More recently, scholarship on the United States' role in imperialism—whether through federal action or through the work of private institutions—provides insight into Jim Crow's global influences on both culture and institutional structure.[31]

Situating southern segregation in a broader geographical frame highlights the problem of terminology, which was—concerning the context of South Africa—vigorously debated in *"Race," Writing, and Difference*. In response to Jacques Derrida's description of "apartheid" as a term that "no tongue has ever translated . . . as if all the languages of the world were defending themselves," Anne McClintock and Rob Nixon have called for closer attention to "the politically persuasive function that successive racist lexicons have served in South Africa."[32] For Derrida, the term "apartheid" appeared distinctive for its explicitness as a "state racism . . . *inscribed in the constitution* and in an impressive judicial apparatus"; in that sense, it was also useful as an oppositional tactic, as this notorious word enabled a global audience to visualize what he sought "to condemn, to stigmatize, to combat, to keep in memory."[33] For McClintock and Nixon, however, this emphasis on what "apartheid" meant to readers irresponsibly ignored its rather brief usage by the South African state, which had enforced numerous segregationist policies before the institution of apartheid in 1948, and very quickly changed its terminology—while intensifying many of its policies—into phrases suggesting that those it oppressed were actually being granted autonomy: "separate development" or "self-determination."[34] Put together, these essays demonstrate the lexical problem scholars face when dealing with policies that have been named in ways that not only shift over time but also obscure their effects. One cannot readily dismiss either Derrida's desire to highlight oppressive policies in stark—albeit rhetorically strategic—relief or McClintock and Nixon's plea for scholarly precision. As Rita Barnard argues, this problem is compounded when one considers comparative work on South African and U.S. segregation.[35]

This national context, after all, also exemplifies a lexical lack deriving from the use of ideologically fraught naming practices. The name "Jim Crow" was appropriated from a minstrel song and character from the slavery era, a stereotypical figure that would seem to have little to do with state practice. While this term seems dauntingly insufficient for the civic and spatial constraints placed on black southerners, the more formal term "segregation" (like the Afrikaans word *apartheid*) means, etymologically, only "separateness," with no direct or inherent link to citizenship rights. In the post–Civil Rights Movement United States, such usage of the term seemed almost to replace its long-standing reference to social structure. Though Douglas S. Massey and Nancy A. Denton opened their influential 1993 study, *American Apartheid: Segregation and the Making of the Underclass*, by complaining that "during the 1970s and 1980s" the word "segregation" "disappeared from the American vocabulary," it actually remained prominent in school research, a fitting exception given that efforts to desegregate schools had constituted an early and highly visible challenge to Jim Crow and that such efforts continued nationwide during this era.[36] But this usage almost necessarily strayed quite far from the meanings associated with de jure segregation: research on education sought to understand how students were faring with regard to "academic achievement, self-esteem, and intergroup relations"—apt pedagogical concerns but only a subset of the goals of the Civil Rights Movement, which included such basic aspects of citizenship as political and juridical representation.[37]

In time, such research and even conversation began to focus on questions of social segregation, and Massey and Denton despaired that "beliefs about the voluntary and 'natural' origins of black segregation are . . . deeply ingrained in popular thinking."[38] Noting that U.S. residents were typically very critical of South African apartheid, they used this term in their title to highlight intensifying residential segregation; notably, however, even this well-intentioned usage elided the overt political disfranchisement that had been central to both southern "Jim Crow" and South African apartheid.[39] Writing about southern literature and Jim Crow in 2006, at a time when literary-critical monographs that foregrounded de jure segregation were still unusual, I often used the word "apartheid" in order to emphasize that these practices were not simply cultural habits (as even the majority opinion in *Plessy v. Ferguson* implied) but rather state-sponsored policies.[40] Today, in the context of greater research on this topic, I would choose differently for reasons that reflect the guiding concerns of both McClintock and Nixon—in that the current need for greater specificity in understanding Jim Crow in both space and time seems increasingly acute—and Derrida. As Brian Norman argues, the terms "segregation" and "Jim Crow" stand out more starkly amid references—in journalistic, political, and even academic culture—to the newly prominent idea that the United States might be "postracial."[41]

Ideally, however, expanding scholarship on segregation will yield a broader and more richly contextualized vocabulary. As suggested by the critical history outlined here, humanities scholars have many veins for research available to them, some of which have barely been initiated. One helpful focus would be the vague temporal and spatial borders of Jim Crow: its complex "more-or-less" existence in nonsouthern parts of the United States (where it preceded, in some areas, the onset of the Civil War), its complicated pre-history in the decades between the Civil War and *Plessy v. Ferguson*, its similarities with and even influences from and on international strategies for constraining racialized workers, its commonalities and overlaps with restrictions placed on other demographic groups within the United States, and, as already suggested, its similarities to and differences from contemporary forms of exclusion. How has cultural expression tracked, explored, absorbed, decried, or parodied these institutions and relationships? Answering these questions will certainly require learning from historians and from scholars of other geographic areas, but it will also benefit from explorations across media. Many of the analytic rubrics that Elizabeth Abel applies to Jim Crow's visual and especially photographic culture, for example, can be productively employed by literary critics as well, and Karl Hagstrom Miller's study of genre in recorded music may help to parse the pressing question of how segregation influenced the marketing of print texts. The responses of local audiences, local theaters, black filmmakers, and Hollywood to racial segregation provide especially vivid demonstrations of the relationship between culture and polity.[42] Some relatively recent methodologies in literary studies appear especially useful in exploring Jim Crow: understanding literature as a distinctive contribution to social and cultural geography, for example, or as a discourse contrapuntal to that of the law. But hoarier approaches to cultural expression may also yield fresh insights in this context, as segregation constitutes a particularly complex and stressful circumstance through which to explore the relationship between subjectivity and society or the affective components of interpersonal exchange.

Occasionally in this century, as they encounter representations of the acute economic and political disfranchisement that black sharecroppers confronted in the 1930s, my students mistakenly describe these workers as "slaves."[43] Such slippage is not so surprising when we consider that Depression-era sociologists also described sharecropping as barely postfeudal, a kind of residual slavery, but it does emphasize the need to understand and convey clearly the paradoxical and troubling relationships between our history's continuities and discontinuities. Setbacks follow triumphs, and the differences that do obtain between one form of oppression and its successor necessitate new strategies for resistance. On both "ends"—such as they are— of its history, southern "Jim Crow" exemplifies this problem, but for that reason, it provides a crucial staging ground for efforts to understand what has been gained and to imagine and assess options for the future.[44]

NOTES

1. See, for examples, Cell, *Highest Stage of White Supremacy*; Gilmore, *Gender and Jim Crow*; Hale, *Making Whiteness*; and Kelley, *Hammer and Hoe*.

2. Wall, afterword, 265, 267.

3. See Smethurst, *African American Roots of Modernism*, and Bow, *Partly Colored*.

4. Davis, *Southscapes*, 6.

5. Yaeger, *Dirt and Desire*, 34; Romine, *Narrative Forms of Southern Community*, 18.

6. Rubin and Holman, preface; Rubin and Holman, appendix.

7. Kreyling, *Inventing Southern Literature*, 41; Rubin, "Southern Literature and Southern Society," 19, 11.

8. Rubin, "Southern Literature and Southern Society," 12.

9. F. J. Griffin, "'Race,' Writing and Difference," 1517; Gates, "Writing 'Race,'" 6.

10. In the special issue of *Critical Inquiry*, the term "segregation" appears in four essays: Hazel Carby's on the United States, Jacques Derrida's on South Africa, Edward Said's on Israel, and Henry Louis Gates's introduction. In the latter, however, the word occurs solely in reference to Dominique de Menil's support for civil rights; Gates dedicated the issue to her.

11. Appiah, "Uncompleted Argument," 33.

12. Some work on southern literature also followed this pattern; see, for example, McKay Jenkins, *South in Black and White*. Kreyling argues, however, that during this period, scholars of southern literature tended more often to appropriate texts by African American writers into preexisting paradigms for regional literature; see *Inventing Southern Literature*, 76–97. A few essays on southern white writers did invoke Jim Crow directly; see, for example, Thomas, "*Plessy v. Ferguson*"; Metress, "Fighting Battles One by One"; M. N. Sullivan, "Persons in Pieces"; and Watson, "Uncovering the Body."

13. Norman, *Neo-Segregation Narratives*, 14.

14. Appiah, "Uncompleted Argument," 36.

15. Ibid., 35; Gates, "Writing 'Race,'" 13.

16. H. A. Baker, "Caliban's Triple Play," 195.

17. Appiah attributed this politicization to the belief that "representation in the canon is mistaken . . . for political representation"; see "Conservation of 'Race,'" 54. Gates retrospectively described *"Race," Writing, and Difference* as a way to confront "jim crow in the academy;" see "Reading *'Race,' Writing and Difference*," 1535.

18. Todorov, "'Race,' Writing, and Culture," 177; Gates, "Talkin' That Talk," 207; Griffin, "'*Race,' Writing and Difference*," 1518.

19. Warren, *What Was African American Literature?*, 146, 61, 8, 84.

20. Davis, *Southscapes*, 6, 37, 40, 17, 6.

21. Warren, *What Was African American Literature?*, 67.

22. Massey, Rothwell, and Domina, "Changing Bases of Segregation," 87; Gary Orfield, "Reviving the Goal."

23. Saporito and Deenesh, "Mapping Educational Inequality," 1227–53; Massey, Rothwell, and Domina, "Changing Bases of Segregation," 87–89; Orfield, "Reviving the Goal," 9.

24. Alexander, *New Jim Crow*, 175, 9, 11.

25. Forman, "Racial Critiques of Mass Incarceration," 52–64. Although she focuses almost exclusively on African Americans, Alexander notes that Latinos are also disproportionately disenfranchised through mass incarceration. Stephen A. Berrey approaches this question from a historical perspective, noting that southern segregationists promoted narratives of African American criminality as part of their efforts to preserve "Jim Crow"; already prominent in the nation's racial discourses, this aspect of segregationist ideology has had a lasting impact. See Berrey, *Jim Crow Routine*, 177–217.

26. Carby, "'On the Threshold of Woman's Era,'" 265.

27. Gunning, "Nancy Prince," 33.

28. Nightingale, *Segregation*, 1–17.

29. Siegel, "Beyond Compare," 65. Though vigorously critiqued in recent years, comparative inquiry does, of course, continue, and may be experiencing methodological innovations; see Friedman, "Why Not Compare?," 753–62.

30. Nixon, *Homelands, Harlem, and Hollywood*; Campbell, *Songs of Zion*.

31. See Stecopoulos, *Reconstructing the World*; Zimmerman, *Alabama in Africa*.

32. Derrida, "Racism's Last Word," 292; McClintock and Nixon, "No Names Apart," 142.

33. Derrida, "But, beyond," 163, 158.

34. McClintock and Nixon, "No Names Apart," 142.

35. Barnard, "Of Riots and Rainbows."

36. Massey and Denton, *American Apartheid*, 1.

37. Prager, Longshore, and Seeman, *School Desegregation Research*, 76.

38. Massey and Denton, *American Apartheid*, 9–10. As a teaching assistant in the 1990s, I often heard students comment on their observations of "self-segregation" in the hallways and lunchrooms of their earlier schooling; though such evidence is anecdotal, it aligns well with the interview data gathered by Eduardo Bonilla-Silva in the late 1990s; see *Racism without Racists*, 12–14.

39. By 1993, when *American Apartheid* was published, the South African government and the African National Congress party were negotiating and planning a transfer of power through the nation's first postapartheid multiracial election, which was held in 1994.

40. Duck, *Nation's Region*, 4.

41. Norman, *Neo-Segregation Narratives*, 159–72.

42. Abel, *Signs of the Times*; Miller, *Segregating Sound*; J. N. Stewart, *Migrating to the Movies*; McGehee, "Disturbing the Peace," 23–51.

43. These students assure me—honestly, I believe—that they have been schooled in this history, but their experiences undoubtedly vary. I have not tracked these errors over the years, but they occur among students from diverse backgrounds.

44. See Litwack, *How Free Is Free?*

SUGGESTIONS FOR FURTHER READING

Chafe, William H., Raymond Gavins, and Robert Korstad, eds. *Remembering Jim Crow: African Americans Tell about Life in the Segregated South.* New York: New Press, 2001.

Dailey, Jane, ed. *The Age of Jim Crow.* New York: W. W. Norton, 2008.

Klarman, Michael J. *From Jim Crow to Civil Rights: The Supreme Court and the Struggle for Racial Equality.* New York: Oxford University Press, 2004.

Lofgren, Charles A. *The Plessy Case: A Legal-Historical Interpretation.* New York: Oxford University Press, 1987.

Woodward, C. Vann. *The Strange Career of Jim Crow.* 1955. 3rd ed. New York: Oxford University Press, 1974.

PART II   Places

KEITH CARTWRIGHT

Black Atlantic

One of the most aptly titled books in all of southern literature is *Things Fall Apart* (1959) by the Nigerian novelist Chinua Achebe. *Things Fall Apart* shouts out across the Atlantic to a poem from another Anglo-colonized, postapocalyptic space, "The Second Coming" by W. B. Yeats: "Things fall apart; the center cannot hold; / Mere anarchy is loosed upon the world." Here, from the mourned wake of lost worlds, causes, and centers, we recognize that postcolonial and postplantation cultures across the globe have managed to find second comings of artistic and creative energy from shatter zones resistant to the hold of an overextended metropolitan authority. The true-north orientation of our navigating instruments has been put in question via all sorts of creolizations, and we (who study the U.S. South) are also beginning to look away from Greenwich Standard time, away from certain enshrinements of historical time (in chronologies calibrated to 1607, 1776, or 1865), and away from nation-bound mappings and periodicities. Texts such as Achebe's can help us in the way they present fabulous avatars like Tortoise or Turtle, familiar to narrative communities across the Atlantic world. Consider the following passage from a tale within the novel in which Tortoise attends a yam fest in the sky, accompanying his bird friends after having adopted the name All-of-you (or for our purposes, Y'all):

> When everything had been set before the guests, one of the people of the sky came forward and tasted a little from each pot. He then invited the birds to eat. But Tortoise jumped to his feet and asked: "For whom have you prepared this feast?"
> "For all of you," replied the man.
> Tortoise turned to the birds and said: "You remember that my name is *All of you*. The custom here is to serve the spokesman first and the others later. They will serve you when I have eaten."[1]

Achebe's Y'all can work to alter our reading and teaching practices. If readers of southern literature have been heaping their plates lately with victuals from across the Gulf, the Caribbean, and the Atlantic, we can do much more to set a disciplinary table for other temporalities and orientations, repressed kinships, newfound relations, and vexing questions of service and spokesmanship.

One of the key monographs in helping readers move beyond feasts set around the old tables of nationally rooted patria has been Paul Gilroy's *The Black Atlantic: Modernity and Double Consciousness* (1993). Here, Gilroy advocates attentiveness to transatlantic routes in the making of a "counter-culture of modernity."[2] Gilroy's sea chartings and sea changes encourage us to read a text such as Achebe's *Things Fall Apart* for its enmeshment in a matrix of black Atlantic literature and performance. Following publication of *The Black Atlantic*, the old white-captained Atlantic and the rediscovered black Atlantic of traveling intellectuals and choirs and record albums opened up to a rainbow-hued Atlantic. We began to hear, for instance, of green (Irish and ecological) and red (American Indian and proletarian) Atlantics.[3] All these Atlantics have circulated in a body of literature uniting Achebe and Tortoise (or Birago Diop and Hare) to authors such as Florida's Zora Neale Hurston, Cuba's and Miami's Lydia Cabrera, the Creek Nation's Earnest Gouge, and Georgia's Joel Chandler Harris. Still, neither departments of English nor programs in southern studies have given the circum-Atlantic base of our literary imaginations serious attention. This famine of the cross-cultural imagination has, of course, long been treated by Tortoise himself (a.k.a. Terrapin, Turtle, Cowain, Jicotea, Ayapá), who provides as good a figure as any to mark creolizing challenges of authority and spokesmanship confronting both southern studies and the black Atlantic in a hungry time of crisis within the humanities.[4]

Achebe's tale of Tortoise's opportunistic self-fashioning as All-of-you is set in a time of famine, when resources are scarce. Tortoise has heard tell of a great feast in the sky, to which all the birds have been invited. Possessing a "sweet tongue," he talks the birds into each giving him one feather apiece so that he might fly up to attend the great sky feast. Well known for being "a widely-traveled man who knew the customs of different peoples," Tortoise explains that it is the custom for guests to choose new names when they attend such feasts, and he announces his own new name of All-of-you. Since the feast, of course, is for "all of you," Tortoise hijacks the greater portion of the Sky-people's hospitality, and the bird guests each retrieve their proffered feather from Tortoise and return home, leaving him to plunge helplessly earthward on his return: "His shell broke into pieces. But there was a great medicine man in the neighborhood. Tortoise's wife sent for him and he gathered all the bits of shell and stuck them together. That's why Tortoise's shell is not smooth."[5] The tale does not simply address Tortoise's hubristic greed. It also calls for cognizance of his ability (with significant medicine help) to pull his broken pieces back together. In his scarred patchwork reassembly, he steps forward as a mosaic avatar carrying powerful medicine. Perhaps we can think of the fallen All-of-you as Humpty Dumpty's put-back-together-again Other, a wonderful figure of remixed second and third comings in an Atlantic/global world given over to visions of apocalyptic brokenness. Tortoise reminds us that if things fall apart, they may also reassemble.

75

What English departments have taken to be "the Tradition" (the canon of national British and American literatures, foregrounded by certain "World" classics) was never the whole and has always been only a set of pieces assembled around specific interests. Rather than decry the anarchy of such a situation (the "heap of broken images" of a certain St. Louis–born poet's *The Waste Land*), recent work on black Atlantic and circum-Atlantic worlds urges us to take stock of our composite cross-culturality, our holistic pharmacy. Robert Farris Thompson's path-charting work, *Flash of the Spirit* (1983), which introduced the notion of a "black Atlantic" ten years ahead of Paul Gilroy, identifies the powerful "medicine man" who helps reassemble Tortoise's busted pieces. Thompson shows us how this divinity of the deep forest and its herbal medicines, Osanyin (or Osain), wields repertoires that are "now indelibly Atlantic" since in Nigeria, Benin, Cuba, Brazil, and across the Caribbean and the United States, "most of his followers speak of a one-legged, one-armed, one-eyed appearance and his tiny, high-pitched voice."[6] These are readings of plantation cross-culturality that force us to borrow feathers from a rainbow cotillion of hosts (English and Igbo, French and Choctaw, Wolof and Spanish, Yoruba and Creole) if we are to appear at the gumbo feast of a deep southern literature. And here, too, we must take care not to construct an All-of-you who would eat what should be shared and who would silence other appetites, other voices of witness.

Gilroy's *The Black Atlantic* has been crucial to the sea changes marked by the New Southern Studies. In the wake of *The Black Atlantic*, readers of what had been regionally, racially, and nationally isolated literatures (be they "southern" or "African American") have been pushed to examine previously unexplored modes of double consciousness and countercultural modernity. Largely because Gilroy privileges an archival literary record—even as he gestures toward a lower grounding in black music's "politics of transfiguration" and "slave sublime"—and because he works within familiar matrices of North Atlantic Anglophone relations (the black United States and Britain), *The Black Atlantic* has circulated fairly well within English departments. Gilroy's work, however, must be supplemented by the anthropologically oriented work of scholars such as Melville Herskovits, Sidney Mintz, Richard Price, as well as Thompson. Thompson's study of ritual arts of Nigeria, Mali,

Congo, Togo, Cuba, Haiti, the U.S. South, Suriname, and Mexico originally theorized an "art and philosophy connecting black Atlantic worlds."[7] What Gilroy does in departing from Thompson's focus on an Afrocentric art history and philosophy (via genealogies and analyses of sequin arts, architecture, ironwork, iconography, and patchwork textiles) is to underscore the cosmopolitanism of black Atlantic countercultures of modernity. Gilroy presents an intellectual history examining "the circulation of ideas and activists as well as the movement of key cultural and political artefacts: tracts, books, gramophone records, and choirs."[8] Gilroy's artifacts fit in closer alignment with the intellectual currency of a North Atlantic academic mainstream than do those Thompson routes through more southerly currents.

Linking ports and their hinterlands along the whole Atlantic rim, "the rhizomorphic, fractal structure of the transcultural, international formation I call the black Atlantic," as Gilroy insists, marks a massive extension of scale for the scholarship of a long modernity. The ship is Gilroy's black Atlantic chronotope, pushing us beyond our geographic and national comfort zones to study "the Atlantic as a cultural and political system" emergent from transatlantic plantation slavery.[9] The resultant "fractal patterns of cultural and political exchange and transformation," creolizations and transculturations, turn us away from notions of plantation slavery as a peculiar institution and into an awareness of intricate relations between regions, nations, ethnicities, and "races." From perspectives established by *The Black Atlantic*, the Deep South of New Orleans, Charleston, Savannah, Mobile, St. Augustine, and Pensacola starts to look less like an exotic cultural backwater and more like the Atlantic norm—with kin in Nassau and Havana, Port-au-Prince and Veracruz, Rio de Janeiro and Lagos, Monrovia and Freetown, Seville and Liverpool.

Gilroy presents a resilient black Atlantic emergent from the most abject chattel slavery, fostering a resocializing "rapport with death" and a call-and-response "ethics of antiphony." In response to traumas of the Middle Passage and slaveholders' claims to utter possession of human chattel, black Atlantic reassemblies of agency—via the development of creole languages, religion, and music—proved crucial to sustaining other sets of relation. A performative, musically infused "slave sublime" provides the base for what Gilroy calls a black Atlantic "politics of transfiguration" different from a politics demanding mere "fulfillment" of Euro-metropolitan legal and scriptural code. The politics of transfiguration cannot be reduced to scripture. It must get "played, danced, and acted, as well as sung and sung about, because words," Gilroy insists, "will never be enough to communicate its unsayable

claims to the truth." The politics of transfiguration is oriented "to the formation of a community of needs and solidarity which is magically made audible
in the music itself." This focus on performance, especially in danced rites of
black Atlantic music, is a particular strength of *The Black Atlantic*, which
insists that black musics "produced out of the racialized slavery that made
modern civilization possible, now dominate its popular cultures."[10]

Gilroy focuses on the role played by travel, displacement, and exile in
the development of a black intellectual legacy that exceeds any territorial
boundary. However, his choices of focus on specific writers and thinkers
(Martin Delany, Frederick Douglass, James Weldon Johnson, W. E. B. Du
Bois, Richard Wright, and Toni Morrison) create an Atlantic centered on
the United States. The easiest critique to make of Gilroy's project is that his
Atlantic is not only a *North* Atlantic but also one largely piloted and traveled by Anglophone intellectuals. In Gilroy's black Atlantic, the Caribbean,
South America, and even Africa remain routed through the United States
and Britain. Within this charting, the American South and the Caribbean
tend to be presented as spaces from which modern black intellectuals and
musicians have migrated rather than spaces of ongoing circum-Atlantic destination and intraregional travel.

For an example of work fed by Gilroy (even as it points to cultural histories outside his primary interest or expertise), we can turn to J. Lorand
Matory's *Black Atlantic Religion*. Matory presents a "trance Atlantic" world
linking Brazil to Cuba, Haiti, Trinidad, the United States, Nigeria, Benin,
and a long-globalizing world. With a focus on Brazil, Matory studies not just
the impact of the African slave trade and plantation system on religion and
culture in Brazil but also steady patterns of trade, reverse migration (back to
West Africa), and cultural exchange that have linked Brazil to Nigeria, Benin,
and Sierra Leone from around the 1830s to the present day. He illuminates
the key roles that returning Afro-Brazilians (Yoruba and Yoruba-affiliated
Creoles) played in the development of British colonial Lagos, and he attends
to the reach of this British colonial/Yoruba-creole culture back into Brazil.
Most interesting is Matory's notion of a black Atlantic cultural dynamic that
crosses racial boundaries to shape regional and national identity. He observes
an old pattern whereby white (or even "talented tenth") elites may embrace
localized black Atlantic repertory to speak and consume for All-of-you:

> Paralleling the Afro-Brazilianist emphasis of Regionalism in Northeastern
> Brazil is an important strand in the regionalism of the U.S. South from 1889
> onward, during a period strikingly parallel to the emergence of Afro-Brazilian

studies . . . [as] elite southern whites beleaguered by economic and political decline, and domination by the elites of a whiter region, generated a sizable literature demonstrating their knowledge of and investment in African-American culture. Like so many anti-colonialist "*negrigenismos*," this southern regionalism was intent on demonstrating the legitimacy and beneficence of southern whites' sovereignty over local Blacks.[11]

Matory's insistence that Joel Chandler Harris, Newbell Niles Puckett, and DuBose Heyward, as well as Charleston's lily-white Society for the Preservation of Spirituals, all had their counterparts in regional spaces within Brazil and Cuba seems crucial to any understanding of the creations and appropriations of complex countercultures of modernity.

Gilroy's wariness of racial and ethnic essentialisms leads him to a cautionary distancing from the structures used by colonial and white supremacist systems of oppression. He is, therefore, wary of nationalisms grounded in notions of an idealized family of shared language, culture, and ethnicity, since "a defensive reaction to racism can be said to have taken over its evident appetite for sad symmetry from the discourse of the oppressor. European romanticism and cultural nationalism contributed directly to the development of modern Black Nationalism. . . . Here, the image of the nation as an accumulation of symmetrical family units makes a grim appearance amidst the drama of ethnic identity construction."[12] Gilroy points to the dangers and misrepresentations of the family analogy, which often allows a Tortoise-like patriarch or "race man" to speak for All-of-you. In spite of Gilroy's concern over redeployments of tropes of family, though, two of the most compelling monographs on southern and postplantation literatures have turned to the family model to foster alternative readings of texts from the U.S. South, the Caribbean, and Latin America. These two works are George Handley's *Postslavery Literatures in the Americas: Family Portraits in Black and White* (2000) and Valérie Loichot's *Orphan Naratives: The Postplantation Literature of Faulkner, Glissant, Morrison, and Saint-John Perse* (2007).

Handley's *Postslavery Literatures in the Americas*, in the wake of Gilroy and Caribbean artist/theorists such as Édouard Glissant and Wilson Harris, calls us away from southern and African American narratives of peculiar institutions to "read across borders" into dialogue with texts from "transcultural spaces that are legacies of hemispheric slavery and plantation ideologies."[13] Handley attends to cross-cultural "Genealogies of Narrative" and to creole narratives of genealogy in readings of a number of Cuban writers (a couple of whom happen to have deep connections in nineteenth-century New Orleans and Tampa), the Puerto Rican Rosario Ferré, and the West Indian–born and raised Jean Rhys, alongside texts by George Washington Cable, Charles Chesnutt, Frances Harper, William Faulkner, and Toni Morrison.

Valérie Loichot's *Orphan Narratives* follows up on Handley's work, drawing even more on the work of Glissant than on Gilroy. Loichot takes up Turtle's task of reassembly, reading "Morrison—Saint-John Perse— Faulkner—Glissant as a single calling-responsive unit that emerges from the pieces of their authors, fragmented by the common experience of the Plantation." Since plantation families and cultural genealogies in their full array work more as fractal rhizomes than as clearly legitimized patronymic lineages, postplantation narrative "develops around the complication, multi-plication, and confusion of sites of authority." Examining how reconstituted fictive kinships "create innovative family patterns," Loichot observes that "an 'orphan narrative' is thus not only a narrative without a parent but, more important, a narrative initiated by the orphan." Readers of the texts of plan-tation zones thus face a compelling responsibility. It will not do simply to present these texts for legitimization by a canonical patrilineage in accredited departments such as English, French, Spanish, Portuguese, or even African American studies. Rather, these orphaned texts, their affiliations often vio-lently and strategically submerged, "require special attention." "The critic needs to *foster the text*," Loichot states, in "active close reading [that] recreates kinship between the texts themselves and between the texts and the commu-nity of readers."[14] Black Atlantic and postplantation orphan texts find new networks of relation in being read outside their naturalized academic and national housings.

It makes sense that the Atlantic turn in southern studies has been more of a Gulf and Caribbean turn than a transatlantic turn. In the wake of Handley's Hispano-Caribbean and Loichot's Franco-Caribbean comparative vantage points on postplantation literatures of the U.S. South, much work in circum-Caribbean studies remains to be done, most obviously within the Anglophone literature of the region. Scholars will be bringing creative expression from the Bahamas, Guyana, Trinidad, Grenada, and Jamaica into contrapuntal and confluent engagement with works such as "A Worn Path," *Shell Shaker*, and *Mississippi Masala*.[15]

One would think that more work would have been done to address ways in which the mosaic roots of the South's plantation cultures grew from sources in African literature and orature. John Cullen Gruesser—espe-cially in *Confluences: Postcolonialism, African American Literary Studies, and the Black Atlantic* (2005) and *Black on Black: Twentieth-Century African American Writing about Africa* (2000)—has undertaken cogent work on

Africa in the American literary imagination. My own *Reading Africa into American Literature: Epics, Fables, Gothic Tales* (2002) and Babacar Mbaye's *The Trickster Comes West: Pan-African Influence in Early Black Diasporan Naratives* (2009) work from groundings in African orature to read invisi-
80   bilized transatlantic cultural migrations *into* the archive of American literatures. Active foster-readings may restore something to literature (and its systemic erasures) even as we work toward what Gilroy might call transfigurational evocations. Gay Wilentz's *Binding Cultures* (1992) and Henry Louis Gates's *The Signifying Monkey* (1988) made headway in this direction. Two recent studies—La Vinia DeLois Jennings's *Toni Morrison and the Idea of Africa* (2008) and K. Zauditu-Selassie's *African Spiritual Traditions in the Novels of Toni Morrison* (2009)—offer vital reorientations to the submerged African structures of thought informing America's most celebrated living writer. This work along transatlantic ritual/cultural gateways is only beginning to find meaningful institutional support.

Advancing Gilroy's circum-Atlantic chartings, Ifeoma Nwankwo's *Black Cosmopolitanism: Racial Consciousness and Transnational Identity* (2005) holds its focus steadily on the nineteenth century and the challenge that the Haitian Revolution (1791–1804) presented to black writers' articulations of national and transnational community formations. The Haitian Revolution, according to Nwankwo, heightened desires of enslaved and free black peoples to build far-reaching affiliations of racial identity, as one can see with a writer such as David Walker. At the same time, however, Nwankwo engages black writers' quests for an inclusive sense of national belonging, especially in Cuba and the United States. She addresses the Cuban poets Plácido and Juan Francisco Manzano alongside study of the work of Martin Delany, Frederick Douglass, and the West Indian Mary Prince. Nwankwo would have us attend to a black Atlantic "cosmopolitanism from below" that shares certain features with what Leigh Anne Duck has identified in *The Nation's Region* as "provincial cosmopolitanism."[16] Nwankwo's work is among the best of those that extend Gilroy's call to address a countercultural black Atlantic cosmopolitanism.[17] It is precisely this confluence of a black Atlantic cosmopolitanism from below and a provincial cosmopolitanism from southern backwaters that black Atlantic trickster tales can reveal to us. Who could be simultaneously more cosmopolitan and more folk-country than Brer Terrapin or Anancy or Bugs Bunny, or the griots and diviners and blues musicians who have narrated so many of these tales?

In Brer Rabbit's and Turtle's tales, we can access a mytho-poetic literary base of Atlantic contact zones: the South's Ovid, its Genesis. Here we find a body of work shared by Joel Chandler Harris, Zora Neale Hurston, the Creek writer Earnest Gouge, the Louisiana Creole Alcée Fortier, the Cuban Lydia Cabrera, the Senegalese Birago Diop, and the Nigerian Amos Tutuola, among many others. We must foster such texts beyond the national categorizations that consign them (and ourselves) to minoritarian orphan status. Lodged within these repeating tales are some of the mechanisms whereby black subjects evaded reduction to consumable chattel within the symbolic order of plantation slavery and remained consuming subjects within a world of their own making. For their ability to swing multiperspectival visions of reality and for their heating the pots of agency and innovation, the plantation tales may be as valuable as the blues and early New Orleans swing. Attentiveness to these tales of plantation and wilderness reveals a multilingual, transnational literature that is unquestionably circum-Atlantic. Such repertoires, however, remain orphaned, having not received their due as essential grounding of literatures that have emerged from our early contact zones.

Yoruba divination narratives direct us to follow Tortoise's (or Turtle's) ambit across the Atlantic. The Yoruba narrative for the divination figure Irete Owonrin tells of how Ajapa (Tortoise) used his ventriloquial and masking skills during a famine to disrupt and terrify the marketplace, thereby giving him access to vacated food stalls. No one can face the dread spectacle of Ajapa singing and dancing from a hollowed-out palm tree until Osain, the herbalist deity of medicine (the Medicine Man of Achebe's tale) exposes Tortoise's masquerade and brands him with a hot iron (thus marking his shell), after which he makes Tortoise his junior partner in medicine.[18]

From the first published stories of *Afro-Cuban Tales* (1936) to her work in Miami dedicated to him in *Ayapá: Cuentos de Jicotea* (1971), Lydia Cabrera accorded Turtle an emblematic trickster agency that migrates across the Florida Straits. In "One-Legged-Osain" from her first collection, Cabrera introduces the maimed, one-legged, one-armed, one-eyed pharmacological activator of all initiations: Osain, and his helper Jicotea or Ayapá (Turtle's Cuban Yoruba appellation). Here we find that Turtle has lodged himself comfortably in a yam pile beneath the house of newlyweds. When the wife goes to fetch yams for a meal of fufu, she is met with Turtle's territorializing cry from the yam pile itself. The husband reports the talking yam to his king, who arrives and sends his own representatives to face this strange, talking food staple, the ultimate subaltern: "Under no condition can we allow yams the privilege of speaking."[19] After many others' failed attempts, it is finally one-legged Osain who restores order by exposing Tortoise at the bottom of the yam pile. Osain gives Jicotea a thorough beating with his stick, satisfying the king and the newly married couple, who may eat their fufu in peace. Later that evening Jicotea does a familiar limbo dance of recovery: "Tiny sounds began to multiply, the sounds of body parts that had been mutilated, killed, and spread far and wide beginning to seek each other out, to piece themselves back together and come back to life!" (148). This is the manner in which Jicotea pulls his fragmented self together to join the disfigured, ventriloquial Osain for a good cigar with coffee around a fire deep in the bush. In the multiplied sounds of Turtle's body parts seeking one another out, piecing themselves together, and coming to life, we get a model of the transfiguring work of black Atlantic music routed through a submerged folk authority.[20]

In "Arere Marekén" from the same collection, Turtle falls in love with the king's wife, following "the waves of skirts and petticoats" as she comes singing and dancing down the path (119). He asks only, "Let my eyes enjoy you Arere" (119). But what is it that his eyes enjoy? When Arere explains herself to the king, "Today the road was full of puddles. I held up my train for fear of soiling it" (120), the direction of puddle-dwelling Turtle's gaze becomes clear. For the affront of penetrating the secret of the king's wife with his eyes' enjoyment, Turtle is clubbed to pieces, while Queen Arere, grinding her corn and coffee in a mortar and pestle, grieves. That night, Turtle's many pieces come back to life, reassembling his shell marked and lined with "so many scars for Arere's love" (121). Turtle has a carnal tricksterish knack for discovering the secrets of others. This quest is also sacral, about desire and knowledge, growth and reproduction, as well as about uncovering the truth.

Turtle's vision quest takes us back to the ritual question, "What is the truth?" posed in Hurston's *Tell My Horse*. We recall how the vodou *manbo* answered: "revealing her sex organs," and bearing witness that "there is no mystery beyond the mysterious source of life." We recall, too, the scene in *Their Eyes Were Watching God* beneath the blossoming pear tree, where Janie was called "to come and gaze on a mystery."[21] Turtle, his shell cracked to hell, keeps coming back for second and third visions of this truth. A mosaic body of circum-Atlantic literature, myth, and history has been covered up, kept from our sight, allowing smaller or more partial national and ethnic signs to be held up as wonders. Turtle can help us reenter these gulf abysses. But we will have to loosen our habits and boundaries and be ready to step across puddles, if we are to become Turtle's *iyawo*, or initiate "bride."

Carrying bush knowledge of Turtle from *Cuentos negros de Cuba* and from the Miami volume, *Ayapá: Cuentos de Jicotea*, we can attend to the talents that Turtle and Tortoise possess for crossing boundaries (marine, riverine, earthly, and subterranean), as well as to Turtle's capacity to reassemble his broken parts (the ultimate task of the creole) via a "potent vitality" as Cabrera puts it: "the miracle of a resurrection."[22] We may read this resurrection in texts of exile and retraversal from narrators in Miami and in Havana, or from the Oklahoma lands of Creek and Seminole removal—and as far as Brazil, Puerto Rico, and Nigeria.

Turtle's courting of initiatory vision from beneath women's dresses appears in a collection of tales by Earnest Gouge, written in Muscogee Creek in Oklahoma in 1915 but not published until the University of Oklahoma Press presented it in the dual-language edition *Totkv Mocvse / New Fire* in 2004. In Gouge's rendition of "Turtle Tries to Look up Women's Dresses," Turtle hunkers low, trying to gain vision of women's private parts, and gets beaten to a pulp as a result, his shell shattered, his parts scattered. He manages, however, with a shell-shaking stomp song ("I come-come together / I shake-shake together"), to sing and shake himself back together: "Cvte-li-li, / Cvte-sokoso"[23] (114). Turtle keeps hauling his cracked shell back for another vision of the truth, and caught at it again (hiding down low beneath the mortar and pestle where he knows the women will pound corn), he begs the women—no matter what mode of punishment they choose for him—to please, please not wrap his neck in a necklace made of their pubic hair and sling him into the river. Born and bred in that briar patch, Turtle gets his initiatory necklace and his swim. "When they do that to me, I just die!" Turtle says, "creating a wake" over the water (115). The Muscogee turtle's vision quest offers a powerful perspective for rereading Janie beneath the creaming pear tree, Caddy Compson muddy drawered in a Yoknapatawpha pear tree, and the stomp grounds of LeAnne Howe's Choctaw novel *Shell Shaker*. Why we do not study our trickster lore more often and more carefully than we do is a key question. When tides of the black Atlantic are extended along the coasts and rivers of Afro-Indian contacts, we have to rethink the contact zone more locally and also more systemically—well beyond habitual Euro-colonial and national ethnic habits.

Attentiveness to cultural bubblings from street culture points to this underacknowledged figure of New Orleans Creole identity and desire: turtle (or *cowan* or *cawain*), whose flesh makes a lovely sherry-splashed soup, whose shells Choctaw women shook at stomp grounds and perhaps in Marie Laveau's backyard, and whose tales circulate across the black Atlantic.[24] Turtle is an apt totemic figure of Crescent City's *longue durée*. In *Hearing Sappho in New Orleans: The Call of Poetry from Congo Square to the Ninth Ward* (2012), Ruth Salvaggio uncannily pairs Sappho's tortoise-shell lyre and her lyrics of eros, loss, and desire with an old New Orleans lullaby in a call to reimagine "the delicate bond of person and creature and thing that made up the city."[25] Salvaggio turns us to the following old Creole lyrics of New Orleans's flood-prone streets:

Gae, gae soulangae	Gae, gae Soulangae
bailé chemin-là.	Sweep the road.
M'a dit li, oui,	I tell her, yes,
m'a dit li,	I tell her,
cowan li connais parlé	The turtle knows how to talk,
ti cowan li connais parlé.	The little turtle knows how to talk.[26]

Like many lullabies, this song codes adult knowledge born of Mama's erotic travels. Mama knows Turtle is not so innocent. And she knows this from tales circulated about Turtle/Tortoise from West Africa to Cuba, New Orleans, and the Indian nations surrounding Creole City. Turtle likes to talk. This is what the Creole lullaby's mother has in mind by calling Soulangae to sweep the road of its minefield of turtles.

Like Sappho and the mother of the Creole lullaby, the New Orleans women of Mona Lisa Saloy's Seventh Ward know how to evoke Turtle to speak their own longings. Accessing a Creole pharmacy in *Red Beans and Ricely Yours* (2005), Saloy knows too that Turtle (*Cawain*) is the source of erotically powered Easter eggs and a potentially botchable aphrodisiacal stew:

Springtime brought *cawain*,
and Daddy's expert taking of its head,
then gently removing the neck gland—
a purple thing of poison if burst.
He hung the headless turtle, it still
kicking for three days on the wooden fence,
even its head snapped for hours in the grass.
Never lost a *cawain*, its 21 meat flavors tasting
of beef, pork, fish, and then some.
The turtle eggs, Mother's favorite, promised
youth, health, and sexy eyes, Daddy said.
When he shooed aunts, uncles, and Mother
out of the kitchen, he blended herbs for
sauté and his special roux before stewing.[27]

Springtime brings Daddy's becoming-Turtle, his roux knowledge and egg promise to Mother: youth, health, sexy eyes. Uniting sexual healing and tricksterism, Turtle simmers as communion chronotope of Mother's desire and Daddy's secret seasonings.

The collective Tortoise/Turtle assemblage that has pulled its pieces together and moved from famine to feast does, however, bear the potential for becoming a spokespersonly All-of-you who would devour what should be left out for others and who would use his knowledge of others' private parts to shame and control them. Nevertheless, Turtle carries a powerful medicine of reassembly, one that we may need to read beyond black Atlantic perspectives. A red Atlantic perspective could trace the New Orleans, Muscogee, Cuban, and Puerto Rican Turtle narratives in different Gulf loop currents of Taíno/Timucuan/Muscogee repeating time. An Iberian or Irish Atlantic focus would show us other sets of patternings of a Deep South, and we need to tap into Pacific and Indian Ocean currents of migration in framing a more holistic and inclusive vision that need not aim at gobbling up all the yams at the feast.

To conclude, I would turn us to a culinary master of New Orleans, to hear from Leah Chase (of Dooky Chase restaurant) how Creole time was marked by Turtle since "Easter dinner was never complete without cowan," with "Females . . . preferred and . . . always prodded around the rear legs for eggs . . . cooked right along with the turtle in the spicy gravy." Creole Easter makes its feast of complete assemblage around Turtle's flesh and eggs, a fete that nevertheless comes at considerable cost. Chase adds her thoughts on belief and payback:

> Like my mother and all others who enjoy eating this tasty, spicy dish, I always get the turtle alive. Remove the head and meticulously clean the meat from the shell. If there are any eggs, remove and set aside. I know of no chef willing to take on such a task, but you can believe that this dish is well worth the work. It was always served over rice with a good potato salad on the side and a glass of claret—and that's heaven![28]

This is a heaven to believe in indeed. But let us never forget—as Leah Chase underscores—the demanding economy behind the ritual production and imagination of heaven. Neither the state's nor the nation's miserly trickle-down economy will support the costs, but most of us still demand asymmetrical consumer access to productions (real and symbolic) of New Orleans's, the Gulf's, and the black Atlantic's hospitality. We must embrace both the prerequisite work and the subsequent political/social/spiritual commitments—the fostered reaffiliations—that genuine approaches to Atlantic history and performance may bring. Our *we* must be ready to offer up something for the feathers we borrow. We must also be ready to transgress certain boundaries and be beat to pieces, to host and be hosted, to renegotiate relations to mapped territoriality itself. Heavenly feasting and the powerful truths of erotic musication are ample reward for the reassembled All-of-us who recognize parts of ourselves in a long-tested body of narrative emergent from Atlantic shatter zones.

NOTES

1. Achebe, *Things Fall Apart*, 98.

2. Gilroy, *Black Atlantic*, 36. The opening chapter of Gilroy's book is titled "The Black Atlantic as a Counterculture of Modernity," 1–40.

3. See Lloyd and O'Neill, *Black and Green Atlantic*; J. Weaver, *Red Atlantic*; Linebaugh and Rediker, *Many-Headed Hydra*.

4. I take the term "cross-cultural imagination" from the brilliant work of Wilson Harris, *Womb of Space*. For more of Turtle's repertory, beyond the works by Cabrera, Gouge, Bascom, and Salvaggio addressed in detail in this essay, see also Owomoyela, *Yoruba Trickster Tales*, and Lugo, *De Arañas, Conejos y Tortugas*, as well as Cartwright, *Sacral Grooves, Limbo Gateways*.

5. Achebe, *Things Fall Apart*, 99.

6. R. F. Thompson, *Flash of the Spirit*, 43. Something of Osain's form and pharmacy appear in a tale from Creole Louisiana published by the Modern Language Association back in 1895; see Fortier, *Louisiana Folk-Tales*, 117–19.

7. R. F. Thompson, *Flash of the Spirit*, xvii.

8. Gilroy, *Black Atlantic*, 4.

9. Ibid., 4, 15.

10. Ibid., 198, 200, 131, 137, 37, 80.

11. Matory, *Black Atlantic Religion*, 296. By "talented tenth," I am referring to W. E. B. Du Bois's notion in *The Souls of Black Folk* (1903) of a "talented tenth percent" of the race that would constitute its elite, its leadership. As Frantz Fanon observed, the postcolonial elite may wield a nationalist discourse in such a manner in order to hold on to the colonialists' positions of power and to speak and consume as "All of You." Francois Duvalier of Haiti (with his negritude rhetoric and manipulation of vodou) makes for one of the best examples. Any hold on authenticity or custodianship of folk authority runs these potential dangers.

12. Gilroy, *Black Atlantic*, 97.

13. Handley, *Postslavery Literatures in the Americas*, 25–26.

14. Loichot, *Orphan Narratives*, 29, 30, 3, 30, 12.

15. Strangely, neither English departments nor programs in southern studies are well (dis) positioned to foster this kind of Anglophone comparative work, given their orientations around traditional periodicities and canons of nation.

16. Nwankwo, *Black Cosmopolitanism*, 14; Duck, *Nation's Region*, 177.

17. Edward Pavlić's *Crossroads Modernism* and Heather Russell's *Legba's Crossings* must be mentioned for moving in this direction and for their tending to elements of the black Atlantic sacred performative arts that are deeply aligned with Robert Farris Thompson's notion of the black Atlantic.

18. Bascom, *Ifa Divination*, 399–405.

19. Cabrera, *Afro-Cuban Tales*, 146; text hereafter cited parenthetically. This scene shares much with a Yoruba talking-skull tale and Hurston's "High Walker and the Bloody Bones" in *Mules and Men*.

20. See W. Harris, "History, Fable and Myth," 152–66. Harris notes the need of the West Indian artist to risk identification with "the limbo dance" (162), "the gateway complex between cultures" (165), "this trickster gateway," in "a risk which identifies . . . with the submerged authority of a dispossessed people" (166).

21. Hurston, *Tell My Horse*, 370; Hurston, *Their Eyes Were Watching God*, 10.

22. Cabrera, *Ayapá*, 11, 12.

23. Gouge, *Totkv Mocvse / New Fire*, 114.

24. Marie Laveau is said to have let Choctaw market women encamp in the backyard of her New Orleans St. Ann Street home. See Long, *New Orleans Voudou Priestess*, 35–38.

25. Salvaggio, *Hearing Sappho in New Orleans*, 32.

26. Ibid., 32–33. Salvaggio's source for the Creole song of Ti Cowan is Monroe, *Bayou Ballads*, 6.

27. Saloy, *Red Beans and Ricely Yours*, 45.

28. Chase, *Dooky Chase Cookbook*, 36.

SUGGESTIONS FOR FURTHER READING

Cartwright, Keith. *Sacral Grooves, Limbo Gateways: Travels in Deep Southern Time, Circum-Caribbean Space, Afro-creole Authority.* Athens: University of Georgia Press, 2013.

Gilroy, Paul. *The Black Atlantic: Modernity and Double Consciousness.* Cambridge, Mass.: Harvard University Press, 1993.

Matory, J. Lorand. *Black Atlantic Religion: Tradition, Transnationalism, and Matriarchy in the Afro-Brazilian Candomblé.* Princeton, N.J.: Princeton University Press, 2005.

Nwankwo, Ifeoma. *Black Cosmopolitanism: Racial Consciousness and Transnational Identity in the Nineteenth-Century Americas.* Philadelphia: University of Pennsylvania Press, 2005.

Thompson, Robert Farris. *Flash of the Spirit: African and Afro-American Art and Philosophy.* New York: Vintage, 1983.

Ward, Brian, Martyn Bone, and William A. Link, eds. *The American South and the Atlantic World.* Gainesville: University Press of Florida, 2013.

NATALIE J. RING

Tropics

The tropics are both a place and an ideological concept at first discernible from a global view. They are neither local nor contained. In cartographic terms, the term "tropics" refers to a portion of the globe on either side of the equator that is bordered by two parallel lines running on an east-west axis around the earth. The equator is zero degrees latitude. North of the equator is the latitude 23° 26' N known as the Tropic of Cancer, and south of the equator is the latitude 23° 26' S known as the Tropic of Capricorn. The geographical band circling the globe between Tropics—"the tropics"—became legible as a coherent space only from the perspective of modern empire, with transoceanic navigation, colonization, and intercontinental travel. Thus the tropics have been a subject of fascination since the early days of European global exploration and colonization—at least since the fifteenth century. As attention to global contexts has increased in contemporary scholarship, as well, the concept of the "tropical" has been reinvigorated in an array of disciplines including history, literature, cultural studies, geography, American studies, sociology, philosophy, anthropology, and Southeast Asian studies.

Depictions of the tropics typically have drawn on a complex of themes such as climate, race, landscape, and disease. The early imperial idea that some places, peoples, and plants were tropical and some were not generated a set of recognizable tropes, metaphors, and symbols of the tropics—including representations of the tropics as enervating, medically pathological and contagious, cursed with racial degeneration, overgrown with prolific vegetation, dominated by a plantation economy and race slavery, prone to despotic government, and poverty stricken. Yet the discourse of tropical spaces often was unstable and marked by representational duality. As David Arnold notes, "The symbolism of the tropics was deeply ambivalent, for a landscape of seeming natural abundance and great fertility was also paradoxically a landscape of poverty and disease."[1]

Descriptions of the tropics as fertile and profitable acted as a spur to investment in the expansion of European empire, while depictions of the tropics as depraved bolstered arguments for imperial management and discipline of the space. The tendency to paint the tropics as both pathological and paradisiacal also generated what one geographer has called a "moral climatology."[2] Images of the tropical world frequently offered moral judgments on tropical lands and peoples, even while those seeking to master the tropics often did so under the guise of scientific objectivity. The use of moralistic idioms contributed to the construction of the tropics as Other, a geographical entity often deemed inferior to the temperate regions of the world.[3]

89

Indeed, the idea of tropicality has a long history, which grew out of the expansionist tendencies of European and later American imperialism. As far back as the fifteenth century, Portuguese and Spanish explorers of equatorial Africa and the Americas found the climate an unhealthy one. New scholarship by Nicolás Wey Gómez shows that Christopher Columbus did not travel a western route as conventional understanding suggests but rather sailed south consciously guided by geographical knowledge of the tropics that identified social and political differences between hot, frigid, and temperate climates. Columbus's vision of the tropics drew on two competing beliefs: that the "torrid zone" constituted the "hot, infertile, and uninhabitable fringes of the world" dominated by "marvels" and "monsters"; and that it was a fecund and productive place brimming with natural resources ready to be exploited by those seeking wealth.[4] In the nineteenth century, the French conquest of Algeria and the British interest in India, the West Indies, and Africa brought Europeans into contact with tropical climates and diseases.[5] In the late nineteenth and early twentieth centuries, several developments, including further British exploration of Africa; the U.S. acquisition of the Philippines, Puerto Rico, the Hawaiian Islands, and Guam; the American presence in Cuba during the Spanish-American War; and the United States' role in the development of the Panama Canal, guaranteed that the allure of the tropics in the context of colonialism would persist.[6]

Itinerant travelers, naturalists, social scientists, and political theorists also classified and analyzed the tropicality of the New World. In the late eighteenth century, Enlightenment thinkers revisited classical theories about the relationship between climates and political institutions and social customs. In his 1748 essay "Of National Characters," Hume suggested that all nations located in the tropics were "inferior to the rest of the species," and this could be traced to racial differences. He identified "indolence" as a problem in the southern parts of the world and saw no "ingenuity" in black slaves.[7] The same year Montesquieu published *On the Spirit of the Laws*, which argued that climate played a central role in determining the character of nations and that hot, humid weather made people servile and engendered the rise of despots. In the eighteenth and nineteenth centuries, European naturalists such as Alexander von Humboldt, William Burchell, and Charles Darwin began to collect and document tropical plants, insects, and birds through writing, painting, sketching, and photography after touring the Americas.[8]

Their efforts to map so-called exotic countries like Paraguay and Brazil reinforced the belief that tropicality was a subject worthy of social scientific study.

Europe's long-standing interest in tropical geography involved not only South America but also North America, and in particular the American South—even though, it is important to note, no part of the mainland United States falls within the actual cartographical definition of the tropics. As early as the seventeenth century, the conceptual category of the tropical had become transportable to other geographic spaces of relative climatic warmth, including the southern North American colonies. Colonists considering transplantation to Virginia and South Carolina harbored anxieties about the dangers that hot climates posed to European constitutions. In the early nineteenth century, discussions of European settlement in the southern states of Louisiana, Mississippi, Alabama, and Georgia also manifested a concern with health and climate.[9] Both Europeans and Americans singled out certain tropical features of the southern states such as the climate, topography, fever diseases, the plantation household, and race slavery and its effect on both slave owners and the enslaved. One of the most recognized references to the regional and implied tropical distinctions between the U.S. North and the U.S. South was made in 1785 by Thomas Jefferson in a letter he wrote to his Parisian friend Marquis de Chastellux on regional character traits. Jefferson explained that northerners were "cool, sober, laborious, persevering, independent, jealous of their own liberties and just to those of others," while southerners were "fiery, voluptuary, indolent, unsteady, independent, zealous for their own liberties, but trampling on those of others."[10]

A more pertinent early American example of the idea of the tropics is that of J. Hector St. John de Crèvecoeur, a former French lieutenant, British Loyalist, farmer in rural New York, and self-proclaimed artist, who published *Letters from an American Farmer* (1782). On the cusp of the American Revolution, Crèvecoeur assembled twelve "letters" that provided the British with an exposition on the nature of American character and identity. This transatlantic author with a multinational audience did more than write a canonical text in early American literature about the republican yeoman farmer. Crèvecoeur's art and writing placed the U.S. South in a global framework that underscored the significance of the tropical plantation to a transatlantic economy rooted in slave labor. His travel abroad, including in the

Caribbean, influenced his assessment of the southern colonies of Virginia and South Carolina. In one of his letters detailing life in Charleston, South Carolina, Crèvecoeur portrayed the city as a warm, fertile, "barbarous" tropical space.[11] However, U.S. writers in the late eighteenth century at the moment of nationalization were caught in a bind. They worked very hard to throw off the tropical associations of the U.S. South since by definition the tropics were a marker of political coloniality rather than independence. But the development of a distinctly southern plantation economy, the enduring torrid climate and fecund topography, and the expanding population of African descent repeatedly pulled the U.S. South back into the orbit of the global tropics, underscoring the protean boundaries distinguishing it from foreign locales.

Thus the icon of the "tropical plantation colony" and its origin story in the theory of climatic determinism is powerfully connected to the belief that the U.S. South has always been a distinctive region in the United States. Yet paradoxically the U.S. South's long-standing contact with New World plantation colonialism makes the region transnational and a quintessential feature of the global tropics.[12] Southern tropicality is not a new idea in southern history and literature, but the term has assumed recent importance in the field of southern studies, particularly in recent scholarship on the "Global South" influenced by postcolonial theory (a key strand of the New Southern Studies). In 2004, Jon Smith and Deborah Cohn edited a volume titled *Look Away: The U.S. South in New World Studies* designed to draw attention to the ways in which a comparative framework on the study of the movement of peoples, ideas, and patterns of governance between the U.S. South, the Caribbean, and Latin America could illuminate the nature of postcoloniality. Three years later, Deborah Cohn explained the motive behind this edited collection:

> The U.S. South has not traditionally been studied as part of the postcolonial world. Recently, however, scholars have begun to note how the region calls into question a number of the binary oppositions upon which postcolonial theory has been predicated: it is both victor and defeated, colonizer and colonized, empire and colony, center and periphery; it is white and nonwhite. The region is simultaneously "South" in relation to the U.S. North and "North" in relation to its geopolitical south: in the antebellum years, it cherished a dream of creating a great slave empire that would include Puerto Rico and Cuba; long after the Civil War, white southerners viewed the South as a conquered, occupied, and colonized by the (U.S.) North; and as the U.S. expanded into the Caribbean at the turn of the twentieth century, the region became part of the imperial North, which did after all exert its political muscle through the

Global South, in part through the deployment of plantation discourses and modes of domination.[13]

This theoretical understanding of the U.S. South as intrinsically and multiply involved in global imperial contexts has opened the door to scholarship on the "hemispheric South," which similarly privileges the shared tropical characteristics of the southern states with other American nations to their southward.

While "Global South" and "hemispheric South" are fairly recent additions to the critical vocabulary of southern studies, the U.S. South has been figured as tropical Other since the beginning of national history, and southern tropicality has contained a host of contradictory meanings, both negative and positive. Across the nineteenth century, many Americans viewed the region as a tropical Eden, a therapeutic escape from the alienation engendered by the rise of corporate capitalism in the North. A spate of promotional books and pamphlets focusing on the salubrious climate, the edenic landscape, and the availability of exotic fruits and vegetables welcomed tourists and real-estate developers to the region. Florida, in particular, was often portrayed as a bountiful tropical paradise.[14] Yet underneath the allure of southern tropicality lurked a dark side, a dangerous and pestilential character that needed to be tamed, a land and people ravaged by what one writer in the *North American Review* called "tropical poverty."[15]

Many northern travelers who ventured south or social scientists interested in southern topography often commented on the dangerous, dank, and primitive characteristics of the environment. In his travel diary titled *From Cape Cod to Dixie and the Tropics* (1864), John Milton Mackie from Massachusetts described the "primeval aspect of things" and marveled at the fecundity of the vegetation in the tropics. In Louisiana he noticed that "it [wa]s the beauty of the garden and the desolation of the waste combined" that drew his attention to the local scenery. Yet while Mackie was enthralled with the paradoxical combination of spectacular beauty and decay in the U.S. South, he was glad to leave behind what he called the "pet nursery of fever and pestilence" and return to New England.[16] More than fifty years later, Ellsworth Huntington, a geographer at Yale University, published a book titled *Civilization and Climate* (1915) illustrating how tropical and subtropical climates inhibited the development of modern civilization around the globe. Huntington discussed the connection between environment and progress in a number of locales including the Caribbean, Mexico, South America, Latin America, and the southern states. What all the inhabitants in these areas had in common, Huntington asserted, was a certain "tropical inertia," a state of mind and physical constitution that sapped men's virility, engendered backwardness and disease, and contributed to the degeneration of the white race.[17] Thus the U.S. South was considered as primordial and treacherous as any distant foreign nation.

One of the most noticeable connections between the U.S. South and the tropics was the intersection of race, place, and disease in the late nineteenth and early twentieth centuries. The need for healthy bodies in military combat and imperialist expeditions to the tropics generated an interest in a scientific field called "tropical medicine" designed to facilitate these goals. Various schools, including one in London and others in the United States—such as at Tulane University, Harvard University, Johns Hopkins, the National Institutes of Health, the Walter Reed Army Institute of Research, and the Rockefeller Institute for Medical Research—formed in response to the imperatives of global expansion and the need to master the danger of tropical diseases in colonial settings. A popular medical text by Patrick Manson titled *Tropical Diseases: A Manual of the Diseases of Warm Climates* (1898), published at the height of Western imperialism, offered doctors and public-health reformers a new tool for interpreting foreign environments and cataloging disease. Michel Foucault has described the development of this kind of perception as a "historical and geographical consciousness of disease."[18] The need to know, to look, to catalog, and to map the place (and ultimately the body) would make it possible for Western colonizers to survive the perils of the tropics.

As the scientific and medical communities began to focus on the connections between insects, climate, and disease in their surveys of foreign tropical locales, many Americans began to associate the U.S. South with tropical pathology. Tropical diseases included hookworm, yellow fever, malaria, and pellagra, illnesses widespread throughout the southern states and considered distinctive to the region. The United States' acquisition of the Philippines, Puerto Rico, the Hawaiian Islands, and Guam, as well as the American presence in Cuba and the Panama Canal Zone, raised questions about the nature of infectious diseases thought to have entered North America in the bodies of American soldiers, missionaries, businessmen, sailors, and diplomats who had been traveling abroad. Doctors warned that southern ports in particular were potential hotbeds for diseases indigenous to the damp, hot climate of tropical regions.[19] Relying on a military metaphor, the *Southern Medical Journal* declared that as a consequence of imperialism, "it falls to the lot of southern physicians to act as outpost sentinels, guarding the land from being unconsciously invaded by devastating diseases."[20] In one moment, in the 1880s and 1890s, public health reformers and U.S. government officials implicated Havana, Cuba, in yellow fever outbreaks in Mississippi, Louisiana, and Alabama, a claim that fueled anxiety about the invasion of tropical disease in the U.S. South and ultimately played a role in inciting the Spanish-American War in 1898.[21] A number of physicians and public health officials who wound up working in public health campaigns in the southern states after the war had previously been stationed in colonial governments in tropical countries. A transnational circuit of peoples, colonial models of reform, patterns of governance, and scientific ideas traversed the borders of nation-states and contributed to the idea of a global tropical "South." As historian of medicine Warwick Anderson explains, "These colonial technicians were prepared to find the modern in the colony, the colonial in the metropole."[22]

Shortly after the end of the Spanish-American War, Col. Bailey K. Ashford, an American army surgeon in Puerto Rico, identified and treated almost three hundred thousand Puerto Rican patients infected with hookworm. Inspired by Ashford, Charles Wardell Stiles of the U.S. Public Health Service and Marine Hospital Service began searching for the "germ of laziness" since he was convinced it contributed to the lethargy and idiocy of poor white southerners. Through the assistance of Walter Hines Page, a social reformer from North Carolina, Stiles galvanized the Rockefeller philanthropies in 1909 to establish the Rockefeller Sanitary Commission for the Eradication of Hookworm (RSC), which would initiate a five-year effort to treat hookworm in the South. The southern-based RSC proved to be successful and gave rise to the formation of the International Health Commission (later renamed the International Health Board), which broadened the effort to eradicate not just hookworm but also malaria and other tropical diseases abroad in such places as Mexico, Brazil, and the Caribbean. Public health work done in the tropics underscored the similarities between the U.S. South and distant tropical locales, and efforts to eradicate diseases in the U.S. South then encouraged reformers and philanthropists to expand their activities in other sites in the tropics. One did not need to travel abroad to discover an exotic disease or to experience the enervating effects of a tropical climate. Americans had a tropical country thriving in their own backyard. In general, physicians, reformers, and social scientists writing and talking about disease in the U.S. South did not always make the distinction between imported diseases and diseases native to the region. The tendency to blur the line between the two modes of origin and geographical manifestation in scientific and popular discourse contributed to an image of the tropics as a place that had long harbored unusual and potentially life-threatening diseases. The idea that diseases have histories and are not timeless entities often became lost in discussions of tropical areas.

Indeed, Walter Hines Page published an article in his widely distributed magazine *World's Work* titled "The Hookworm in Civilization," which made comparisons between the "disease belts" of the world, including the U.S. South and Puerto Rico, and described the way in which public health work in the U.S. South seemed likely to lead to "the reclamation of other tropical peoples." The subtitle of the piece, touching on several key points, reads, "The work of the Rockefeller Sanitary Commission in the southern states making men of anaemics [*sic*] and adding incalculable wealth as well as health to our national assets—the way toward the reclamation of all tropical peoples and the utilization of their lands—the prodigious part that this parasite has played in the history of all warm countries."[23] The idea of reclaiming "tropical peoples" intimately linked the U.S. South with the Caribbean, South America, Latin America, and eastern countries, drawing the southern states into a wider global "South." This transnational circuit of rhetoric and reform encouraged American cultural imperialists to construct the U.S. South as a tropical space in need of colonial uplift, much like the tropical possessions acquired as a result of American imperialism. As Page notes, the key to tropical uplift was the extraction of profit from a productive workforce no longer burdened by the enfeebling effect of hookworm. The interest in an efficient, healthy, productive workforce reflected a broader imperial effort to dominate economically the global tropics.

The commitment to "civilizing missions" in the tropics and uplifting backward races through public health applied not only to African Americans in the U.S. South but also to poor southern whites. One of the objectives of tropical medicine was to explain the various interactions between racial constitutions and environment. Racialized manifestations of disease proved highly dangerous to Anglo-Saxon civilization, whether they involved nonwhite peoples in the colonies or African Americans in the United States, 90 percent of whom lived in the South. Colonial physicians and reformers presumed that people of color were plagued with contagious disease. Science also promised answers to the medical conundrum posed by the threat of specific tropical diseases and climates: Why did the white man demonstrate a relative lack of immunity to foreign contagions given the asserted superiority of the Anglo-Saxons? This medical paradox was especially apparent in the southern states because a conspicuous portion of the poor white population suffered from hookworm and pellagra. Physicians and travelers to the tropics had always worried about possible expressions of white degeneration as a result of the hot, humid climate, particularly mental and moral retrogression. Ellsworth Huntington argued that certain tropical diseases native to the southern climate of the United States had exacerbated the penchant for laziness that had caused poor southern whites to "fall below the level of their race" and become "Crackers."[24] Wickliffe Rose, the secretary of the RSC, noted the degeneracy of the white race during a trip to Richmond County, Virginia, in 1911. He reported that poor whites in this community, called "Forkemites," were known for their extreme poverty, lack of thrift, "dense illiteracy," and "low moral tone" and subsequently had begun to take on the appearance of a "distinct race."[25] Were poor whites in the South true Anglo-Saxon Americans or tropical peoples in need of "reclamation," as Walter Hines Page asserted?

The existence of poor whites in the U.S. South exhibiting tropical characteristics in need of uplift drew attention to the inherent postcolonial tension and contradiction between race and place. Just when the Western imperial project abroad was helping to contribute to the construction of a white national identity through its dominance of the nonwhite races in the tropical world, the distinctive problems of the U.S. South, magnified by the new interest in tropical medicine, including the pathology of poor whites, threatened to weaken this ideology from within. Mastering disease in the tropics—whether in the U.S. South or abroad—was a crucial part of the imperial project, a step taken toward saving white civilization and extracting profitable economic resources by way of healthy labor.

In a broad sense, then, viewed from the northern industrialized hemisphere the tropics were always located south of temperate regions. From the perspective of the United States, the southern tropics included the Caribbean, Mexico, Central America, and South America. Yet throughout the history of the United States, the boundary between the temperate and the tropical has shifted farther north, and the southern region of the country has been incorporated into a broader vision of the tropics that includes all of the Americas south of the Mason-Dixon Line. In his theoretical work on the rise of the modern capitalist world system, Immanuel Wallerstein explains how "this new peripheral region" could be envisioned as "the extended Caribbean, stretching from northeast Brazil to Maryland."[26] The historical fascination with the tropical South or the "extended Caribbean" suggests the fluidity of the categories of region, nation-state, and empire. The U.S. South was simultaneously viewed as alluring and perilous, exotic yet familiarly American. In the past fifteen years, as scholars have moved away from the North/South binary that has long dominated the field of southern studies, the idea of the tropical South has regained prominence. This global view of tropicality suggests that rather than framing the relationship between the U.S. South and the nation on a regional and national scale, we need to broaden our units of spatial analysis.

NOTES

1. Arnold, "'Illusory Riches,'" 7. For other examples addressing this duality see Arnold, "Inventing Tropicality," and Frenkel, "Jungle Stories."

2. See Livingstone, "Race, Space and Moral Climatology."

3. See Stepan, *Picturing Tropical Nature*, 17; and Frenkel, "Geographical Representations of the 'Other.'"

4. Gómez, *Tropics of Empire*, 50.

5. See Curtin, *Death by Migration,* and Arnold, *Tropics and the Traveling Gaze.*

6. For some histories of American imperialism and tropicality, see Espinosa, *Epidemic Invasions,* and Moran, *Colonizing Leprosy.*

7. Hume, *Political Essays*, 86. See also Gerbi, *Dispute of the New World*, 35.

8. See Stepan, *Picturing Tropical Nature*; Driver, "Imagining the Tropics"; and Martins, "Naturalist's Vision of the Tropics".

9. Kupperman, "Fear of Hot Climes," and Livingstone, "Human Acclimatization."

10. Thomas Jefferson, letter to Marquis de Chastellux.

11. See Greeson, *Our South*, and Iannini, "'The Itinerant Man.'"

12. Quotations taken from E. T. Thompson, "Climatic Theory of the Plantation," 53; and Smith and Cohn, "Introduction," 2.

13. Cohn, "U.S. Southern and Latin American Studies," 39–40.

14. See Dunn, "Florida"; Tarr, "Eden Revisited"; and Grunwald, *Swamp.*

15. Westerberg, "Revolt of the Tropics," 263.

16. Mackie, *From Cape Cod to Dixie*, 153, 169.

17. Huntington, *Civilization and Climate*, 17, 42.

18. Michel Foucault, *Birth of the Clinic*, 24.

19. John D. Swan, "Tropical Diseases," 400.

20. "American Society of Tropical Medicine," 175–76.

21. See Espinosa, *Epidemic Invasions.*

22. W. Anderson, "Pacific Crossings," 278.

23. Page, "Hookworm in Civilization."

24. Huntington, *Civilization and Climate*, 24, 35.

25. Wickliffe Rose, letter to Frederick T. Gates.

26. Wallerstein, *Modern World-System*, 2:167.

SUGGESTIONS FOR FURTHER READING

Cocks, Catherine. *Tropical Whites: The Rise of the Tourist South in the Americas*. Philadelphia: University of Pennsylvania Press, 2013.

Greeson, Jennifer Rae. *Our South: Geographic Fantasy and the Rise of National Literature*. Cambridge, Mass.: Harvard University Press, 2010.

MacIntyre, Rebecca C. "Promoting the Gothic South." *Southern Cultures* 11 (Summer 2005): 33–61.

Ring, Natalie J. *The Problem South: Region, Empire, and the New Liberal State, 1880–1930*. Athens: University of Georgia Press, 2012.

Rothman, Adam. "Lafcadio Hearn in New Orleans and the Caribbean." *Atlantic Studies* 5 (August 2008): 265–83.

Smith, Jon. "Hot Bodies and 'Barbaric Tropics': The U.S. South and New World Natures." *Southern Literary Journal* 36 (Fall 2003): 104–20.

ANNA BRICKHOUSE

Haiti:

When Edgar Allan Poe wrote a pro-slavery book review for the Richmond-based *Southern Literary Messenger* in 1836, lashing out against northern as well as transatlantic critics ("false, ignorant, and malignant accusers" of the South) and defending its "much abused and partially-considered institution" of human bondage, he referred circumspectly to a troubling matter that he apparently believed weighed heavily on the minds of his readers. The unnamed problem involved what he called "recent events in the West Indies." Poe never specified which events he meant, noting only, in the vaguest of terms, that they gave "an awful importance to these thoughts in our minds," along with "the parallel movement here." It is possible that one of the recent events Poe had in mind was the abolition of slavery in the British West Indies in 1834, which gave strength to the parallel U.S. abolitionist movement, which he saw as central to the "assault" on the South. But Poe clearly had other "events in the West Indies" in mind as well, to which he could refer only elliptically as a source of "something like despair," "a sort of boding," a set of "vague and undefined fears."[1] The term "West Indies" was Poe's proxy, in other words, for an unspoken historical phenomenon, as it was for William Faulkner's Quentin when, in *Absalom, Absalom!* (1936), he condensed Thomas Sutpen's biographical turning point to a single phrase: "He went to the West Indies."[2]

What both Poe and Faulkner evoke, but without specifying directly, is the Haitian Revolution of 1791–1804, which occurred in the richest colony of the New World, Saint-Domingue. Located on the Caribbean island of Hispaniola, Saint-Domingue—often referred to in English as St. Domingo or San Domingo—was colonized in the late fifteenth century by the Spanish and then in the 1600s by French settlers, who brought the western portion of the island under recognized French colonial rule in 1697. (The eastern portion of the island remained a Spanish colony and was known as Santo Domingo and is today the Dominican Republic.) When a coalition of black slaves and mixed-race free people (*gens de couleur libres*) took up arms and threw off French colonial rule at the end of the eighteenth century, they restored to their country the indigenous name it had once been

talking about without saying — slave revolts that the U.S. South feared called by the Taino population living on the island when the first European colonizers arrived: Haiti.

Born of what the Trinidadian historian C. L. R. James once called "the only successful slave revolt in history," Haiti was the second nation in the Americas (after the United States) to declare its independence from its European colonizer and the first to abolish slavery. The Canadian political philosopher Peter Hallward, writing in 2004, in the bicentennial year of the Haitian revolution, explains its significance this way:

> Of the three great revolutions that began in the final decades of the eighteenth century—American, French and Haitian—only the third forced the unconditional application of the principle that inspired each one: affirmation of the natural, inalienable rights of all human beings. Only in Haiti was the declaration of human freedom universally consistent. Only in Haiti was this declaration sustained *at all costs*, in direct opposition to the social order and economic logic of the day. Only in Haiti were the consequences of this declaration— the end of slavery, of colonialism, of racial inequality—upheld in terms that directly embraced the world as a whole. And of these three revolutions, it is Haiti's that has the most to teach those seeking to uphold these consequences in the world today.[3]

Yet, as the Haitian anthropologist and philosopher of history Michel-Rolph Trouillot has argued, the Haitian revolution was from its own moment silenced in a variety of ways within Western history; it "entered history with the peculiar characteristic of being unthinkable even as it happened" and has been often inadvertently and sometimes systematically erased by historians from the early nineteenth century onward.[4] The Haitian Revolution, unlike the American and the French Revolutions, was often told in the nineteenth and twentieth centuries as a story beyond the pale of politics or philosophy—a gothic story about animalistic slaves brutally avenging themselves against their white masters, unleashing the so-called "Horrors of St. Domingo."

The official U.S. relation to Haiti was openly hostile from the beginning of its revolution. Thomas Jefferson, who was secretary of state when the Haitian Revolution broke out and had served his first term as president before it was over, offered aid to the French in reestablishing colonial rule. A half century of active U.S. undermining of Haiti's independent government ensued, through means ranging from official disavowal of its legitimacy and sovereignty to trade embargoes designed to crush its war-ravaged economy and ensure that, as Jefferson's son-in-law, Congressman John Wayles Eppes, put it, "the Negro government should be destroyed." While the United

States was ultimately unsuccessful in putting an end to Haitian independence, its official foreign policies vis-à-vis the "Negro government" contributed profoundly to the historical impoverishment of that republic. Not until the Lincoln administration—and the abolition of U.S. slavery—was the American government willing to establish diplomatic relations with Haiti.

As Poe's ominous reference to the Haitian Revolution suggests, the relation of the U.S South to Haiti was especially vexed, for the reality of what he called "the parallel movement here"—organized slave insurrection in the South, modeled specifically on the Haitian Revolution—could not be denied. Jefferson had made the connection between the revolution that produced Haiti and the response of those enslaved in the U.S. South almost immediately, observing that "the West Indies appear[ed] to have given considerable impulse to the minds of the slaves . . . in the United States."⁵ Southern slaveholders were painfully aware that Haiti had constituted a model for the major slave insurrections led by Gabriel Prosser and Denmark Vesey, in 1820 and 1822 respectively. Saint-Dominguean creole protest songs, reported to have been sung on Louisiana plantations, were but one measure of the pervasive cultural transmission of the Haitian Revolution among the enslaved even while it was still occurring. The largest slave revolt in U.S. history, which occurred in southern Louisiana in 1811, was in fact led by at least one free immigrant from Saint-Domingue, Charles Deslondes, and some slaveholders identified traveling "French Negroes" specifically as a threat to their peculiar institution. In 1829, David Walker's *Appeal* made explicit references to Haiti in its call for resistance to slavery and racial oppression, instructing the "colored citizens" of the United States to "go to [their] brethren, the Haytians, who, according to their word, [were] bound to protect and comfort [them]."⁶

The Haitian Revolution shaped the contours of nineteenth-century U.S. literary culture in profound ways, from explicit representation of the revolutionary atmosphere in Leonora Sansay's *Secret History, or The Horrors of St. Domingo* to far more subtle engagements. In 1837, the Louisiana-born Victor Séjour, the son of a free man of color from the former Saint Domingue, published the earliest known story of the African American literary tradition, "Le Mulâtre." Written in French, this powerful tale played upon the prevailing horror of slave revolt and anxieties about Haiti while elaborating the Haitian Revolution as a dark family romance. That same year, Poe completed *The Narrative of Arthur Gordon Pym*, a strange novella about a voyage "to the southward," in which a shipboard insurrection and the eponymous protagonist's eventual predicament—finding himself one of "the only living white men upon [an] island"—allegorically refracted popular anxieties about the fate of colonial slaveholders in Saint-Domingue.[7] In 1852, Herman Melville's novella "Benito Cereno" also featured a shipboard insurrection, this one explicitly a slave rebellion, aboard a vessel whose name immediately signaled its implied historical reference: the *San Dominick*.

At the same time, the history of the Haitian Revolution figured prominently in much abolitionist literature, from Harriet Beecher Stowe's *Uncle Tom's Cabin* (1852), with its Caribbean-inflected villain (Simon Legree, who had "learned his trade well . . . in the West Indies") and its ominous warnings about the terrors that might occur "if ever the San Domingo hour" came; to Wendell Phillips's poem honoring the revolution and its leader "Toussaint" (Toussaint-Louverture); to the first novel by an African American writer, William Wells Brown's *Clotel, or, The President's Daughter* (1853). Though Haiti is never referenced explicitly in the novel, Brown clearly had its history in mind, for he cites from John R. Beard's study of the Haitian Revolution in a key chapter on Clotel's arrest as a fugitive slave. Two years later, Brown issued his own history, *St. Domingo: Its Revolutions and its Patriots*, in which he fashioned Toussaint-Louverture as an American revolutionary superior to his U.S counterpart, George Washington. Brown also lectured and published widely in support of African American migration to Haiti and considered repatriating there himself. After the Civil War, the storied Frederick Douglass—whose only work of fiction, a historical novella titled *The Heroic Slave* (1853), had conjoined the theme of slave revolt to the proximity of U.S. and West Indian shores—served as ambassador to Haiti and wrote extensively on its history and politics in his journalism.

But Haiti shaped early U.S. literary history in other ways as well. In the early nineteenth century, the ever-present possibility of Haitian-influenced slave insurrection occurring in the United States led to vigilant new legal restrictions prohibiting the immigration of Haitians and other free people of color from the French Caribbean. Of particular concern were mixed-race Saint-Domingueans—such as Séjour's father—many of whom had already fled the island during the revolution and relocated in the United States, particularly Louisiana. These anxieties about the permeability of national and racial borders led a "Franco-Africanist" shadow to fall across the U.S. literary landscape of the nineteenth century: a series of racially indeterminate francophone or French-identified figures proliferating in works ranging from Walt Whitman's early novel *Franklin Evans* (1842) to Stowe's *Uncle Tom's Cabin*, in which the tragic quadroon Cassy is New Orleans born, French speaking, and associated with the powers of vodou, while Madame de Thoux, introduced by the narrator as a "French" woman traveling between the United States and Canada, turns out in fact to be George Harris's mulatta sister, formerly the slave and then the wife of a West Indian creole master. Lydia Maria Child, said to have inaugurated the tradition of mixed-race plotlines in U.S. literature, favored French-inflected names for her heroines in the early story "The Quadroons" (1842); by the time she wrote *A Romance of the Republic* (1867), her racially mixed, polyglot heroines were explicitly linked with the francophone West Indies. Similarly, both Kate Chopin and George Washington Cable drew on the creole francophonie of Louisiana in fiction and essays to thematize the relation between linguistic and racial hybridity. Even in a northeastern-set work such as Herman Melville's *Pierre* (1852), the connections between Haiti and a U.S. literary tradition of Franco-Africanism shadow the text: the eponymous hero is haunted by the Franco-Africanist figure of Isabel, a ghostly stranger claiming kin as the daughter of Pierre's father and an exotic French immigrant purported to have fled the Reign of Terror. Yet Isabel's "dark, olive cheek" and "Nubian" eyes that threaten to "desecrat[e] the whitest altar" of the Glendinning name suggest that her Frenchness, like Mme de Thoux's, may have come by way of revolutionary Saint-Domingue rather than revolutionary France.[8]

Melville invokes the Haitian revolution explicitly in the novella published three years later, "Benito Cereno" (1855), the story of Amasa Delano, the New England–born captain of a U.S. whaling vessel, who encounters a storm-tossed slave ship off the coast of Chile and attempts to lend help to its eponymous and erratically behaving Spanish captain. Set in 1799, the story takes place almost entirely on Benito Cereno's ship, which is called the *San Dominick*—a thinly veiled reference, of course, to Saint-Domingue and the Haitian Revolution. Readers who don't grasp the reference may not foresee the novella's stunning reversal: it turns out that a revolution has in fact occurred on Cereno's slave ship; the slaves have seized control of their former masters as well as the vessel. Neither the reader nor Delano knows the true state of affairs until near the end of the story, at which point the novella offers a searing allegory of the early American attitude toward the emergence of Haiti when Delano calls on his sailors to quell the insurrection, restore the revolutionaries to slavery—and keep the profit for themselves: the sailors "were told that the Spanish captain considered his ship as good as lost. . . . Take her, and no small part should be theirs."[9]

"Benito Cereno" brilliantly interweaves the dominant American discourse of racially defined horror at the revolution ("nothing but a total massacre of the whites could be looked for") with an incisive commentary on the hypocrisy of America's own historical self-perception as typified by Delano's point of view. Little by little, the novella unmasks Delano's own supposedly revolutionary ideals—his "generous" "democratic conclusion" and "republican impartiality"—as self-congratulatory and self-interested. In the final pages of the novella, after order has been restored and the black insurrectionaries tortured and executed, Captain Delano remains untroubled by what he has witnessed (and indeed destroyed with his intervention), while Benito Cereno, to the contrary, is unable to recover from the trauma of the slave revolution. In the most famous lines from the novella, Captain Delano, "more and more astonished and pained," cries out, "You are saved, Don Benito . . . you are saved; what has cast such a shadow upon you?" Benito Cereno's two-word reply—"The negro"—succinctly encapsulates Trouillot's thesis about the sheer incomprehensibility of the Haitian Revolution within the terms of Western modernity and historical thought.[10]

The American intervention into Haitian affairs foreshadowed by "Benito Cereno" became a historical reality in 1915, when U.S. Marines were ordered to Port-au-Prince by President Woodrow Wilson. The deployment was touted as a peacekeeping mission but was widely recognized as a military occupation to safeguard the economic interests of U.S. corporations and their investors by gaining control of Haiti's customhouses, banks, national treasury, and—not least important—its exploitable laborers who, now further impoverished by the U.S. redirection of a staggering 40 percent of Haitian national income toward the repayment of international debt, worked as virtual slaves for companies such as the U.S. sugar company HASCO.

Early twentieth-century literary texts meditated on Haiti and the occupation from a variety of perspectives, particularly during the Harlem Renaissance. In Claude McKay's *Home to Harlem* (1928), for example, the black protagonist, Jake Brown, has been to Europe as a soldier but cannot point to Haiti on a map until, in one of the book's major turning points, he meets the exiled Haitian intellectual, Ray, on a train. Jake, who embodies the fragile values of folk life in the rural U.S. South now displaced to the modernized streets of New York City, finds new moral sustenance in Haiti's revolutionary history. Before meeting Ray, Jake is "very American in spirit and share[s] a little of that American contempt for poor foreigners," but as his Haitian interlocutor speaks about Toussaint-Louverture, the French Revolution, and the "beautiful ideas of the 'Liberté, Egalité, Fraternité' of Mankind," Jake is transported beyond the confines of the world as he has known it. He "felt like one passing through a dream, vivid in rich, varied colors. It was revelation beautiful in his mind." To Jake it is a "romance of his race," one that allows him also to place Haitian revolutionary history in a comparative context, appreciating "that Black Hayti's independence was more dramatic and picturesque than the United States' independence": its revolution was "fought for collective liberty," rather than for landed white men; was threatened not only by the French but by "the Spanish and the English vultures" (not to mention potential American ones); and was shaped by "laws for Hayti that held more of human wisdom and nobility than the Code Napoleon." But when Jake asks Ray why he is living in the segregated United States instead of Haiti, his sense of historical euphoria is quickly deflated. "Maybe you didn't know that during the World War Uncle Sam grabbed Hayti," Ray tells him. Ray's father protested the U.S. occupation and found himself imprisoned; then "American marines killed [his brother] in the street."[11] Like his family, Ray suggests, the ideals of the Haitian Revolution have been destroyed by U.S. intervention.

Ten years later, Harlem Renaissance writer Zora Neale Hurston published the book *Tell My Horse* (1938) based on her ethnographic research on zombies and vodou in Haiti as well as Jamaica. Unlike McKay, whose anti-imperial stance resonated clearly in the voice of his character Ray, Hurston produced a text with a far more ambiguous position on U.S. intervention in Haiti—a book that earned her what J. Michael Dash has called "the dubious distinction of being the only black writer who actually approved of the American occupation."[12] Based on her fieldwork in Haiti during 1937, a few years after the end of the occupation, *Tell My Horse* offers a number of positive observations about the effects of the occupation: in her stated view, "Haiti [was] left with a stable currency, the beginnings of a system of transportation, a modern capitol, the nucleus of a modern army."[13] Staging a conversation between herself and a Haitian man critical of the occupation, Hurston stacks the deck against the anti-imperial point of view and allows her own narrative persona to trump all criticism of the occupation with sly questions and observations. Yet as Barbara Ladd and others have suggested, Hurston's apparent endorsement of the American intervention in Haiti may well have masked a subtle critique of the discourse of "black degeneracy" that sustained both racial violence at home and U.S. imperialism in the Caribbean during the first half of the twentieth century.[14] Indeed, *Tell My Horse* drew much of its language and some of its actual material from sensationalist, popular U.S. works about Haiti such as William Seabrook's travelogue *Magic Island* (1929), which titillated American audiences with stories of zombies and bloody vodou ceremonies. In Hurston's parodic text, this mode of gothic, exotic primitivism allowed her to comment obliquely on the uncanny relation between the

United States and one of its many neo-plantation "Souths" throughout the hemisphere: its Haitian heart of darkness.

The contemporary period of U.S. literature has also seen several powerful contributions to the tradition of imaginative writing about Haiti. Of particular note is Madison Smartt Bell's widely acclaimed Haitian Revolution trilogy—*All Souls' Rising* (1995), *Master of the Crossroads* (2000), and *The Stone That the Builder Refused* (2004)—which recounts the revolution across three novels spanning the slave insurrection of 1791 through the arrival and ultimate vanquishing of Napoleon's forces and the 1804 declaration of Haitian independence. Told through multiple points of view, including the slave-owning *grand blanc*, or white Frenchman, Doctor Hébert; the vodou-practicing and formerly enslaved military leader, Riau; and Hébert's mixed-race mistress, Nanon, the meticulously researched trilogy offers a stunning and often brutally graphic portrait of the cruelties of Enlightenment Saint-Domingue followed by the violent emergence of the second independent state in the Western Hemisphere and the world's first free black republic. Bell himself was born and raised in Tennessee, and as some critics have observed, his trilogy brings to bear on Haitian revolutionary history the author's contemplation of the legacy of slavery in the U.S. South.

Finally, no account of Haiti in the U.S. literary imagination would be complete without mentioning the important contributions of the Haitian American writer Edwidge Danticat, who has written widely on the country of her birth and the experiences of Haitian immigrants to the United States in both her fiction and her nonfiction. Danticat's work explores a range of historical moments in Haitian and Haitian-U.S. history, beginning with her first published novel, *Breath, Eyes, Memory* (1994), and its poignant depiction of the sexual identity of a young Haitian American woman who must come to terms with her mother, her origin in an act of rape, and the meaning of her cultural inheritance from Haiti. It is perhaps a measure of how far U.S. literary history has come that Danticat has recently edited an anthology (for the noir crime fiction series published by Akashic Books) called *Haiti Noir* (2011)—a title that in some sense recalls the Haitian southern gothic mode popularized in the nineteenth century while proffering a very different poetics of relation. Indeed, with its locally inflected stories by both Haitian and U.S. writers, the collection ultimately constitutes a series of what Danticat calls "elegies to lost, broken, and destroyed neighborhoods" in the wake of the devastating earthquake that struck Haiti in 2010.[15]

NOTES

1. [Poe], "Slavery," 339, 337.
2. Faulkner, *Absalom, Absalom!*, 194.
3. Hallward, "Haitian Inspiration," 2.
4. Trouillot, *Silencing the Past*, 73.
5. Thomas Jefferson, letter to Rufus King, 9:383.
6. D. Walker, *Walker's Appeal*, 63.
7. Poe, *Narrative of Arthur Gordon Pym*, 216.
8. Melville, *Pierre*, 46, 145, 91.
9. Melville, "Benito Cereno," 235.
10. Ibid., 235, 207, 257.
11. McKay, *Home to Harlem*, 134–38.
12. Dash, *Haiti and the United States*, 60.
13. Hurston, *Tell My Horse*, 74.
14. See Ladd, *Resisting History*, 108–31.
15. Danticat, quoted in Lee, "Dark Tales Illuminate Haiti," C1.

SUGGESTIONS FOR FURTHER READING

Buck-Morss, Susan. *Hegel, Haiti, and Universal History*. Pittsburgh: University of Pittsburgh Press, 2009.

Dash, J. Michael. *Haiti and the United States: National Stereotypes and the Literary Imagination*. New York: Palgrave McMillan: 1997.

Dubois, Laurent. *Avengers of the New World: The Story of the Haitian Revolution*. Cambridge, Mass.: Harvard University Press, 2005.

Fischer, Sybille. *Modernity Disavowed: Haiti and the Cultures of Slavery in the Age of Revolution*. Durham, N.C.: Duke University Press, 2004.

James, C. L. R. *The Black Jacobins: Toussaint L'Ouverture and the San Domingo Revolution*. New York: Vintage, 1989.

Trouillot, Michel-Rolph. *Silencing the Past: Power and the Production of History*. Boston: Beacon Press, 1995.

Begining with the slave revolts in Haiti, The U.S. + its southern literary history have expressed a mirrored fear — As in Haiti is a mirror of the U.S.

America

DEBORAH COHN

In her 1998 presidential address to the American Studies Association (ASA), Janice Radway posed the question, "What's in a name?" The question served as a gateway to an examination of the discipline of U.S. American studies, and to what constitutes both the discipline and the idea of "America." Radway began by drawing her audience's attention to the meaning of "American" in the association's name, which, she argued, obfuscates the awareness of difference by assuming—presuming, even—"the coherence of a distinctly 'American' history." She further asked if "the perpetuation of the particular name, 'American,' in the title of the field and in the name of the association continue[s] surreptitiously to support the notion that such a whole exists even in the face of powerful work that tends to question its presumed coherence"; this, in turn, led her to wonder if the field should be reconceptualized, and the association itself renamed "in order to prevent this imaginary unity from asserting itself in the end, again and again, as a form of containment." For Radway, the use of the term "American"—and, I would add, "America"—is problematic both because it overlooks difference and presupposes a singular and coherent referent, and because it is in itself an "imperial gesture" that claims the name of the hemisphere for the United States alone.[1] Kirsten Silva Gruesz has elaborated on both aspects of this dilemma with her assertion that "part of what has been repressed in the United States is its location within a hemisphere *also* known as America (or, to inflect it with an appropriate Spanishness, América), a name it has appropriated synechdochically unto itself."[2]

The conflation of "America" with "United States," the subsuming of the full geographic and cultural expanse encompassed by the former within the carefully delimited borders of the U.S. nation-state, is hardly unique to the discipline of U.S. American studies; if anything, the discipline's usage is symptomatic of how the term is used in common parlance. By bringing this question to the fore, though, and inscribing it within the moment of disciplinary self-reflection constituted by the genre of a presidential address, Radway's words marked an important moment in the transnational and hemispheric turn that has characterized U.S. American studies over the past twenty years—even as her own persistent use of "America"/"American" to refer exclusively to "the United States" throughout her speech bears witness to just how deeply ingrained the usurpation of the term by the nation-state is.[3]

To address the concerns that she put forth in her speech, Radway proposed renaming the ASA. She offered three alternative names, all of which invited reflection on how the discipline of U.S. American studies has actively constituted its object of study within a geopolitical context of U.S. hegemony. Radway suggested that the ASA become the International Association for the Study of the United States; the Inter-American Studies Association; or the Society for Intercultural Studies. The most pertinent of these options to the present discussion are the first two, which focus on the object of study (rather than the method of analysis) as the linchpin that orients scholars in their research. Both, however, also speak to the difficulties of addressing the question of "America" within this institutional context. The "International Association for the Study of the United States" acknowledges the international context for producing scholarship on the United States and demands that scholars from abroad, as well as other associations focusing on the Americas, play an important role. At the same time, though, it runs the risk of fostering isolationism by situating the association's center of gravity within the political borders of the United States, rather than focusing on the transnational flows of people and ideas that pass back and forth across these borders.[4] The "Inter-American Studies Association," in turn, foregrounds the transnational dimension of the discipline and would likewise entail establishing connections with other national and international scholarly associations. However, it privileges the hemisphere over other important transnational connections even as it runs the risk of reinscribing the very power imbalances that Radway sought to avoid by renaming the field—for, as Sophia McClennen asked in 2004, "Is it possible for such a field of study, which is squarely located within U.S. academic institutions and often practiced by scholars working in departments of English and History, to avoid a further replication of the unequal relations of power that have dominated the Inter-American literary scene?"[5] In the years since McClennen articulated this question, the discipline has started to engage with a number of these issues, but the question of unequal relations of power, both within and outside U.S. institutions and among disciplines, still remains a concern.

Perhaps not surprisingly, Radway's address did not ultimately prompt the ASA to change its name. It was, nevertheless, a timely and provocative intervention at a moment when U.S. American studies scholars were turning their attention ever more toward the need to situate the study of the United States within transnational and hemispheric frameworks. Just four years earlier, Amy Kaplan and Donald Pease's monumental coedited collection, *Cultures of United States Imperialism* (1994), had made an important contribution to catalyzing this transnational turn by placing the question of imperialism within the United States (and within U.S. American studies) front and center: empire by definition, of course, involves the study of multiple nations yoked together within unequal power relations. (The work was itself fittingly sparked, as Pease details, "in the shadow of three macropolitical events—the end of the Cold War, the Persian Gulf War, and the Columbian quincentennial.")[6] And it is hardly coincidental that Radway suggested recentering the study of the United States within an international context the year after her predecessor, Mary Helen Washington, called on the ASA to "put African American studies at the center" of U.S. American studies, and to commit to collaborating with and supporting ethnic studies groups, as well as fostering relationships with American studies scholars in Africa, Latin America, and the Caribbean. This was an act that challenged the monolithic conceptualizations of "America" that Radway likewise sought to break down. It also challenged the hegemony and privileges of those who anchored the discipline's traditional institutional identity, even as it spoke to "a commitment to the deeper project of *reconstructing* the definition of America—and not merely 'expanding' or 'including' so-called others [emphasis in original]."[7]

Washington's idea of "*reconstructing* the definition of America" is absolutely key to fostering the production of scholarship within U.S. American studies about the Americas (and beyond) that does not automatically privilege the United States. Great strides have been made in this direction with both the research and the activism of scholars such as McClennen, Ralph Bauer, Anna Brickhouse, Debra Castillo, Amaryll Chanady, Jane Desmond, Brian Edwards, Emory Elliott, Claire Fox, Susan Gillman, Kirsten Silva Gruesz, Matthew Guterl, George Handley, Robert Irwin, Djelal Kadir, Caroline Levander, José Limón, Claudia Sadowski-Smith, José David Saldívar, Ramón Saldívar, Ricardo Salvatore, Micol Seigel, Jon Smith, Diana Taylor, Sonia Torres, and many others. However, the extent to which "America" is used even now by some of the most accomplished scholars in U.S. American studies—and some of the most attentive to questions of empire and transnationalism—to refer to "the United States" speaks to the fact that this is a work still in progress.

Washington and Radway alike spoke of the complicity of U.S. American studies in overlooking differences and power imbalances, both within the United States and in an international arena, and of thereby participating

110

in broader systems of oppression and discrimination. Both likewise sought ways of redressing this situation, the former through deeper commitment to ethnic studies and international exchange, and the latter by engaging more deeply and sensitively with the position of the United States within a transnational context. It is thus no coincidence that both scholars invoked Cuban writer José Martí's 1891 essay, "Nuestra América" ("Our America"), as a challenge to practitioners of U.S. American studies and a way of pushing them to open their understanding of both the idea of "America" and the field as a whole.[8] First published in *La revista ilustrada* in New York, where Martí was exiled for his efforts to secure Cuban independence from Spain, and where he was able to observe from the inside as the United States sought to extend its political influence throughout the hemisphere, the essay reclaims "America": "nuestra América," "nuestra América mestiza," and, simply, "América," with no modification, are the sole terms used to designate Spanish America, whereas the United States is identified as "los Estados Unidos" and "América del Norte" (with Canada here falling victim to the powers of metonymy) and is thereby prevented from being the default referent of "America."[9]

Martí's essay is framed by his concern about the rise of U.S. expansionism in Spanish America. He urges those who live in the region to look beyond their local concerns and join forces with one another to resist the encroachment of the giant with the seven-league boots, as Martí refers to the United States, and he suggests that the new republics will find the strength to sustain themselves in the international arena by drawing on their own histories and cultures as foundations for their political structures and leaders. The essay has had a powerful and galvanizing effect throughout Spanish America, as well as in the United States. Indeed, Martí himself has become a touchstone throughout the Americas. Long an important figure for those working in Spanish American literary studies, he has also become central to U.S. American studies. Published the same year that Radway gave her presidential address, Jeffrey Belnap and Raúl Fernández's collection, *José Martí's "Our America": From National to Hemispheric Cultural Studies* (1998), speaks to the rise in important scholarship on the writer being produced within this discipline, as well as to the efforts to situate his work within a hemispheric context. The collection brings together an impressive roster of distinguished Latin Americanists, U.S. Americanists, and Latino studies scholars alike. Belnap and Fernández sought to incorporate Martí's work "into the general reexamination of the borders, parameters, and purposes of 'American Studies,'" and to "explore the tension in Martí's work between

national and transnational perspectives, a tension that makes his analysis
of the Western Hemisphere's different national formations and their intra-
hemispheric relations extremely significant for reconfiguring the way we
think about 'America.'"[10] The essays in the collection place the writer's work
in dialogue with writers on and from the United States and its frontier
zones, such as Helen Hunt Jackson (whose novel *Ramona* Martí translated),
Alexis de Tocqueville, Frederick Jackson Turner, Walt Whitman, and María
Amparo Ruiz de Burton (1832–1895), whose own experience of U.S. expansionism as a native of Baja California who spent much of her life in the
United States provides an interesting complement to that of Martí. The
collection is an exciting and fruitful project that invites us to remap not just
U.S. American cultural studies, as the title of José David Saldívar's essay
suggests, but "America," too. At the same time, though, it relies almost
exclusively on scholars based in the U.S. academy for the vision of hemispheric cultural studies that it articulates and thus, however inadvertently,
perpetuates an imbalance that it had set out to redress.

So, then, what is in a name? Consideration of the name of an academic
association and of research directions for U.S. American studies may seem
peripheral to an effort to characterize what is "America," but, in fact, studying this institutional history brings to the foreground many of the key issues
and forces that have long determined (and overdetermined) the use and
understanding of the term. Simply put, names matter, and they are inscribed
within a hierarchy of power that both reflects and conditions political relations as well as the production and circulation of knowledge. Technically,
"America" encompasses the hemisphere, although it has, as we have seen,
been co-opted within the United States in both popular and scholarly contexts and used to designate "the United States." This has not always been the
case, though: when the term first appeared in Martin Waldseemüller's 1507
world map, it was used to designate not North America or even the hemisphere but rather South America. Only later was the referent of "America"
broadened to include North America as well. (The term is, in fact, absent
from Waldseemüller's 1516 "Carta Marina," in which the southern continent
is labeled "Terra Nova," while the northern continent is identified as "Cuba,"
which, in turn, is identified as part of Asia.)

The co-optation of "America" by "the United States" came with time. It
was, as McClennen demonstrates, already under way in documents such as
Thomas Paine's *Common Sense*, the Declaration of Independence, and the
Articles of Confederation, which refer to "America," "the American states,"
"the United Colonies," "the thirteen united States of America," "the United

Colonies of North America," and "the United States of America," among others. With the nation-state itself still inchoate, it is, as McClennen notes, not surprising that its name had not yet fully taken shape, but she reads the incipient divorce (within the United States) of "America" from its hemispheric referent as pointing toward the future, that is, toward a "story of a semantic slippage that serves the interests of U.S. expansionism and hegemony."[11]

Gruesz has observed that "the self-evidence of 'America' is . . . troubled from the start by multiple ambiguities about the extent of the territory it delineates, as well as about its deeper connotations."[12] Such connotations are ever present but not always troubling, it seems, and may bleed easily into the expansionism-enabling slippage referenced by McClennen, for they include claiming the ability to designate what is, and what is not, "American," as can be seen in the following examples. In 1966, when Chilean poet Pablo Neruda gave his first poetry reading in the United States, Archibald MacLeish told the audience that he "should be considered 'an American poet' since the word 'American' belonged to both continents and since South America was too small to lay exclusive claim to such expansive myth-making."[13] Several years later, Neruda's compatriot and fellow poet Nicanor Parra was introduced in the United States by Stanley Kunitz, with apologies for "a parochial convention" that prevented him from speaking of the Chilean as "an American poet," although he did declare Parra to be "a poet of the Americas, one of the very finest."[14] Both hosts clearly felt that the work of their guests transcended national boundaries, laying the groundwork for a hemispheric conception of poetic accomplishment. And yet the compliments—however unconsciously—were backhanded, wrapped within a presumption of U.S. hegemony that privileged the nation-state's ability to decide what counts as "American," whether by casting South America as "too small" to be able to claim the term for itself (when the area of Brazil alone is greater than that of the contiguous United States), or by invoking a convention that prohibited the continent from being able to claim the term at all.

The implications of the slippage between "America" and "the United States"—the presumption of the predominance of the United States and the assumption that there is only one "America"—were brought home to me quite clearly when my family moved from the United States to Nicaragua in 1980. Soon after my arrival, new friends asked where I was from. "America," I replied. Blank stares ensued, followed by "America? But where do you think you are now?" Their response profoundly—and appropriately—decentered my world. It both resisted and revealed the underlying arrogance of my terminology and the concomitant erasure of the America in which they, too, lived. This exchange pulled back the curtain for me on a much longer history of U.S. imperialism in Latin America and the efforts to seek autonomy that this history had inspired, including the very recent Sandinista revolution, which was at the time still in a euphoric stage, and which had played a formative role in raising the consciousness of my interlocutors. This is a primal memory for me of my years in Central America, where the seeds of my later pursuit of training in Latin American studies were sown, and it is one that I share with my students—undergraduate and graduate alike—each semester as a way of conveying to them clearly and directly the political stakes and implications of the usurpation of "America" by those whose frame of reference is "the United States."

The lesson is one that is worth repeating as a means of consciousness-raising in the United States, for the conflation of the two terms is all pervasive, deeply ingrained, and reinforced constantly at all levels of culture, society, and politics. Politicians ask their constituents—"fellow Americans"—to "believe in America"; they present themselves as champions of "American values," they seek to rebuild "the American economy" and create jobs for "Americans," and so on. (The current crackdown on undocumented immigrants in the United States, many of whom are from Spanish America, would make the broader implications of the promises of jobs for "Americans" ironic if it weren't ultimately so tragic.) The media likewise reinforce this (mis)usage, thereby underscoring the primacy of the United States as a nation-state. Across the board, standard weather maps in the United States gray out Canada and Mexico, thus representing weather patterns as neatly circumscribed within the national borders of the United States. This only underscores the idea of "American" (i.e., U.S.) exceptionalism: the nation, such maps seem to imply, has its own weather system, which is not a part of nor party to the weather patterns affecting the rest of the hemisphere, even as winter's arctic blasts (from Canada) and El Niño, among other phenomena, remind us that the United States is not, climatologically speaking, an island unto itself. And then, of course, there is baseball, which pits National League teams against American League teams in its "World" Series. The irony of two "American" leagues playing against each other in a "world" championship in a sport that is fundamentally associated with the United States and that has only recently begun to attract a following outside the nation is clear, even though the blindness of most within the United States to this sleight of hand—or of names—renders it largely invisible.

It is also worth examining the terms used to designate other regions within the American hemisphere, as well as their pitfalls. "Spanish America" is generally used to refer to the Central American, South American, and Caribbean nations that were formerly under Spanish colonial rule, while "Latin America" refers to the region that includes both Spanish America and Brazil (although it excludes the English Caribbean, which has yet to find a place in this nomenclature). Even these designations, though, break down. It is, for example, common in both Spanish America and the U.S. to use "Latin America" to refer to Spanish America—a tendency that is resisted by those who would rather not see Brazil subsumed under an umbrella that does not recognize the nation's different history and culture. Through much of the twentieth century, moreover, conceptualizations of Latin America were, as George Handley points out, unifying and homogenizing, overlooking indigenous cultures as well as differences of race and class.[15] And, of course, the term "Latin America" is itself embedded in a set of imperial dynamics: it was coined by the French, "who thought that since their culture, like that of Spanish and Portuguese America, was 'Latin' (i.e., Romance language speaking), France was destined to assume leadership throughout the continent."[16] If the concerns about French imperialism have long since faded, leaving "Latin America" a less contested term (when used properly), the long history of U.S. intervention in the region has served as a continuous reminder that "America" is not coextensive with the United States alone.

The question of what is "America" intersects at a number of points with issues involved in the use of the term "South" as a regional designation. Over the past few years, scholars associated with the New (U.S.) Southern Studies have both questioned and expanded the meanings of "South." They have moved away from the paradigm of (U.S.) southern exceptionalism, often invoking C. Vann Woodward's assertion that in contrast to the United States as a whole, with its myths of innocence, prosperity, and success, "the [white] South had undergone an experience that it could share with no other part of America—though it is shared by nearly all the peoples of Europe and Asia—the experience of military defeat, occupation, and reconstruction."[17] Woodward's "America" is, of course, the United States, and while he clearly meant here to assert the region's difference from its national context, one could easily flip his statement around and argue that the experience of conquest and subordination is indeed shared with another part of America: Latin America. Commonalities aside, though, it is precisely the efforts of scholars associated with the New (U.S.) Southern Studies—of which this collection is a part—to acknowledge the region's position within an "America" that refers not just to the United States but to the hemisphere as a whole, as well as within the history of the Global South, that prompted the evolution of the term used to identify the southern United States within the discipline from "the South" to "the American South" to "the U.S. South."[18] This represents a convergence with the terminology of Latin Americanists, for whom "South" has always had a more global referent.[19]

If it is fitting that this shift in terminology coincides with increased scholarly attention to the region's position within a hemispheric and transnational context, and to the corresponding move in U.S. American studies, it is also paradoxical: the label of "U.S. South" underscores the region's positioning within the United States as simultaneously "South" in relation to the U.S. North and "North" in relation to the nation's geopolitical south. As Jon Smith and I have observed, the U.S. South is "a space simultaneously (or alternately) center and margin, victor and defeated, empire and colony, essentialist and hybrid, northern and southern (both in the global sense) . . . a zone where the familiar dichotomies of postcolonial theory—unstable enough since the early 1990s—are rendered particularly precarious."[20] The U.S. South is at once part of the imperial North, which exerted its political muscle through the Global South, and situated within this same Global South.

The reconsideration of the significance of "America" at all levels of American studies scholarship has thus been contemporaneous with other scholarly endeavors that further this discussion, and it echoes and expands, both in time and space, Edmundo Paz-Soldán and Alberto Fuguet's declaration that "it is not possible to talk about Latin America without including the United States. And it is not possible to conceive of the United States without necessarily thinking about Latin America."[21] Deeply comparative, transnational, and trans-American work by scholars such as Brickhouse, Gruesz, and Seigel, among others, has made significant progress in recent years in reinscribing the Americas within the United States and vice versa, and thereby setting models of how U.S. Americanist scholarship can—indeed, must—also be American in a hemispheric sense. Rachel Adams, in turn, uses the North American continent as a frame for studying the Americas, bringing Mexico, Canada, and the United States into dialogue with each other even as she downplays the use of nation-based models and instead "grants new centrality to people and places that have been marginalized by official histories of conquest and nation building"; her work speaks to the rising importance of Canadianists' contributions in reconceptualizing both "America" and American studies.[22] Scholars such as Edwards and Dilip Parameshwar Gaonkar, among others, have made a concerted effort to globalize American studies in a manner that includes scholars from outside the United States on equal footing. Comparative and diasporic studies of the black presence in the Americas realized by Latin Americanists, Caribbeanists, comparatists, and scholars in U.S. literature have also been fundamental to expanding our understanding of American studies: Michael Bérubé says that the discipline is today "defined emphatically by its wholesale rejection of exceptionalism, its success at putting American race relations at the center of cultural analysis, its increasing willingness to expand its intellectual inter- ests beyond the borders of the U.S. nation-state."[23] This approach brings the Caribbean, Latin America, Canada, and the United States into dialogue with one another and opens the door to reading the hemisphere through the Global South, and vice versa.

Organizations such as the International American Studies Association have also made important contributions to our understanding of "America" and American studies by holding conferences in venues outside the United States, organizing panels in multiple languages, sponsoring journals such as the *Review of International American Studies*, and fostering collabora- tive efforts among scholars from different regions that are aimed at inte- grating international scholars into the discipline. The Tepoztlán Institute for Transnational History of the Americas and the Hemispheric Institute of Performance and Politics have likewise demonstrated their commitment to truly transnational collaborations and scholarship. The ASA has also con- tinued its efforts to broaden its scope while trying not to incite concerns about reduplicating in the academy the neocolonial patterns of domina- tion and imperialism that have long characterized the relationship between the United States and Latin America. The association has increased efforts at outreach to international scholars and has made transnational scholar- ship central to its mission, as is evident in the topics of several recent con- gresses: "The United States from Inside and Out: Transnational American Studies" (2006), "América Aquí: Transhemispheric Visions and Community Connections" (2007), and "Dimensions of Empire and Resistance: Past, Present, and Future" (2012), held, significantly, in Puerto Rico. In the same way that Washington noted in the late 1990s that many ethnic studies schol- ars had found a home for their work in the ASA's annual conventions, a growing number of Latin Americanists likewise now choose to present at ASA as well as at the Latin American Studies Association's congresses, believing that it may be possible to begin finding common ground in the visions of "America" that are being put forth.

The process of rapprochement must not be rushed, though, for it takes place within and must be careful to avoid perpetuating the broader power dynamics between "North" and "South," as well as the "global hierarchies of knowledge production" that frame the production of institutional discourses on Latin America within the U.S. academy.[24] Latin Americanist scholars such as Walter Mignolo, as well as Irwin, Antonio Cornejo Polar, Néstor García Canclini, Nelly Richard, and others, have criticized how the production of knowledge about Latin America for the U.S. academy, which has come to

dominate the field of Latin American studies, in effect turns this knowledge into primary materials that are then exported to the United States, where they are published, often in English, in a reinscription of the neocolonial cycle of the United States' mining of Latin America for its primary resources, with the finished product—the published scholarship—often remaining in the United States and not being shared with scholars in the region.[25] Irwin thus asks: "If Latin American Studies has been unable to resolve issues of cultural and intellectual imperialism exacerbated by globalization and the dominance of English in the global academy, along with the relative wealth and international prestige of the U.S. academy and the U.S. academic publishing industry, how can U.S.-based American Studies . . . even think about throwing itself into the fray?" For Irwin, the path to a more evenly balanced inter-American studies is to be found in projects that conceive of the Americas as a contact zone. As such, he argues that the projects, and the training necessary to execute them, must of necessity be multilingual and draw on theories and delve into archives originating both north and south of the U.S. border; they should also be published and presented on in venues both north and south.[26] This would make such projects both of interest and, critically, accessible to Latin Americanists and U.S. Americanists alike. Sadowski-Smith and Fox, in turn, recommend "close collaboration" among Canadian studies, Latin American studies, and U.S. American studies "and a 'critical internationalist' awareness of our own institutional locations so as to position the United States' neighboring geographies and the fields that study them as protagonists rather than mere recipient sites of U.S. policies and of U.S.-based theoretical perspectives and comparative paradigms."[27]

North America is unlikely to find itself in South America's shadow again, as it was in the Waldseemüller map, but it is only by taking such steps as these, by self-consciously questioning and reconsidering both terminology and methodologies, and the conceptualizations of "America" that these reflect and perpetuate, that imbalances of power may start to be rectified and that we may begin to find common ground—with differences and similarities alike—across the disciplines and the continents.

NOTES

1. Radway, "What's in a Name?," 2, 6.

2. Gruesz, *Ambassadors of Culture*, 10.

3. Similarly, even as scholarship in U.S. American studies has turned a critical eye to the idea of "American exceptionalism" as a driving force in the formative years of the discipline, the use of the phrase nevertheless reflects, compounds, and, in effect, enacts a similar set of problems: the notion of exceptionalism foregrounds the different origins and destiny of the nation while the use of "American," rather than "U.S.," simultaneously arrogates the designation for the nation and proleptically suggests the spread of the social and political model that it represents through the hemisphere.

4. Radway, "What's in a Name?," 18–19.

5. McClennen, "Inter-American Studies or Imperial American Studies?," 394; see also Handley, "Oedipus in the Americas," 161.

6. Pease, "New Perspectives," 22.

7. Washington, "'Disturbing the Peace,'" 21.

8. Washington, however, grossly misreads the essay as forming part of Martí's "claims for hemispheric unity"; see "Disturbing the Peace," 2. Martí does call for unity, but within Spanish America, not the hemisphere as a whole.

9. Very soon after its publication in New York, the essay was published in Mexico's *El partido liberal*, thus simultaneously reaching numerous readers throughout both the United States and Spanish America.

10. Belnap and Fernández, "Introduction," 2, 3–4.

11. McClennen, "Inter-American Studies or Imperial American Studies?," 397.

12. Gruesz, "America," 17.

13. Rodman, "All American."

14. Quoted in M. Phillips, "Amid City's Hum, Poetry."

15. Handley, *New World Poetics*, 34–37.

16. Skidmore and Smith, *Modern Latin America*, 3.

17. Woodward, *Burden of Southern History*, 190.

18. Hobson, introduction, 1.

19. Indeed, in the 1930s, Uruguayan artist Joaquín Torres García called the notion of "South" into question altogether. In 1935, he spoke of founding a "School of the South" in Uruguay: "I have said School of the South; because in reality, *our North is the South.* There should be no North for us, except in opposition to our South. That is why we now turn the map upside down, and now we know what our true position is, and it is not the way the rest of the world would like to have it. From now on, the elongated tip of South America will point insistently at the South, our North. Our compass as well . . . This is a necessary rectification; so that now we know where we are" (qtd. in Ramírez, *El Taller*, 53). Torres García's famous inverted map (1936) illustrated this image, challenging the viewer to remember that "North" and "South," their histories, and the relations that bind them, were constructs, labels placed by Europeans that better showcased their own positions, and thus had, to paraphrase Simone de Beauvoir, become, rather than being born.

20. J. Smith and Cohn, "Introduction," 9.

21. Quoted in Castillo, *Redreaming America*, 3–4.

22. R. Adams, *Continental Divides*, 7.

23. Bérubé, "American Studies without Exceptions," 109.

24. Irwin, "¿Qué hacen los nuevos americanistas?," 315.

25. Ibid., 309–10, 319.

26. Ibid., 310, 311–12.

27. Sadowski-Smith and Fox, "Theorizing the Hemisphere," 7.

SUGGESTIONS FOR FURTHER READING

Guterl, Matthew Pratt. "South." In *Keywords for American Cultural Studies*, edited by Bruce Burgett and Glenn Hendler, 230–33. New York: New York University Press, 2007.

Limón, José E. *American Encounters: Greater Mexico, the United States, and the Erotics of Culture*. Boston: Beacon Press, 1998.

Smith, Jon, and Deborah Cohn, eds. *Look Away! The U.S. South in New World Studies*. Durham, N.C.: Duke University Press, 2004.

Stecopoulos, Harilaos. *Reconstructing the World: Southern Fictions and U.S. Imperialisms, 1898–1976*. Ithaca, N.Y.: Cornell University Press, 2008.

WANDA RUSHING

Region

Discussions of region in southern studies usually begin by acknowledging social science research conducted by Howard Odum and his
multidisciplinary colleagues at the University of North Carolina at
Chapel Hill. Beginning in the 1920s and ending in the post–World
War II era, regionalist scholars produced a body of work about the
South that attained a high level of recognition and influence among
scholars and policymakers. The University of North Carolina at
Chapel Hill became the first academic center associated with this
research aimed at understanding regional distinctiveness and promoting institutional change. But the era produced "an outburst of
regional expression" among academics, artists, writers, and observers
at other sites.[1]

For Odum and his colleagues, the methodology of regionalism involved collecting social science data not only for advancing
knowledge about the region and its problems but also for advocating
planning, intervention, and education to achieve regional balance
and convergence. Regionalism involved collecting and interpreting descriptive information about "folk-regional society," as well as
compiling statistical indicators to guide social action. According to
Odum's assessment, the South possessed an abundance of natural
resources, as well as social inadequacies: "as to science, skills, technology, organization—deficiency; as to general economy—waste; as
to culture—richness, with immaturity and multiple handicaps; as to
trends—hesitancy and relative retrogression in many aspects of culture."[2] Hence, from the outset regionalism took on a social-problems
framework. This approach to viewing so-called southern backwardness in terms of economics and culture and constructing scientific
measures of economic efficiency and convergence to guide regional
transformation was compatible with the "sociology of modernization" gaining acceptance in academia, government, and philanthropy
during the 1930s and 1940s. Visions of modernization and progress
as normative processes of development guided many domestic and
foreign policy initiatives in the United States. These visions both
informed and constrained regionalism.

Regionalist scholars and planners adopted a social science approach for understanding problems and proposing solutions for advancing the most impoverished region of the United States, identified by President Franklin D. Roosevelt as the nation's number one economic problem. By focusing theoretical and empirical research on social problems occurring in the least urbanized and industrialized part of the United States and in the agricultural economy, regionalists diverged from their contemporaries associated with the Chicago School of Sociology, whose research in cities and metropolitan regions emerged at the same time.[3] In both cases, scholars advanced the discipline by concentrating on place, ecology, and culture; however, in the postwar era, regional sociology faded into obscurity. Sociological studies of U.S. regions and case-study analysis declined in the 1950s and 1960s, and the nation's most rural region became more urbanized, hence more modern, in the postwar era. With a few notable exceptions, most mainstream social scientists did not pursue regional analysis in the 1970s and 1980s as primary research areas, although literary scholars and historians never lost interest.

Wendy Griswold compares regionalist social science research of the 1930s and 1940s to the regionalist movement in art, describing it as "a sharply distinctive and celebratory depiction of the culture of place, as in the Midwest regionalist painters . . . of the 1930s." Basically, however, by setting aside both interventionist aims and celebratory depictions characterizing that particular era, Griswold adopts a more general view of regionalism, befitting contemporary arts and sciences scholarship, as "a recognized association between culture and place."[4] Significantly, however, most mainstream social science during the second half of the twentieth century not only eschewed interventionist intentions but also neglected associations between culture and place. Place became an abstraction, left in the background or taken for granted in social science research at a time when research methods were dominated by "general linear reality" and variables analysis.[5]

At present, twenty-first-century social scientists, intrigued with theories of space and place, are making new associations between culture and place, and in doing so, have refocused attention on the significance of region, not only in the United States but throughout the world. Today, few if any social scientists describe themselves or their work as regionalist, but many who study globalization, economic development, demography, culture, group identity, immigration, mobility, and even urbanization are examining place and region in the context of globalization and social change, using a variety of research methods. Recent theoretical and empirical approaches have informed discussions and stimulated research in the U.S. South, still perceived as the most distinctive region in the nation. Many contemporary studies of regional differences have been influenced by world-systems perspectives and postcolonial studies, which reject hegemonic assumptions underlying "the sociology of modernization," provide structural analyses of persistent social inequalities, and offer alternative frameworks for understanding cultural diversity.

In this essay, I examine social science perspectives associated with southern studies, starting with regionalism in the 1920s, continuing with shifts in social science research in the second half of the twentieth century, and ending with a discussion of contemporary frameworks for studying the region. My goal is to analyze contributions and contradictions within regionalism, as well as trends in social science research, to explain how they have influenced studies of the U.S. South, and how they are likely to continue doing so.

Howard Odum: Regional Distinctiveness

The work produced by Howard Odum, his students, and his colleagues was influenced by early twentieth-century regionalists in Europe and the United States who believed that wide-ranging social science research should inform public policy and offer solutions to social and economic problems. Their desire and "intent to do sociology *for*, as well as *of* and *in*, the South" attracted scholars willing to focus on problems, particularly those related to the moribund agricultural economy.[6] Proponents of regionalism saw their systematic scientific approach to southern studies as differing from sectionalism or parochialism. They especially disagreed with a traditional southern perspective known as Agrarianism expressed by scholars at Vanderbilt University. For Odum sectionalism, based on antipathy toward the New Deal and an assertion of rural values, "would encourage interregional conflict, controversy, and separation."[7] But regionalism, influenced by early twentieth-century progressivism and the southern education movement, encouraged federal intervention and regional planning to achieve the South's economic and social integration with the nation. Regionalists supported New Deal programs. Agrarians did not. To put the two schools of thought in perspective, one writer described Agrarianism as "the conservative aestheticism of Nashville," contrasting it with "the liberal sociology of Chapel Hill."[8]

The Tennessee Valley Authority, one of the largest social programs to emerge from the New Deal, became identified with regionalism and the

South. The TVA supported the study of regional problems, involving land-grant colleges and state departments of education in a series of comprehensive research initiatives.[9] It was an excellent example of how the tools of social science research could be applied to social problems for increasing knowledge about the region and raising the standard of living within it. The Columbia-trained Odum and his colleagues believed that the South and social scientists had much to offer each other. The South served as a kind of regional laboratory where social scientists could expand knowledge about social processes.

Odum's most valuable contribution, according to Dewey W. Grantham, "was the impetus he gave to the concept of the region and to the identity of the contemporary South."[10] In fact, regionalism influenced a generation of scholars who produced so many books and monographs from the 1920s through the 1940s that Larry J. Griffin describes that period as the golden age for "sociological and anthropological studies *of* the South."[11] Scholars such as Hortense Powdermaker, John Dollard, Charles Johnson, Liston Pope, Arthur Raper, Rupert Vance, Howard Odum, and others used their expertise in the social scientific theories and methods of the day for advancing knowledge *of* the South. Not all of them were based *in* the South, and not all of them saw themselves as doing research *for* the South. But their work called attention to the damaging institutions of sharecropping and tenancy, the effects of paternalism in mill towns, patterns of racial and class discrimination, and the lives of rural southerners, black and white. These studies also benefitted from and contributed to an institutional and research framework based in the South for collecting and disseminating information about the region. Many of the regionalists won research grants from large foundations, owing to mutual understandings that emerged between members of the academic community and organizations interested in regional reform. In 1924, grants from the Laura Spelman Rockefeller Memorial of New York funded the Institute for Research in the Social Sciences (IRSS) at UNC, now known as the Odum Institute, supported research assistants, and subsidized the University of North Carolina Press, whose influential publications included monographs about the region, as well as the journal *Social Forces*, established by Odum in 1922. Regional sociology flourished, and Odum attained national and international recognition when members of the American Sociological Society elected him president in 1930 and ranked the Department of Sociology at UNC among the "most distinguished" in the United States in 1934.

During the same period, Fisk University became the major African American center for social science research on the South under the leadership of Charles S. Johnson. While earning his PhD at the University of Chicago, Johnson studied with Robert Park and published research on urban riots. A scholar and an activist, Johnson first served as director of research with the National Urban League, where he founded its first magazine, *Opportunity*, and became its first editor. At Fisk he became the first chair of the Department of Social Science. Like Odum at UNC, Johnson secured outside funding for research and recruited outstanding scholars whose work became part of the golden age of regional sociology. Johnson and his colleagues at Fisk published twenty-three books between 1928 and 1940. Johnson conducted field research in southern black communities and published his findings in two monographs that became classics: *The Shadow of the Plantation* and *Growing Up in the Black Belt*. In 1942, Johnson began an annual seminar at Fisk known as the Race Relations Institute. Its purpose was to lead a national discussion on race by bringing together social scientists, community leaders, educators, and policymakers for discussions on racial parity in housing, education, and earnings. In 1946, he was elected president of the Southern Sociological Society; in 1948, Johnson became the first African American president of Fisk University.[12]

By the 1960s, regionalism and interventionism had fallen out of favor among social scientists. Odum died in 1954, Johnson died in 1956, and by 1960, increasing economic activity in the region had convinced many problems-oriented regionalists that their subject matter (i.e., regional distinctiveness) was disappearing. Claims were made and widely believed that modernization processes were transforming the region and New South initiatives were bringing about economic convergence. Institutional support for regionalist research shifted as the University of North Carolina Press, the IRSS, the UNC sociology department, as well as government-sponsored and philanthropic research "invested in other fields and other locales."[13] Griffin concludes that "neither sociology of the South nor Odum's kind of regional sociology would ever again achieve this level of visibility and influence, and since the 1950s they ha[d] sadly slipped into near obscurity."[14] Charles S. Johnson's research and his accomplishments also slipped into relative obscurity.

John Shelton Reed: Regional Groups

John Shelton Reed joined the UNC Department of Sociology in 1969 straight from graduate school at Columbia University. His expertise in quantitative survey research and social psychological theory, combined with his discovery of almost-forgotten regional sociologists, informed Reed's efforts to understand an increasingly complex region and the people who identify as southerners during an important time of social transformation. Reed's dissertation became his first book, *The Enduring South: Subcultural Persistence in Mass Society*. Published in 1972, *The Enduring South* "recast the defining presupposition of southern studies, the distinctiveness of the region, by presenting white southerners as an 'ethnic' or 'quasiethnic' group."[15] The book title also identifies a concept that informs his later research—the enduring South. His first book, and the second one, *Southerners: The Social Psychology of Sectionalism*, published in 1983, employed social psychological theories and social survey data for measuring attitudes about group identity among white southerners. Focusing on *regional groups*, not regionalism, and employing a different set of theoretical assumptions and methodological tools, both books won respect from sociologists and historians. Reed's subsequent publications moved away from survey research, adopting innovative and often humorous approaches to observing and interpreting associations between culture and place. His work won attention from a broader intellectual and popular audience, renewing and expanding interest in regional sociology at a time when it had become increasingly obscure.

Wendy Griswold and Nathan Wright credit John Shelton Reed as the sociologist who "almost single-handedly kept regional studies in sociology alive over the lean decades of the 1970s and 1980s."[16] He did so by writing eighteen books and more than one hundred journal articles, book chapters, and essays. While pursuing his research, Reed also played a prominent role in maintaining the institutional framework established by Odum and his contemporaries and expanding it. Reed directed the Odum Institute for Research in Social Science and served as book review editor for *Social Forces*, both founded by Odum. He served as president of the Southern Sociological Society in 1989, an organization founded by Odum and his colleagues in 1936. Additionally, Reed has advised the National Endowment for the Humanities, helped establish the Center for the Study of the American South, and was a founding coeditor of *Southern Cultures*. Today Reed is professor emeritus, and the University of North Carolina honors him with an endowed chair in the Department of Sociology, the John Shelton Reed Distinguished Professorship. Reed's many honors include such things as election to the Fellowship of Southern Writers, a Guggenheim Fellowship, and lectureships in universities throughout the world. Celebrating his retirement from UNC in 2001, southern writers joined social scientists with contributions to a special issue of *Southern Cultures* published in spring 2001 titled "The South according to Reed." In that volume, Griffin recognized Reed as the "most accomplished and influential living sociologist of the U.S. South."[17]

In addition to publishing his own research about white southerners and regional group identity, on occasion Reed has commented on the state of regional research and the state of the discipline, reminding sociologists of the importance of region. He poses the question, "Whatever became of regional sociology?" in an essay published in a 1982 collection titled *One South*. Reed credits Odum and his colleagues with producing a "vast and apparently enduring body of work on regional variation in the United States— work that, to all appearances had established a legitimate school within American sociology and claimed a place for sociologists as equal partners in the cross-disciplinary enterprise of regional studies." From Reed's perspective, the regionalists' most remarkable contribution consists of descriptive material emphasizing regional differences "which will provide a base line for studies of continuity and change for years to come."[18] However, by 1970, regional sociology had disappeared from specialties listed by the American Sociological Association, vanished from sociology journals (including *Social Forces*), and faded from professional meetings (including those of the Southern Sociological Society).

Reed attributed the decline of regional sociology to several things, including shortcomings in the theoretical and methodological underpinnings of regionalism, describing it as "not very good *sociology*." And, in their efforts to avoid sectionalism, the regionalists had avoided aspects of "Southern culture that probably had historical rather than economic or demographic roots, and largely ignored the perplexing subject of regional identity or regional consciousness." A few of Odum's contemporaries had published similar critiques in *Social Forces* and in the *American Economic Review* in the 1940s. Moreover, Reed criticized the "problem" orientation of the regionalists as being insufficient for sustaining research interest in the South, citing Rupert Vance's remarks in 1960: "Many of the basic conditions that gave rise to regional disability and differences have simply evaporated on our doorsteps. The New Deal has been dealt. . . . As the affluent society crosses the Mason-Dixon line, the regionalist of the 1930s turns up as just another 'liberal without a cause.'"[19]

Reed notes a modest revival of interest in regional studies beginning in the 1970s. He cites Norval Glenn at the University of Texas, whose work demonstrated that regional differences in terms of social problems might not be decreasing at all, and publication of Lewis Killian's book *White Southerners*, which "challenged the conventional view that American regional groups were sinking into the national mainstream."[20] Reed also welcomes scholarship applying Immanuel Wallerstein's approach to the political economy of the world system to the internal structure of the United States as well as to the developing world. He notes that some of the early regional sociology, such as Edgar Thompson's plantation studies and Rupert Vance's work on the South's colonial economy, had introduced a political economy approach that was abandoned by the regionalists.

Reed's 1989 Presidential Address to the Southern Sociological Society takes stock of theories, methods, and research priorities in the discipline.

> I suggest that there are two kinds of sociology: call them "ideal types" if you think I am oversimplifying. On one hand is the sort of hypothesis-testing and theory-building that we hold in highest esteem—rewarding it, for example, with publication in our major journals. On the other is work that applies the concepts and methods of our discipline to the understanding of particular societies, particular groups, particular institutions. In general, this narrative or interpretive sociology is less highly valued than the other, less highly valued than it once was, and (I would argue) less highly valued than it should be, if for no other reason than because it is the kind of sociology our fellow-citizens most often find worthwhile. Most of them would agree with Immanuel Wallerstein's assertion that "the purpose of abstractions is to arrive at specificity," not the other way around. In other words, they like it when we tell them sociologically informed stories: about themselves, about other men and women in their society, about other times and places.[21]

The Continuing Significance of Region

Contemporary social scientists, including sociologists, are paying more attention to place and space; subsequently, much of their research contributes to new understandings of regional differences and the South, both Old South and New (or Newest) South. And some, following Reed's suggestions, are paying attention to narrative or interpretive sociology as well as hypothesis testing. Many contemporary scholars recognize that social phenomena, including identity, interaction, as well as community, social movements, crime, health disparities, urbanization, migration, and cultural innovation are *emplaced*. Because place matters in all aspects of social life, "it is something more than just another independent variable."[22] If place matters more than was thought fifty years ago and perhaps in different ways, it is also true that region still matters. Persistent regional distinctiveness, dynamic southern urbanization, record Hispanic immigration, and African American reverse migration call attention to regional studies and to the South as a distinctive region in the nation and its position in the global economy.

Much of the scholarship emerging from the resurgence of interest in place and region, like the work of Odum and his colleagues, tends to be cross disciplinary; however, it differs significantly in other ways. First, theoretical and methodological approaches to these emplaced social phenomena vary as much as the topics. Social scientists use diverse theoretical frameworks as well as methods such as demography, ethnography, surveys, interviews, case studies, and other techniques to produce knowledge about place, region, and the South. Some scholars have raised questions about the limitations of mainstream techniques for understanding the region, some have challenged assumptions made by previous scholarship on the South, but none have recommended the resuscitation of regionalism as defined by early regionalists in the 1930s and 1940s. Influence from the problems of orientation of regionalism and assumptions from modernization perspectives may have declined, but they linger in stereotypical ideas about the South and continue to frame some scholarship of place and region, treating the South as an American Other. This is particularly true with regard to underlying assumptions about backwardness, internal regional characteristics, and racial dichotomies. But these assumptions have been challenged and reframed by critical race theorists and world-system theorists and have contributed to debates about the impact of globalization. Mounting empirical evidence of dramatic changes in the racial and ethnic composition of southern populations and in regional patterns of urbanization reveals additional limitations of regionalism and southern exceptionalism. The reverse migration of African Americans to southern destinations and the influx of immigration from Latin America could not have been foreseen by regionalists. Nor could they have anticipated that urban scholars would view southern urbanization as a significant social phenomenon. Because of regional change and innovative theoretical and methodological research strategies, scholars are finding new ways to interpret the Old South and understand the New South.

Some scholars contend that external global economic demands, not internal economic institutions, fostered the "southern" plantation labor system of the Old South, which included slavery and its successors in sharecropping and tenancy. Recent scholarship on Appalachia critiques earlier assumptions about isolation and internal processes. Wilma Dunaway applies world-systems theory and a rigorous research methodology to evaluate regional economic development within a global framework. Her studies of indigenous peoples, African Americans, and even the role of children as workers in a region long ago incorporated into the global economy are supported by exhaustive data in her analyses of the antebellum mountain South. Consequently, when Appalachia is viewed through the lenses of world-system and feminist theories, a richer picture emerges of the region's diversity and its incorporation into the world system.[23]

Race and class are viewed differently by contemporary scholars who study social movements as significant historical events occurring in the region. Vincent Roscigno and William Danaher's *The Voice of Southern Labor: Radio, Music, and Textile Strikes, 1929–1934* offers an account of the experiences of southern textile workers and the sharing of collective grievances through the music they sang and heard played on local radio stations. The book challenges old assumptions about the absence of class consciousness in the region. Similarly, Aldon Morris's *The Origins of the Civil Rights Movement*, published in 1984, gained national attention and accolades for its analysis of black protest between 1953 and 1963. Although the civil rights movement is considered a national movement, Morris's book is a case study of southern black communities. These studies of the South prior to 1960 link the region to national and international events and show black and white southerners, as well as Native Americans, as agents of change.

Now social scientists are recognizing dramatic changes in the urban South. Rupert Vance, a regionalist, described southern cities as "unremark-able," and the Chicago School focused primarily on New York, Chicago, and Los Angeles as "real cities," ignoring the South. But contemporary scholars are seeking new approaches for understanding southern urban-ization.[24] Southern communities now are being changed by a significant migration of African Americans to the metropolitan South from cities out-side the region, especially Detroit and Chicago. In a dramatic turnaround, the Great Migration out of the rural South that took place during the first half of the twentieth century has been reversed. The South has become "a regional magnet for blacks, more so than for whites or the population as a whole."[25] Regional economic growth and cultural diversity now operate as "pull" factors replacing "push" factors associated with declining agricultural production and Jim Crow in the era of regionalist sociology. Early research on reverse migration tended to focus on the "return" of African Americans to rural southern communities.[26] But the unprecedented migration of African Americans to southern cities and suburbs has opened up new research pos-sibilities for understanding different trajectories of reverse migration, espe-cially for non-southern-born African Americans.[27] Reverse migration to the

South, as well as Hispanic immigration to new communities, has created interest in new associations between place and culture, with such topics as the return of hip-hop to its southern roots and the spread of *norteño* music in new immigrant communities.[28] And recent case studies of southern cities are contributing to discussions of white flight, housing, tourism, globalization, and disasters.[29]

Regionalism lost its appeal nearly three-quarters of a century ago, and declining interest in regional sociology is unlikely to recover. But evidence of persistent regional distinctions, as well as interesting, lingering questions about the South take on new significance in an era of dynamic urbanization and new immigration. Mainstream social scientists who neglected southern studies for decades, based on assumptions of convergence, are seeking new approaches for understanding regional transformations. Interdisciplinary institutional support for this kind of research has shifted and expanded to research centers at the University of North Carolina, the University of South Carolina, the University of Mississippi, the University of Virginia, Virginia Polytechnic Institute, Emory University, and others. A number of academic presses, including those of the University of North Carolina and the University of Georgia, publish innovative scholarship. All these intellectual pursuits and institutional supports suggest a promising future for the study of the U.S. South.

NOTES

1. Grantham, *South in Modern America,* 149.
2. Odum, *Southern Regions,* 151.
3. Rudel and Fu, "Requiem for the Southern Regionalists."
4. Griswold, *Regionalism and the Reading Class,* 13, 11.
5. See Abbot, "Transcending General Linear Reality."
6. J. S. Reed, *One South,* 36.
7. Grantham, *South in Modern America,* 150.
8. O'Brien, *Idea of the American South,* xv.
9. Grantham, *South in Modern America,* 153.
10. Ibid., 153.
11. L. J. Griffin, "Promise of a Sociology," 52.
12. See Gilpin and Gasman, *Charles S. Johnson.*
13. Goldfield, *Region, Race, and Cities,* 32.
14. L. J. Griffin, "Promise of a Sociology," 53.
15. Ibid., 58.
16. Griswold and Wright, "Cowbirds, Locals," 1414.
17. L. J. Griffin, "Promise of a Sociology," 50.

18. J. S. Reed, *One South*, 33, 43.

19. Ibid., 34, 36, 38.

20. Ibid., 39.

21. J. S. Reed, "On Narrative and Sociology," 2. Quotation from Wallerstein, "What Can One Mean?," xi.

22. Gieryn, "Place for Space in Sociology," 463, 467.

23. See Dunaway, *First American Frontier* and *Women, Work and Family*.

24. See Rushing, *Memphis and the Paradox of Place*, and R. Lloyd, "Urbanization and the Southern United States."

25. Frey, "New Great Migration."

26. See Stack, *Call to Home*, and Falk, Hunt, and Hunt, "Return Migrations of African-Americans."

27. See Pendergrass, "Routing Black Migration."

28. See Robinson, "Crunk and Hip-Hop Culture," and Winders, "Nashville's New 'Sonido.'"

29. On white flight, see Kruse, *White Flight*; on housing, see Gilderbloom, *Invisible City*; on tourism, see Gotham, *Authentic New Orleans*; on globalization, see Rushing, *Memphis and the Paradox of Place;* on disasters, see Hartman and Squires, *There Is No Such Thing*, and Gotham and Greenberg, "From 9/11 to 8/29."

SUGGESTIONS FOR FURTHER READING

Dollard, John. *Caste and Class in a Southern Town*. 1937. New Haven, Conn.: Yale University Press: 1957.

Falk, William W. *Rooted in Place: Family and Belonging in a Southern Black Community*. Brunswick, N.J.: Rutgers University Press, 2004.

Gilpin, Patrick J., and Marybeth Gasman. *Charles S. Johnson: Leadership beyond the Veil in the Age of Jim Crow*. New York: State University of New York Press, 2003.

Robinson, Zandria F. *This Ain't Chicago: Race, Class and Regional identity in the Post-Soul South*. Chapel Hill: University of North Carolina Press, 2014.

Rushing, Wanda. *Memphis and the Paradox of Place: Globalization in the American South*. Chapel Hill: University of North Carolina Press, 2009.

ERIC LOTT

Global South

"The Global South" has replaced "the Third World" as a way of talking about global inequality. There are several reasons for this. Foremost among them is the end of the Cold War (1945–89), which in the 1950s brought about a nonaligned movement of countries dedicated to independence from both their former colonizers and the orbits of the Western, capitalist "First World" and the Eastern-bloc, state-communist "Second." The initial period of Third World jubilance and solidarity gave way to widespread state dictatorship and corruption across Africa, South America, and South Asia; and by the time of the Berlin Wall's fall, marking the Second World's end and thus the return of "One World, Ready or Not" (in one writer's phrase), the idea of a Third World gave way to talk of "the globe," "globalization," and globalization's capital flows and unequal relations of trade and distributions of wealth.[1] At the same time, inequalities between North and South produced economic powerhouses in countries like China and India, where manufacturing had migrated from the Global North, immiserating millions in global sweatshops but also introducing class disparities within such nations and between them and poorer nations elsewhere. Any remaining sense of a nonaligned community crumbled in the face of new geopolitical realities.

Yet if the Global South seems a by-product of post-1989 globalization discourses and developments, scholars have been eager to explore its precursors and earlier historical shapes. American studies scholars in particular have sought to bridge studies of the U.S. South and postcolonial studies of Global South formations across many moments and periods, linking Cotton Belt and Sun Belt to the "color line [that] belts the world," in W. E. B. Du Bois's fine phrase.[2] Since the Global South is a useful heuristic device as well as political-economic description, one way of configuring it is to consider broadly "southern" formations in three conceptual frames: a subnational U.S. section with a distinctive, historically changing political and cultural economy (chattel slavery, debt peonage, New South industrialism, post-Fordist neoliberalism); a hemispheric formation extending across the Caribbean and Latin America to which these modes were exported (as in Henry Ford's Amazon rubber manufacturing venture Fordlandia) even as labor, commodities, and cultures were extracted (as in cultural forms such as reggae music and the so-called Latin American Boom in literature); and finally that relatively new imaginary called the Global South that has its antecedents in everything from spice extraction in Indonesia to oil extraction in the Congo but is keynoted today by that Bastard Out of Arkansas, Wal-Mart. The internal dynamics of these formations are as complex as their interrelations and interconnections with one another. Even the briefest inventory suggests how considering these formations together enriches the study of each of them. Our understanding of the idea of southern exceptionalism, what used to be called the "mind" of the South, and its cultural expressions (the plantation romance, the rape-lynching nexus, the work of William Faulkner and Zora Neale Hurston, the blues, the film *Deliverance*, rapper Lil Wayne) gains much in comparison with plantation economies and caste-based impoverished areas elsewhere. The U.S. South's various and extensive cultural-political relations with its southern neighbors (the wrangling of what became the state of Texas from Mexico, the corporate-driven epic drama behind the vogue of the banana, the itinerant career of Cuban independence fighter José Martí, the emergence of Miami's Little Haiti, postrevolutionary Cuba's bifurcated Havana/Miami metropole, Faulkner's influence on Gabriel García Márquez, the invention of the Caribbean steel drum out of the U.S. oil drum, Caribbean poet Derek Walcott's volume *Arkansas Testament*) suggest the contours of a broader postnational South, revealing new aspects of both the southern United States and of regions to its south (for which it becomes a sort of new North). Finally there is the place and role of the U.S. South in a global North-South divide, including Richard Wright's report on his trip to the 1955 Bandung conference of non-aligned nations, the post-1965 Pacific Rim remaking of states like Virginia with the voluminous in-migration of Asian nationals, the "Toyotization" of North Carolina auto plants, and Wal-Mart as perhaps the primary template for twenty-first-century capitalism—a tale of bar codes, containerization, pop-up factories, and sweated labor there and here.

What follows is a necessarily speculative itinerary or genealogy of Global South coordinates. Italian Marxist Antonio Gramsci's essay "Some Aspects of the Southern Question" (1926) discusses the matter of Italian regional unevenness with regard to economic and political development and is thus a useful starting point from which to theorize connections among many modern Global Souths.[3] Gramsci's insights into the way a "backward" South is produced by and tightly bound up with a national-popular dispensation find striking resonances with the well-known contemporaneous U.S. volume *I'll Take My Stand: The South and the Agrarian Tradition* (1930), with of course the crucial difference that the Twelve Southerners who authored that volume were defending their beloved, defensively white social formation from northern industrial incursion. Gramsci for his part (in an echo of W. E. B. Du Bois's 1935 *Black Reconstruction in America*) envisioned a reconstructed nation-state by way of embracing a southern subaltern peasantry. Any number of subsequent texts speak to (and revise) such visions, from *Gone with the Wind* (both book and movie) to *The Help* (ditto) to artist Kara Walker's plantation romance–killing *Pictures from Another Time* (2002). One possible postscript to this tradition comes with the emergence of the Tennessee corporate behemoth Federal Express (slogan: The World On Time)—a spatially expansive and temporally acute company that the Tom Hanks–Robert Zemeckis vehicle *Cast Away* (2000) links to a *longue durée* of Global South imagining. Hanks's character is a Fed Ex employee who goes down in a plane crash and lives Robinson Crusoe–like for a number of years on a deserted South Pacific island before being rescued, a narrative arc that stretches symbolically from prenational to postsectional understandings of the U.S. South and brings them together back home.

In fact what is striking about so much southern and Global South narrative is how allusively self-conscious it is about its status as story, its discursive construction of the South, as in (to take but one of many examples) William Faulkner's *Absalom, Absalom!* (1936), a historical novel of southern foundations that unfolds as a series of tales told (or imagined, or outright invented) by various speakers from often incompatible perspectives, what we might think of as Telling Time. Perhaps the most widely remembered depiction of southern atavism, *Deliverance*, the James Dickey novel put indelibly on film in 1972 (and thus midway between 1930s debates and more recent Global South ruminations) is surprisingly self-reflexive about what it means to "get our story straight"—as the vacationing suburban Atlanta sportsmen describe their not altogether honest words to the local sheriff in the wake of their fatal encounters with backwoods southern whites during a white-water rafting trip.[4] Though the film has often been regarded as a nasty piece of southern essentializing, such gestures indicate that it is in fact a critical account of Sun Belt suburban fantasy caught in the act of that essentializing. "Getting our story straight" might be taken as a scholarly injunction when it comes to historicizing the South. Jennifer Rae Greeson's *Our South: Geographic Fantasy and the Rise of National Literature* (2010) adduces the long backstory of the kind of othering and pathologizing of the South implicitly critiqued in

Deliverance, while Harilaos Stecopoulos's *Reconstructing the World: Southern Fictions and U.S. Imperialism, 1898–1976* (2008) helps connect that critique to the contemporaneous Vietnam War, a disastrous Global South venture before it had a name.

Such works, in other words, open lines of inquiry to geographies farther south, to a broader southern imperium whose plantation economies across the Caribbean and Central America gave rise to the gangsterism of the United Fruit Company as well as such literary works as Gabriel García Márquez's *One Hundred Years of Solitude* (1967), which in a Faulknerian register engages the devastations visited on the region by U.S. corporate agricultural interests. Thinking through the humble banana, an unknown quantity in the United States until it was introduced by such interests in the first decades of the twentieth century, produces connections between Faulkner's *As I Lay Dying* (1929), García Márquez's *Leaf Storm* (1955), Josephine Baker's banana-skirt performances, Carmen Miranda's elaborate fruit hat, the pop song "Yes! We Have No Bananas" (1922), Harry Belafonte's "Banana Boat Song (Day O)" (1956), and banana-peel slapstick comedy. Other sorts of connection are pursued by a great variety of Caribbean intellectuals, including poet Derek Walcott's "The Arkansas Testament" (1987), which reflects in parallax fashion on this region and its relations with the Old South; critic Edouard Glissant, who thought of Martinique and Mississippi in the same frame of reference; and novelist V. S. Naipaul, whose travelogue *A Turn in the South* (1989) finds all sorts of cross-regional resonances.

These can be extended even farther south through texts and scholarly studies that evidence just how interlinked and elaborate these interconnections are. The plot thickens, for instance, with Henry Ford's fantastical (and industrial) venture Fordlandia, not just an Amazon-based rubber manufacturing plant but a whole company town set down in the middle of the South American jungle, a kingdom of rubber given useful treatment in Greg Grandin's *Fordlandia: The Rise and Fall of Henry Ford's Forgotten Jungle City* (2009). There are curious and instructive parallels here with Werner Herzog's film *Fitzcarraldo* (1982), the tale of a somewhat unhinged visionary (Klaus Kinski) who dabbles in various schemes (including the Amazon rubber trade) and who dreams of building an opera house deep in the Amazon jungle. In order to reach the remote parcel of land where he wishes to build the structure, he must have his steamboat hoisted over a steep hillside by a small army of indigenous men, which results in several casualties; the transcendent scene of Fitzcarraldo subsequently cruising downriver blasting Caruso from a Victrola thus becomes a critical image of a "document of civilization" become a "document of barbarism," in Walter Benjamin's well-known words.[5] Yet as is depicted in the Les Blank documentary *Burden of Dreams* (1982), Herzog's film production mimicked much of the madness portrayed in his film, exploiting the local laboring population and placing impossible demands on cast and crew. From Ford to Herzog, a certain strain of Global South imagining bears the distinct impress of empire.

137

This is why it is crucial to locate counterdiscourses that dislodge or at least complicate imperialist visions of a Global South. One might turn here to certain U.S. southern cultural figures and a series of broader global political movements and political affinities. There is, for example, the ethnographic and travel writing of Zora Neale Hurston in *Tell My Horse* (1938), her studies in and of Haiti and Jamaica, and Richard Wright in *Black Power* (1954), his account of decolonizing Ghana, and *The Color Curtain* (1956), his report on the 1955 Bandung conference. There are also the cultural-ambassadorial tours undertaken by such figures as Louis Armstrong, Duke Ellington, and Dizzy Gillespie, Cold War cultural exchanges given very fine treatment in Penny Von Eschen's *Satchmo Blows Up the World* (2006). These examples, while not without their contradictions and complications, offer interesting counterpoints to Faulkner's forays as a State Department ambassador to Venezuela and Japan. By the turn of the 1960s, one can point to an emerging U.S./Global South revolutionary nexus, when Robert Williams, Harold Cruse, LeRoi Jones/Amiri Baraka, and others visited Cuba soon after the 1959 revolution. Jones/Baraka's "Cuba Libre" (1960) is the great essay of this moment, helping to radicalize his bohemian cohort in New York; but it is Williams's *Negroes with Guns* (1962), generated out of connections he drew between Ku Klux Klan violence against African Americans in his hometown of Monroe, North Carolina, and the experience of Cuban revolutionaries during the Batista regime, that set in motion new tendencies in U.S. black radical thought—Maoist and Third-Worldist among others—and action throughout the 1960s. In a similar vein, the Rumble in the Jungle—the 1974 prizefight between Muhammad Ali and George Foreman—had a radicalizing effect on both its U.S. principals and radicals beginning to suffer from the Mobutu regime in Zaire, where the fight was held. In all its extraordinary performative dimensions, from the media circus surrounding the larger-than-life personae of the fighters themselves (both of them U.S. southerners, incidentally) to the spectacular prelude concert featuring James Brown, Miriam Makeba, The Crusaders, and others, the occasion became a high-water mark of black cultural-nationalist efflorescence on a global (pay-per-view) stage. The Leon Gast documentary *When We Were Kings* (1996) offers up a fascinating and problematic look at this episode in the unfinished struggle for democracy.

As a number of scholars have argued, however, the world we live in today is in no small part the world the Waltons made—by way of Arkansas and Wal-Mart. The folksy southern fantasies put forward in TV's *The Waltons* in the 1970s, it turns out, provided ideological cover stories or false screen memories for the contemporaneous emergence of the retail leviathan that has remade global capitalism, the condition in and against which the Global South struggles. Wal-Mart is the face of twenty-first-century capitalism, as one historian has termed it, and the connections here between nonunion/low-wage U.S. southern labor standards, evangelical Christianity, the rise of the chain store, and a neoliberal capitalism that imports nearly all its manufactured goods from abroad are the earmark—and challenge—of the Global South in our time.

NOTES

1. See Greider, *One World, Ready or Not.*
2. See Du Bois, "Color Line Belts the World."
3. See Gramsci, "Some Aspects of the Southern Question," especially 316–17.
4. Dickey, *Deliverance*, 219.
5. Benjamin, *Illuminations*, 256.

SUGGESTIONS FOR FURTHER READING

Chapman, Peter. *Bananas: How the United Fruit Company Shaped the World.* Edinburgh: Canongate Books, 2007.

Grandin, Greg. *Fordlandia: The Rise and Fall of Henry Ford's Forgotten Jungle City.* New York: Metropolitan Books, 2009.

Lichtenstein, Nelson, ed., *Wal-Mart: The Face of Twenty-First-Century Capitalism.* New York: New Press, 2006.

Lowe, Lisa. *The Intimacies of Four Continents.* Durham, N.C.: Duke University Press, 2015

Moreton, Bethany. *To Serve God and Wal-Mart: The Making of Christian Free Enterprise.* Cambridge, Mass.: Harvard University Press, 2009.

Prashad, Vijay. *The Darker Nations: A People's History of the Third World.* New York: New Press, 2007.

———. *The Poorer Nations: A Possible History of the Global South.* New York: Verso, 2013.

Von Eschen, Penny M. *Satchmo Blows Up the World: Jazz Ambassadors Play the Cold War.* Cambridge, Mass.: Harvard University Press, 2004.

Young, Cynthia A. *Soul Power: Culture, Radicalism, and the Making of a U.S. Third World Left.* Durham, N.C.: Duke University Press, 2006.

PART III

Peoples

SHIRLEY ELIZABETH THOMPSON

Creole/Creolization

When visiting Southern University in Baton Rouge, Louisiana, for a stint in 1989, the Martiniquan poet and theorist Édouard Glissant made it a point to travel to Oxford, Mississippi, the birthplace of William Faulkner. It was for him a mission of sorts, an attempt to commune with the legacies of Faulkner for his own writerly imagination. As if "controlled by Faulkner's thinking," Glissant and three friends entered Mississippi along its less beaten paths. At every turn, they confronted a "tragic and irremediable thickness" despite the American ordinariness of roads lined with "encampments of Burger Kings, fried chicken places, bars, and gas stations." Glissant's party —"three Antilleans and a very slight French woman"—followed the traces of racial and sexual danger in Faulkner's real and imagined landscape. Surveying the main square of Oxford/Jefferson, Glissant recognized its similarity to haunted squares in towns throughout the Americas, a particular "feeling of intimacy (and infinity), a feeling of silent pleasure or of hard times and injustice, endured." It was only during the return trip from Mississippi to Louisiana, "moving toward the bayous once again, toward the mouth of the river, toward the Cajuns, Black Indians, and zydeco" that Glissant more deeply realized the predicament haunting Faulkner's oeuvre: "It had a name, Creolization."[1]

Although the idea of "creolization" and related terms such as "Creole" (spelled with lower- and uppercase *c*) and *creolité* (or Creoleness) circulate most conspicuously in the context of the Caribbean, as Glissant's intervention implies, the concepts have a long history in the context of the U.S. South. Particularly along the Gulf Coast and within the city of New Orleans, the term "Creole" has evoked political, cultural, and territorial struggles among former French and Spanish colonial subjects, enslaved and free people of African descent, indigenous Choctaw and Houma residents, and agents of Anglo-American empire. As a Creole place, New Orleans has a reputation for cultural fluidity, racial hybridity, and moral permissiveness. Promoting a performance and culinary culture that includes Mardi Gras, gumbo, and jazz, the city's thriving tourism industry has conspicuously cultivated a Creole identity since the late nineteenth century. For generations of writers, artists, and casual tourists alike, Creole New Orleans has exemplified a spirit of *métissage* in the national imagination and has served as an antidote to the Protestant propriety and strict racial etiquette that seem to operate elsewhere within the United States. As a budding author living in New Orleans in the 1920s, Faulkner himself appropriated the term "Creole" to describe his circle of writers, many of whom labored on the brink of national and international acclaim.

When Glissant deploys the concept in reference to the southern United States, he is not simply reiterating these popular usages, where Creole infers fluidity and mixture but often serves as a mere container for predictable and socially sanctioned combinations. Instead, he mobilizes the somewhat static term "creole" into "creolization," an active and haunting agent of racial memory and retribution. Emerging within the challenges posed by racial, linguistic, and cultural contingency, creolization encompasses an unpredictable, multivalent set of processes. In Faulkner and elsewhere in southern literature and culture, creolization, according to Glissant, is a felt presence: it "lingers menacingly at the county's horizon," forming an "unstoppable conjunction despite misery, oppression and lynching, [a] conjunction that opens up torrents of unpredictable results." Elsewhere, Glissant identifies these conjunctures as "points of entanglement," multilayered impasses forcing artists, scholars, and political actors to mediate contradiction and move within the interstices between disciplines. Focus on creolization bypasses the frame of the nation, opening out onto transnational spaces of diaspora and exchange. Along these lines, Glissant insists on a shared system of meaning and experience among those of the U.S. South—said "emphatically . . . with a capital 'S' as though it represents an absolute"—and "we other people of the south, to the south of this capitalized South."[2] Zeroing in on intensely local sites of intimate struggle such as the plantation, an emphasis on creolization exposes "race relations" as being a pitifully inadequate discourse for situating the ongoing and structural antagonisms between blacks and whites or, more broadly, between nonwhites and whites. Creolization seeks to identify and articulate what is at stake in the struggles between colonial agents and slave masters, on the one hand, and the colonized and enslaved, on the other. It especially helps illuminate subaltern quests for freedom and identity in the midst of violent and suppressed histories and intimacies. Rather than addressing how individuals from various social groups within the fixed social system of the nation might "get along," the rubric of creolization illuminates how, specifically, these antagonisms have been constituted and resisted amid local and global contingencies.

Defining Terms

One should not venture too far into a discussion of things Creole without attempting to clarify the murky history of the concept. It has operated across various figures of speech. The adjective form, "creole," as mere descriptor has in many historical contexts hardened into the noun "Creole," signifying an essential component of identity. Subsequent noun forms such as *creolité* (creole-ness) have confirmed this essential, inalienable quality, whereas others, such as "creolization," emphasize processes of becoming over states of being and begin to mobilize the concept as a verb ("to creolize"). As many scholars have pointed out, "creole/creolization" is a "found" concept, a historical term specific to particular moments and places that has nonetheless gained widespread theoretical currency beyond them. In its wide array of theoretical applications, creole/creolization has been a "model of" historical and cultural phenomena and a "model for" thinking through social and political confrontation."[3]

Deriving from the sixteenth-century Portuguese *crioulo* and Spanish *criollo*, the term "Creole" in its earliest colonial iteration refers to those of Old World parentage born in the Americas. It distinguished such persons from indigenous populations, on the one hand, and from Europeans and Africans, on the other. The term helped colonial subjects grapple with cultural and biological adaptation and the processes by which the physiological constitutions of migrants from elsewhere transformed to accommodate their new environments. Rooted in the Spanish verb *criare* and the Portuguese *criar*, "to create," creole/creolization discourse wrestles with the meaning of newness, understood alternatively as a cultural asset or a cultural burden. On the one hand, the notion of creole novelty implies a territorial and juridical tabula rasa. It allows colonizers to erase indigenous claims on the land and casts imperial conquest as the advance of civilization. However, it also, especially when referring to Europeans, encodes fears of moral and physical degeneracy. It tracks a disturbing movement away from the mores and traditions of the metropole toward dangerously exotic practices on the colonial margins. In the early colonial period, the term most consistently referred to people of African descent and was perhaps first used by enslaved people themselves. Planters and slave traders often indicated a general preference for the temperament of those Creoles habituated to American contexts. In this sense, they drew on another meaning of *criare/ criar*: to "breed" or to "raise"—an etymology that reminds us that processes of adaptation did not take place in a vacuum. Planters and officials sought to manage and direct these processes in order to best serve the interests of slavery and empire.

The term "Creole" did not originally imply hybridity or mixture; however, it gained currency amid challenges posed by the radical diversity of convergent empires and markets trafficking in a stunning variety of commodities, including human beings. Within this dynamic system, historical actors invariably found themselves in interstitial places, forced to negotiate their status amid rapid change. This predicament of "in-between-ness" highlights the relational aspect of identity formation and frames language and other cultural aspects as tools and strategies that might help any individual actor achieve a contingent, contestable advantage. Marked by acts of translation, creole practices and languages developed from the urgency of communication among people from a variety of places who suddenly found themselves on common ground or bound together in the "anomalous intimacies" within the carceral spaces of the Atlantic world system. Along these lines, historians have identified a class of polyglot "Atlantic Creoles" whose hybrid cultural practices, cosmopolitan sensibilities, and intermediary functions helped them thrive in an atmosphere of fluid identification. This context reached its apotheosis along the West African littoral and well into the interior of the continent; in Caribbean, Latin American, and North American port cities; on slave ships at sea; and in the harsh fields of New World plantations.

Even though creole practices have taken shape within an atmosphere of diversity and mixture, they have also, paradoxically, helped to set the terms of political, social, and racial exclusion. Creole/creolization discourse has often attempted to order these sites of exchange, to fix national, racial, and cultural multiplicity by a locally particular exclusionary logic. Creole exclusions have proliferated throughout the hemisphere. Reflecting a condition of what Mimi Sheller has called "achieved indigineity," creole status has necessarily displaced and appropriated the claims of indigenous peoples to territory and identity throughout the Americas.[4] The national mythology of Mexico, for example, has historically adopted a mestizo identity, privileging the perceived mixture of *indio* and European to the exclusion of *indios* and people of African descent. An exclusionary creole logic was also a feature of colonial Trinidad, where the "creole" designation sought to manage a legacy of sexual and cultural exploitation of enslaved Africans by European masters and has often failed to acknowledge subsequent labor regimes that depended on forced migrations from Asia. Because it has been formulated along a black-white continuum, the politically salient term "Creole" has obscured the presence and voices of Indo-Trinidadians. As Aisha Khan has demonstrated, their illegibility within the postcolonial Trinidadian state has continued within the country's "Callaloo nation" paradigm.[5]

In the context of the U.S. South, the term "Creole" has been both capacious and exclusive. In early nineteenth-century Louisiana, those "Creoles of Louisiana" born in the territory allied themselves politically and culturally with francophone migrants to meet the challenge of U.S. dominion and the "Americans" who came streaming into the city after the Louisiana Purchase of 1803. The massive 1809 influx of San Domingans from Cuba, where they had originally fled the upheavals of the Haitian Revolution, doubled the francophone population of New Orleans and contributed to a landscape of fraught interracial intimacy and kinship. The city's creole faubourgs harbored a culture marked by a perceived racial fluidity; Catholic, spiritualist, and vodou-inflected religious traditions; and intertwined artistic and performance traditions of French Romanticism and West African polyrhythm. The historiography of the city has portrayed a deep cultural division in antebellum New Orleans in which Creoles mounted a valiant resistance against "Americanization." However, mutual class interests and an investment in white supremacy aligned New Orleans with the rest of the United States in powerful ways. As a bustling port center, New Orleans acculturated countless immigrants to the restrictions and possibilities of an American identity. As the nation's largest domestic slave market, New Orleans processed around one million enslaved people from elsewhere as commodities.

Beginning in the middle decades of the nineteenth century, a number of prominent New Orleans "Creoles" fought publically to establish the purity of their white identities and to bar people of African descent from the perceived cultural advantages conveyed by "Creole-ness." Creoles of African descent have often likewise asserted their francophone heritage and "creole" identities to exclude and oppose English-speaking African Americans. Even in the face of the continued adaptation of the term by New Orleans's residents of color, "white" members of New Orleans's literary establishment maintained that a "Creole" was a native solely "of European extraction, whose origin was known and whose superior Caucasian blood was never to be assimilated to the baser liquid that ran in the veins of the Indian and the African native."[6] Using a formulation reiterated over and over again in the late nineteenth and early twentieth centuries, they argued that while the noun "Creole" was to be reserved for whites, the adjective "creole" could be made to modify lesser beings and inanimate objects: "creole horses, creole cattle, creole eggs, creole corn, creole cottonade," and creole "negroes."[7] Thus, in the 1920s, when Faulkner, Sherwood Anderson, and others deemed themselves "Creole," they indulged in a well-worn and safe brand of racially pure exoticism.

If notions of Creole and creolization have historically encapsulated the difficulty of pinning down stable identities and enacting complicated struggles over history, power, and representation within an Atlantic system, the terms have been no less slippery for scholars and theorists working in a wide variety of disciplines, from linguistics to cultural anthropology and from history to cultural studies. In taking up the question of what, exactly, happens at the intersection of cultures, creole/creolization discourse has encompassed a wide range of often-contradictory scholarly formulations. In the field of linguistics, where the term has had its longest currency stretching back to the late nineteenth century, scholars have charted a highly technical process by which "pidgin" languages of contact transformed into "creoles," "former pidgins that [had] acquired native speakers." Betraying a colonialist bias, the earliest of these studies tended to figure Creoles as failed attempts by speakers to achieve fluency in their "target" Western language.[8] Aiming to distinguish the European lexicon from the underlying African grammar and semantics, linguistic theories have heavily influenced the development of anthropological theories of cultural change and historical analyses of the survival of Africanisms in African American culture. As Stephan Palmié has argued, seminal scholarship on the Gullah and Geechee communities of the Georgia and South Carolina Sea Islands has perhaps adapted linguistic models of creolization too literally in efforts to recover in Sea Islanders' creolized language, kinship practices, and work rhythms evidence of a "deep structure" of "African grammar."[9]

More recently, theorists, building on Sidney Mintz and Richard Price's influential work on the Anglophone Caribbean widely disseminated as *The Birth of African American Culture* (1992), view creolization as a process that significantly restructures received meanings and innovates qualitatively novel forms of expression in response to historical, political, and geographical contingencies. When seen in this light, creole/creolization discourse reaches beyond concerns over mixture and "survival" and interrogates the differentials of power giving rise to cultural production and performance. Of special concern for many theorists are the ways in which creolization has constituted race as a category of colonial administration and governance. For these theorists, "issues of domination and subalternity, mastery and servitude, and control and resistance" are placed in the foreground.[10] The objective within this theoretical enterprise is not to uncover the ultimate origin or source of any given cultural practice or to place it along a simple historical and geographical vector from "Old World" to "New." Rather, it is to unpack the "points of entanglement" produced by the operations of the

146

slave trade, the plantation economy, and colonial expansion. Furthermore, it is to demonstrate how these entanglements have both hastened the formation of racialized hierarchies of knowledge and identification and provided the grounds for collective resistance to them.

In an explosion of scholarship since the early 1990s, a number of theorists have found "creolization" to be—alongside such related terms as hybridity, *métissage*, and bricolage—an apt conceptual tool for thinking through the cosmopolitan circuits of economic, cultural, and intellectual exchange characteristic of late modern capitalism. In this vein, Ulf Hannerz has determined that "we are all Creoles now," and historian James Clifford has made a metaphor of the Caribbean context of creolization, suggesting that "we are all Caribbeans now in our urban archipelagos."[11] In his insistence on countering static, essentialized notions of creole-ness with a somewhat vague and literary formulation of agency, Glissant has also prompted criticism for producing a limited and "defanged" account of creolization.[12] In response, a number of Caribbeanists and scholars of the black diaspora have insisted on the "concrete local and historical specificity of their Caribbean contexts" as an essential aspect of creolization's critical role (as theory) in unearthing and exposing those disavowed regulatory and disciplinary processes so central to the histories of colonialism and slavery.[13]

Well aware of the potential pitfalls of such a flexible concept, Glissant does not deploy the term "creolization" lightly in reference to Faulkner's "Capital S" South. Attending to local exigencies of place, he surveys the edges of Faulkner's "postage stamp of a world" in order to sift through the complex and intimate legacies of slavery and mastery. Faulkner's anxious narratives invite this engagement even as they recoil in horror from it. What Glissant finds in Faulkner is a South of uneven geography, the contradictions of which pose productive challenges to standard national narratives and the narrow politics they engender. From a creolized perspective, the South does not merely present a regional variation on a larger theme, exhibiting a "local color" easily reconciled to national norms. Nor is it a repository of ideological or racial purity as neo-Confederates would have it. Following Glissant's diagnosis of a creolized South, southern studies might better understand the South as frontier, border, or crossroads. Forming what Joseph Roach, speaking of New Orleans's culture, called the "selvage" of American civilization, the South is a rough seam, a geographical, ideological, and political terrain characterized by a return of the repressed and the unpredictable irruption.[14]

Creolization and Colonial Violence

"Frontier" is the recurring term in Glissant's work, and like Roach's "selvage," it functions as a three-dimensional space of overlapping colonial legacies and intimacies of private rule. Within this complicated intersection, French, Spanish, British, and U.S. imperial projects have confronted Native American quests for sovereignty and identity and the fugitive struggles of free and enslaved blacks against commodification. As in other creolized contexts, enmities and alliances cut across and within lines of class, status, race, and national/tribal affiliation. Recent historical work has detailed, for example, how shifting terms of ownership created deep cultural and class divisions within the Creek Nation; how Indians' involvement with the institution of slavery, as plantation owners and slave traders, intersected with the politics of removal and sovereignty; and how free people of African descent secured their free status by owning slaves and other property and by attempting to pass as white. As a means of interrogating frontier spaces, the lens of creolization exposes the fictions and violence necessary to achieve status and recognition and, with them, claims to "legitimate" possession of territory.

The lens of creolization also identifies the plantation as a significant "cultural matrix" for legitimating and contesting these claims.[15] Under the principles of private property rights, plantation culture cast institutionalized violence and command as private spheres of affection and production rather than state-sponsored and market-based regimes. Thus, a hegemonic plantation culture helped to insulate the public ideal of the homogenous nation from its creolized reality. As an "author of the plantation" and an heir to its legacies, Faulkner grappled with the psychic and historical consequences of unacknowledged creolization. In the "Bear" section of *Go Down, Moses*, for example, Ike McCaslin struggles to name the origin of the land's possession and discredits any firm basis for his own repudiation of it: "It was never Father's and Uncle Buddy's to bequeath me to repudiate because it was never Grandfather's to bequeath them to bequeath me to repudiate because it was never Ikkemotubbe's to sell to Grandfather for bequeathment and repudiation."[16] However, "nevertheless and notwithstanding" the illegitimate claim, Ike and his cousin, as heirs, feel compelled to interpret the sins and burdens of ownership. In the yellowed pages of the "scarred cracked leather" plantation ledgers, they discern the techniques their forefathers used to dispossess the enslaved: commodification, false equivalency, rape, and incest among others. In Faulkner's hands, landscape is a palimpsest where the past not only haunts the present. It also offers up its narratives as strategies, in Ike McCaslin's case, for naturalizing history and resisting the future.

As the McCaslin predicament shows, Glissant's creolized frontier is not merely physical, "offering new space to colonize." It is also an "intellectual and mental frontier between Western ideals and the threatened realities of colonized peoples"—a frontier that "generates problems and anguish on both sides of the border." In the U.S. South, as in the Caribbean, the "adventure, rape and murder" constituting everyday life for masters of slaves gives rise to convoluted anxieties, which many scholars, from W. J. Cash to Nell Irvin Painter, have suggested form a bedrock of the collective white southern psyche. As an "author of the Plantation," Faulkner keeps track of the dynamic relations of power operating in such spaces and demonstrates how those who "refuse the very idea, if not the temptation, to mix, flow together, and share" run the risk of their own "damnation." For Glissant, Faulkner's genius lies in his ability to render artistically the habits of mind of former masters and their despondent heirs, those "prefer[ing] the torments of withdrawal into self and the damned solitude of a refusal that does not have to speak its name."[17]

In this respect, Thomas Jefferson's *Notes on the State of Virginia* is as instructive as Faulkner's oeuvre and offers an exemplary account of Glissant's creolized mental frontier. In Query 18, Jefferson portrays the plantation household as a place where one might witness "a perpetual exercise of the most boisterous passions, the most unremitting despotism on the one part, and degrading submissions on the other." As a domestic environment, the plantation household is a troubling site of moral instruction: "The parent storms, the child looks on, catches the lineaments of wrath, puts on the same airs in the circle of smaller slaves, gives a loose to his worst of passions, and thus nursed, educated, and daily exercised in tyranny, cannot but be stamped by it with odious peculiarities."[18] Jefferson's description prefigures Faulkner's depiction of a scene at Sutpen's Hundred, in which Clytie and Judith watch unseen from the hayloft as their father, stripped to the waist, brawls with one of his "wild negroes" from the francophone Caribbean before a crowd of local men. His "odious peculiarities" are stamped all over their "Sutpen faces."[19]

According to political theorist Barnor Hesse, creolized points of entanglement manifest themselves in the political as well as the aesthetic realms. Both Jefferson's circle of childhood tyranny and Faulkner's ritual of masculine domination lift the veil of "civility [from] a pronounced public sphere and a secluded private sphere" to reveal "a regulatory civilization resourced by and defined against a subaltern sphere—the slaves, the colonized, the natives, the racially segregated others."[20] By distinguishing among different frames of thought and action and mapping the interstices between them, a creolized perspective demonstrates how the structural exclusion of the colonized and enslaved from the realm of the political has helped to constitute white masculine citizenship at the deepest registers of social interaction. Keeping track of what Hesse calls a "creolized political" should guide southern studies scholars to address how the whim, caprice, and local impressions of masters have asserted themselves as politics, providing a foundation for public policy, law, and liberal doctrine.

Again, Jefferson provides a blueprint for how this might happen. His unease over the tyranny of slavery notwithstanding, Jefferson rejects the notion of incorporating emancipated blacks into the state of Virginia as free persons. "Deep rooted prejudices entertained by the whites; ten thousand recollections, by the blacks, of the injuries they have sustained" under slavery had produced an enmity between blacks and whites too entrenched to be mitigated by politics. He further encodes his discussion of the "administration of justice and description of the laws" with an infamous series of observations regarding black physical, mental, and intellectual inferiority and a charge to natural scientists to pursue further research on "the races of black and of red men." For Jefferson, scientifically mastering nonwhite bodies, "even where the subject may be submitted to the anatomical knife, to optical glasses, to analysis by fire, or by solvents," keeps them at a safe remove from the political body.[21] By the mid-nineteenth century, a new generation of scientists had elaborated on his formulations, informing everything from Indian Removal policy to the majority opinion in *Dred Scott v. Sandford* (1857).

Creolization and Subaltern Restructuring

If creolization is a productive rubric through which to view the cultural production and political practice of masters and their heirs, it is perhaps because it illuminates a process of cultural "restructuring" especially suited to assess the cultural and political legacy of the enslaved. Colonialism and slavery have produced a racial and moral binarism positing whiteness (and "goodness") against an antithetical blackness. Under this representational schema, blackness has been devalued as opaque and inscrutable or as transparent and imminently knowable. Thus Jefferson describes the countenances of black people as an "eternal monotony," in which "that immoveable veil of black . . . covers all the emotions."[22] And Faulkner, after urging the NAACP and other civil rights organizations to "Go slow now," could attempt a racial ventriloquism in the pages of *Ebony* magazine: "The white man has devoted three hundred years to teaching *us* to be patient; that is one thing at least in which *we* are his superiors."[23] In the insurgent and playful disciplines of masking, tricksterism, signifyin', and the blues among others, black artists and writers from a range of political perspectives have, to paraphrase Ralph Ellison, changed the joke and slipped the yoke of Western modernity's master narratives. Michel-Rolph Trouillot has referred to these cultural, spiritual, and artistic innovations as "the African American miracle."[24]

As an instance of creolized restructuring, black artists' refiguration of Topsy, the wild-child slave from Harriet Beecher Stowe's *Uncle Tom's Cabin*, demonstrates an ongoing attempt to reverse and redirect the violent logics of commodification and mastery operating on black bodies. More than a sentimental depiction of slavery's "natal alienation" or a stock figure of blackface minstrelsy, Topsy functions instead as an opportunity for strategic circumvention and a theorist of black cultural production. When prompted to account for her existence, she responds, "I spect I grow'd. Don't think nobody never made me." In the early twentieth century, as James Weldon Johnson noted in the *Book of American Negro Poetry*, the formulation "like Topsy, Jes' grew" captured the generative but disruptive aspects of black musical culture from ragtime to the blues. In his 1972 novel, *Mumbo Jumbo*, Ishmael Reed portrays Jes' Grew as an "anti-plague . . . electric as life and . . . characterized by ebullience and ecstasy . . . seeking its words. Its text," as it spreads throughout the country from New Orleans.[25] In this novel and throughout his "Neo-HooDoo" oeuvre, Reed casts this specialized knowledge and its techniques not as African survivals but as instances of creolized restructuring. Drawing on the historical and moral multidimensionality of black diasporic spiritual traditions such as vodou, *candomblé*, and Santeria, the "lost American church" of Neo-HooDoo builds on previous uses of conjure by other black writers such as Zora Neale Hurston and Charles Chesnutt and asserts itself against the binary moralism of American culture.

Within the frame of creolization, black politics and black expressive culture issue what Hesse calls an "irruptive challenge" to the civilized veneer of plantation society and Western history.[26] Of the American, French, and Haitian Revolutions, only the Haitian was both anticolonial and truly antislavery, and yet, as many scholars have noted, Western thought and historiography has actively disavowed and silenced the Haitian Revolution and its influences. As a primary point of creolized entanglement, Haiti has long been a signal and model for black politics and agency throughout the diaspora, from the insurrection planned by Gabriel Prosser in Virginia in 1800, to the Charles Deslondes rebellion in 1811 territorial Louisiana, to the 1812 Aponte

Revolt in Cuba and beyond. When viewed from the vantage of creolization, southern history is replete with other such examples of marginalized peoples mobilizing at national and imperial margins to oppose their subjugation. In Spanish and U.S. territorial Florida, black Maroons, Seminoles, and Haitian revolutionary exiles sought to create spheres of independent influence and creativity in the face of U.S. military encroachment. In Reconstruction-era Louisiana, French-speaking *gens de couleur* infused radical discourse with antiracist and utopian socialist formulations circulating throughout the francophone Atlantic.

As these examples show, "creolization" tends to evoke a transnational or diasporic framework. However, as Glissant sensed on his journey to Oxford, creolization might also be a useful lens for analyzing local spheres of black political action. For example, in mid-1940s Alabama, white men raped black women with impunity. As historian Danielle McGuire has detailed, a young Rosa Parks traveled rural routes at her own peril to bring these crimes to light and to give victims voice. A half century before, Ida B. Wells-Barnett had described a system of intimidation in the U.S. South whereby the public lynching of black men as alleged rapists of white women provided a cover for the widespread and unacknowledged rape and sexual humiliation of black women.[27] Following in this critical tradition, Parks and other activists investigated the sexual violation of black women as *rape*, thus refusing to transfer the stigma of creolized intimacies onto the bodies and reputations of black women. In doing so, they sought to expose and resist a doubly unintelligible crime. They challenged a legal culture that perpetuated mastery by granting white men unimpeded access to black women's bodies. They also labored against a black cultural politics chiefly concerned with the public perception of black feminine virtue. Tellingly, as McGuire notes, traditional histories of the civil rights movement have obscured this context of antirape activism, preferring instead to detail the quest for civil rights as a "struggle between black and white men."[28] Delving beneath the surface of official histories, southern studies might limn creolized local contexts and intimate histories for counternarratives of mastery and resistance.

When Glissant first identifies the challenge that creolization poses to Faulkner's South, he describes it as one would describe a haunting, a menacing lingering that will not be stopped. Just as ghosts threaten the boundaries between life and death, creolization threatens the sanctity of the geographical boundaries of nations and empire, the political boundaries of public and private, and the psychic and racial boundaries purporting to separate master and slave. It also troubles disciplinary knowledge and its historic commitment to the intellectual work of empire and nation building, including its role in the creation, management, and valuation of racial categories. When taking up the challenges posed by creolization, southern studies scholars would therefore do well to pursue a radical interdisciplinarity. By forging critical and contingent methods and theories from history, literary criticism, anthropology, linguistics, political theory, and a range of other fields, the field may equip itself to discern, with Faulkner, the "the curse of this 'menace' and the damnation of those who fight it."[29] More importantly, by more precisely articulating the disruptive knowledge of subalterns, southern studies may be able to glean from the history of colonization and slavery the means by which the colonized and enslaved have improvised alternative visions of freedom and justice.

NOTES

1. Glissant, *Faulkner, Mississippi*, 7, 26, 29–30.
2. Ibid., 30.
3. Khan, "Creolization Moments," 238.
4. Sheller, "Creolization in Discourses of Global Culture," 276.
5. Khan, "Creolization Moments," 238.
6. Gayarré, *Creoles of History*, 2–3.
7. Ibid.
8. P. Baker and Mühlhäusler, "Creole Linguistics from Its Beginnings," 95, 100.
9. Palmié, "Is There a Model?," 187–92.
10. S. Hall, "Créolité and the Process of Creolization," 29.
11. See Hannerz, "World in Creolization," 12–18; Clifford, *Predicament of Culture*, 173.
12. See Khan, "Good to Think?," 653–73
13. Palmié, "Is There a Model?," 193.
14. See Roach, *Cities of the Dead*, 179–202.
15. Trouillot, "Culture on the Edges," 198.
16. Faulkner, *Go Down, Moses*, 246.
17. Glissant, *Faulkner, Mississippi*, 30–31.
18. Jefferson, "Notes on the State of Virginia," 288.
19. Faulkner, *Absalom, Absalom!*, 22.
20. Hesse, "Symptomatically Black," 59.
21. Jefferson, "Notes on the State of Virginia," 264, 270, 269.
22. Ibid., 264–65.
23. Faulkner, quoted in Hale and Jackson, "'We're Trying Hard as Hell,'" 40.
24. Trouillot, "Culture on the Edges," 191.
25. I. Reed, *Mumbo Jumbo*, 6.
26. Hesse, "Symptomatically Black," 59.
27. See I. B. Wells, *Red Record*.
28. McGuire, *At the Dark End*, xx.
29. Glissant, *Faulkner, Mississippi*, 30.

SUGGESTIONS FOR FURTHER READING

Cohen, Robin, and Paola Toninato, eds. *The Creolization Reader: Studies in Mixed Identities and Cultures*. London: Routledge, 2009.

Glissant, Édouard. *Faulkner, Mississippi*. Translated by Barbara B. Lewis and Thomas C. Spear. Chicago: University of Chicago Press, 2000.

Lionnet, Françoise, and Shu-mei Shih, eds. *The Creolization of Theory*. Durham, N.C.: Duke University Press, 2011.

Stewart, Charles, ed. *Creolization: History, Ethnography, Theory*. Walnut Creek, Calif.: Left Coast Press, 2007.

Thompson, Shirley Elizabeth. *Exiles at Home: The Struggle to Become American in Creole New Orleans*. Cambridge, Mass.: Harvard University Press, 2009.

Trouillot, Michel-Rolph. "Culture on the Edges: Caribbean Creolization in Historical Context." In *From the Margins: Historical Anthropology and Its Futures*, edited by Brian Keith Axel, 189–210. Durham, N.C.: Duke University Press, 2002.

SUZANNE W. JONES

Black and White

Continued popular perception and past scholarly analysis of the South as a region to be mapped in black and white is not surprising, given that African slaves were brought to Virginia in 1619, a Civil War was fought over the enslavement of black people, a bloody civil rights movement was needed to end the de jure racial segregation and racial violence that followed, and much ink continues to be spilled over the de facto social segregation that lingers outside the workplace. But since the turn of the twenty-first century, many scholars have come to view this biracial rendering as a problematic "obsession," "diverting attention from the varieties of multiracial, transnational experiences" that have equally been part of the region's history and culture.[1] As a term, "biracial" can be restrictive because it often posits separation rather than mixing and blending of people but even more so because it may only suggest the possibility of two absolute, flattening categories in a world of complex ethnic origins and makeups. However, as we turn our attention to analyses of races and ethnic groups that have been omitted in southern studies, we should not ignore issues in black and white that are still ongoing, even as they are changing in significant ways.

During the twentieth century, scholars examined the relationship of black and white to the South in different and contested ways. Historian U. B. Phillips's 1928 assessment contended that white supremacy, "whether expressed with the frenzy of a demagogue or maintained with a patrician's quietude, is the cardinal test of a Southerner and the central theme of Southern history."[2] Anthologies, even those published as late as the 1950s, assured that southern literature would be thought of as white as well.[3] The civil rights movement ushered in a more inclusive southern literary canon, beginning with Louis D. Rubin Jr.'s *The Literary South* (1979), although black women writers were noticeably absent from his table of contents. Anthologies that followed have been progressively more inclusive. The most recent, *The Literature of the American South* (1998), edited by a more diverse team (William L. Andrews, Minrose C. Gwin, Trudier Harris, and Fred Hobson) was admirably integrated, at least as regards black and white authors, although the biracial focus persisted.

Sadly the racial revision of southern literature anthologies has been slow to result in more racially integrated southern literature classes, no doubt because the terms "South" and "southerner" still trail burdensome baggage. The enrollment demographic has everything to do with the lingering connotations of "South" and "southerner," at least in the popular imagination. As Nell Irvin Painter has pointed out, during the era of segregation, "*the South* meant white people, and *the Negro* meant black people. . . . *The South* did not embrace whites who supported the Union in the Civil War or those who later disliked or opposed segregation."[4] For some today, both native and nonnative to the South, such limited and limiting connotations still hold. Others, both white and black, have attempted to broaden the definition of "southerner" beyond white (and racist). On the publication of *Soldier's Joy* (1989), white writer Madison Smartt Bell told a reporter for the *Atlanta Constitution* that after listening to a smooth-talking Ku Klux Klansman on a radio show and hearing of the arrest of a friend who participated in an anti-Klan demonstration, he was so angry that he began a novel set in the South, not just to denounce the Klan but to reclaim the South as a place for whites who are not racist.[5] On the other side of the color line, African American literary critic Thadious Davis has also argued for a more inclusive redefinition of the South, asserting that the return migration of African Americans to the rural South is not just "flight from the hardships of urban life" but also "a laying claim to a culture and a region that though fraught with pain and difficulty, provides a major grounding for identity."[6]

Attempting to fit black southerners into accepted definitions of "southern culture" and their work into conventional paradigms of "southern literature" has posed unnecessary dilemmas.[7] For some, African American interest in the South has produced limiting definitions of racial authenticity. John Oliver Killens has argued that "the people of the black South are much closer to their African roots, in its culture, its humanity, the beat and rhythms of its music, its concept of family, its dance and its spirituality."[8] In contrast, in *Turning South Again* (2001) Houston Baker reminds those too nostalgically inclined toward the life of the folk that the South imprisoned black minds and bodies. And yet in their anthology *Black Southern Voices* (1992), Killens and Jerry W. Ward Jr. embrace the term "southern," declaring that the "Southern imagination" has always been articulated by black voices, but that these voices have been ignored. They argue that without black voices, "it is impossible to discern fully the beauty and values of Southern literature and imagination." Although Killens focuses on difference, broadly defining "the black Southern voice" as angry, in opposition to white southern voices of "complacency and contentment," in his 1991 study, *The Southern Writer in the Postmodern World*, Fred Hobson points to similarities in order to bring black writers into the southern canon.[9] Using the traditional paradigm of southern exceptionalism as outlined by southern historian C. Vann Woodward, Hobson argues that a writer such as Ernest Gaines "might be seen as the quintessential southern *writer*—with his emphasis on family and community, his essentially concrete vision, his feeling for place, his legacy of failure, poverty, defeat, and those other well-known qualities of the southern experience."[10] Other scholars have questioned such attempts at inclusion, either in definitions of "southern literature" or "southerner." In *Inventing Southern Literature* (1998), Michael Kreyling argues that black writers, no matter their gender, will always sit uneasily in the southern canon because for them race always comes before region. Scott Romine has rightly argued in *The Real South* (2008) that, whether separatist or inclusive, such models "produce a positivist, fundamentalist model of culture that is increasingly distant from the cultural operations of the late South."[11]

Romine's focus, however, is on the production of southern cultural narratives, not on specific southern places. And yet particular places are often the avenues by which contemporary African Americans find their way back to the South, which is not to say the "real South." In Tony Grooms's *Bombingham* (2001), a black male character speculates about the reverse migration of blacks to the South: "I can see it in their eyes when they come for a visit how much they miss down here. They always talking about country cooking. . . . Can't they cook collards in Detroit? It's not the collards they're craving—it's the whole thing. It's home."[12] Ernest Gaines perhaps best explains the ambivalence of African Americans to "the South" when he speaks of his own love of Pointe Coupee Parish, Louisiana, where he grew up, but his alienation from the South as an ideological region. His nuanced response is similar to that of white writer Ellen Douglas, for whom the specificity of a locale allows for a narrative complexity that myths and stereotypes mask. When discussing the importance of "place" in her fiction, Douglas emphasized that "*place*, in the sense of the specific, is absolutely essential," remarking, "I don't think *regionalism* is important."[13]

Although research that broadens race and ethnicity beyond the biracial paradigm is vital, there is still work to be done in analyzing the South in black and white. For example, New Orleans hip-hop artist Jay Electronica, who channels New York rap artists, has worried publicly that his southern background has been a "career liability."[14] Scholars might examine in more detail and complexity the contemporary relationships of blacks and whites to the South, but also their attendant variations when age, sexual orientation, and socioeconomic status are considered. I have argued elsewhere that instead of worrying about who qualifies as a "southern writer" or rigidly delimiting "southern literature," we might more fruitfully ask questions about who is writing about the U.S. South (no matter their birthplace or residence), what stories they are telling, what images they are conjuring up, and, most important, why.[15] Continued investigations of black and white can provide a fruitful rubric for the study of the U.S. South in many literary genres. Travel writing by black outsiders to the South, such as Eddy L. Harris in *South of Haunted Dreams* (1993), often springs from the intersections of stereotyped expectations and more-complex realities encountered on their travels. The discussion about and subsequent change in identification on the 2000 U.S. Census, allowing citizens to mark more than one racial category, has spurred the publication of more racially inclusive family histories and memoirs of racially mixed people, such as Thulani Davis's *My Confederate Kinfolk* (2006) and Gregory Howard's *Life on the Color Line: The True Story of a White Boy Who Discovered He Was Black* (1995). African American writers once reluctant or uninterested in their racially mixed ancestry, such as Neil Henry and Carrie Allen McCray, have begun searching for the white roots on their mixed family tree, and a few writers who assumed they were white, like Bliss Broyard in *One-Drop: My Father's Hidden Life—A Story of Race and Family Secrets* (2007), are also making forays into formerly forbidden territory. Contemporary fictions about black-white relationships and racially mixed characters, such as those I highlighted in *Race Mixing: Southern Fiction since the Sixties* (2004), continue to be published and need analysis. And classic southern narratives in black and white that we thought we could not say another word about need reexamining.

Take, for example, the representation of the Jefferson-Hemings relationship and the way in which racial stereotypes have likely obscured a more complex historical narrative about white and black, master and slave.[16] Cultural critic bell hooks argues that "no one seems to know how to tell the story" of white men romantically involved with slave women. The realities of white exploitation and black solidarity have made it difficult to imagine consensual sex and impossible to imagine love of any kind across the color line in the plantation South. Hooks predicts that the suppressed story, if told, would explain how sexuality could serve as "a force subverting and disrupting power relations, unsettling the oppressor/oppressed paradigm."[17] Barbara Chase-Riboud's novel *Sally Hemings* (1979), the Merchant-Ivory-Jhabvala film *Jefferson in Paris* (1995), the Haid-Andrews TV movie *Sally Hemings:*

An American Scandal (2000), and Annette Gordon-Reed's family history, *The Hemingses of Monticello* (2008) attempt to do just that by postulating answers to the questions most often asked about the Jefferson-Hemings liaison: What attracted Thomas Jefferson to Sally Hemings? What attracted Hemings to Jefferson? Why would Jefferson give up the cosmopolitan artist Maria Cosway for a relationship with a slave? Why would Hemings leave France, where she was a free woman, to return to slavery in Virginia? Could a slave owner love a slave? Could a slave love her enslaver? That these questions are always generalized in this way—with the erasure of individual identities, as Gordon-Reed points out—illustrates the difficulty of representing such a relationship, or getting beyond what bell hooks terms the "oppressed/oppressor paradigm."

Such a reduction of the two people to symbols of the institution of slavery and to prevailing ideas about racial identification does little to penetrate the historical mystery of their intimate relationship. While Sally Hemings would not have thought of herself as white, she may not have thought of herself as simply black or considered her identity in terms of black solidarity with African Americans of varied skin tones.[18] Similarly, although Jefferson may have written in *Notes on the State of Virginia* that dark-skinned people were unattractive and intellectually inferior, he surrounded himself with racially mixed people at Monticello.[19] Gordon-Reed believes that Jefferson viewed the extended Hemings family "in a light different from the one in which he viewed other enslaved people," perhaps because they were blood kin to his wife, Martha. Gordon-Reed points out that he gave them certain freedoms within their slave status: training them to be skilled artisans, allowing them to earn their own money, and housing them away from the slaves who labored in his fields.[20]

But the relationship between Jefferson and Hemings, who as a fourteen-year-old slave accompanied his daughter Polly to France, may never have begun had they not been together in Paris for two years. Paris brought Jefferson into close personal contact with Hemings with no wife to take care of his servants' well-being while he was foreign minister to France. Furthermore, Jefferson read French but spoke it poorly, so he may have been drawn to those in his household, like Sally and her brother James, with whom he could speak English, especially since Sally brought news from home. Perhaps most importantly, Sally Hemings was legally free in France, and for the first time in her life, she earned wages for her work. Many years later, her son Madison recounted in his reminiscences that Jefferson had to bargain with his mother to get her to return to Virginia.[21]

Thus thinking of Sally Hemings simply as a black slave does not explain her return to Monticello or Jefferson's attraction to her. Although no likeness of Sally Hemings survives, it is important to remember that she was the half sister of Jefferson's deceased wife, that she had only one-quarter African ancestry, that she was described as beautiful by both blacks and whites, and that in 1830 she was listed in the U.S. Census as white. Ironically, Chase-Riboud's novel, a medium of words, depends on the visual (Hemings's "pale complexion" and her resemblance to Jefferson's deceased wife) and the auditory (her "soft Virginia accent," described as "a relief to his ears from the harsh beauty of the French") to make the fictional case for Jefferson's attraction to Hemings, while the more visual and auditory medium of film exaggerates Hemings's African features and renders her speech as different in order to mark her slave status for viewers.[22]

In contrast to the films, the novel *Sally Hemings* allows for the reader to imagine the quite likely possibility that Hemings physically resembled Jefferson's wife. In the novel, such a statement of resemblance does not depend on casting and so ironically can be more realistically evoked by the written word. In the made-for-television movie, *Sally Hemings: An American Scandal*, Sam Neil, who plays Jefferson, is mesmerized when he first sees Sally, asking his slave/servant James, Sally's brother, who she is. This scene perfectly captures the uncanny feeling Jefferson may have experienced on first seeing Hemings in Paris. Jefferson is depicted as initially glimpsing her reflection in a mirror, almost as if his wife had been brought back from the dead. Later when he verbalizes his thoughts to Sally ("You look exactly like my wife. The resemblance is uncanny"), I suspect that most viewers are struck, not by the possibility of physical similarity but by racial difference, given Carmen Ejogo's African features and skin tone (her mother is Scottish and her father Nigerian). Unlike fiction, film fixes the visual image, offering what literary critic Fredric Jameson calls "a translation" and therefore para-doxically something "closer to language" than reality in presenting a "materi-alized subjectivity."[23] But both filmic and fictional representations of racially mixed people warrant closer examination.

Leni Sorenson, a researcher at Monticello and historical consultant for *Sally Hemings: An American Scandal*, thought that Ejogo, despite her beauty, was miscast. As historical consultant, Sorenson, who is herself racially mixed, raised the concern before filming began that the actress playing Hemings should have a lighter skin tone, but her suggestion was made to no avail. Sorenson was similarly dismayed about the casting of Thandie Newton in *Jefferson in Paris*, although Sorenson was not the historical consultant for that film. Like Ejogo, Newton is half white and half black; her mother is British and her father Zimbabwean. Sorenson worries that such casting does not reflect the "nuances" of the historical truth of Hemings's racial ancestry and so perpetuates the myth than one "can always tell if someone has African ancestry"—a myth first born of white fear of impurity and later perpetuated out of black desire for racial solidarity.[24]

Unlike Chase-Riboud, who renders Hemings's speech like that of the white characters in her novel, in the film *Jefferson in Paris* Ruth Prawer Jhabvala creates a slave dialect for Hemings. She and her fellow British filmmakers drew a bright line between their well-spoken Jefferson and his slave, using Hemings's highly inflected speech, ungrammatical and singsong, to remind both Jefferson and their audience of plantation life at Monticello. In making this choice, their Sally Hemings entertains Jefferson and thus becomes, as more than one reviewer noted, the stereotypical "pickaninny" distracting the master with song and dance.[25] Interestingly Gordon-Reed believes that speech patterns may have been one more way that Sally reminded Jefferson of Martha. Besides resembling each other physically, half sisters can resemble each other "in the tone and timbre of voice, and mannerisms." Furthermore, Gordon-Reed points out that "even before they were together in Paris, the Hemingses and Jeffersons lived in close proximity to one another and interacted on a daily basis, creating as this did all over the South, a mixed culture of shared language, expressions, sayings, and norms of presentation." She argues that Hemings's "manner of speaking was probably not markedly different from either of theirs."[26] The British filmmakers' decision to render Hemings's speech so different from Jefferson's in *Jefferson in Paris* may stem from a desire to find as many ways as possible to remind viewers of Hemings's slave status and surely originates in stereotypes about the "essential differences" between white masters and black slaves fostered no doubt by "conventional" renderings. A decade after *Jefferson in Paris* was released, historian Melvin Patrick Ely's research revealed how much alike the idioms and speech patterns of slaves and masters actually were in Virginia during the late eighteenth and nineteenth centuries.[27]

Despite filmmakers' reliance on their audience's senses of sight and hearing to reveal identity, racial ancestry is not always audible or visible, which Chase-Riboud emphasizes by opening her novel with the perspective of Nathan Langdon, the 1830 white census taker. He is "unnerved" by Hemings's physical beauty and startled to discover that she is "fair enough to be his [own] mother."[28] Chase-Riboud's purpose is not so much to "insinuate into the consciousness of white readers the humanity of a people they otherwise constructed as subhuman," which, as Ann duCille argues, was the strategy of earlier African American writers who employed the mulatta figure.[29] Rather Chase-Riboud creates through her description a very specific individual, Sally Hemings, whom earlier white male historians had reduced to an abstraction.

Nathan, who is half Sally's age, literally becomes addicted to her presence, returning day after day until he convinces himself he has fabricated her race on the census form, not to protect Jefferson from miscegenation, his original reason, but to protect Hemings, a freed slave, from having to leave Virginia and proximity to him. This behavior provides another possible similarity to Jefferson who, in one way or another, freed his children with Sally, but not Sally, leaving that task to his daughter. Virginia law required freed slaves to leave the state unless special permission was granted by the state legislature. In the novel, after Sally spurns Nathan when she discovers that he has falsified her race, he becomes obsessed with her and her relationship with Jefferson, interviewing all who might have met her. Thus he becomes the first in a long line of historians, amateur and professional, many determined to suppress her story, others more recently to penetrate the mystery of her allure.

Chase-Riboud's representation of the beginning of Jefferson and Hemings's sexual relationship, like the screenplays of Jhabvala and Andrews, breaks the link with a master-slave narrative of forcible sex, even as it reminds readers of Hemings's slave status. The novel complicates one-dimensional racial concerns by raising matters not only of color but also of class. A French character who does not know Sally is African American, although she does know she is a servant, admires her grace, expecting "her manners and gentleness and soft, charmingly accented French" to convey a "breeding" that will "surely attract a gentleman of property and improve her station in life." By the time Jefferson leaves Paris for Monticello in 1789, two years after Hemings's arrival, Chase-Riboud, like Tina Andrews, represents Hemings as a French lady with a southern accent, who reminds Jefferson of both the beautiful "rare objects" that he purchased in Paris and the "sweet breath" that draws him to Monticello.[30] In his remembrance of his mother, Madison Hemings remarked how often she spoke of life in France, proof perhaps that she was changed by her sojourn there. To one degree or another, in all the imaginative renderings of their liaison, Jefferson, like Pygmalion, creates Hemings into his ideal life partner. Gordon-Reed speculates that when Thomas Jefferson left Paris, Sally Hemings, not Maria Cosway, "represented the place and way of life he expected to return to . . . a shared universe in which he would be the unquestioned center."[31]

Interestingly neither Chase-Riboud, Jhabvala, nor Andrews suggests that Hemings's attraction to Jefferson was physical, perhaps because of the thirty-year age difference, perhaps because prevailing narratives and contemporary racial ideologies have rendered this interpretation unimaginable. Instead Chase-Riboud imagines that as a teenager far from home, Hemings sees Jefferson, a powerful man in his forties, as a protector. Jhabvala spotlights as attractive Jefferson's influential position, both at home and abroad. Andrews portrays Hemings as an eager pupil to Jefferson, a willing teacher—knowledgeable in all subjects from language and ideas to manners and haute couture. Only the historian Gordon-Reed posits that Sally may have been physically attracted to Jefferson given the physical features of her racially mixed family members and the fact that all the Hemings women had long-term relationships with either high-status white males, white workers, or racially mixed servants from other plantations. Just as the 1979 novel, the 1995 film, and the 2000 television movie exhibit the social and political concerns of their day, Gordon-Reed's 2008 interpretation of the liaison reflects America's current fascination with the racially mixed figure and scholars' willingness to move beyond the racial dichotomies of the twentieth century.

In Eric Foner's review of *The Hemingses of Monticello*, he points out that although "most scholars are likely to agree with Gordon-Reed's conclusion that Jefferson fathered Hemings's seven children (of whom three died in infancy)," he believes that her portrait of the "enduring romance" (his phrase) is questionable.[32] Gordon-Reed makes the case that Jefferson's liaison with a much younger woman was not out of the ordinary, that a long-term relationship with a woman of color was within the norm of southern plantation society, and that his attraction was based on something more than sex. Gordon-Reed views Hemings's return to Virginia as reasoned, not coerced, a way for a slave simultaneously to become mistress of Monticello and to ensure her children's freedom. Has Gordon-Reed been too early influenced by her reading of Barbara Chase-Riboud's historical romance? Or has Foner's thinking been indelibly marked by the very master narrative that Gordon-Reed seeks to unsettle? What is clear is that each generation of writers, to one degree or another, continues to fashion the Jefferson-Hemings narrative in a way that reveals as much about the racial preoccupations of their own era as those of the eighteenth century.

What is equally clear in multiple renderings of the Jefferson-Hemings relationship is that there is still much to write about regarding the racially mixed black-white figure. In the novel *Half a Heart* (2000), for example, Rosellen Brown examines Miriam Vener's attempt to assuage white liberal guilt by tracking down Ronnee Reece, the child of her interracial love affair with Eljay Reece, a music professor at a black college in Mississippi where she taught briefly during the 1960s. When she was a baby, Eljay abducted Ronnee, claiming that since she was black, she needed to grow up with her black father in New York. Brown leavens her take on contemporary racism and identity politics with the hopeful story of interracial reconciliation between mother and daughter, which takes place primarily in Houston. In Ronnee, Brown creates a racially mixed protagonist, who, as has been the convention, identifies as African American. But Ronnee is different in that her reunion with her white mother sets her on a course to forge a new self-concept. Brown's decision to alternate the focalization of her narrative between Miriam and Ronnee allows her to illuminate the evolution in their thinking about each other, about race relations, and perhaps most significantly about racial identity. At the end of the novel, Brown gives Ronnee two choices that earlier racially mixed protagonists did not have: the chance to have a relationship with the white parent and the opportunity to identify herself racially. The ending suggests that the growing presence of both parents in the racially mixed child's life may change the old one-drop rule, although Ronnee's conflicts show that existential angst, if not tragedy, will continue to plague racially mixed people as long as society's demand to define them as black clashes with their attempts to define themselves.

NOTES

1. Perdue and Green, *Columbia Guide*, 136; see also E. G. Anderson, "Red Crosscurrents."

2. U. B. Phillips, "Central Theme of Southern History," 31.

3. See, for example, Beatty, Watkins, and Young, *Literature of the South*. Only one black writer, Booker T. Washington, was included in the first edition. The revised edition added a few white women writers (Glasgow, Porter, Roberts, Gordon, Welty, O'Connor, Grau) but no black women. In *One Homogeneous People*, Trent A. Watts summarizes the whitewashing of southern history and literature.

4. Painter, "'The South' and 'The Negro,'" 43.

5. O'Briant, "Anger at Klan," B1.

6. Davis, "Expanding the Limits," 6.

7. Many such definitions originate from C. Vann Woodward's argument that distinguishing southern characteristics included emphasis on family and community, love of place, a concrete as opposed to abstract view of life, and a history of poverty and defeat; see *Burden of Southern History*.

8. Killens, introduction, 3.

9. J. W. Ward, preface, 5; Killens, introduction, 3.

10. F. Hobson, *Southern Writer in the Postmodern World*, 101.

11. Romine, *Real South*, 103.

12. Grooms, *Bombingham*, 131.

13. Speir, "Of Novels and the Novelist," 236.

14. Caramanica, "Hip-Hop Traditionalism."

15. See S. Jones, "Who Is a Southern Writer?," 725.

16. In Paris in September 2009, I gave a talk on this topic. A longer article, "Imagining Jefferson and Hemings in Paris," based on the talk appears in *Transatlantica*.

17. hooks, *Yearning*, 57, 58.

18. Gordon-Reed, The *Hemingses of Monticello*, 335. Information about Jefferson and Hemings in this paragraph and the two that follow is based on this source.

19. Jefferson, *Notes on the State of Virginia*, 186–93.

20. Gordon-Reed, The *Hemingses of Monticello*, 90.

21. Ibid., 299, 270. The "Reminiscences of Madison Hemings," which first appeared as "Life among the Lowly, No. 1," in the *Pike County (Ohio) Republican* on March 13, 1873, is included as an appendix in Brodie, *Thomas Jefferson*, 471–76.

22. Chase-Riboud, *Sally Hemings*, 90–91.

23. Jameson, *Signatures of the Visible*, 3.

24. Telephone interview with Leni Sorenson, Charlottesville, Virginia, October 10, 2008.

25. Zibart, Review of "Jefferson in Paris."

26. Gordon-Reed, *Hemingses of Monticello*, 284, 285.

27. See Ely, *Israel on the Appomattox*. Gordon-Reed summarizes Ely's research in *Hemingses of Monticello*, 290–95.

28. Chase-Riboud, *Sally Hemings*, 8.

29. DuCille, *Coupling Convention*, 8.

30. Chase-Riboud, *Sally Hemings*, 112, 130, 89.

31. In *The Hemingses of Monticello*, Gordon-Reed quotes Jefferson's May 11, 1788, letter to Anne Willing Bingham, which forms the basis of her argument about why Jefferson turned away from Cosway (278).

32. Foner, "Master and His Mistress."

SUGGESTIONS FOR FURTHER READING

Davis, Thadious M. "Expanding the Limits: The Intersection of Race and Region." *Southern Literary Journal* 20, no. 2 (Spring 1988): 3–11.

———. *Southscapes: Geographies of Race, Region, and Literature*. Chapel Hill: University of North Carolina Press, 2011.

Hale, Grace Elizabeth. *Making Whiteness: The Culture of Segregation in the South, 1890–1940*. New York: Pantheon Books, 1998.

Jones, Suzanne W. *Race Mixing: Southern Fiction since the Sixties*. Baltimore: Johns Hopkins University Press, 2004.

Kreyling, Michael. *Inventing Southern Literature*. Jackson: University Press of Mississippi, 1998.

Painter, Nell Irvin. "'The South' and 'The Negro': The Rhetoric of Race Relations and Real Life." In *The South for New Southerners*, edited by Paul D. Escott and David R. Goldfield, 42–66. Chapel Hill: University of North Carolina Press, 1991.

Native

ERIC GARY ANDERSON

In a recently published essay on "writing the indigenous Deep South," Janet McAdams (Alabama Creek) observes,

> An Alabama Cherokee friend tells me she is "Cherokee, Creek, German, and English," but that "Southern is a layer over all of that." She's not suggesting a hierarchy here, but pointing to something I, too, know well. That Southern mixedbloods don't exist at intersections of identity categories. "Southern" isn't something that taints an otherwise authentic Creek- or Cherokee-ness. One is indigenous *through* one's Southernness.[1]

McAdams finds that these layers of "southern" and "native" cultural identities strongly suffuse each other; the former does not contaminate the latter, and the latter does not disaffiliate the former. Instead, southern mixed-bloods remain, despite countless legislative and extragovernmental efforts to dilute or eradicate them, "indigenous *through* [their] Southernness." The critical term or concept "native" typically defines and claims *more* than one personal, cultural, geographic, regional, or national identity; "native" refers to a plurality rather than a singularity, and "native" also bespeaks "nonnative," whether the latter stands separate from the former or whether, as in McAdams's example, these two complex and often ambiguous categories intermingle. McAdams's passage also makes plain that mileage may vary when it comes to nomenclature. Though it does not crop up in the passage above, the term "native" has cultural as well as scholarly traction, but so do the terms "indigenous" and "Indian," along with the specific tribal names that citizens of tribal nations often, though not always, prefer. Moreover, as the inclusion of "native" in *Keywords for Southern Studies* demonstrates, indigenous cultures and perspectives are much more visible and audible to twenty-first-century southernists than they were to our precursors. The wonder of it all is that the presence of an "indigenous" South has been, for so many decades, an absence in southern studies, and a particularly conspicuous absence in southern literary studies.

To explain why this is so, and to sketch the career of the term "native," I'll begin by making a transcontinental leap from Rabun

County, Georgia, the setting of McAdams's essay, to Lame Deer, Montana. In a 2000 essay on the maintenance and revitalization of Native languages, Richard Littlebear (Northern Cheyenne), president of Chief Dull Knife College in Lame Deer, comments, "Right now we have children who are mute in our languages, who are migrants to our languages, who are like extraterrestrials to our cultures."[2] As he suggests, a home language helps define and strengthen a home culture—helps make natives "Native"—while, correlatively, language loss destabilizes and threatens it to the extent that children, detached in various ways from their heritage language, come to seem less like Natives and more like aliens. The proximity of "native" and "alien" also plagues Littlebear in the more general, deconstructive sense suggested in the previous paragraph: the two terms, both baggage laden and both articulating a relationship between home place and self, cannot be uncoupled. Indeed, as Hilary N. Weaver (Lakota) points out, "There was no Native American identity prior to contact with Europeans." "Alien" and "native," considered as critical terms, invent and sustain each other.[3] As James Cobb puts it, "Historically, identities have not existed in isolation, but always in relation to other perceived oppositional identities against which they are defined," though "this has not always been a purely reciprocal process."[4] As such, even Native children who learn Native languages and solidify their indigenous cultural identities are both "native" and "not alien." The term "native" always carries this colonial baggage, in the South as elsewhere.

As an expression of cultural identity, however, "native" is far from empty or impossibly dualistic. As Weaver asserts, "Indigenous identity is connected to a sense of peoplehood inseparably linked to sacred traditions, traditional homelands, and a shared history as indigenous people."[5] "Native" works most powerfully as an indigenous self-representation: a declaration and affirmation of orientation, community, and survival. But "native" in colonial contexts also evokes removal from traditional homelands, including large swaths of the Southeast, and removal places indigenous people, cultures, and histories at risk of being de-nativized and rendered culturally as well as geographically homeless. McAdams affirms that the Georgia she writes from "is, [and] always will be, Indian land," but the complexity of "native" as a critical term centers on its ability to encapsulate these histories of dispossession and survival, of intercultural exchange and violence, of an indigeneity that filters through a non-Native language but also, to at least some extent, defines itself.[6] Amy Kaplan, in a study of nineteenth- and early twentieth-century U.S. imperialism, suggests another turn of the screw when she discusses the rootlessness and the self-enclosed mobility necessary for the efficacy of middle-class domesticity to redefine the meaning of habitation, to make Euro-Americans feel at home in a place where *they* are initially the foreign ones. Domesticity inverts this relationship to create a home by rendering prior inhabitants alien and undomesticated and by implicitly nativizing newcomers.[7]

Viewed in this light, "native" functions not only as a way of defining self against other but also as a way of misdefining, if not masking, both natives and aliens by transforming them into each other.

In the South, certainly, "native" denotes both Native Americans and non-Native "native southerners." Indeed, throughout the United States, as Philip Deloria has demonstrated, newcomers nativize not only by alienating actual Natives but also by playing Indian, calling themselves "natives" and/or performatively appropriating traits they associate with the very peoples and cultures they remove.[8] In late eighteenth- and early nineteenth-century novels, for example, both Charles Brockden Brown in Philadelphia and William Gilmore Simms in South Carolina use "native" to refer to non-native Americans. Brown, in his preface to *Edgar Huntly* (1799), states, "The incidents of Indian hostility, and the perils of the western wilderness, are far more suitable [as subject matter for the emerging American novel]; and, for a native of America, to overlook these, would admit of no apology."[9] Simms, in *The Yemassee: A Romance of Carolina* (1835), writes, "But perseverance at length triumphed over all these difficulties, and though Sayle, for further security, in the infancy of his settlement, had removed to the banks of the Ashley, other adventurers, by little and little, contrived to occupy the ground he had left, and in the year 1700, the birth of a white native child is recorded." Granted, in *The Yemassee* "native" refers to Indians as well—"The Indians were fairly defeated, Ishiagaska slain, and Chorley, the pirate, uninfluenced by any of those feelings of nationality which governed the native red men"— and, not stopping there, Simms also gives us "native" birds, woods, vigor, superstition, acerbity, and alligators.[10] Writing in the thick of the removal crisis, as countless indigenous Native Americans face the loss of the home-lands and cultural practices that make them native, Simms scatters the term "native" widely, expanding its reach as actual Native cultures are forcibly dispossessed and contracted. Perhaps the term itself mutates into a metaphor for a colonial process of displacement and subsumption that, once launched, provokes non-Natives to identify themselves as "native" Americans com-pelled to ward off "alien" threats more like than unlike the ones they them-selves recently posed. As a critical term for southern and American studies, "native" has often if not always encapsulated and restaged such complex and contradictory engagements between selves and "others."

"Native" sometimes works anachronistically as well as paradoxically. Much like the notion of "the South before 'the South,'" so too with "the Native before 'the native'": we apply the term "native" retroactively, across twelve thousand years of indigenous cultural presence and history in the present-day South, although the people in question almost certainly did not refer to themselves this way, any more than they called themselves "southern." That said, we remain largely in the dark about what southeastern Indigenous peoples *did* call themselves, either tribally or individually, for the vast majority of this twelve-thousand-year history. Even after European invasion, Theda Perdue and Michael Green tell us, "we do not know precisely which of the peoples De Soto met became the Choctaws, Creeks, Cherokees, and other historic tribes."[11] "Native" and its counterparts "Indian" and "indigenous" thus operate as necessary generalizations or placeholders.

Although, so far as we know, the term "native" comes into being late in the cultural histories of the first peoples of the Americas, Indians retell origin stories that affirm their indigeneity. Western academics, primarily non-Natives, offer different accounts of the peopling of the Americas; these accounts often conflict with the information transmitted in Native stories. At stake in these debates about nativity are claims to both native and national identity. Space prohibits a detailed recounting, but in a nutshell, many non-Native archaeologists and historians hew to the Bering Land Bridge theory, which asserts that in an inexactly demarcated distant past, the ancestors of present-day American Indians and Inuits migrated from Africa to Asia to Siberia and then into North America across an enormous land bridge formed of exposed continental shelves of the Bering Strait. The proposed migration trajectories include the present-day U.S. South, which appears to have been one of the last places to be settled. Moreover, as Colin Calloway writes, "Migration via land from Asia offers only one explanation of the peopling of America: maritime people would have been more likely to make the trip by sea, expanding back the time when migration may have taken place. Native traditions say the ancestors have always been here."[12] Like the Bering Land Bridge migration theory, indigenous origin stories are often worldly in scope, though vastly different in the particulars.[13] Origin stories tell of the creation of the world as well as the people; their orientation is often both local and planetary. In Cherokee earth diver stories, Choctaw emergence stories, and the land bridge theory, to mention but three accounts of the peopling of a Native America, seismic global events precede or are coterminous with the formation of local Native cultures and identities.

For southeastern Indians, as for Indians elsewhere, the stories also transmit the cultural-historical knowledge that "native" means "here first" and that, prior to the arrival of Europeans and other aliens who would be or become natives, this Native world was complex, dynamic, and fully functioning. But, as David Moltke-Hansen points out, "the emergence of a creole culture reflects the subordination or elimination of many aspects of the creole population's antecedents as well as accommodations to an often oppressive and alien cultural hegemony."[14] Vine Deloria Jr. (Standing Rock Sioux) contends that the Bering Land Bridge theory is driven by European ideology that swirls around two core beliefs: "that the Western Hemisphere, and more particularly North America, was a vacant, unexploited, fertile land waiting to be put under cultivation according to God's holy dictates" and "that American Indians were not original inhabitants of the Western Hemisphere but latecomers who had barely unpacked before Columbus came knocking on the door. If Indians had arrived only a few centuries earlier, they had no *real* claim to land that could not be swept away by European discovery."[15] In this light, the Bering Land Bridge theory renders Natives non-native by redefining them as immigrants. "Here first," as a Native definition of "native," thus occupies crucial indigenous cultural and political ground as it honors Native history, celebrates Native survival, and pointedly resists ideological maneuvers against Native cultures and claims.

"Native" also gets tangled up in social constructions of race. Nancy Shoemaker notes that "it was southeastern Indians who first adopted a self-identification as red people, while southeastern European colonists were also early proclaimers of a white identity." This was happening by the mid-1720s, and its occurrence in the Southeast might indicate that Indians applied existing cultural structures to their diplomatic interactions with Europeans. Shoemaker speculates that "*red* and *white* were metaphors for moieties, or complementary divisions, within southeastern Indian society, suggesting that Indians might have thought *red* a logical rejoinder on meeting these newcomers who introduced themselves as white people." That said, clearly the association of "red" with identity of any kind, let alone racial and "native" identity, does not happen right away, or even particularly early, in southeastern Indian-European interactions. But, as Shoemaker asserts, over the course of the eighteenth century, "in the world of ideas, there emerged one absolute, indelible mark of identity: skin color."[16]

By the end of the eighteenth century, red and white and black were "racial categories." It will come as no surprise that these new categories of identity, along with the concomitant racialization of "native," made (and also exacerbated) trouble. Perdue and Green write, for example, that white racists in the late nineteenth and early twentieth centuries regarded Southern Indians as subversive of the caste system. Refusing to accept the notion that many Native people survived in the South, they insisted that individuals claiming to be Indians were merely African Americans establishing a racial way station to "passing" as whites. Virginia went to the greatest extreme in attempting to thwart this challenge to white racial purity.[17]

Though "most Native people . . . resisted classification in every way they could," Virginia began "to take measures to eradicate Native identity in the 1920s," culminating in the Racial Integrity Act of 1924, which, as Karenne Wood (Monacan) explains, "prohibited marriage to whites by people of color, including Indians."[18] One of the major anti-Indian crusaders in the state at this time was Walter Plecker, a eugenicist physician who from 1912 to 1946 served as state registrar of the Virginia Bureau of Vital Statistics. Plecker, writes Wood, "believed that there should be only two races of people in Virginia, white and 'colored,' that white people were superior, and that people of 'mixed' race would produce defective children." By 1925, he also "had decided, based mainly on conjecture, that there were no 'pure' Indians in Virginia" and altered numerous Indians' birth certificates to redefine them as 'colored.'"[19] Plecker's doctoring of the records was eventually exposed, and the Racial Integrity Act was ruled unconstitutional in 1967. In July 2015, the Pamunkey Indian Tribe of Virginia was granted federal recognition; bills to grant several other Virginia Indian tribes federal recognition are advancing through the U.S. House and Senate. The Virginia Indian Heritage Program, housed at the Virginia Foundation for the Humanities and headed by Wood, is going strong, as are a number of Native American and Indigenous studies programs at Virginia universities. But versions of Plecker's biracial imperative remained active throughout the twentieth century, and, all in all, the baggage "native" carries remains heavy, in the South and throughout the Americas.

In the spring of 2002, the Society for the Study of Southern Literature (SSSL) biennial conference met in Lafayette, Louisiana, to explore the theme "The South in Black and White." I went to SSSL as a Native American literature scholar, and in that capacity, I was impressed that the conference theme encouraged a scholarship of integration and inclusion that could not be more passionately opposed to the Walter Pleckers of the world, but I was also curious about the apparent limits of that inclusiveness. Published that same year, the Blackwell *Companion to the American South*, a collection of field surveys by historians, also acknowledges the biracial much more than the multiracial.[20] Though this volume leads with Amy Turner Bushnell's essay on "The First Southerners: Indians of the Early South," the twenty-eight essays that follow Bushnell's do not regard Indians as major players in the *Companion*'s version of southern history and culture. Neither did American Indians make lengthy appearances at another event held in 2002, the American Literature Association/SSSL Symposium on "Postcolonial Theory, the U.S. South, and New World Studies," which convened at Puerto Vallarta, Mexico. However, this gathering clearly signaled a sea change in southern literary studies that, more indirectly than directly, prepared the way for consideration of "native" literatures and cultures, mainly by enlarging prevailing theories and practices of southern studies to argue that "the South" both reflects and shapes American, hemispheric, global, postcolonial, and multiethnic studies. Put another way, Puerto Vallarta launched a "New Southern Studies" committed to reconceiving "'Southern Culture' in the singular" as "'Southern Cultures' in the plural."[21] No longer hewing to southern exceptionalism, this paradigm shift has also by and large rejected binaristic approaches (North/South, black/white) and pressured received wisdom to the extent that "the South" has begun to melt into air. In the process, the New Southern Studies has helped deconstruct Native southern studies into re-existence.

To put it mildly, conditions were ripe for a Native southern studies intervention. In "Native American Literature, Ecocriticism, and the South: The Inaccessible Worlds of Linda Hogan's *Power*," which appeared in another 2002 project, Suzanne Jones and Sharon Monteith's edited collection, *South to a New Place*, I contend that

> in presenting her readers with an invented tribe of Florida Indians, the Taiga, whose lives are entirely predicated and centered on their intimate, knowing experiences of particular southern homeplaces, Hogan reminds us of how much we don't know, and how decentered, how inaccessible, how fictive, indeed how absent such lives and experiences can be in non-Native cultural histories of the South.[22]

My implicit point here is that the intensive, extensive, necessary attention to a biracial South perpetuated and ratified, however inadvertently, the invisibility and absence of Native Souths. Here and elsewhere, however, I have argued that the work of making Native cultures and Native studies more present, visible, and substantive within southern studies needs to be undertaken with a healthy respect for all that remains unknown or inaccessible about "native," as well as a necessary caution about the dangers of choosing a single angle of vision.[23] Neither southern nor Native studies should be the only lens. That said, "native" contributes greatly to the work of understanding cultural, intercultural, hemispheric, transnational, and global multiplicity, in and of the South. In reclaiming southeastern Native cultural identities and helping to deconstruct "southern," "native" as a critical term also opens up space for more-expansive literary and textual histories of the South, allowing us to begin well before the early-nineteenth-century, plantation-shadowed invention of the South and to focus less intently on such historical markers as antebellum/postbellum.

Put another way, reading "southern" through "native" enables us to begin to see the scope and expansiveness of both. Indeed, centuries before the relatively recent invention of the United States and its subdivision into regions, the people who first lived in the present-day South crafted eloquent objects and structures for themselves and others to see, use, read, and (in some instances) exchange. I argue that textuality began in the South during the Archaic Period, with pottery and earthworks, and continued with later circum-Mississippian earthworks of dazzling architectonic distinction and rhetorical power. Much later, when Sequoyah completed the Cherokee syllabary in 1821, Cherokees quickly learned it, acquired alphabetic literacy, and started writing. Print texts gave Cherokees and other Native peoples new forms and venues for prosecuting what was, by 1821, the familiar, long-standing work of both making texts and conducting countercolonial negotiation and resistance. Writing afforded Native people new means of doing some of the things they had been doing outside print: determining and representing their own cultural identities, articulating tribal and intertribal points of view, surviving colonialism and genocide, and otherwise conducting Native business on Native terms to the extent possible. The term "native" works as shorthand for these often-neglected cultural and textual histories.

Published in 2010, *The People Who Stayed: Southeastern Indian Writing after Removal* backlights many of the issues raised above and illuminates some of the challenges and fault lines of a twenty-first-century Native southern literary studies. This anthology presents 350 pages of southeastern Indian writing, nearly all of it produced in the twentieth or twenty-first century.[24] As the title suggests, the editors prefer the term "Indian" to the term "Native," but the book resoundingly affirms that "native" as a critical concept remains a strong and vital element of "southern" while "southern" continues to be challenged and enriched by "native." The title of the volume makes a concise argument about southeastern indigenous volition and presence: some Indian people stayed in the South, this was to some significant extent a choice they made, and the people who stayed have produced a considerable body of writing. As this book makes abundantly clear, "Native" identity in the South remains firmly tied to place—to traditional homelands—as well as to oral and written literacies, (still) often used tactically for decolonizing purposes. The sheer existence of this book makes a powerful pedagogical point about Indigenous southern texts and contexts that, for many students as well as many southernists, will be visible for the first time.

174

The People Who Stayed collects southeastern Indian poetry, fiction, drama, and nonfiction, but in an important sense it does not forward an argument about literature so much as it urges consideration of cultures and contexts. As the editors say early in their introduction to the book,

> This anthology seeks to tell some of . . . the stories of the people who stayed. The forces of disappearance have been, and remain, strong. Yet Indian people of the South resist, survive, persist. Through song, story, picture, declaration, and declamation, they use language and art to claim—and reclaim—their identities and homelands, to say: "We are still here."[25]

As such, the editors take up "Indians in Southern Literature" and the persistent problem of non-Native representations of Indians in both literature and mainstream culture, but they do not limit their introductory remarks to these subjects, and the anthology as a whole betrays little concern with situating southeastern Indian writing within southern literature. The book decenters so that it may recenter; the more urgent work at hand is to insist on southeastern Indian presence and self-representation; to that end, two of the book's editors, Janet McAdams and Geary Hobson (Cherokee-Quapaw/ Chickasaw) are themselves noted southeastern Indian writers.

The editors break the Southeast into four subregions: "Virginia, Maryland, and Delaware"; "Carolinas, Tennessee, and Kentucky"; "Deep South: Georgia, Florida, Alabama, and Mississippi"; and "Arkansas, Louisiana, and East Texas." As McAdams observes in the passage that opens this essay, "One is indigenous *through* one's Southernness." But to what extent does this state-bound map of the U.S. South write over other maps? To what extent do associations with particular southern states illuminate "native" beyond, say, demographics? What does it mean to be a Native writer from Louisiana as distinct from a Native writer from Virginia? Likewise, how does one cluster of states differ from another when it comes to southeastern Indian writing after removal? In that this anthology collects pieces written and published in the years after all the above-mentioned states were granted statehood, this organizational strategy works in principle; in that the anthology's structure reflects the complicated superimpositions of "native" and "southern" cultures and contexts on each other, the subregional clusters lend the book an honest respect for literary-historical messiness and a refreshing rejection of straight linear chronology.

Further, the editors explain, "We are purposely omitting the writings   175
of Indian people who are descended from Southeastern tribes that were removed to Indian Territory and whose orientation is essentially from "Oklahoma" rather than from the southeastern United States." More controversial than their decision to organize by subregions, this omission raises the question of whether removal from the Southeast in the 1830s is sufficient cause for excluding writers from an anthology of southeastern Indian writing published in the early twenty-first century. For one thing, writers such as LeAnne Howe (Choctaw), Craig Womack (Oklahoma Creek-Cherokee), and Joy Harjo (Mvskoke), all of whom have much to tell us about past, present, and future Native Souths, do not appear in *The People Who Stayed*. For another thing, as the editors acknowledge, "It might . . . seem ironic, if not contradictory, that many of the writers featured in *The People Who Stayed* are presently residing outside the Southeast."[26] The editors also point out that we have at our disposal Daniel Littlefield Jr. and James Parins's *Native American Writing in the Southeast: An Anthology, 1875–1935* (1995), which offers a healthy sampling of Oklahoma Indian writing about (rather than "in") the Southeast. Still, the distinction between an Oklahoma orientation and a southeastern orientation is a federally imposed consequence of Indian removal; and even though numerous writers included in *The People Who Stayed* speak powerfully about removal, the exclusion of Oklahoma writers with southeastern connections comes at a cost. As I write elsewhere, "How can American Indians, very much including American Indian writers and the enterprises of American Indian literature and criticism, repossess dispossessed southeastern homelands and retell the stories of and from these home places? In what ways do indigenous people and stories take control of their own comings and goings?"[27] *The People Who Stayed* demonstrates that these are difficult, perhaps impossible questions. It also emphasizes, by way of its principles of selection and organization, the complexity of "native" and the challenges of reading and writing "native" and "southern" into each other.

All in all, the deconstruction of "the South" as a category happens alongside the "reconstruction" of the Southeast as Indian country. *The People Who Stayed* performs both of these tasks to some extent but also holds fast to at least some prevailing non-Native mappings of the South; though distinct, "native" and "southern" are also inextricable. As mentioned above, the anthology also resists conventional chronological literary history. In a piece first published in the Carlisle Indian Industrial School newspaper, *The Red Man and Helper*, in 1898, Wilson H. Welch (Cherokee) archly concludes, "Many Indians are in the United States, but not of it. My people are here and are citizens. Why not let all the Indians immigrate to the United States?" In "Surviving Document Genocide" (1999), which appears earlier in the book, Rose Powhatan (Pamunkey) explains that "document genocide regulates your relationship to others with whom you interact on a daily basis. It's not easy to be upbeat about your tribal identity when most people around you constantly remind you that you are not supposed to exist."[28] From its title on, and as the quotations from the late nineteenth-century boarding school student Welch and the late twentieth-century teacher Powhatan indicate, *The People Who Stayed* intervenes strongly in the continuing effort to turn back the rhetoric of indigenous disappearance. Necessary and dazzling, this anthology makes interaction between Native studies and southern studies more possible; as it takes its place as part of the longer histories of indigenous cultures in the South, it also teaches us much about the ways "native" and "southern" texts and contexts both repel and create each other.

Much has happened in the still-emerging field of Native southern studies in the years since Puerto Vallarta and *South to a New Place*. In 2004, Annette Trefzer and Kathryn McKee hosted a symposium at the University of Mississippi titled "The U.S. South in Global Contexts," at which I spoke about Indian removal and the importance of rethinking southern Indigenous communities. With its Winter 2006–7 special issue, "American Indian Literatures and Cultures in the South," *Mississippi Quarterly* became the first southern studies journal to dedicate an issue entirely to American Indians. The 2008 SSSL prominently featured Native southern writers, with a keynote address by Craig Womack and readings by LeAnne Howe and Allison Hedge Coke. Trefzer's *Disturbing Indians: The Archaeology of Southern Fiction* (2007) is the first monograph to take up Native southern literary studies, while Melanie Benson Taylor's *Reconstructing the Native South: American Indian Literature and the Lost Cause* (2011) breaks further new ground by doing so with an emphasis on Indigenous writers. And the journal *Native South*, edited by Taylor, anthropologist Robbie Ethridge, and historian Greg O'Brien, published its first issue in 2008. It is now possible to be a southern studies person who works primarily on Native studies, or vice versa.

But as my discussion makes abundantly apparent, regional as well as racial categories still hold a great deal of power, very much including the power to do harm. In the excerpt from "Betty Creek: Writing the Indigenous

Deep South," published in *The People Who Stayed*, Janet McAdams rehearses all-too-familiar questions about blood quantum ("How much?") and "authenticity." To what extent, she wonders, does even a well-intentioned simulacra such as "'a re-enactment of a Creek village'" provide some sense or experience of the "native" in the South, particularly given the many less benign "moments when the weight of the inauthentic pulls down the very air around you, thick, intangible, undeniable." She tells us, "My own parents affirm their Indian blood but think of themselves as white people with Creek and Cherokee ancestors," and while "Mixedblood families in the South approach their Indian ancestry in all kinds of ways," some of these ways involve passing as white, self-removing the "native" from the "southern."[29] In her conclusion, McAdams links "native" to place, to land, to home. But the roads to and from Indian Country's southeastern precincts remain twisted and obstacle laden, impossible to traverse without being "indigenous *through* one's Southernness."

NOTES

1. McAdams, excerpt from "Betty Creek," 253. Along with McAdams, others (Melanie Benson Taylor, myself) have used versions of the singular, definite-article-laden phrases "the Indigenous Deep South" and, more commonly, "the Native South." Like the monolithic phrase "the Native American perspective," phrases such as these do not adequately reflect the pluralistic diversity of southeastern Indian cultures. But they also sometimes seem unavoidable, at least pending the development of phrases that reflect and represent both indigenous southeastern cultural histories and the academic field of Native southern studies. In the meantime, phrases such as "the Native South" help provoke larger considerations, some of which I take up in this essay, that center less on the "the" and more on the problems and prospects of the terms "native" and "South."

2. Littlebear, "Just Speak Your Language," 91.

3. H. N. Weaver, "Indigenous Identity," 29. As Betonie says in Leslie Marmon Silko's classic 1977 novel *Ceremony*, "white people are only the tools that the witchery manipulates; and I tell you, we can deal with white people, with their machines and their beliefs. We can because we invented white people; it was Indian witchery that made white people in the first place;" see Silko, *Ceremony*, 132. In this version of the story, for reasons the novel makes apparent, Betonie does not make the counterclaim that white people invented Indians.

4. Cobb, *Away Down South*, 6–7.

5. H. N. Weaver, "Indigenous Identity," 31.

6. McAdams, excerpt from "Betty Creek," 256.

7. A. Kaplan, *Anarchy of Empire*, 34.

8. See P. J. Deloria, *Playing Indian*.

9. C. B. Brown, *Edgar Huntly*, 3.

10. Simms, *Yemassee*, 10, 340.

11. Perdue and Green, *Columbia Guide to American Indians*, 43.

12. Calloway, *First Peoples*, 16.

13. Other early Native texts—mounds and effigies and marks on the land, some built three thousand or more years ago—are also quite literally of the world: earthworks.

14. Moltke-Hansen, "Intellectual and Cultural History," 219.

15. V. Deloria, *Red Earth, White Lies*, 67–68.

16. Shoemaker, *Strange Likeness*, 131–32, 131, 137. Shoemaker also points out that "Houma" translates as "red" (132), to which I would add that the name "Oklahoma" derives from two Choctaw words, *okla* (people) and *humma* (red).

17. Perdue and Green, *Columbia Guide to American Indians,* 139.

18. Ibid., 140, 139; Wood, "Virginia Indians," 20.

19. Wood, "Virginia Indians," 20.

20. See Boles, *Companion to the American South.*

21. Moltke-Hansen, "Intellectual and Cultural History," 215.

22. E. G. Anderson, "Native American Literature," 166.

23. See E. G. Anderson, "Native American Literature" and "South to a Red Place."

24. Along with the contemporary works, the anthology includes a few late nineteenth- and earlier twentieth-century selections as well as a small number of transcribed oral stories, of unknown vintage, as performed by contemporary storytellers.

25. Hobson, McAdams, and Walkiewicz, "Introduction," 2.

26. Ibid., 19.

27. E. G. Anderson, "On Native Ground."

28. Welch, "People Who Would Not Be Driven," 78; Powhatan, "Surviving Document Genocide," 24.

29. McAdams, excerpt from "Betty Creek," 254, 253.

SUGGESTIONS FOR FURTHER READING

Hobson, Geary, Janet McAdams, and Kathryn Walkiewicz, eds. *The People Who Stayed: Southeastern Indian Writing after Removal.* Norman: University of Oklahoma Press, 2010.

Lyons, Scott Richard. *X-Marks: Native Signatures of Assent.* Minneapolis: University of Minnesota Press, 2010.

Perdue, Theda, and Michael Green. *The Columbia Guide to American Indians of the Southeast.* New York: Columbia University Press, 2001.

Smith, Linda Tuwahai. *Decolonizing Methodologies: Research and Indigenous Peoples.* London: Zed Books, 1999.

Taylor, Melanie Benson. *Reconstructing the Native South: American Indian Literature and the Lost Cause.* Athens: University of Georgia Press, 2011.

Trefzer, Annette. *Disturbing Indians: The Archaeology of Southern Fiction.* Tuscaloosa: University of Alabama Press, 2007

Latin

At the close of the nineteenth century, historian and bibliophile Hubert Howe Bancroft (1832–1918) acknowledged that a part of Anglo-Americans' dislike of Spanish-speaking Californians stemmed from their ties to "the Latin races in America and Europe."[1] Latin, of course, has a vast genealogy, extending long before the United States existed as a nation or Spain claimed California as part of its empire.

Latin, the *Oxford English Dictionary* delineates, pertains to Latium, a country in ancient Italy and capital of the Roman Empire (27 BCE–476 CE). Latium encompasses the home of the early Latins, meaning, the Romans. As the Roman Catholic Church became the Roman Empire's scion, Latin functioned as the worldwide medium of communication and a sign of global unity for worship. Latin corresponds with the tongue of ancient Rome's people, "the Latins," and is employed as a designation for European persons who speak Latin-descended languages. Latin also references a printing typeface. This Latin font, in newspaper readerly format, developed into the "Times Roman" design, originally conceived for the *Times of London* in 1932. For our immediate aims, the *OED*'s parameters that concern us are found in this precept: Latins are members of various communities in Europe, specifically France, Italy, and Spain, as well as Latin America. These regions' lingua francas, known as Romance languages, derive from Latin. But this scrutiny is not a record of how Latin, as a canonical language, has played out in the West's cultural history and development. Even so, this Latin provenance is insinuated in the U.S. iteration of the panethnic *Latino* category. Latin metastasizes as a system of communication within the realm of American racialization practices and geographies, primarily as they cling to popular projections of peoples of U.S. Latino or Latin American descent through a "Latin" denominator. The U.S. propagation of this sort of Latinness has engendered a cohesive oneness around an exultant and default Americanism that culturally depends on an English-speaking, Protestant-not-Hispanic-Catholic Anglo America. This précis begins with Latin as a synonym for a Latino body politic that coevally taps into individuals who may speak any of the aforestated Romance languages. It conceptually proceeds by linking U.S. Latin semiotics—the everyday body language, the cultural references, the signs, the messages, and the assumptions that structure and give life to these tenets—to a Global South that melds with the American South.

Latin has culturally and ethnoracially jelled to Latino bodies north and south of the American hemisphere, often in stereotypical and othering ways that collapse all these subjects as foreign and exotic to the U.S. landscape. Renowned scholar Américo Paredes (1915–1999), as a brief illustration, sketched "little Latins" in his foundational *George Washington Gómez: A Mexicotexan Novel* to highlight assimilatory struggles by Mexican Americans in Texas and the Southwest, a terrain that was annexed during western expansion and the 1846–48 U.S.-Mexican War. This war's final stage brought a formal agreement, the 1848 Treaty of Guadalupe Hidalgo, legally incorporating Mexicans who lived in the present-day states of Arizona, California, Colorado, Nevada, New Mexico, Utah, and Texas into the United States. Despite their American citizenship, Mexicans became a conquered population through a new racial and class structural order. The "Mexicotexan" rubric captures the oneness of a national and regional subjectivity, as it straddles a monumental American history. Paredes's category for little Latin Americans—abridged to "little Latins" or "little things"—brings life to "a polite term" that has concealed the violence of a pejorative lexicology uniting skin color with animal fat and fatty oils, as is the case with "greaser," or a racialized nationality like "Mexican." Under Paredes's pen, "little Latins," inured to American racism since elementary school, do not only learn English. They also invariably think as Americans, in English, despite feeling "infinitely dirty."[2] Dirt can be read as the grimy substance, the matter that matters in the historical narration and interpretation of a people who have been scaled down, reduced, to a collapsible Latinness-cum-Mexicanness presumably speaking its abject status in a "Latin" tongue.

In a phenotypic vein, sociologist Clara E. Rodríguez has dubbed the perceived U.S. visual economy of commodified Latino difference as "Latin looks." These conventional characteristics amount to a "Latin or Latino look that everyone recognizes. This person is slightly tan, with dark hair and eyes. Upon further thought, we find other factors that contribute to the 'Latin look,' for example, Spanish usage, accented English, occupation, education, residence, relationship to Anglos, self-identification, and identification by others."[3] Rodríguez cleaves together dark-looking Latins and Latinos. This interchangeability dialogues with the Hollywood industry and the U.S. mainstream media's representations, from the twentieth century onward, of a passionate population, as evinced through the sensual screen images of the "Latin lover." The fictional and legendary Ricky Ricardo of the classic CBS television comedy *I Love Lucy* (1951–57) served as a type of Latin lover. Ricardo, a bandleader portrayed by the Cuban American actor and musician Desi Arnaz (1917–86), satisfied, as essayist Richard Rodriguez puts forward, a 1950s American infatuation with "the Copacabana curtain—all the nightclub gaiety of Latin America in old black-and-white movies."[4] But not all Latin lovers with their impressed Latin looks have been Latinos of Latin American descent. The pantheon of this erotic, made-in-Hollywood tradition is traced to Italian American actor and sex symbol Rudolph Valentino (1895–1926). The female counterpart to this Latin twinning spans a racialized and promiscuous sexuality, a hot-blooded disposition, a spitfire, or a tittuping figure like the Portuguese-born Brazilian performer Carmen Miranda (1909–55). Miranda's gendered body, as Myra Mendible has it, operated as a "synecdoche for Latin America" since "her banana-laden headpieces" enacted the region's assumed agricultural reductionism.[5] Miranda's millennial representation is actualized today through Sofia Vergara's impersonation of Gloria Delgado-Pritchett—a heavily accented and curvy trophy wife whose televised biography scripts an underdeveloped and rural nationality, Colombian—in the hit ABC sitcom *Modern Family*. At the aural level, Latin shapes U.S. popular music discourses and consumption. The Latin Grammy Awards is a prototype where particular sounds, forms of expression, and performers collapse into "Latin" acts, "Latin" rhythms, and a generic "Latin" genre.

Such comprehensive Latin characteristics have signified a set of looks, mental maps that define and catalog this social group's existence from the perspective of a U.S. northern gaze looking at its southern constructions, both domestically and abroad. These discursive appropriations can be invoked, in Charles Ramírez Berg's phraseology, as "Latinism." This framework ought not be confused with the social media hashtag "#Latinism," which is used by public interlocutors to foster Latino views on current sociopolitical events and cultural representations as well as Latino participation on technology and entrepreneurship. Ramírez Berg's Latinism, more concretely, borrows and departs from Edward Said's notion of Orientalism, wherein imperial expansion and a style of thought have ingrained differences between the East-West—or, "the Orient"/"the Occident"—dyad and produced a tactical mode of knowing and ruling over "orientals." Latinism likewise disentangles the precepts that construct Latin America, its inhabitants, and Latinos in the United States. Hollywood is implicated in this process of meaning making because, in Ramírez Berg's assessment, it has "endorsed North American dominance of this hemisphere and as often as it depicted the hegemony uncritically, movies helped to perpetuate it."[6] Using everyday symbols as a new resource for how "they" appear in the U.S. world, a sociocultural and political language by Latins has been remade. In other words, the conventions that pattern an array of Latins have generated a response countering U.S. Latino invisibility and misrecognition. This unknowability is conjectured, as a Latino comedy group announces it under its name, a dexterous collectivity of "Latins Anonymous" (1996).

182

Latin American decolonization theorist Walter D. Mignolo advances the notion of "Latin" America, charting the course of the "Latin" noun in Latin America with scare quotes, to give visual and analytic prominence to how the gazes of the West and the United States have ordered the modern world, or Europe's "New World." As an idea, "Latin" America differs from "Anglo" America, since the former has taken an inferior role, most substantially after the geopolitics and continental division of the 1898 Spanish-American War. During this conflict, the United States consolidated its imperial power, seizing the Philippines, Guam, and Puerto Rico. And yet as historian Louis A. Pérez Jr. has appraised, "it was Cuba that mattered the most and, indeed, what the matter was mostly about" due to U.S. regional interests.[7] This war, Mignolo proffers, created North/South and Anglo/Latin binaries where imperial national identities were established to rank and devalue colonial differences responsible for the invention of America (in the U.S. *and* continental sense) and "Latin" America. The pressing need arises for what Mignolo dubs as a distinct "geography of knowledge" that elicits new cartographies and sources of understanding.[8] The U.S.-Mexican War, paired with the Spanish-American War, may have crafted a continental "American" Latin, one that is indigenous to "the" American outlook in U.S. terms. Latins have been geographically split and can be found, under this grid, to the west of the U.S. Southeast and to the south of the U.S. South. "They" are distinguishable—apart—from the U.S. national imaginary.

But Latin life practices have not been at a U.S. distance. And what if, from a south-south vantage point, corollaries can be forged between regional ways of living, distinctive norms and practices, food preferences and traditions, plantation economies, tropical/humid climates, and language and speech patterns? Together with this query, what if there are more Latins in "Anglo" America than "those" we already know? Are nationless Latins, to put it differently, only bound and applicable to the American continent south of the United States? Can Latins be extended to broader American processes of "Latining," one where a *Latined* America in the United States hosts a pan-Latin economy of dynamic elements and signifiers?

This Latined America features peoples, geographies, and practices usher-ing in the particularities and peculiarities of comparative Souths. Considered this way, Latin significations branch out to the black-white syntax that has historically omitted a brownness-cum-blackness as well as varying shades between black and white. These hues have resonances among Latinos and Latinas and the African American diaspora. Latin can be a powerful catalyst for new flows of intercultural exchanges that open up a rereading of America, its black-white populations, and its regional formations. Latin peoples and origins, Gustavo Pérez Firmat has suggested in the context of Cuban atmo-spherics, fuse into a "generalized geography" of a "pan-Latin 'somewhere,' a locale without a location."[9] To this Latin nowhere, or anywhere, a Latin anyone who also becomes a Latin somebody can be appended. This "new" Latin contingent situates and resists the terms that simply explain and clearly organize the worlds of blackness in connection to African Americans and brownness with regard to Latinos and Latinas. How do we, in effect, admit blackness as a visual and linguistic signifier of Latin? Even more: What are the "new" locations and possibilities of this Latinness? And, truly, how new are these iterations of Latinness?

Marshall C. Eakin reminds us that a nearsighted definition of the Old South would confine this region to eleven states, if one adheres, that is, "to membership in the Confederacy as the ultimate measuring stick." But exci-sions based on geography, sociocultural patterns such as language and reli-gion, and a sense of identification would surface, thereby erasing Missouri, Kentucky, Maryland, and West Virginia out of the South's sui generis. Eakin's premise places paramount importance on what qualifies as southern inside and outside the region. As he deems it, the topographies of southern Florida, northern Virginia, or sections of Appalachia, "clearly within even the most traditional political boundaries," do not "fit" the normative defi-nition trumping southernness. Latin Americanists, he adds, face parallel dilemmas with those of southern studies specialists, as they struggle with the detrital geographic boundaries of the U.S. South and Latin America. Texas and Florida, Eakin fleshes out, "are on everyone's list of Southern states, yet they were parts of the Spanish Empire in the Americas for three centuries. Despite their long histories under Spanish colonial rule, scholars of American studies count them as part of the U.S. South. In spite of their long histories under Spanish colonial rule, many scholars of Latin America do not include them in standard treatments of Latin America. These regions do not suddenly become Southern and leave Latin America in the 1820s and 1830s."[10]

In Eakin's outline, a concise overview tallies southern U.S. entanglements with southern neighbors in "Latin" America, namely, through the 1840s ideological doctrine of Manifest Destiny. This notion's spirit in antebellum America relied on the principle that the United States had the obligation to expand territorially and gain control of the American continent. U.S. westward expansion during this period is one precedent, with filibustering activities by soldiers of fortune in Cuba, Mexico, Nicaragua, and the Dominican Republic functioning as a related link to "Latin" frontiers. The Tennessean adventurer William Walker (1824–60), as a relevant instance, exposed a heyday of U.S. pursuits in Latin America that exceeded the Southwest. Walker sought economic opportunities in Mexico and Central America, overthrowing Nicaragua's government, becoming that republic's president from 1856 to 1857, and attempting to Americanize that nation by making English the official language and reinstituting slavery. Not only this, but Nicaragua was also an important site particularly after the mid-nineteenth-century gold rush and quests to facilitate the travel between the U.S. East and West Coasts. Prior to the U.S. completion of the Panama Canal in 1914, Nicaragua offered the potential to connect the Pacific and the Atlantic Oceans. Certainly there are power structures and dynamics at work here between a hegemonic "North" (that is southern) and a Central American nation (that was "southernized").

A codicil to this Latin historical formation also lies in what Kirsten Silva Gruesz calls "the 'Latinness' of New Orleans," which situates this port city, with its British, French, Spanish, and Anglo-American influences, in a "liminal zone between the Anglo and the Latin worlds." This Latin seaport's access to the Gulf of Mexico sets forth a complex Latino-Anglo border system signified through "New Orleans as the *ultima thule* of Southern regionality," paired with "the reified map of the land border, *la línea*," that facilitated U.S. expansion in the Caribbean.[11] Latin life practices in New Orleans include thriving Hispanophone literary communities wherein "a multitude of visions of Manifest Destiny and national expansionism were hotly contested," as Gruesz imparts in her seminal *Ambassadors of Culture*. New Orleans coalesces into "the heart of a vital system of communication and language, the system of the national print body." That being so, this city housed, in 1806, the first Spanish-language newspaper in the United States: *El Misisipí*. Other international Hispanophone publications there include the *Diario del Gobierno de la República Mexicana* (1844), *El Telégrafo* (1849), and *El Independiente* (1853). And, as Gruesz submits, New Orleans's self-identifying "Creole" population had integrated a noticeable degree of Spanish speakers into the aforesaid group.[12]

The task at hand is to critically engage with expansive southern Latinings. Take Evelio Grillo's *Black Cuban, Black American* as an archetype of an interdependent Latinness, blackness, and Latinoness and as a southeastern landscape homing Cubans, Spaniards, and Italians. The octogenarian's scrutiny heralds the detours of vicissitudes in Ybor City, Florida, a region that is not generally hypothesized as part of the South and whose economic boom is attributed to Latin migrants and the cigar industry. Grillo's unsettled black and Latin instabilities are neatly halved and assigned into his black American and Cuban American sides. The memoir unearths the story of a twentieth-century Latino voice and his Latino racial uplift. Grillo (1919–2008), a contemporary of renowned African American historian John Hope Franklin (1915–2009), returns to the 1920s, an era in which Afro-Latinos sought to establish American roots. He graduated from a Catholic school for blacks and a historically black college, Xavier University in Louisiana. Tapping into a distinct black Americanness, Grillo chiseled an epistemological nexus with African American literary and intellectual thought, including such canonical figures as Nat Turner, Frederick Douglass, Harriet Tubman, Sojourner Truth, Paul Laurence Dunbar, John Brown, Paul Robeson, Langston Hughes, W. E. B. Du Bois, Allison Davis, Alain Locke, James Weldon Johnson, and James Rosamond Johnson.[13] Considering the rigidity of Jim Crow, a black/white binaristic gaze informs Grillo's outlook. But his black-brown passages demonstrate another timbre that does not follow the traditionally anticipated forms and norms of adhering to one ethnoracial identity. Grillo's Latin equivalencies slide through blackness and brownness. African Americans conceive his Latinness linguistically. Seen as such, Latin as a shared signifier for Latinoness and blackness is substantiated, embodied through the inseparability of Grillo's twoness. His book was published as part of Arte Público Press's Recovering the U.S. Hispanic Literary Heritage, a national archival project that documents and preserves this group's written culture in the United States from the sixteenth century to the 1960s. Yet Grillo's self-articulation is equally immersed in an American blackness that forms a part of the African American canon. This chronicle anchors an urgent question: How does Grillo's recovered Latined tradition coevally fit in the African American literary tradition? Can black and blackness also be bearers of Latin?

Literary figures such as James Weldon Johnson (1871–1938) explored what can be gauged as a Latined South. Give close attention to his limning of the anonymous protagonist in the fictional enterprise *The Autobiography of An Ex-Coloured Man*. There, shades of African American blackness appear as iterations of a Latined existence, depicted through his character's keen capacity to become a cigar maker and to speak Spanish like a native in Florida. The cigar industry served a pivotal role in Latin centers such as Ybor City, as Cuban poet, patriot, and Pan-American thinker José Martí (1853–95) exhibited upon garnishing support for Cuban independence in Florida. The Latin identity Johnson confers on the leading figure is as good as the Latino "original." This portrayal testifies that the "ex-coloured man" is not so free from color, nor is he monolingual. Johnson had a knowledge of Spanish from a young age, having learned the language from his father, James Johnson, an autodidact who was born a freeman in Richmond, Virginia. During his tenure as principal of the Stanton School in Florida, Johnson also introduced Spanish as a modern language in courses. Not purely moving into whiteness, *The Autobiography*'s protagonist passes through Latinness—tapping into a Latin life that has not been admitted into Americanness. Through Johnson, the tertiary shade affixed to Latinoness parallels his brown world of difference. Johnson describes his father's aspect, in his own life narration, *Along This Way*, as "light bronze, a number of shades darker than that of my mother." His grandfather's disposition was recorded as "dark brown." The coloring of his maternal grandmother's side of the family was pictured as "lighter in complexion" and "light brown." Certain neighbors were also perceived as "brown." Others "looked white but were not." Upon arriving at Atlanta University, Johnson remarked that "the bulk" of his classmates "ran the full gamut of all the shades and nuances of brown."[14] As broached with Grillo earlier, an analogous query is suitable here, too: How does the African American canon yield passage to Latinness?

Gayl Jones's late twentieth-century novel set in a south Texas border town, *Mosquito*, documents a muted world of Latinos and blacks in connection to the U.S.-Mexico border zone. Mosquito, the titular main character, is a woman truck driver with an auditory memory who speaks in black vernacular and Spanglish. She also smuggles undocumented migrants into the United States as part of a new political movement that Mosquito christens as "the new Underground Railroad." Jones relocates mid-nineteenth-century clandestine networks that assisted slaves in escaping southern plantations for the northern United States and Canada to contemporary migration struggles. The North-South axis of America, as previously diagrammed, now flourishes as a South-South one. So doing, the author patterns a common Latin ground for the multiple Americas and diverse Souths within the United States. Jones aligns the nuances, experiences, and interactions among Latinos and African Americans at the dawning twenty-first century, taking Du Bois's color line to its intersecting borders through the contours of ethnicity, race, gender, sexuality, religion, migration, "illegality," and class. Jones illuminates a Latined

South that veers toward multidirectional routes, ranging from Southeast-Southwest, North-South, South-South, U.S. South–"Latin" South, and "local" South–"global" South. Mosquito's vision constitutes a "Nuevo" South not simply because Latinas and Latinos take part in it but also because of the cultural transformations that warrant new ontologies of the present.   187

The region's history of Jim Crow pre-civil-rights segregation discloses similarities with what some public intellectuals have now designated as "Juan Crow" due to strict anti-immigration laws and attitudes in places like Alabama and Georgia. Juan Crow—note the bilingual name—is an adaptation of Jim Crow, the appellation for segregation in the South. This moniker infers forms of sociopolitical control that target and detain migrants, often violating their human and constitutional rights. The Juan Crow era, as a regime, is "the matrix of laws, social customs, economic institutions and symbolic systems enabling the physical and psychic isolation needed to control and exploit undocumented immigrants."[15]

Our American moment reveals two contradictory impulses: first, to contain and limit the Latin presence and, second, to categorize and absorb Latins so they fit previous patterns of U.S. incorporation. Yet at the level of social experience and the realm of signification, endless permutations and reproductions of Latinness abound. Latin is malleable and opens up in multiple geographies. We are now witnessing copious manifestations of Latinness, try as we may to pin down the Latin essence.

NOTES

1. Bancroft, *History of California*, 7:701.
2. Paredes, *George Washington Gómez*, 149, 118, 148–49.
3. C. E. Rodríguez, introduction, 1.
4. R. Rodriguez, *Brown*, 108.
5. Mendible, "Introduction," 10.
6. Ramírez Berg, *Latino Images in Film*, 4.
7. Pérez, *War of 1898*, 3.
8. Mignolo, *Idea of Latin America*, xiv.
9. Pérez Firmat, *Havana Habit*, 18.
10. Eakin, "When South Is North," 17, 18.
11. Gruesz, "Gulf of Mexico System," 469, 470.
12. Gruesz, *Ambassadors of Culture*, 109, 123, 111, 112.
13. Grillo, *Black Cuban, Black American*, 17.
14. J. W. Johnson, *Along This Way*, 18, 20, 46–47, 32–33, 75.
15. Lovato, "Juan Crow in Georgia."

SUGGESTIONS FOR FURTHER READING

Delgado, Grace. *Making the Chinese Mexican: Global Migration, Localism, and Exclusion in the U.S.-Mexico Borderlands*. Palo Alto, Calif.: Stanford University Press, 2012.

Fink, Leon. *The Maya of Morganton: Work and Community in the Nuevo New South*. Chapel Hill: University of North Carolina Press, 2007.

Gruesz, Kirsten Silva. *Ambassadors of Culture: The Transamerican Origins of Latino Writing*. Princeton, N.J.: Princeton University Press, 2002.

Guridy, Frank. *Forging Diaspora: Afro-Cubans and African Americans in a World of Empire and Jim Crow*. Chapel Hill: University of North Carolina Press, 2010.

Milian, Claudia. *Latining America: Black-Brown Passages and the Coloring of Latino/a Studies*. Athens: University of Georgia Press, 2013.

ERICH NUNN

Folk

For a term that has occupied such a central place in American culture—particularly that of the U.S. South—since at least the nineteenth century, "folk" remains remarkably multivalent and slippery. It has at times been used to describe subcultural forms ostensibly isolated from the mainstream of American culture, while also serving as a marker of regional and/or racial traditions that serve as an edifice on which a national culture might be built. It has been applied to musical practices held in opposition to those of the commercial mainstream and co-opted as a set of generic signifiers by the very culture industry against which it was once defined. Recent scholarship has approached the shifting meanings of the term to consider it as a reflection of changing understandings of race and racial difference and the importance of those understandings in defining the South in relation to the nation as a whole.

The word "folk" features prominently in the title of one of the twentieth century's key works, W. E. B. Du Bois's 1903 *The Souls of Black Folk*, and Du Bois's book offers us a starting point from which to begin to unravel the term's varied and often contradictory significations. As Du Bois declares in that famous book's central claim, "the problem of the twentieth century is the problem of the color-line," and this felicitous phrase provides a key into the cultural and ideological work that the term "folk" has performed.[1] For Du Bois, the term "folk" is intimately bound up with what he calls "the unifying ideal of Race," which involves "fostering and developing the traits and talents of the Negro . . . in large conformity to the greater ideals of the American Republic." He derives this conception of "folk" as expressing racial and national characteristics from such nineteenth-century European thinkers as Johann Gottfried von Herder, who, as Benjamin Filene explains, "contrasted the *Kultur des Volkes* ('culture of the people') with *Kultur der Gelehrten* ('learned culture')" and argued for the superiority of folk culture.[2] The "traits and talents" that Du Bois ascribes to the black folk are universal, exemplifying "the pure human spirit of the Declaration of Independence." At the same time, they take on racially specific forms: "American fairy tales and folk-lore," which are "Indian and African," and, most importantly, "the wild sweet melodies of the Negro slave." Echoing Herder's idea of the *Kultur des Volkes* as a pure alternative to learned culture, for Du Bois the cultural and artistic products of African American folk offer an alternative to a corrupt commercial culture, prompting him to propose that America replace "her vulgar music with the soul of the Sorrow Songs"—that is, songs of southern slaves and their descendants. In Du Bois's view, then, "folk" is a property both of race ("the Negro") and place (the South). In positing "folk" music as an authentic locally and racially grounded corrective to the debased, inauthentic products of commercial culture, Du Bois sets the tone for subsequent conceptions of folk authenticity. At the same time, this very idea of authenticity evinces an anxiety about the ever-present threat of the debasement, contamination, and racist expropriation of this autochthonous culture. He laments that "caricature has sought again to spoil the quaint beauty of the music, and has filled the air with many debased melodies which vulgar ears scarce know from the real."[3] The artistic products of the folk, then, lay claim to a tenuous authenticity, one that depends on the ability of those both inside and outside the folk group to correctly apprehend them and to distinguish them from the corrupt products of popular culture. As Eric Sundquist explains, part of the significance of Du Bois's project is its positing spirituals as a "core expression of African American culture . . . to create a foundation for modern African American culture as an extension of slave culture." In *Souls*, Sundquist argues, Du Bois models "the centrality of song to African American culture, both its extension of the folk traditions of slavery into a later era and its incorporation of the tonal semantics of vernacular culture into modern literary form." By identifying affectively with the music of southern slaves, Du Bois positions the folk culture of enslaved black southerners at the center of American culture writ large. In the process, Sundquist continues, Du Bois rejects the tension between the concepts of "Negro" and "American" and between elite and folk cultures. In the process, the notion of "folk"—grounded in a "sense of [southern] soil and place"— eventually gives way to a broader idea of "nation."[4]

Crucial to this project is the idea that both the aesthetic beauty and the meaning of the slave songs are audible to white listeners both inside and— crucially—outside the South: "these weird old songs" are the means through which "the soul of the black slave spoke to [white] men." Not only does "the true Negro folk-song" live on "in the hearts of the Negro people" but also, crucially, "in the hearts of those who have heard them truly sung."[5] Jon Cruz terms this process, whereby folk song allows for an affective response across the color line, "ethnosympathy." Beginning in the nineteenth century, Cruz argues, ethnosympathy allowed slaves to "adapt and modify for their own needs this [emerging] cultural arena" and at the same time allowed "sympathetic whites . . . to further reconceptualize slaves as culturally expressive subjects."[6] Du Bois's notion of the Sorrow Songs furthers this aim, affirming the humanity of African Americans by establishing their affinity with the nation as a whole. This dual identification of the Sorrow Songs as at the same time distinctively "Negro" and characteristically American is Du Bois's key intervention into the musicological debate about African American folk music in the late nineteenth and early twentieth centuries. In reconceiving the diverse songs of southern slaves as a unified body of Sorrow Songs, Du Bois places the music of African Americans at the center of the cultural life of the United States at the same time that Jim Crow segregation worked to prevent black Americans' full participation in political and civic life. He declares that "the Sorrow Songs" "came out of the South unknown to me, one by one, and yet at once I knew them as of me and mine."[7] This emphasis on the South's centrality to struggles over black identity in *Souls* sets the stage for attempts by both African American intellectuals and their white interlocutors to grapple with the legacy of the South's history in shaping conceptions of black people and the music associated with them, from slave songs and minstrelsy to the popular music that followed.

An early example of such an attempt is German American musicologist Henry Edward Krehbiel's 1914 *Afro-American Folksongs*. Krehbiel explicitly invokes Du Bois's "The Sorrow Songs" in his chapter on "Songs of the American Slaves." "Why are not the songs of the American negroes American folksongs?" he asks rhetorically, "Can anyone say?" For Krehbiel, the spirituals are in fact fundamentally "American folksongs," just as Du Bois's *Souls of Black Folk* is exemplary "'American' prose."[8] Krehbiel echoes Du Bois's idea that the musical products of black folk stake a claim to African Americans' participation in American culture. In turn, Krehbiel's work served as a touchstone for African American writers like James Weldon Johnson and Alain Locke as they worked to define an African American cultural heritage rooted in folk sources (Locke calls Krehbiel's *Afro-American Folksongs* the "first serious and adequate musical analysis" of the spirituals).[9] The idea that African American folk music—first spirituals, then the blues—was emblematic of a folk culture on which an African American literary culture could be modeled has served as a touchstone for a remarkably diverse group of black writers and intellectuals, from Du Bois, Johnson, and Locke to Langston Hughes and Zora Neale Hurston. These writers all perceived black folk culture as a precious resource, though they disagreed about whether it was a renewable one and what particular forms best exemplified this folk tradition.

One influential conception of African American folk culture's relationship to industrial modernity is exemplified by Jean Toomer's account of the genesis of his 1923 *Cane*, a cornerstone text of the Negro renaissance (despite Toomer's later objections that he was "not a negro") and a key achievement of American literary modernism.[10] Like Du Bois, Toomer encounters black folk culture as a product of the South and understands its significance as rooted in both race and place. Upon arriving in rural Georgia, Toomer encounters "a family of back-country Negroes." He recalls, "This was the first time I'd ever heard the folk-songs and spirituals. They were very rich and sad and joyous and beautiful." Breaking from Du Bois's emphasis on the universality of the Sorrow Songs, Toomer instead laments that the "folk-songs and spirituals" of the rural folk are threatened by the encroachment of technological modernity. "I learned that the Negroes of the town objected to them," he continues. "They had victrolas and player-pianos. So, I realized with deep regret, that the spirituals, meeting ridicule, would be certain to die out. With Negroes also the trend was toward the small town and then toward the city—and industry and commerce and machines. The folk-spirit was walking in to die on the modern desert. That spirit was so beautiful. Its death was so tragic."[11] A vestige of slavery, black folk culture was doomed to extinction. T. Austin Graham argues that Toomer's aesthetic engagement with the folk song forms he encountered in Georgia "is perhaps best understood as a field recording, an attempt on Toomer's part to catch a disappearing musical culture in words and to preserve it in literary form."[12] Graham's observation situates Toomer's literary engagement with the music of rural southern African Americans in a preservationist tradition that was in the process of being revolutionized by the very recording technologies whose influence Toomer bemoans.

Henry Louis Gates Jr. and Gene Andrew Jarrett term this notion "romantic culturism," an "ideological turn within the New Negro movement" that "pivoted on . . . hegemonic tropes of the 'folk.'" "Romanticized as ahistorical, lower-class, and authentically black," they continue, "the folk served as metonym or synecdoche of the African American community."[13] Gates and Jarrett identify this ideological move with Alain Locke, a key architect of the New Negro renaissance, although its roots lie with Du Bois, Johnson, and other of Locke's predecessors and collaborators. In such works as *The New Negro* (1925) and *The Negro and His Music* a decade later, Locke articulates an understanding of black folk culture as a resource to be mined and refined. Following Du Bois, Krehbiel, and Johnson, he posits folk music as a "precious musical ore" to be mined by classically minded composers, as well as a source that is corrupted by its transformation into popular forms. These two lines of development—classical and popular—are in Locke's model directly opposed. Folk music's value lies in its potential for development as a characteristically "racial" strain in a larger classical idiom. This process, he argues, is universal; Negro composers should follow the models of Liszt, Brahms, Dvořák, and Smetana in incorporating "the characteristic folk spirit" (of their respective folk—Hungarian for Liszt, German/Austrian for Brahms, Czech for Dvořák and Smetana) into their music without losing "its rare raciness and unique flavor." [14] Refined and adapted to conform to European models, Negro folk music would achieve parity with these other national traditions. Paul Burgett describes this attitude toward folk materials as indicative of what he calls a "vindication syndrome": Locke and others attempted "to vindicate the value of Negro folk music . . . by pointing out their use in a musical form not endemic to the spiritual's culture of origin but, rather, [in] a highly valued form of western European culture, i.e., the symphony." [15] The threat of corruption and expropriation again rears its head in this scenario. Eric Lott points out that in the nineteenth century blackface minstrelsy was often "claimed as the *completion* of black [folk] culture, its professional emergence"; the phenomenon Burgett describes offers an alternative path—presumably a less vexed, more authentic one—for black folk culture's development. [16]

Locke's conception of the New Negro was not universally shared; such important Harlem Renaissance figures as Langston Hughes conceived of the relationship between African American literary production and the larger realm of black folk and popular culture quite differently. Hughes's famous proclamation in "The Negro Artist and the Racial Mountain," published in the *Nation* a year after *The New Negro*, articulates a view of African American culture diametrically opposed to the one Locke had articulated and in fact issues a direct challenge: "Let the blare of Negro jazz bands and the bellowing voice of Bessie Smith singing Blues penetrate the closed ears of the colored near-intellectuals until they listen and perhaps understand." [17] Locke is a rather obvious target of Hughes's epithet "colored near-intellectuals." Nonetheless, Samuel A. Floyd Jr. claims that the "youthful and eloquent defiance" of Hughes's statement "harmonized with the ambiance of the Harlem Renaissance." [18] Such an assessment obscures the dissonance between Hughes's proclamation and Locke's own ideas concerning the role of music in the renaissance and illustrates the continuing appeal of a romantic culturalist conception of black folk culture to contemporary critical assessments.

While Krehbiel's appreciative reading of Du Bois points to the influence of *The Souls of Black Folk* on musicological thinking, the work of Newman Ivey White illustrates the recalcitrant racism of the critical mainstream. White, along with contemporaries such as Dorothy Scarborough, Howard Odum, and John Lomax, sought in the 1920s and 1930s—that is, at the same time that "New Negro" intellectuals sought to transmute African American folk culture into literary and other high cultural forms—to collect and analyze African American folk materials from both sociological and literary perspectives in order to reveal what were posited as racial characteristics. Echoing—in some cases quite literally—the stereotyped caricatures of minstrelsy, these collectors both produced invaluable documents of African American folk culture and perpetuated racist stereotypes. White's "Racial Traits in the Negro Song," published in 1920, reveals its prejudices up front, as it purports to derive from an examination of collections of African American folk songs "a few of the characteristics of that buoyant and invincibly likeable person, the illiterate Southern 'darky.'" White emphatically denies the emotional transparency that Du Bois and Krehbiel ascribe to the spirituals; rather than offering a means through which the soul of the black slave could speak to sympathetic listeners, for White, slave songs instead attest to African Americans' emotional simplicity and sensuous atavism. At the outset of his piece, White outlines a quasi-scientific methodology: "Surely we may regard a large body of negro songs as fit material out of which may be evolved some conclusions as to the lives and characters of the singers." The songs of a folk group, in this conception, serve as a window into the character of that group. Almost immediately, though, this method is revealed as tautological. To counter the idea that the supposed "melancholy" of the spirituals' musical form speaks to an emotional melancholy or despair, White argues that "the negro, outside of his songs, is not of a brooding and pensive disposition."[19] Rather than deriving "the negro's" character from an analysis of his songs, in other words, White analyzes the songs through the lens of racial stereotype. For White, analysis (almost exclusively textual, not musical) of "negro songs" reveals the character of "the negro." Unsurprisingly, the character thus revealed is, White proposes, indistinguishable from the stereotypes of minstrelsy. Ignoring the warning that Du Bois had issued almost two decades earlier, White willfully conflates caricatures and "debased melodies" with actual African American folk songs. White's magnum opus, *American Negro Folk-Songs*, published in 1928, likewise purports to analyze a large body of folk songs in order to get at "the character of the folk Negro," yet begins with an epigraph taken not from a "Negro" folk song but rather from what White himself identifies as an "Old Minstrel Song."[20] In White's hands, the concept of black "folk" becomes a tool for racial caricature and stereotype.

Bearing out Du Bois's prediction of the "problem of the color-line" in structuring twentieth-century life, scholarly and popular interest in white folk operated in parallel, but with few intersections with investigations of black folk life and culture. "I know many souls that toss and whirl and pass," he observes in "The Souls of White Folk" from 1910, "but none there are that puzzle me more than the Souls of White Folk. Not, mind you, the souls of them that are white, but souls of them that have become painfully conscious of their whiteness."[21] While the title of Du Bois's essay mirrors that of his earlier book, his invocation of "white folk" is not merely fortuitous. From the turn of the century until at least the 1930s, changing understandings of "folk" authenticity and isolation worked to define racial whiteness and to insulate it from the cultural interracialism threatened by popular culture. Writing at the beginning of the twentieth century, Du Bois accurately predicts that uses of the term "folk" will reflect the cultural logic of Jim Crow segregation; for much of the ensuing century, understandings of folk culture would exemplify "the problem of the color-line."

Anxieties concerning the purity of cultural forms understood as white influenced John Lomax's *Cowboy Songs and Other Frontier Ballads* (1910), for example, which purported to document the survival in the American Southwest of "the Anglo-Saxon ballad spirit that was active in secluded districts in England and Scotland even after the coming of Tennyson and Browning." This "Anglo-Saxon ballad spirit," Lomax maintains, "is manifested both in the preservation of the English ballad and in the creation of local songs."[22] Lomax collected hundreds of such local songs—the most famous of which was "Home on the Range"—which he understood as part of an ancestral inheritance, despite the fact that he collected many of these songs, including "Home on the Range," from African American singers.[23] The (white) singers of these songs, he explains, evince "the gallantry, the grace, and the song heritage of their English ancestors."[24] Lomax's argument that the U.S. Southwest was a repository for a transplanted "Anglo-Saxon" ballad tradition, though, proved less influential than the closely related idea that a folk culture had taken root among the isolated descendants of English, Scottish, and Irish folksingers in Appalachia.

An influential articulation of this idea may be found in William Goodell Frost's "Our Contemporary Ancestors in the Southern Mountains," published in the *Atlantic Monthly* in 1899, which maintained that "the 'mountain whites'" lived "to all intents and purposes in the conditions of the colonial times."[25] Working in part to counter stereotyped depictions of mountain residents as backward "poor white trash," Frost defines "'Appalachian America' . . . as a unique and distinct social and cultural entity" that represented a transplanted English (or "Saxon") culture uncorrupted by industrial American modernity.[26] While the idea that "Appalachian America" represents a preindustrial folk culture untainted by industrial modernity (not to mention African American influence) has been thoroughly debunked, as Bill C. Malone explains, "the possibilities for romantic speculation [are] almost endless, and observers . . . have not hesitated to make bold and sweeping judgments about the South, its people, and their music."[27] Famously, folklorists such as Olive Dame Campbell and Cecil Sharp sought (and found) English and Scottish folk songs in the mountain communities of Virginia, North Carolina, Tennessee, and Kentucky, lending credence to the idea of Appalachia as "'Anglo-Saxon,' a pure racial strain that preserved both the speech and folkways of Elizabethan England."[28] Later scholars (including Malone, David E. Whisnant, and Benjamin J. Filene) have dismantled this notion, however, noting that in their search for ballad survivals among mountain folk, Sharp, Campbell, and their followers ignored and in some cases actively suppressed musical evidence that did not support their hypotheses. Despite the conscious attempt by Sharp and others to collect songs from sources who had been denied intercultural or interracial contact, such folk collectors were consistently mortified to find their informants—white and black—singing songs of hillbilly or, worse, vaudeville, origin. Charles Seeger sums up this idea succinctly: "You have to keep a tight rein on things or else you hear nothing but jazz."[29] In an interesting twist, as what Malone terms "the Anglo-Saxon myth" was falling out of favor, it was largely supplanted by "the Celtic myth, the belief that southern character was the product of people who came from the 'Celtic Fringe' of Great Britain (Northern England, lowland Scotland, Ulster, Wales, the Hebrides, and Ireland)." This theory's proponents argue that not only folk music but also a wide range of other cultural practices were transplanted from the Celtic Fringe to Appalachia. Malone argues convincingly to the contrary, granting that while early immigrants brought cultural practices from both the "Celtic Fringe" and elsewhere in the British Isles and Ireland, "both music and consciousness of ethnic distinctiveness eventually became subsumed in a larger folk culture that encompassed virtually all the inhabitants of the South."[30] Including, of course, black folk. So while in 1959 D. K. Wilgus could confidently dedicate nearly 350 pages to "Anglo-American Folksong" while dedicating a single appendix to the question of interracial musical exchange in

"The Negro-White Spirituals," current scholars are less interested in defining and policing discrete racialized folk traditions than in exploring the complex interactions between black and white, rural and urban, "folk" and commercial practices.

Lawrence Levine, for example, has argued that the ostensible divide between "folk" culture and mass-mediated popular culture is chimerical, and that the latter in fact constitutes what he calls the "folklore of industrial society."[31] In a marked departure from earlier conceptions of folk culture as threatened by industrial modernity, historian Karl Hagstrom Miller argues that recording technology has helped preserve folk culture by making it available to wider audiences, helping "people to craft unique individual and group identities, preserve collective memory, and maintain living traditions."[32] Popular culture, in other words, fulfills many of the functions once understood to be unique attributes of authentic folk culture. Robin D. G. Kelley takes this idea a step further, pointing out that "'folk' has no meaning without 'modern,'" both serving as terms around which our understanding of "the dynamic process by which culture is created" revolves.[33] In a similar vein, Benjamin J. Filene reconsiders how ideas revolving around the term "folk" have influenced twentieth-century popular music. In Filene's rethinking, the term "folk music" describes not intrinsic properties of musical forms or performances but rather a set of attitudes toward that music—the term itself is troublesome due to the "contradictory meanings" it has accrued throughout the twentieth century.[34] In an attempt to forestall the difficulty that these contradictions raise, Filene substitutes for "folk" other terms: "vernacular music" and "roots" music. These substitutions sidestep the problem of distinguishing between "folk" and "nonfolk" musical forms and authentic and inauthentic performances that plagued many earlier efforts, but these new terms pose additional challenges.

In the afterword to his 2010 *Segregating Sound: Inventing Folk and Pop Music in the Age of Jim Crow*, Karl Hagstrom Miller revisits an aphorism credited to musician Big Bill Broonzy and originally published in *Time* in 1962: "I guess all songs is folk songs. I never heard no horse sing 'em." Miller traces citations and glosses of Broonzy's bon mot through a half century of music criticism and scholarship, revealing in the process "both the central interpretive role that the folkloric paradigm has continued to play in American music scholarship and the persistent inadequacy of [the] central dichotomies" of black and white, folk and commercial "to explain or contain U.S. musical history."[35] In other words, a half century ago Broonzy was already aware of what Filene, Miller, and other current scholars have only recently begun exploring in earnest: the failure of the category of "folk" to adequately account for the diversity of actual musical practice. Perhaps the substitution of terms such as "vernacular," "roots," or the even more recent "Americana" are attempts to catch up with Broonzy by employing a new vocabulary. Nominations for the 2013 Grammy Awards include the categories "Folk," "Regional Roots," "Americana," "Bluegrass," and "Blues," among others.[36] As Miller observes, the performances represented here in popular music's annual celebration of itself "may be more broad and diversified than previous writers had acknowledged. They may be more modern and commercialized, hybrid and omnivorous, but they remain knowing and knowable communal cultures bounded by race and sound."[37] The terms may have changed, but the legacies of the musical color lines delimited by twentieth-century conceptions of the "folk" are still audible.

NOTES

1. Du Bois, *Souls of Black Folk*, 13.
2. Filene, *Romancing the Folk*, 10.
3. Du Bois, *Souls of Black Folk*, 11, 12, 253.
4. Sundquist, *To Wake the Nations*, 458, 459, 461, 465, 459–460.
5. Du Bois, *Souls of Black Folk*, 154–155, 156.
6. Cruz, *Culture on the Margins*, 3, 4.
7. Du Bois, *Souls of Black Folk*, 250.
8. Krehbiel, *Afro-American Folksongs*, 27–28.
9. Locke, *Negro and His Music*, 20.
10. Toomer, quoted in Michael North, *Dialect of Modernism*, 150.
11. Toomer, "*Cane* Years," 123.
12. Graham, *Great American Songbooks*, 117.
13. Gates and Jarrett, *New* Negro, 9.
14. Locke, *Negro and His Music*, 12, 130.
15. P. Burgett, "Vindication as a Thematic Principle," 33.
16. Lott, *Love and Theft*, 56, emphasis in original.
17. Hughes, "Negro Artist," 694.
18. Floyd, "Music in the Harlem Renaissance," 9.
19. White, "Racial Traits in the Negro Folk-Song," 396, 397.
20. White, *American Negro Folk-Songs*, v; see also Nunn, "Country Music," 633.
21. Du Bois, "Souls of White Folk," 339.
22. Lomax, *Cowboy Songs* (1910), xvii.
23. See Nunn, "American Balladry."
24. Lomax, *Cowboy Songs*, rev. ed., xviii.
25. Frost, "Our Contemporary Ancestors," 311.
26. Harkins, *Hillbilly*, 11–14.
27. Malone, *Singing Cowboys and Musical Mountaineers*, 10.

28. Ibid., *Singing Cowboys and Musical Mountaineers*, 10.
29. Seeger, quoted in Whisnant, *All That Is Native and Fine*, 206.
30. Malone, *Singing Cowboys and Musical Mountaineers*, 10, 12.
31. Levine, "Folklore of Industrial Society," 1369–99.
32. Miller, *Segregating Sound*, 9.
33. Kelley, "Notes on Deconstructing 'The Folk,'" 1402.
34. Filene, *Romancing the Folk*, 3–4.
35. Miller, *Segregating Sound*, 275, 276.
36. "55th Annual GRAMMY Awards Nominees."
37. Miller, *Segregating Sound*, 279.

SUGGESTIONS FOR FURTHER READING

Filene, Benjamin. *Romancing the Folk: Public Memory and American Roots Music*. Chapel Hill: University of North Carolina Press, 2000.

Kelley, Robin D. G. "Notes on Deconstructing 'The Folk.'" *American Historical Review* 97, no. 5 (December 1992): 1400–1408.

Kirshenblatt-Gimblett, Barbara. "Folklore's Crisis." *Journal of American Folklore* 111, no. 441 (Summer 2008): 281–327.

Levine, Lawrence W. "The Folklore of Industrial Society: Popular Culture and Its Audiences." *American Historical Review* 97, no. 5 (December 1992): 1369–99.

Miller, Karl Hagstrom. *Segregating Sound: Inventing Folk and Pop Music in the Age of Jim Crow*. Durham, N.C.: Duke University Press, 2010.

MICHAEL P. BIBLER

Queer/Quare

How does one go about queering a region that many people regard as already queer? As a theoretical tool, "queer" does far more than simply describe particular inflections of gender, desire, and sexual identity. Rather, by exposing the incoherencies and inconsistencies within and between these three terms, a queer analysis demands a much broader critique of culture and power that must be central to any discussion of the South's regional peculiarities. Indeed, it is precisely where gender and sexuality are most unstable that the wider complexities of culture and society within the South become most apparent.

In the early 1990s, scholars and activists found rich potential in "queer" because of the way it has been used historically to signify both sexual and/or gender deviance (typically homosexuality) as well as a general, unaccountable oddness or strangeness—a difference from the familiar, the conventional, and the expected. The reappropriation of "queer" not only reclaimed an abusive, homophobic term for progressive sexual politics but also opened possibilities for discussing the full spectrum of sexual and gender expression beyond the limited categories of "lesbian" and "gay." In Eve Kosofsky Sedgwick's widely quoted formulation, "one of the things 'queer' can refer to [is] the open mesh of possibilities, gaps, overlaps, dissonances and resonances, lapses and excesses of meaning when the constitutive elements of anyone's gender, of anyone's sexuality aren't made (or *can't be* made) to signify monolithically."[1] This expansiveness has enabled theorists to position the queer in opposition not just to the prescriptive norms of heterosexuality but to the wider regimes of the normal. Consequently, many have argued that the job of queer theory is, in Ruth Goldman's words, "to challenge the racist, misogynist, and other oppressive discourses/norms, as well as those that are heterosexist and homophobic. We must not simply challenge heteronormativity but must instead question the very system that sustains heteronormativity."[2] Rather than a stable identity, "queer" is thus better understood as an active denaturalization of identity categories and an unsettling of the power structures that support them. Indeed, Lee Edelman has pursued this notion of queer antinormativity to its logical extreme by mapping the queer's structural relation to the death drive and embracing its power to disrupt and resist the fantasies of stability and coherence that define both sociality itself and the political hope of "forging some more perfect social order" in the future.[3] Other theorists and critics have expanded, complicated, and refined the uses and meanings of "queer" by exploring its relationship to affect, temporality, performance, and more. But scholars interested in the literatures and cultures of the U.S. South should already see the usefulness of this term, not least for interrogating the norms of gender, eroticism, and desire within the region but also for reconsidering the gaps and fissures that emerge where southern regional differences intersect and overlap with national (or global) normativities.

Although discussions of gender and sexuality in the South are growing in number, southern studies and sexuality studies were slow in finding each other. This disjuncture can be attributed in part to the discomfort, even homophobia, of an earlier generation of southernists who avoided or disparaged representations of queer desires and identities, as Gary Richards has argued.[4] And many queer scholars have neglected the South largely out of their prejudices against nonmetropolitan, regional, and rural cultures and spaces, as John Howard and Scott Herring have discussed.[5] Another explanation for this disciplinary gap is the enduring stereotype that the South is the most virulently conservative region in the country, where queers are pervasively, sometimes brutally oppressed and thus forced to remain invisible. As Donna Jo Smith writes, this myth of a deeply homophobic or queer-phobic South is a "myth that is particularly southern *and* queer," and more and more scholars are confronting this image by mapping the histories and cultures of homosexual and other queer communities that have thrived in the South for much of the twentieth century, if not before.[6]

The stereotype of a queer-phobic South is linked to the long-standing view that the South is the nation's backward and perverse regional Other. In the early national period (and, indeed, before), this othering of the South exaggerated the violent and regressive elements of southern culture, especially in the context of slavery, to enable the formation and functioning of the nation as a place otherwise allegedly (and falsely) free of such problems, as Jennifer Rae Greeson has discussed.[7] Ironically, however, notions of a strange and backward South are also supported by the predominance of queerly gothic and grotesque motifs in countless representations of the region from both inside and outside its borders, including the works of modern "southern gothic" writers such as Tennessee Williams and Carson McCullers. Flannery O'Connor famously wrote that "anything that comes out of the South is going to be called grotesque by the Northern reader, unless it is grotesque, in which case it is going to be called realistic."[8] And as Leigh Anne Duck has shown, national debates about the alleged social, racial, and economic differences of the region in the early twentieth century inspired "a proliferation of gothic tropes, as editors, artists, and even social scientists described the 'tremendous and ghastly visions' of the South's white supremacists, the Dantean 'inferno' of its agricultural districts, the 'lunatic, disintegrating wildness' of its evangelical Protestantism, and its culture 'linger[ing] in the dark backward abysm of time.'"[9] Likewise, the South has been portrayed for centuries as a hotbed of sexual obsession and degeneracy: from abolitionists' depictions of rapacious slave owners, to southern whites' mythification of the black rapist during the Jim Crow era, to the darkly comic images of incest and debauchery in the modernist works of William Faulkner and Erskine Caldwell, and the gratuitous sexuality of films like *Mandingo* (1975) and television shows like *True Blood* (2008–14). Queerness is woven into the discourses of southern regionalism in such complex ways that both sexual perversion *and* queer phobia simultaneously register as signs of the South's *social and cultural* perversity within the United States.

This conflation of southernness with backwardness and perversity is exactly what R. Bruce Brasell believes makes queer theory particularly useful for studying southern culture:

> Rather than resist the popular alignment of the South with perversion and attempt to replace it with a positive image founded on post-colonialism, theorists of the South should embrace it. Such a move denaturalizes the process of normalization used to stain only the South's regionalism with perversion of the American national ideal through reliance on enduring memories of the region's nineteenth-century failure at nationalism.[10]

However, treating the South as a perversion of U.S. nationalism—whether to demonize it or to highlight its distinctiveness—muddles the terms by which southern deviance and normalcy can be understood, especially where sexuality is an issue. As Donna Jo Smith writes, for some people, "the term *southern queer* is redundant: Since the South is already an aberration, what is a southern queer but deviance multiplied? In other words, did Truman Capote really need to tell the world that he was a pervert? After all, he was from south Alabama."[11] But these kinds of associations obscure the ways that southern queers, including Capote, might be marked as deviant *within* the region. In any discursive opposition between regional queerness and national normalcy, the southerner who deviates from both sets of cultural expectations becomes doubly queered. Yet her queerness is never "redundant." Brasell's form of queer southern studies might still ignore issues of sexual or gender deviance just as easily as a queer-phobic concept of region. Moreover, most queer people in the South probably see little difference between southern and national forms of conservatism and intolerance. Any queer analysis of region must therefore be attentive to the ways that narratives of regional difference can also support regional power structures, and it must be sensitive to the ways that regional systems of normativity can overlap and merge with national ones, even when the South seems perversely different.

"Queer" presents other theoretical pitfalls as well. Some critics question the extent of its power to disrupt the social order. And many women and racial and ethnic minorities find that the word too easily "homogenizes" and "erases" the differences between individuals, as Gloria Anzaldúa writes.[12] Despite its deliberate recuperation as an umbrella term lacking a single, coherent referent, "queer" often becomes synonymous with white, middle-class male homosexuality, eliding or excluding lesbianism and other racial, ethnic, gender, or class differences, as well as other forms of sexual practice or identity, such as cross-dressing, transsexuality, sadomasochism, bisexuality, and asexuality. As Judith Butler writes, even the political recuperation of "queer" inevitably "retains and reiterates the abjected history of the term" as a term that "signified degradation"; thus, it is all too possible to use "queer" "in ways that enforce a set of overlapping divisions" within queer politics.[13] For Butler, then, an ongoing critique of the "exclusionary operations" of the term is absolutely necessary: "queer" will "have to remain that which is, in the present, never fully owned, but always and only redeployed, twisted, queered from a prior usage and in the direction of urgent and expanding political purposes."[14] Critics who use "queer" to redress national histories of injury *to* the South must not ignore how the term has also served various histories of injury *within* the South. "Queer" does not automatically deconstruct regional paradigms and power structures, so it must also be the subject of rigorous deconstructive scrutiny in its own right.

Butler writes that the term "queer" "will be revised, dispelled, rendered obsolete to the extent that it yields to the demands which resist the term precisely because of the exclusions by which it is mobilized."[15] And some scholars who write from or about the region we collectively call "the South" have already begun this kind of revision. Cherokee scholar Daniel Heath Justice proposes a theory of "anomaly" that connects queer and two-spirit Native American identities with Mississippian Indian traditions of hybrid and anomalous human beings and other creatures: "[A] queer theory that draws inspiration from Mississippianism offers intriguing and tribally oriented interpretive possibilities for understanding diverse sexualities and genders among Southeastern Indians of today, and it provides a tribal challenge to the category of the toxic queer to which we've too long been subjected."[16] E. Patrick

Johnson similarly proposes an alternative to "queer" by borrowing from the vernacular of his western North Carolina grandmother: "quare." While it functions in other ways like "queer," Johnson's theorization of "quare" foregrounds the positionality of the subject "within an oppressive system" so that queer "ways of knowing" are recognized not only as mediated by discourse and ideology but also as "historically situated and materially conditioned" by the subject's involvement in the "practice of everyday life." Showing how his grandmother uses "quare" "to connote something excessive" to the discursive meanings grounded in "African American cultural rituals and lived experience," Johnson offers a model of quare studies that focuses on the ways that race, ethnicity, and other factors attached to the material body shape knowledge and behavior.[17] Following these theoretical models, a quare analysis of southern queerness and anomaly must address how racial and Indian national and tribal differences influence both physical and symbolic deployments of gender and sexuality. Critics who maintain this awareness would thus avoid conflating both southernness and queerness with whiteness and avoid privileging "the position of those whose subjectivity and agency, outside the realm of gender and sexuality, have never been subjugated."[18]

Furthermore, a quare analysis offers a useful approach for taking into account economic and geographic differences within the South, for "quare" and "quar" are also part of the vernacular of the (mostly white) Appalachian South—a linguistic phenomenon that extends across the Atlantic to Ireland, where "quare" is also part of the dialect.[19] If southern Appalachia occupies a queer relation to the nation because it is regional, and if it occupies a *different* queer relation to the region (for example, because it is viewed as the most "backward" part of the South, or because there is a debate about whether Appalachian literature counts as a subset of southern literature), how can the word "queer" function clearly? What does it mean to be queer when there are already competing norms and power structures against which queer must define itself? Borrowing from the Appalachian vernacular itself and shifting from "queer" to "quare" may help capture the nuances of these differences better. By insisting on the historical and material situatedness of regionalized and racialized bodies and practices, a quare study demands a more precise consideration of the multiple dimensions of culture and identity that are inevitably combined under the broad labels "southern" and "queer."

The interlocking registers of gender, desire, identity, and region are readily apparent in Truman Capote's 1948 short story "Children on Their Birthdays." But as the following analysis demonstrates, a close reading of these interconnections also requires a quare sensitivity to the different responses that readers might bring to Capote's depiction of race. The story begins and ends with the death of the ten-year-old girl Miss Lily Jane Bobbit, whose unconventional behavior shakes up the sleepy southern town where she spends only a single year. The opening line explains: "Yesterday afternoon the six-o'clock bus ran over Miss Bobbit." And the narrator, who is identified as "Mr. C.," then recounts how "nothing she ever did was ordinary, not from the first time we saw her" when she arrived "on that same six-o'clock bus" a year before.[20] In addition to establishing the story's distinctive blend of serious and comic tones, the randomness of Miss Bobbit's death is crucial because it forces readers to consider all the "queer things" that she did strictly in terms of the instability and disruption that she caused when she was alive (143). That is, by starting with her death, Capote creates a circular plot that prevents readers from anticipating some other narrative or political trajectory in which Miss Bobbit's enigmatic queerness might become a matter of secondary importance. Unlike most depictions of children, the story does not define Miss Bobbit's actions in terms of the grown-up she will become, nor does it make her into a political symbol of a future that should be built on her behalf.[21] Therefore, her queerness has to be evaluated solely in relation to the immediate southern context in which we see it. On the one hand, although Mr. C. explains that "whatever she did she did it with completeness, and so directly, so solemnly, that there was nothing to do but accept it" until it "gradually seemed natural" (143), the story never reframes Miss Bobbit's queerness as a stable or stabilizing component of the southern social norms she disturbs. On the other hand, Miss Bobbit's queerness also never constitutes an absolute *rejection* of the social order. Instead, Capote compels his readers to recognize the unresolvable tensions between queerness and normativity by highlighting the constant interplay between them.

The way that Miss Bobbit queers gender is immediately visible in her Shirley Temple–like exaggeration of feminine characteristics. When she first steps off the bus on her arrival in town, she is wearing a "starched, lemon-colored party dress," and her walk is excessively stylized: "She sassed along with a grown-up mince, one hand on her hip, the other supporting a spinsterish umbrella" (135). Her bodily appearance also suggests a theatrical femininity like that of a drag queen: "Tangee gave her lips an orange glow, her hair, rather like a costume wig, was a mass of rosy curls, and her eyes had a knowing, penciled tilt; even so, she had a skinny dignity, she was a lady, and, what is more she looked you in the eye with manlike directness" (136). An adult knowingness shows through her deliberate performance of girl-ish femininity, destabilizing the notion that gender is naturally and innately tied to biological sex. Indeed, her queerness becomes most visible when the descriptors of her identity fail to explain or reveal her character fully, and especially where those descriptors contradict each other, such as when her biological age clashes with her "grown-up mince" and where her hyperfemi-ninity clashes with the "manlike directness" of her gaze.

This fractious multiplicity persists throughout the narrative. At a talent show organized by the shyster Manny Fox, she wows the audience with a burlesque song and dance but then reassumes the guise of purity by singing "The Star Spangled Banner." Her act begins with a tap dance again reminis-cent of Shirley Temple: "Out she came, tossing her hips, her curls, rolling her eyes. . . . She tapped across the stage, daintily holding up the sides of a cloud-blue skirt. . . . Aunt El had to agree that Miss Bobbit looked real sweet." But then she launches into a risqué blues number:

> "I was born in China, and raised in Jay-pan . . ." We had never heard her sing before, and she had a rowdy sandpaper voice. ". . . if you don't like my peaches, stay away from my can, o-ho o-ho!" Aunt El gasped; she gasped again when Miss Bobbit, with a bump, up-ended her skirt to display blue-lace underwear, thereby collecting most of the whistles the boys had been saving. (151)

Miss Bobbit's skillful performance of innocence makes her sexual burlesque all the more provocative and alluring. Once the first song ends, however, Miss Bobbit's friend Sister Rosalba runs on stage and hands a lighted Roman candle to Miss Bobbit, who is in the middle of a full split: "The Roman candle burst into fire balls of red, white and blue, and we all had to stand up because she was singing 'The Star Spangled Banner' at the top of her lungs. Aunt El said afterwards that it was one of the most gorgeous things she'd ever seen on the American stage" (151). Together, the bawdy and patriotic parts of Miss Bobbit's act win the whistles and cheers of the entire audience, includ-ing the fickle Aunt El. But the ultimate appeal of this camp performance lies in the way that those contradictory elements accentuate each other through their immediate contrast to each other. As with the queer tensions between her femininity and "manlike directness," her childishness and maturity, Miss Bobbit wins the competition through her deft juxtaposition of the serious and the carnivalesque, the sweet and the sexy.

The story develops this queer meditation on multiplicity and the incompleteness of identity constructions with Miss Bobbit's remarks on the interrelation between good and evil. On a Sunday morning when everyone else is at church, she pays a visit to Mr. C. and explains:

> I've had enough experience to know that there is a God and that there is a Devil. But the way to tame the Devil is not to go down there to church and listen to what a sinful mean fool he is. No, love the Devil like you love Jesus: because he is a powerful man, and will do you a good turn if he knows you trust him. He has frequently done me good turns, like at dancing school in Memphis. . . . I always called in the Devil to help me get the biggest part in our annual show. That is common sense; you see, I knew Jesus wouldn't have any truck with dancing. (144)

Most critics have discussed this passage simply to show how her "philosophy is as unconventional as her behavior," as William L. Nance writes.[22] But this philosophy is also deeply relevant to the story's negotiation of queerness because it validates alternative kinds of "love" that the rest of this southern town normally disparages. And it foregrounds the inextricable connectedness of opposing moral systems. As with Miss Bobbit's performance of incommensurate sexual and gender characteristics, her philosophy contends that no aspect of life is simplistic and pure. There can be no good without bad, no Jesus without the devil, and, by implication, no norms without queerness. Thus, queerness in this story exists not just in opposition to the normal but in the fractures and fissures that occur wherever those queer dynamics intersect *with* the normal—not simply in the rejection of the normative but in the vibrant, irrepressible coexistence of the normative with the antinormative.

Capote further emphasizes this kind of queer multiplicity in his portrayal of Mr. C.'s cousin Billy Bob and his friend Preacher Star. Although they are "the biggest friends in town," both boys become "cross-eyed jealous over Miss Bobbit," and Preacher tries to win her favor by accusing Billy Bob of stealing money from her (139, 146). The accusation starts a fight, and the boys remain alienated from each other until the end of the story, when Miss Bobbit gets hit by the bus as she is about to leave town. An undeniably queer sentimentality shapes the boys' friendship and rivalry. As Mr. C. explains, "There did not seem to be any *straight* way for their friendship to happen again. . . . And when Preacher found himself a new buddy, Billy Bob moped around for days" (147, emphasis added). Sometimes Preacher comes to the house to speak to Aunt El, but "only to torment Billy Bob."

And at Christmas he gives Billy Bob a book of Sherlock Holmes stories with a note written on the flyleaf: "Friends Like Ivy On the Wall Must Fall [*sic*]" (147). Billy Bob pretends that this is "the corniest thing [he] ever saw," but he cannot hide the grief of losing his friend and climbs into a pecan tree to sulk (147). Billy Bob also climbs this tree earlier in the story when his mother punishes him for cutting her best roses and giving them to Miss Bobbit as a get-well present (140). And at the end of the story, Mr. C. describes this emotional tenderness explicitly in terms of queerness: "It had not been easy for him, Miss Bobbit's going. Because she'd meant more than that. Than what? Than being thirteen years old and crazy in love. She was the queer things in him, like the pecan tree and liking books and caring enough about people to let them hurt him. She was the things he was afraid to show anyone else" (153). Despite his masculine façade, Miss Bobbit brings out the sensitive, perhaps feminine aspects of Billy Bob's character, queering his identity almost as much as her own.

However, one should not misconstrue Billy Bob's queer sentimentality, especially in relation to Preacher, as a sign of latent homosexuality. Rather, Capote breaks the usual conflation of queerness with homosexuality by centering the homoeroticism of the story on the character of Mr. C. After Billy Bob gets in trouble over the roses, Mr. C. describes how he came into Mr. C.'s room and "flung himself on the foot of [his] bed. He smelled all sour and sweet, the way boys do, and [Mr. C.] felt very sorry for him" (141). Later, when Billy Bob and Preacher break up their friendship, Mr. C. turns his gaze on Preacher: "Oh, yes, Preacher, you looked so lost that day that for the first time I really liked you, so skinny and mean and lost going down the road all by yourself" (147). By inserting himself into the story as what we would almost certainly read as a gay character, Capote refuses to divorce queerness completely from homosexuality. But he also destabilizes the category of homosexuality itself, for Mr. C.'s vaguely intergenerational affection might seem closer to a chaste form of pederasty than gayness as we typically understand it. And he resists the notion that "queer" should always be read in terms of same-gender attraction, for the boys are the *objects* of this mildly homoerotic gaze and do not themselves explicitly exhibit what we would call gay desires. This story reminds us, in other words, that queerness, homoeroticism, and homosexuality are not all the same thing.

Finally, in addition to troubling the ideologies of gender and sexuality, Miss Bobbit also disrupts the town's larger social order by defying the conventions of morality, law, and race. Her dance at the talent show scandalizes the audience even as it earns a standing ovation; and she stirs up greater

controversy by refusing to attend both church and school (148). More significantly, she flagrantly disregards the rules of racial segregation by befriending
Sister Rosalba, whom Mr. C. describes as "a colored girl, baby-fat and sugar-
plum shaped" (142). Their friendship begins when Miss Bobbit rescues
Rosalba from what is clearly a threat of sexual assault by group of boys led by
Preacher. The boys block Rosalba's way in the road and demand that she pay
a tariff. She asks, "What kinda tariff you talkin' about, mister?" And Preacher
replies with "clenched teeth": "A party in the barn . . . mighty nice party in
the barn" (142). When the boys prevent her from running away, Miss Bobbit
rushes into the street and confronts them by exposing their deviation from
both the chivalric gender roles associated with traditional southern culture
and the codes of urbane sophistication. She queerly joins southern "honor"
with cosmopolitanism to contravene and correct both the myths and histories of the South as a sexually backward place: "It is a well-known fact
that gentlemen are put on the face of this earth for the protection of ladies.
Do you suppose boys behave this way in towns like Memphis, New York,
London, Hollywood or Paris?" (142). The boys walk away sheepishly, and
Mr. C. reports that "for the next year they were never far apart, Miss Bobbit
and this baby elephant, whose name was Rosalba Cat" (142).

Evoking a similar scene in William Faulkner's *Light in August* (1932), the
threat of the "barn party" implies that interracial rape is a normative sexual
practice in the segregated South. Yet Miss Bobbit's condemnation reframes
that threat as a morally repugnant violation of what she claims are the proper
forms of gender and sexual relations in the South and beyond. The story
thus redefines interracial rape as an intolerable act of sexual deviance at odds
with southern norms. Miss Bobbit's defense of Rosalba's femininity is also
highly unconventional—and again intrinsically progressive—because she
calls Rosalba a "lady," a term reserved only for white women during this
time. Moreover, while it is arguable whether Miss Bobbit ever treats Rosalba
as an equal, the constant companions move through the town freely and
never leave each other's side, flouting the racial codes that would prevent
Rosalba from accompanying Miss Bobbit in some public spaces. For example, the girls regularly sit on the front porch of Mrs. Sawyer's house, where
Miss Bobbit and her mother are boarders, a location that would otherwise
be off limits to Rosalba. And Mr. C. reports that, initially, Mrs. Sawyer raises
"a fuss" about it: "She told Aunt El that it went against the grain to have
a nigger lolling smack there in plain sight on her front porch" (142–43).
Ultimately, however, Mrs. Sawyer and the rest of the town grow accustomed
to seeing the two girls together, suggesting that the rules of segregation are

maybe not so rigid here, after all. Miss Bobbit's queering of gender and sexual norms inevitably queers racial norms as well.

Yet neither the town's nor the story's racism disappears completely. Although the town newspaper publishes an angry editorial when Miss Bobbit refuses to attend school, nobody bothers with the fact that Sister Rosalba quits school, too: "She was colored, so no one cared" (148). From this remark and from Miss Bobbit's behavior overall, some readers might thus infer an attack on southern racism—something like an early expression of civil rights politics. But a self-consciously "quare" analysis must challenge this conclusion. Depending on their own relationship to the South's racial inequalities, some readers might quickly recognize that neither Miss Bobbit nor Capote criticizes segregation openly, and that the white townsfolk simply accommodate this interracial pair rather than reconsidering the problems of racism on a larger scale. Also, some might detect an underlying racism in Capote's unflattering descriptions of the "baby elephant" Rosalba Cat. However, the presence of contradictory political impulses in this story does not mean that one necessarily cancels out the other. Capote's treatment of race might be troubling, but it is anything but straightforward. Indeed, rather than blindly praising or condemning the story's politics, a quare reading that takes into account the various perspectives of Capote's readers reveals the extent to which Capote associates queerness with multiplicity, incompleteness, and contradiction. Just as gender and sexual queerness emerge in this story at the junctures between the masculine and the feminine, the childish and the adult, and the normative and the transgressive, the story queers the politics of race by overlapping conservative and progressive attitudes toward race. This is not to excuse any potential racism on Capote's part or to suggest that the story is ultimately noncommittal about race. Rather, this sort of quare reading shows that the politics of race are just one strand in the larger circulation of normative, nonnormative, and antinormative discourses. Instead of subordinating Miss Bobbit's queerness to a singular political message about race or any other social problem, Capote consistently exposes the queer inconsistencies that exist wherever opposing ideologies intersect. That is, while Miss Bobbit's actions implicitly challenge segregation, the story makes no coherent political appeal that would transform her queerness into either a new kind of progressive normativity or a reactionary defense of the status quo. This story preserves the queerness of queerness by refusing to offer any form of narrative or political resolution.

Obviously this brief analysis of "Children on Their Birthdays" is just one example of how one might examine the queer dynamics of southern literature and culture. But the story of Miss Lily Jane Bobbit usefully reveals how making a queer study of the region means doing more than simply pointing out aberrant forms of gender, desire, eroticism, and identity. While "queer" always begins with an analysis of gender and sexuality, it also enables a systemic critique of the larger social and ideological structures that define normativity and transgression both within the region and at the junctures between region and nation. Moreover, a discursive analysis of southern queerness also requires a "quare" recognition of how race, ethnicity, class, and locality shape the materiality of relations and identities, as well as the presuppositions that inform the interpretive process itself. Together, this combination of approaches makes it possible to begin queering the South by revealing what is already queer within southern culture.

NOTES

1. Sedgwick, *Tendencies*, 8.

2. Goldman, "Who Is That Queer Queer?," 174.

3. Edelman, *No Future*, 4.

4. Richards, *Lovers and Beloveds*, 14–21.

5. J. Howard, "Introduction," 4–5; Herring, *Another Country*, 99–124. See also Halberstam, *In a Queer Time and Place*, 36.

6. D. J. Smith, "Queering the South," 381, emphasis in original. For further studies of queer sexualities in southern literature, see Bibler, *Cotton's Queer Relations*; Poteet, *Gay Men in Modern Southern Literature*; Pugh, *Queer Chivalry*; and Amende, *Desire and the Divine*. For more-localized studies of queer communities in the U.S. South, see Sears, *Lonely Hunters*; Buring, *Lesbian and Gay Memphis*; Chenault and Braukman, *Gay and Lesbian Atlanta*; and B. Thompson, *Un-Natural State*.

7. Greeson, *Our South*.

8. O'Connor, *Mystery and Manners*, 40.

9. Duck, *Nation's Region*, 18.

10. Brasell, "'Degeneration of Nationalism,'" 53.

11. D. J. Smith, "Queering the South," 370.

12. Anzaldúa, "To(o) Queer the Writer," 250.

13. Butler, *Bodies That Matter*, 223, 228.

14. Ibid., 228.

15. Ibid., 229.

16. Justice, "Notes toward a Theory of Anomaly," 226. For a discussion of two-spirit identities, see Qwo-Li Driskill, "Doubleweaving Two-Spirit Critiques."

17. E. P. Johnson, "'Quare' Studies," 9, 3, 20, 2.

18. Ibid., 12.

19. "Quar," 130. When discussing this Irish connection, Johnson quotes from Valente, *Quare Joyce*, 126–27.

20. Capote, "Children on Their Birthdays," 135. Text hereafter cited parenthetically.

21. See Stockton, *Queer Child*, and Edelman, *No Future*.
22. Nance, *Worlds of Truman Capote*, 68.

SUGGESTIONS FOR FURTHER READING

Amende, Kathaleen E. *Desire and the Divine: Feminine Identity in White Southern Women's Writing*. Baton Rouge: Louisiana State University Press, 2013.

Bibler, Michael P. *Cotton's Queer Relations: Same-Sex Intimacy and the Literature of the Southern Plantation, 1936–1968*. Charlottesville: University of Virginia Press, 2009.

Dews, Carlos L., and Carolyn Leste Law, eds. *Out in the South*. Philadelphia: Temple University Press, 2001.

Herring, Scott. *Another Country: Queer Anti-Urbanism*. New York: New York University Press, 2010.

Howard, John. *Men Like That: A Southern Queer History*. Chicago: University of Chicago Press, 1999.

Johnson, E. Patrick. *Sweet Tea: Black Gay Men of the South*. Chapel Hill: University of North Carolina Press, 2008.

Poteet, William Mark. *Gay Men in Modern Southern Literature: Ritual, Initiation, and the Construction of Masculinity*. New York: Peter Lang, 2006.

Pugh, Tison. *Queer Chivalry: Medievalism and the Myth of White Masculinity in Southern Literature*. Baton Rouge: Louisiana State University Press, 2013.

Ray, Douglass, ed. *The Queer South: LGBTQ Writers on the American South*. Little Rock: Sibling Rivalry Press, 2014.

Richards, Gary. *Lovers and Beloveds: Sexual Otherness in Southern Fiction, 1936–1961*. Baton Rouge: Louisiana State University Press, 2005.

Whitlock, Reta Ugena, ed. *Queer South Rising: Voices of a Contested Place*. Charlotte, N.C.: Information Age, 2013.

PART IV

Approaches

SCOTT ROMINE

Consumption

Consumption, defined broadly as the exchange of money for goods and services, appears before us initially as a curious object of inquiry. Compared with forms of identification grounded in race, religion, gender, class, and nation, consumption competes badly. Few persons identify themselves primarily—or even importantly—as consumers, while consumerism stands alongside other scandalous isms (sexism, for example) that, although understood to afflict society as a whole, do so mostly by afflicting *other people*. The relationship between consumption and culture is similarly fraught; as Pierre Bourdieu observes, one of the key (and most persistent) "'inventions' of Romanticism" was "the representation of culture as a kind of superior reality, irreducible to the vulgar demands of economics"—although, he adds, this representation was itself a "reactio[n] against the pressures of an anonymous market."[1] But even when culture is conceived as something that cannot be bought or sold, and market forces as a faceless matrix of supply and demand, consumption offers a fairly reliable index of desire, including desires that derive from and reproduce social imaginaries. To some significant degree, consumption both reproduces and shapes conceptions of place, history, and identity.

Discourses of southern cultural identity, originating both inside and outside the U.S. South, have often imagined the region as an alternative to the pressures of Bourdieu's anonymous market. When a Charleston native in V. S. Naipaul's *A Turn in the South* casually describes southern culture in terms of "the agrarian culture versus the industrial" and "the ideals of honor against the crass values of commerce," he positions the South within a long-standing mode of cultural self-definition.[2] In the antebellum era, pro-slavery apologists defended the agrarian plantation as a benign alternative to the impersonal regime of wage slavery. For George Fitzhugh, defending slavery as a mode of production meant altering southern modes of consumption. Warning southerners to avoid "French silks, French wines, French brandy, and French trinkets," he called for the consumption of local goods as a means of "becom[ing] national, nay, provincial, and ceas[ing] to be imitative cosmopolitans."[3] Fitzhugh's early version of "buy local" would undergo revision in the postbellum era.

With the ascendance of New South doctrines preaching industrial progress, the branding of the South came to signal regionalist pride. Noting the ubiquity of "southern" as a marketing device, the northern writer and civil rights activist Albion Tourgée observed in 1880 that, from patent medicines and steamboats to restaurants and barrooms, "everything that courts popularity, patronage or applause, makes haste to brand itself as distinctively and especially 'Southern.'"[4] This mode of identitarian branding and consumption survives to the present, leading the sociologist John Shelton Reed to conclude that the best way to determine the South's borders is to compare "Southern" listings in telephone directories as a percentage of "American" listings. "If you want to know whether you're in the South," Reed writes, "you could do worse than to look in the phone book."[5]

But if buying southern has anchored some practices of cultural self-fashioning, others have sought to exempt the region from, as Naipaul's interlocutor puts it, the "crass values of commerce." The Nashville Agrarians viewed consumption, "the grand end which justifies the evil of modern labor," as a baleful symptom of an alien industrial economy. Inveighing against the "rise of modern advertising," the primary means by which producers "coerce and wheedle the public into being loyal and steady consumers," the Agrarians offered an idea of the U.S. South that would prove durable in academic circles despite its singular lack of success in influencing the region's economy. As a "rebuke to materialism, a corrective to the worship of Progress, and a reaffirmation of man's aesthetic and spiritual needs," Louis Rubin wrote in 1962, *I'll Take My Stand* drew upon the "lingering memory within the Southerner's mind of the tranquil and leisurely Southern life before the machines and the superhighways came."[6] There are multiple ironies here, not least that the South's "rebuke to materialism" was delusive, existing as it did alongside a profit motive that had long extracted labor in ways that were scarcely "tranquil and leisurely." Far from correcting the worship of Progress, the South simply hadn't progressed very far. Moreover, as Ted Ownby shows in *American Dreams in Mississippi: Consumers, Poverty, and Culture, 1830–1998*, rural consumers had long sought imported goods as a bridge to an urban, cosmopolitan culture that, from antebellum times forward, served as an object of desire and aspiration.[7]

That a liberal such as Rubin could reiterate this reactionary critique of materialism suggests the curious consonance of the Agrarian program and rebukes to capital coming from the Left; among other things, the Agrarians had positioned the South within a field of academic labor that has never wanted for tillers. When Andrew Lytle advised his readers to "throw out the radio and take the fiddle down from the wall," he predicted with some precision Theodor Adorno's argument in "A Social Critique of Radio Music," an essay published by John Crowe Ransom in the *Kenyon Review*. There, Adorno argues that music, having been forced "to go to the market" during the late eighteenth century, had come to exist as a commodity—"a means instead of an end, a fetish"—and thus "has ceased to be a human force and is consumed like other consumers' goods."[8] Donald Davidson had sounded the same culture industry note in *I'll Take My Stand*, lamenting that an industrial economy, "seeing the world altogether in terms of commodities, . . . simply proposes to add one more commodity to the list. . . . It will buy art, if any fool wants art."[9] Likewise, the Agrarians' denunciation of advertising looks forward to Herbert Marcuse's *One-Dimensional Man* (1964) and its critique of the "false needs" created by advanced industrial society and its ideology of consumerism.

The overlap between Nashville and Frankfurt suggests that conservative efforts to define consumption as a threat to culture were regional variations on a theme unbounded by geography or even ideology. Ironically, however, the romantic conception of culture as resistant to market homogenization has itself proven highly marketable. As Stephanie Yuhl shows in *A Golden Haze of Memory* (2005), at about the same time the Agrarians were promoting the idea of a traditional South, elite Charlestonians were actually *selling* it by inventing, marketing, and "enshrin[ing] Charleston as a place where remnants of a glorious past lived on, unmarred by the uglier sides of modernity," an effort that culminated in "'Historic Charleston,' a burgeoning tourist industry that lured thousands of history-hungry visitors to the city annually."[10] Yuhl's study exemplifies a number of trends that have emerged in recent southern studies, notably in considering the production and consumption of cultural goods not merely as the industrialization of an authentic prior culture but as a significant field of cultural activity in its own right. Recent scholarship has tended toward the ambivalent position marked out by Mark Paterson, who writes that consumption permits us "to articulate important cultural phenomena such as self-identity and social identity, our identity within a group," but always with the knowledge that "our tastes, desires and aspirations are almost inescapably engineered" by producers and advertisers.[11] To make and market Charleston as an elite group did is to engineer a product with social consequences, among them an *idea* of history selectively culled from actual history and strategically deployed within a social order. As Grant McCracken observes in *Culture and Consumption*, the material realization of categories "created according to the blueprint of culture" renders the blueprint substantial, and thus "plays a vital part in the cultural constitution of the world."[12]

Southern blueprints have not always been native products. As William Taylor demonstrates in his 1957 *Cavalier and Yankee*, the antebellum figure of the southern cavalier emerged in part as a northern response to anxieties about the effects of the "grasping, soulless world of business" on its increasingly materialistic culture.[13] Although Taylor directs only passing reference to consumer goods such as gift books, the imagined South has long been central to national practices of consumption. According to Eric Plaag, antebellum practices of northern tourism and souvenir collection helped to consolidate a national myth of a solid South. "Northern travelers," he writes, "found difference everywhere in the South, and they consistently used a burgeoning souvenir mentality to commemorate that difference" in the years leading up to the Civil War.[14] The mass consumer market emerging after the war drew powerfully on southern iconography associated with the plantation and black labor. In *Dreaming of Dixie*, Karen Cox argues that the numerous industries that "cleverly linked their products—from pancake flour to movies—to the idyllic images conjured up by the Old South" did so mostly from locations *outside* the South, thereby "exert[ing] far more influence over what ideas Americans consumed about the South than did native southerners themselves."[15] But as Grace Elizabeth Hale shows in *Making Whiteness*, while the racialized commodification of southern icons such as the mammy helped to make whiteness the "homogenizing ground of the American mass market," southern purveyors of the new mass culture actually found it more difficult to employ such tactics because African Americans constituted a significant consumer group. Booster and tourist pamphlets, however, were marketed to a different (and whiter) demographic, leading to the creation by 1930 of what Hale calls "DixieBrand, a regional identity made or marketed as southern" that juxtaposed romantic images of black labor, plantation homes, and Confederate iconography alongside signs of modernity such as factories.[16] The branding of "Dixie" declined, however, in the aftermath of the Civil Rights Movement due to its association with white supremacist politics.

Consuming the South, then, has never been an exclusively or even predominantly internal affair but rather a set of practices implicated in national fantasies of the South. Although relatively absent from southern studies until the recent past, advertising, tourism, and souvenirs have become increasingly of interest to historians, sociologists, literary scholars, anthropologists, art historians, and scholars working in adjacent fields. Tara McPherson, a professor of media studies, opens *Reconstructing Dixie*, her "exploration of the South's role in the national imaginary," with an anecdote about a visit in postmodern, placeless Los Angeles to the House of Blues and its reproduction of a Delta blues joint. Grounding her analysis in objects ranging from plantation kitsch to literary fiction, McPherson moves as well beyond national boundaries, asserting that "in an era of increasing globalization, the region circulates as an alternative to the nation-state, shifting in meaning and content."[17]

Increasingly, cultural goods constitute the media through which the region circulates, altering in the process the meaning and content of the region so circulated. As goods pass across cultural boundaries—as Madison Avenue, for example, creates the U.S. South in popular culture and sells it worldwide—cultural blueprints are inevitably redrafted as they are consumed outside the culture of origin. What, for example, do the sounds of a Delta blues joint mean to media experts in Los Angeles, or to working-class Brits? What did they mean for the Rolling Stones, who sent altered sounds back to, among other places, the Mississippi Delta? The global vectors involved can be dizzying. Consider the case of Darky Toothpaste, a Chinese brand drawing from minstrel images of southern blacks developed on the antebellum northern stage, as it appears in a parody commercial ("For a shine that's jigaboo bright!") in Kevin Willmott's *C.S.A.*, a film that mimics a BBC documentary in telling a counterfactual history of a South that won the war, but whose victory generates patterns of consumption uncannily reminiscent of those that emerged in the aftermath of the South's loss: Darky Toothpaste, for instance.

The mutable nature of consumption also occurs when goods reenter or remain in the culture of origin. In order to understand how consumption reproduces but also complicates conceptions of southern culture, I want to consider the example of shrimp and grits, a dish that has come to occupy a central position in the consumption of southern food and the discourse of southern foodways. Perhaps because it is eaten, food has long been a popular subject for scholars interested in how consumption shapes flows of capital and culture. George Ritzer's *McDonaldization*, for example, uses the fast-food chain to example the effects of rationalization and standardization in a globalized market, while "Coca-colonization" has become a catchphrase for U.S. cultural imperialism. But against the assault of Big, Fast Food, counterpractices of small, slow food have emerged to consolidate conceptions of locality and resistance to globalization. The term "foodways," which first appeared in the United States as part of the New Deal Federal Writers' Project to catalog distinctive regional cultures, derives from the earlier term "folkways" and preserves that term's emphasis on cultural practices that are distinctive, deeply engrained, and passed down through generations.

A consensus has emerged, however, that *southern* foodways, although they existed in the past and are cherished in the present, underwent a period of neglect. Employing this gap-ridden chronology, John T. Edge writes in 2007 that "in the two decades since the original *Encyclopedia of Southern Culture* was published . . . the South in particular, has awakened to the cultural import of regional foodways." (Indeed, it has "awakened" enough to justify a separate *Foodways* volume in the *New Encyclopedia of Southern Culture*.)[18] Shrimp and grits follows this pattern, its origin assigned to the South Carolina Low Country (as a breakfast food for shrimpers) prior to its 1980s resurrection in cookbooks and restaurants. The renaissance of the dish can be traced to 1985, when *New York Times* food critic Craig Claiborne lauded the "helpings of history" offered at Crook's Corner, a Chapel Hill restaurant run by classically trained chef Bill Neal. Although Claiborne's article mentions "Shrimp with Cheese Grits" only in passing, it introduces what would become a journalistic convention applied to celebrity chefs in the South: memories of parents who "cured their own hams, smoked their own sausages"; grandmothers who "were marvelous cooks"—a good thing, since no one in Neal's home "community ever thought of going to a restaurant."[19] The transfer of "home cooking" to the restaurant involves a shift from what Karl Marx described as the logic of pre-commodity production, wherein "the social relations between individuals in the performance of their labor, appear at all events as their own mutual personal relations, and are not disguised under the shape of social relationships between the products of labor" to a mode of production and consumption mediated by the commodity.[20] What is lost in this transfer is precisely what the Agrarian Andrew Lytle celebrated about preindustrial eating: that food was "particularly relished" because "each dish has particular meaning for the consumer, for everybody has had something to do with the long and intricate procession from the ground to the table."[21]

Shrimp and grits often signifies, but rarely embodies, that intricate procession, thereby transubstantiating (or fetishizing) the South in its familiar role as antidote to modernity. But the dish also represents other Souths, among them the Camp South (at Jekyll Island's annual Shrimp and Grits Festival and, as we shall see, at the Bubba Gump Shrimp Company) and the Cosmopolitan South (in the various fusion versions of the dish that combine southern ingredients with kimchi, pesto, jalapenos, pimientos del Piquillo, and the like). Even as a regional dish, however, shrimp and grits follows global patterns of food consumption. Writing of contemporary British food cultures, Allison James identifies paradigms of "food nostalgia" (representations of British food as "plain and robust, the family food of farmhouses and firelight") and "food creolization" ("providing for the consumer a global experience of consumption often within a single meal") that could, by swapping out a few ingredients, easily translate to various incarnations of shrimp and grits.[22]

Because the consumption of food is driven by appetite, the South represented tends toward romance and away from abjection. As plated, the South does not usually conjure an imagined land of boors and rednecks, although food continues to represent such Souths. The TLC hit *Here Comes Honey Boo Boo*, for example, draws powerfully on redneck stereotypes, with the family's foodways—consuming roadkill or "sketti" made with ketchup and Country Crock margarine—signaling that, where Mama June and brood are concerned, you are what you eat. Since you probably don't want to be that way, *Mama June's Cookbook* is unlikely to hit bookstores near you. Within the field of cultural production, domains of consumption select differently the cultures they represent: the backward South is apparently more palatable in T-shirts—"A Dolla Makes Me Holla" and "You Better Redneckognize" are both available on TLC's Honey Boo Boo website—than if you actually have to swallow it.

If you want to swallow shrimp and grits in New Orleans, one place you do can do so is the Bubba Gump Shrimp Company, which offers "A whole mess o' Shrimp" alongside andouille sausage, Cajun spices, and "Carolina Grits." But you can't swallow it at the Bubba Gump Shrimp Company in New York City, where the menu includes New England Clam Chowder—unavailable in New Orleans—and substitutes "Shrimp Chimichurri Skewers" for "Kentucky Bourbon Skewers." Both menus recycle southern stereotypes already recycled by the 1994 film and the 1986 novel, with "Mama always said" framing several picturesque observations about life and shrimp. Although "Forrest's favorite meal after a day on the boat" is said to be the Seafood Feast, the shrimp at Bubba Gump don't come from a boat but rather are "sustainably farmed using state of the art methods." The romantic origins of the shrimp are thus exchanged for eco-branding with a southern accent: "No by-catch. No way!"[23]

But if you're in New Orleans, of course, you probably *won't* go to Bubba Gump Shrimp Company. Instead, you'll consult a local resident (or an iPhone app) to find where the locals eat. Perhaps you'll end up at Café Amelie, where, among the "small plates," you might choose "jumbo shrimp

& grits, corn and andouille macque choux over old mill grits 13."[24] Several conventions of the menu—the absence of capital letters, prices rounded to the dollar, at least one ingredient that nonfoodies won't recognize—indicate that, besides food, Café Amelie offers the kind of *distinction* that Pierre Bourdieu identifies as available through modes of consumption that integrate into social habitus markers of taste and group differentiation. Because you're eating at Café Amelie instead of Bubba Gump, you're likely to know what macque choux is, to prefer olive oil to Crisco, and to identify yourself as different from the kind of person who eats at Bubba Gump.

222

You might also be a connoisseur of "old mill grits," which are probably grits from The Old Mill in Pigeon Forge, Tennessee. Dating from the nineteenth century and advertised as "one of the most photographed mills in the country," The Old Mill is part of the tourist trade in a town made famous by Dollywood, the theme park created by country music singer Dolly Parton. At The Old Mill, not only do they grind their grits "the same way the pioneers did," actual "resident millers then hand-fill, weigh and tie each bag of stone ground grain." Here, grits, ground by stone and grounded in premodern fantasy, generate an idea of the South, since, "if there's a warm bowl of homemade white grits on your breakfast table, you know you're experiencing traditional Southern fare and hospitality at its best."[25] The formula is not limited to advertising. Writing in *The Encyclopedia of Southern Culture*, John Egerton claims that "throughout its history, and in pre-Columbian times as well, the South has relished grits and made them a symbol of its diet, its customs, its humor, and its good-spirited hospitality."[26] Although it's doubtful that grits functioned as a symbol for as long as Egerton claims, there is little question that they now signify in a number of ways: as a delineator of cultural boundaries (a food southerners eat and nonsoutherners don't); as representing cultural values ("good-spirited hospitality" and other ostensibly premodern virtues); and, increasingly, as a consumer product through which distinction is available. The title character of the 1992 film *My Cousin Vinny* begins by asking "what the heck is a grit?" and ends having mastered the protocols of grits consumption, a shift that signals his access to southern hospitality and his newfound professional competence as a defense attorney: he forces a hostile witness to recant his timeline on the basis that "no self-respecting southerner" would use instant grits. As a concession to the temporal rhythms of modernity, instant grits don't conjure up the South of hospitality and leisure, which probably explains why the latest grit trend is toward slow-cooked versions that (moving ever farther beyond the twenty-minute threshold that qualifies as respectably southern in *My Cousin Vinny*) can take up to three hours to cook. Going traditional also means going upscale; if you follow The Old Mill's advice to "forget instant grits" and "instead, indulge in grits that are stone ground and slow cooked the old fashioned way," you'll be paying more to put "traditional Southern fare and hospitality" on the table.[27]

Although, as Anthony Szczesiul has shown, the discourse of southern hospitality emerged from a particular discourse of labor relations grounded in slavery, it has survived emancipation to function broadly in the selling of the South.[28] That economy has flourished, in part, by screening the labor behind the goods offered, a function Marx attributed to the commodity fetish generally. Often, however, the properties ascribed to the commodity derive not from an outright disavowal of labor but by its romantic reinscription. If, as Marx (not a foodie) famously observed, "From the taste of wheat it is not possible to tell who produced it," contemporary purveyors of heritage grains take great pains to relieve you of your ignorance. When you order online from The Old Mill, part of what you're paying for is the idea that the "resident millers" hand-filled and tied your bag of grits. Hand-filling and tying bags of grits all day may not be a great job, and it's probably not a superior method of filling and tying bags of grits, but it transfers to the grits the idea that they were made "the same way the pioneers did." If you prefer a non-pioneer mythology of labor, you might consider Anson Mills' Antebellum Coarse White Grits, made from "organic heirloom grains . . . prized historically for exceptional flavor and texture."[29] Anson Mills describes its "mission" as the perpetuation of a cuisine representing "a complex expression of community that emerges in a distinct locale and is dependent on soil, agriculture, preparation, and rites of consumption." Specifically, Carolina Rice Kitchen cuisine

> arose when three distinct rice cultures came together to build rice canals on the sea islands of Carolina and Georgia: Venetian rice farmers who designed the canals, Africans who brought their rice management methods to the endeavor, and Native Americans who worked in the fields. The association of these peoples and their cultures resulted in a vibrant melting-pot exchange that ultimately became a new cuisine.[30]

Portraying Africans as rice management consultants who "brought" their expertise to a "vibrant melting-pot exchange" is, at the least, a *selective* transatlantic history. The selection isn't accidental, because if you're paying heirloom grain prices, you don't really want to think about how slaves got here. Jettisoning that history means enhancing the heirloom effect. Selling a regional cuisine—that "complex expression of community"—depends partially, then, on a configuration of memory that is both broadly repre-sentative (since all cultural memory is selective) and specifically so, since, as Anthony J. Stanonis observes, the discursive memorialization of southern foodways tends to "overemphasize food's ability to unite southerners across racial lines."[31] The line between a poetics of culture and a poetics of advertis-ing is anything but clear.

Multiplied by thousands of products and across millions of exchanges, the symbolic work performed in such transactions is not insignificant. The commodity form through which ideas of culture, and of a cultural past, are increasingly mediated brings to bear a profit motive on cultural memory, despite the fact that the logic of such transactions is often occluded. Anson Mills, for example, prominently features shrimp and grits as part of its "mis-sion" to recover regional cuisine, observing that "the renaissance of regional Southern fare some two decades ago landed shrimp and grits on every menu from Charleston to Savannah—as well as on menus in cities where no shrimp ever swam or spawned."[32] Although their recipe insists on "dayboat shrimp" (the kind of boat Forrest Gump works on), it silently passes over the tem-poral and spatial gaps involved: the cultural product is discontinuous with both the past it idealizes (since the dish and the fare it represents required a renaissance) and its place of origin (since the dish is easily exported from the local community of which it is said to be a "complex expression").

For John Edge, the export potential of shrimp and grits creates the pos-sibility for cultural theft. Writing in *Gourmet* magazine, Edge laments that, "thanks to a legion of trend-happy restaurateurs, the dish's origins as a fish-erman's breakfast are now obfuscated, its subtleties consigned to memory." Granting Bill Neal the license to use garlic (since Neal "was a native of South Carolina"), Edge bemoans the depredations of nonnatives: the Canadian chef, for example, who promiscuously adds Swiss cheese and "a dry rub better suited to Boston butt." Foreigners "bent upon taking liberties with shrimp and grits" are enjoined to "take a moment to consider from whence the dish came," which, presumably, will make adding Swiss cheese (or "heaven for-bid, pesto") a thing too painful to contemplate.[33]

For consumers like Edge who "wish to revel in the provincial," shrimp and grits generates a collective identity grounded in regional and local dif-ference. The sine qua non of nativist shrimp and grits is probably found at Charleston's award-winning Husk restaurant, where celebrity chef Sean Brock insists that "if it doesn't come from the South, it's not coming through the door." Promoting an "ingredient-driven cuisine that begins in the rediscovery of heirloom products," drawing from "a larder of ingredients indigenous to the South," and displaying on a prominent chalkboard the "artisanal products currently provisioning the kitchen" (you get the idea), Husk offers a seasonal shrimp and grits that uses Anson Mills grits among its other (rediscovered) heirloom products.[34] Although the heirlooms involved weren't inherited, the heirloom industry is flourishing. In a recent issue of *Southern Living*, Charleston-based tonic artisan Jack Reitz explains that he began "handcrafting" his Small Batch Tonic because "there weren't any Southern artisan tonics out there." In an almost genealogical sense, markets beget markets, and as the "Slow Food mentality began trickling down to the bar," Reitz capitalized on the trickle.[35] As a consequence, the South is no longer counted among those cultures lacking an artisan tonic—one sold, naturally, to Husk, where it helps to "evok[e] a way of life centered on seasonality and the grand traditions of Charleston life—one lived at a slower pace, preferably with a cocktail and a wide porch in the late afternoon."[36] That evocation, in turn, helps to fuel a local economy driven by tourism. Replenishing the "golden haze of memory," it seems, requires innovation, new products, and updated histories.

As a mode of both material and symbolic exchange, consumption facilitates the reproduction of culture. As the best works of recent scholarship have shown, attending carefully to the feedbacks involved means rejecting two opposing positions: first, the Agrarian fantasy that culture is prior to, separate from, and damaged by the commodity, and second, that the commodity can embody and transmit the culture. As Grant McCracken observes, consumer goods offer bridges to displaced meanings and thus constitute "instruments for the reproduction, representation, and manipulation" of cultures.[37] A poetics of consumption requires, then, an awareness of the displacements and manipulations involved—that representation involves neither simulation (bearing no relation to the "reality" of culture) nor re-presentation (*delivering* the culture) but rather, as in any symbolic act, a complex and dynamic interaction between sign and referent. This recognition is important because, as a culture-bearing medium, the commodity has gained market share and because the South bought is related to the South bought into.

NOTES

1. Bourdieu, *Field of Cultural Production*, 114.
2. Naipaul, *Turn in the South*, 105.
3. Fitzhugh, *Cannibals All!*, 5, 58, 59.
4. Tourgée, *Bricks without Straw*, 383.

5. J. S. Reed, *My Tears Spoiled My Aim*, 27.

6. Twelve Southerners, "Introduction," xlvi; L. D. Rubin, introduction, xxxi–xxxii.

7. See Ownby, *American Dreams in Mississippi*, especially 8–24.

8. Adorno, "Social Critique of Radio Music," 211.

9. Lytle, "Hind Tit," 244; D. Davidson, "Mirror for Artists," 30–31.

10. Yuhl, *Golden Haze of Memory*, 6.

11. Paterson, *Consumption and Everyday Life*, 8–9.

12. McCracken, *Culture and Consumption*, 74.

13. W. R. Taylor, *Cavalier and Yankee*, 18.

14. Plaag, "'There Is an Abundance,'" 42.

15. Cox, *Dreaming of Dixie*, 4, 5.

16. Hale, *Making Whiteness*, 168–69, 146.

17. McPherson, *Reconstructing Dixie*, 2.

18. Edge, introduction, xix–xx.

19. Claiborne, "For a Carolina Chef," c6.

20. Marx, *Capital*, 89.

21. Lytle, "Hind Tit," 223, 27.

22. A. James, "Cooking the Books," 89, 91.

23. "Menus," Bubba Gump Shrimp Company.

24. "Menu," Café Amelie.

25. "About Us," The Old Mill; "Grits—White Corn," The Old Mill.

26. Egerton, "Grits," 495.

27. "Grits—Gourmet Cheddar Cheese Grits," The Old Mill.

28. Szczesiul, "Re-Mapping Southern Hospitality," 127–29.

29. "Antebellum Coarse White Grits," Anson Mills.

30. "What We Do," Anson Mills.

31. Stanonis, "Just Like Mammy Used to Make," 209.

32. "Shrimp and Grits," Anson Mills.

33. Edge, "Kiss My Grits."

34. "About Husk," Husk Restaurant.

35. Bordonaro, "Shop Local," NC10.

36. "About Husk," Husk Restaurant.

37. McCracken, *Culture and Consumption*, xi.

SUGGESTIONS FOR FURTHER READING

Bone, Martyn, Brian Ward, and William A. Link, eds. *Creating and Consuming the American South*. Gainesville: University of Florida Press, 2015.

Cox, Karen. *Dreaming of Dixie: How the American South Was Created in American Popular Culture*. Chapel Hill: University of North Carolina Press, 2011.

Hale, Grace Elizabeth. *Making Whiteness: The Culture of Segregation in the South, 1890–1940*. New York: Pantheon, 1998.

Ownby, Ted. *American Dreams in Mississippi: Consumers, Poverty, and Culture, 1830–1998*. Chapel Hill: University of North Carolina Press, 1999.

Stanonis, Anthony J., ed. *Dixie Emporium: Tourism, Foodways, and Consumer Culture in the American South*. Athens: University of Georgia Press, 2008.

JAYNA BROWN

Performance

I define performance as a broader geography than the theater or the stage. Performance here refers to sets of relations and particular choreographies of interaction through which race and other subject formations are produced and reinforced, but also contested. The examples of performance in this essay are adapted from my book, *Babylon Girls: Black Women Performers and the Shaping of the Modern*, in which I explore processes of racialization and gendering as articulated on and off the black variety stages of Europe and America.[1] My study of the variety stage and social dance is grounded in both cultural studies and feminist approaches. It understands black expressive cultures as crucial articulations of black resilience and transformation, and as operating in a different register than do literature or visual arts. The study interprets expressive cultures in relation to the specific historical conjunctures and geographical locations in which they were performed, and always with the question of what is politically at stake.

To fully understand what is happening on the heterogeneous, unruly black popular stage, we have to locate where black women are in its history. Their presences are often obscured by a masculinist bias toward histories of the lone male instrumentalist, which underplays the importance of dance as a central cultural formation. In black culture, I argue, artistic performance is about inhabiting the body on different terms than are set by dominant regimes. Popular dance, in particular, is about reclaiming the body from the worlds of unfree labor, control, and punishment choreographed to mark the racialized and gendered body. Instead, the black body in creative motion moves through and around these forms of wounding, affirming that although it can be dominated, a body can never fully be owned.

Plantation Time on the Popular Stage, 1850s–1900s

I begin this section with the plantation because histories of plantation slavery form a key topos in the nation's dialectic of racial formation. The fantasy of the plantation returns again and again in popular cultural forms well into the twentieth century. The staged plantation was a prime site of return. Mid-nineteenth-century traveling stage shows, particularly staged versions of Harriet Beecher Stowe's *Uncle Tom's Cabin*, were often referred to as "plant shows," or "take-me-backs," and at the turn of the century the fictive plantation was the setting for nostalgic spectacles of an old South. To understand the cultural meaning of these acts, we must look to antebellum slavery, reading the popular stage acts in relation to the circulating discourses of plantation slavery, civic freedom, and the laboring black body, for these earlier discourses profoundly shaped their significance.

The family was the central trope and problematic in sentimental fictions, and the southern cotton plantation, as a peculiarly American "family," became the prime site at which the racial/sexual drama of chattel slavery unfolded. At the center was the capering black slave child, a key product of this drama. The mischievous and often unruly "pickaninnies," grown on the plantation, would become long-standing stock characters of the popular press, the minstrel stage, and the music score.

Midcentury, ideas of the black child and the childlike races from abolitionist, Christian, and scientific discourses shaped the course and tactics of much sentimental fiction and popular drama. Little black children were an integral part of the domestic space of the (imaginary) southern plantation. They were constantly tumbling, rolling, and getting underfoot. They needed constant supervision, as they refused to behave, defying all order necessary to the smooth running of a "home." Unlike the primitive races that Europeans were subduing in faraway places, African Americans were internal colonial subjects, not only geographically, in the public spheres of nation and colony, but also within the "private" sphere of the home and family. The opening act of Harriet Beecher Stowe's novel *Uncle Tom's Cabin* is the forced cavorting of a small black child, Little Harry. In his act, prompted by his master in the interest of a sale, the popular stage is conflated with the auction block.

A large number of black children frisked and frolicked throughout the pages of Stowe's *Uncle Tom's Cabin* and onto the popular stage. When Topsy is introduced in the novel, she is added to what is already a physical cacophony of small black children, "mopping and mowing and grinning between the railings, and tumbling over the kitchen floor" on the plantation, exhibiting a ubiquitous and disruptive physicality, calling for vigilant discipline and guidance.[2]

Stowe's novel reads thoroughly as a pastiche of numerous sources. Reflecting its influences, the text acted as a condensation point; in turn versions and echoes from this text proliferated, affecting the developing genre of children's literature and the minstrel and variety stages. *Uncle Tom's Cabin* plays became a fixture in the United States, Britain, and Europe. Hundreds of special companies, Tommers, toured for over fifty years. In these "Tom Shows," white actors played the principal roles. Topsy quickly became a main character in the plays. What we need to remember is that the role of Topsy was developed as a blackface role for and by white women; Topsy was not a wench role for men to play.

Stowe's book is intensely theatrical, its melodramatic immediacy marking it as a central text in popular culture's transition to visual mediums. U.S. minstrel stage conventions influenced Stowe's fiction as much as her fiction would then influence the popular stage.[3] The incredible success of Stowe's novel was immediately followed by a myriad of popular stage versions. The decades-long phenomena of *Uncle Tom's Cabin* plays glutenized the tradition of plantation nostalgia, of take-me-backs and plantation fiction. George Aiken's dramatization of Stowe's novel was the longest-running and the most popular stage version. This was a family business, as were most of the Tom companies that followed. Aiken wrote the play in 1852 for the Howard family—his cousin Caroline Howard, her husband, George Cunnabell Howard, and their small daughter, Cordelia—who ran a small stock company with which Aiken worked and traveled.[4] The institution of the traveling Uncle Tom's Cabin shows across the United States was a family affair, either literally or scripted, and Topsy was played by the mother figure of the troupe.

The term "pickaninny" comes from picayune, a coin of small value that circulated in the United States during the nineteenth century. The derivation of the term "pickaninny" signals the interchangeability between the black child bodies and the small bits of money required for their acquisition. Not always purchased but often "made" on the plantation, they embodied the very public marketplace politics of sexualized subjection at the heart of the domestic sphere. Slave children were living currency. The pickaninny was a key symbol of the conflation of sex and commerce, which defined the peculiar institution.

On the plantation, the domestic sphere of the home was fused with large-scale commercial concern. As Hortense Spillers eloquently observes, the private (home) and the public (marketplace) were "useless distinction[s]":

> Deeply embedded . . . in the heart of social arrangements, the "peculiar institution" elaborated "home and marketplace" as a useless distinction since, at any moment, and certainly 1850—the year of the Fugitive—the slave was as much property of the collusive state as he or she was the personal property of the slaveholder. We could say that slavery was, at once, the most public private institution *and* the ground for the institution's most terrifying intimacies,

because fathers *could* and *did* sell their sons and daughters, under the allowance of *law* and the flag of a new nation, "conceived in liberty," and all the rest of it.[5]

U.S. plantation slavery disrupted communities and severed family ties at the same time as it staged itself as a family romance. But in this system of "terrifying intimacies," master and slave relationships were figured as those of parent and child, as well as owner and saleable property.[6] "The Children must be particularly attended to," a plantation record reads, "for rearing them is not only a duty, but also the most profitable part of plantation business."[7] The children, as the most private and miraculous expressions of family life, were the products of the most cruelly public of marketplace rituals. The figure of the pickaninny symbolizes the convergence of the domestic and the commercial at the heart of the American racial drama.

Perhaps the most apt imprint of the "terrifying conflation of sex and commerce," the slave plantation, and the intimate histories it contains sat for years on the back of the American five-cent piece, the modern picayune. Thomas Jefferson's massive slave plantation, Monticello, is engraved on the back of every nickel, this small bit of money that still circulates through millions of daily monetary exchanges. Jefferson himself designed Monticello and worked on it for over fifty years. It is celebrated as a singular feat of architectural genius and serves as a symbol of colonial U.S. nation building—practical, utilitarian, sensible, democratic. Jefferson's engineering and aesthetic innovations are said to "produce domestic democracy"; for instance, an architectural historian of Monticello claims that Jefferson's "simple stairway . . . demands the meeting of those who are equal before the law be conducted on an egalitarian surface, level ground."[8] His claim, that the architecture demands a leveling of social hierarchy, is an obscenely absurd one, considering that it was slaves who staffed the household. Like the dumbwaiters and basement kitchen, the stairwells were designed for the discreet passage of unpaid labor. Monticello's ingenuity for hiding the slaves who lived within it is literally part of the blueprint of American architectural history. Notable also is Jefferson's bedchamber, fitted with a closed alcove for the bed itself, and with a stairwell leading to it. Sally Hemings moved through this "domestic democracy," as her mother had moved through a plantation house before her (she and her children belonged to Jefferson's father-in-law). Their presence leaves ghostlike imprints on the historical record, remaining profoundly unrecognized.

I think it useful to include Jefferson's plantation compound in relation to other racialized regimes, such as the camp, the prison, and the reservation.

Including the "southern household" as a public space whose business was a traffic in "bare life" expands and decentralizes our concept of what constitutes "exemplary places of modern biopolitics."[9] Love was work in this model site of domestic democracy, and bodies for sale were created there, in its most private alcoves.

Why, then, do we see such strange events as a summer-long plantation re-creation called Black America, staged over the summer of 1894 in a Brooklyn city park? Decades after the Civil War, at the turn of the century, the fictive plantation was the setting for inner-city spectacles. The cakewalk in particular was a featured entertainment in plantation reenactments across the nation. This dance was staged as an authentic slave dance, the dance's "origins" as the happy days of servitude, the natural effulgence of the slaves, readily demonstrated for their master's enjoyment. The dance was also formally acknowledged as a national "pastime," acting as the folk expression of a nation. Black dancers competed in huge cakewalk jubilees in New York City's Madison Square Garden, with black sporting celebrities such as Jack Johnson officiating at the proceedings.

Plantation reenactments were fallaciously "historical" re-creations in which "the stage and the political forum easily merged; theatre and politics extended each other's capacity to drain African American culture of . . . civil rights while mapping it onto an idealized display of racial supremacy that transported pastoral nostalgia into a violence-ridden present."[10] These re-creations staged an agrarian topos as the natural homeland for the "hewers of wood and drawers of water." These enactments were one way in which the plantation would return in popular cultural forms, reenvisioning slavery as a prelapsarian innocence rather than as a system that needed to be enforced by violence and coercion. Like the ethnic villages staged at fairs, like the World's Columbian Exposition in 1893, and like the newly designed museums, these restagings required an audience. Strolling through, as they did through the ethnic villages at various expositions, northern white audiences could simultaneously enjoy the imagined pastoral landscape of the South and distance themselves from the practice of slavery, while they denied their own complicity in the practices of segregation.

A Usable Past of Music and Dance in the New Negro Renaissance

Like the cakewalk, for black dancers, the Charleston dance of the 1920s also spoke of the physical memory of place and displacement. Charleston, South Carolina, was one of the first urban ports of call in the dislocation of African slaves to the American continent. Black people were a fundamental presence in the building of this urban center, as the city's geography was organized around the sale of slaves. Analyses of dance as a retention of African aesthetic practices may recognize the complexities of the cultural philosophies developed by various African tribes. But by reading these practices as ahistorical, such readings can easily miss the ways dances function as multisignifying forms of comment on the historical contingencies of forced and violent transportation, voluntary relocation, and the imbrication of black people and culture in the formative building of the nation's urban centers. The polyrhythms of dance embodied a sense of black being in time, a sense of oneself as existing simultaneously in several different timed and spatial zones. The tensions of movement—rural to urban, and transcontinental, both painful and pleasurable—are what the fragmented black body alternately hinges itself to and unhinges itself from.

Dance forms were encoded moments of historical memory, remembrances of historical shifts and their effect on African Americans' lived experiences. Certain steps from past dances were brought into new surroundings and there took on new meanings, at the same time as they referenced former moments. The search to describe and situate particular forms generates multiple tales of origin. The stories of origin are accompanying fictions, necessary for what they reveal about what the dances meant as narratives of African American cultural and social formation. The circle dance can be recognized as containing within it memories of the ring dance and for having the same linked bodies and low, shuffling feet as the ring shout, a devotional dance developed primarily in rural Georgia and South Carolina.[11] But this does not mean that it is the same dance. This dance was very much about geopolitical territory, a politics of claiming community. It was about the streets and city spaces and about the continual movement between "homes."

The New Negro movement of the 1920s was one of conscious self-defining. African Americans responded with various reassessments of their relationship to their dual "homelands": the African continent as well as the rural southern United States. Discourses of return, both literal and figurative, developed around these reassessments. The South or Africa (often the Africa within) became privileged sites of both literal and literary return. Discourses converged and diverged as to the appropriate strategies for going back/home, as well as to the potential meaning of these journeys. Going back meant voyaging to actual lands, but it also required flights back in time. To go home, to return to the self, involved chronological leaps into the past to claim lost and disregarded ancestral heritage. But in the search for an authentic usable past, black artists and writers cleaved to alternative understandings of origin that were often just as fictional as the ubiquitous and virulent racial schemas being drawn around them. Alternative sources for self-definition were an imperative, but a truly restorative return was impossible. This impossibility was denied, sometimes acknowledged, and often mourned with an urgent nostalgia. It also bred a complicated kind of liberty, for African Americans were free to invent themselves.

Literary efforts at representing the race were the fruit of fantastic voyages of discovery and return. African American artists rendered some of the most eloquent expressions of black life in the United States while traveling and living outside it. Hughes wrote "The Negro Speaks of Rivers" as a nineteen-year-old boy on the train to his father's home in Mexico and drafted poems for his collection *Weary Blues* while at sea aboard the ss *Malone*, traveling between New York and the west coast of Africa.[12] He wrote jazz-inflected verse while working as a waiter for Bricktop at the Grand Duc in Paris. Here he observed dancers immersed in the music being produced by the African American musicians working there; they too had brought the sound of home (or homelessness) with them. In 1927 and 1928, Claude McKay wrote his novels *Home to Harlem* and *Banjo* while in Marseilles, amongst the African and West Indian men working at the seaports there. Ten years later, Zora Neale Hurston wrote *Their Eyes Were Watching God* while doing fieldwork in Haiti. Their eloquent renderings were at times nostalgic but always the result of a change in perspective, the development of a modern view, which in turn was the result of purposeful travels. The modern view combined intense intimacy and unbrookable distance and required the ability to record what one saw or felt from above, below, inside, or outside. Modern black self-definition claimed these views, as well as territorial rights to various black diasporic proximities.

In this era of momentous migrations, African American cultural producers were looking for ways to construct a racial inheritance, a usable past. Many of the participants in the Harlem Renaissance movement self-consciously drew on romanticist concepts of the primitive in declaring their cultural legacies. These were familiar, ahistorical notions of the Negro's "psychological complexion," which he had "inherited from his primitive ancestors" and still maintained. Negroes were not a threat to civilization; rather they brought restorative properties to the modern world, an emotionalism, a "luxuriant and free imagination," as well as a close connection with nature. Negro art was great because it remained inspired by a primitive source. But artistic expressions needed to travel away from their primitive sources in order to, as Albert C. Barnes put it, "bea[r] comparison with the great art expressions of any race or civilization."[13] The fine arts of literature, poetry, painting, and sculpture were assigned as the appropriate forms through which African Americans could shape their cultural heritage as well as affirm their place in the civilized world.[14] Intellectuals such as Barnes stressed the spiritual proclivities of their people; carnal, fleshly, and profane manifestations of the primitive within had to be trained or at least contained. The fathers and midwives of the Harlem Renaissance trod anxiously when it came to the expressive arts. Popular developments in stagecraft, music, and dance were constantly contentious.

But not all black artists felt responsible for filtering the raw material of the folk through the refiner's sieve. Zora Neale Hurston, Claude McKay, and Langston Hughes, all in different ways, rejected with their work what they considered an elitist cultural politic. Any real look at black culture, their work acknowledged, had to celebrate collective music, song, dance, and dramaturgy.

Hurston and Hughes both had music, the popular stage, and drama on their minds. Hughes used jazz music and rhythms in his poetry and found both legitimate and variety black theater important sites of black expression. Hurston's involvement in expressive arts is less recognized. She did her first stint of travel at the age of twenty-four, working as a maid for the white actress "Mrs. M——."[15] In 1925 she penned the play *Color Struck*, a satire of the politics of southern racial segregation that follows a troupe of performers on the way to a cakewalking contest. She continued writing plays, and in 1927, as part of her fieldwork in Eatonville, Florida, Hurston directed a documentary film, capturing footage of such "folk" practices as children's games and a baptism. In 1939, after a disastrous collaboration on the play *Mule Bone* with Langston Hughes, Hurston worked briefly as a drama instructor at the North Carolina College for Negroes in Durham. Her attention to expressive forms continued. In 1942, living in Los Angeles and writing *Dust Tracks on the Road*, Hurston worked as a consultant for Paramount Pictures and spent time on the film set of the black-cast musical film *Cabin in the Sky*, where she met and befriended Ethel Waters.[16] The young choreographer and anthropologist Katherine Dunham choreographed for and performed with her dance troupe in this film.

In the United States during the 1920s, forms of romantic nationalism constructed fantasies of a black "folk," sprung from the soil of the South. This notion of a timeless people in the midst of the modern took on crucial importance during the 1930s following the sudden and devastating failure of the U.S. economy in 1929. Black folkways soothed white anxieties; despite the failure of the capitalist system, the United States had a caste to represent a preindustrial innocence, immune to the corrupting seductions of commercialism. In the 1920s, black chorus women of the stage musicals embodied the pleasurable mobilities of the modern age: the primitive infusing the modern with its resilience. But by the 1930s, they were instead associated with the corrupting seduction and betrayal of capitalism.

After the crash of New York's Stock Exchange of 1929 (but before the Harlem "Riot" in 1935), Sterling Brown wrote his most stinging indictments of the modern age. "Nineveh, Tyre / Babylon / Not much lef' / of either one," he wrote in "Memphis Blues." "All dese cities / Ashes and rust / De win' sing sperrichals / Through their dust." Cities like Memphis on the Nile were destroyed "in many ways"; natural disaster was God's wrath visited on the hordes of sinners.[17] In poems like "Tin Roof Blues," the poet/singer states his intent to leave the "do-dirty city," where black people have become a "gang of dicties an' de rest wants to get that way." He yearns for a return to the South, where "the shingles covers folks mo' my kind."[18] Blues singers like Ma Rainey were figures who belonged to the South, who spoke to and for the ethos of her people.[19]

Brown's poems recognize the Southland as no longer a preindustrial utopia and mourn its dissolution. Racial hegira was no longer possible or desirable, as the mudsills of rural poverty and racial oppression threatened slow death and suffocation. "Still it's my home sweet home," the singer/poet mourns in "Cabaret."[20] In 1927 disaster struck on the Mississippi River when a levee broke, flooding the lands below it. Quickly, in sermons, blues songs, and in Brown's poems, the resulting flood took on religious, poetic, and political weight. The flood was both nature's revenge and the concrete effect of industrializing America's neglectful policy toward its black population. The flooding of Mississippi in 1927 became a trope of Old Testament–style revenge for the self-serving materialism of civilization.

A troupe of light-skinned chorus girls wind through Brown's poem "Cabaret (1927, Black & Tan Chicago)," symbols of the seductive, corrupting influence of modernity. They are symptoms of the sins of civilization, which shall make the cities fall, as did the citadels of ancient times. The cabaret is a metaphorical space, recalling Babylon, in whose court the "rich, flashy, puffy-faced / Hebrew and Anglo Saxon . . . overlords . . . sprawl here with their glittering darlings." The light skin of the chorus girls, the "Creole Beauties from New Orleans," is a reproach of sex and commerce, their beauty the result of lust and artifice.

The chorus sways in.
The "Creole Beauties from New Orleans"
Their creamy skin flushing rose warm,
Oh, le bal des belles quarterounes!
Their shapely bodies naked save
For tattered pink silk bodices, short velvet tights,
And shining silver-buckled boots;
Red bandanas on their sleek and close-clipped hair;
To bring to mind (aided by the bottles under the tables)
Life upon the river—

Along with bootlegged liquor, the cabaret offers up the sale of black cultural memory, corrupted in the form of half-naked women with "sleek and close-clipped hair." These women are not rooted in the rural South but rather are the products of a rootless, roaming transurban condition. They come "by way of Atlanta, Louisville, Washington, Yonkers / With stop-overs they've used all their lives." The chorus line is juxtaposed with a chain gang in Arkansas, beleaguered figures of black manhood, *"poor half-naked fools, tagged with identification numbers / worn out upon the levees / And carted back to the serfdom / they may never leave again."* But the poem does not use the analogy to shed light on the sexual servitude suffered by so many young black women or to beg pity for their plight. Rather it pathologizes them, directly situating them as willful and uncaring urban courtiers against a poor, rural black folk. The "too / proud high-stepping beauties" bring no relief to "the black folk" who *"huddle, mute, uncomprehending,"* sheltered at the mouth of the Mississippi River as the flood line recedes. Their dancing forms in fact seem to evoke the demise of their brethren as "the chorus leaps into weird posturings . . . seductive bodies weaving / Bending, writhing, turning." The chorus women embody the modern condition as an illness of spirit and a cultural death. The poet's heart cries out for "MUDDY WATER"; he wishes to be freed from the city's limits, to be down in the mud, and to sacrifice himself with his dying brethren. *"Down in the valleys / The stench of drying mud / Is a bitter reminder of death."*

Brown's literary use of the female chorus line was a dramatization of the class anxieties regularly displaced onto the figures of female chorus-line dancers in films and literature produced after the stock market crash. Sterling Brown's vividly staged cabaret resembles the court of the king of Babylon in both the play and the film versions of Marc Connolly's *Green Pastures.* "Nobody in the world can squirm like those Babylon Gals!" the king of Babylon cries, as three dancing women enter his court. One, clad in a grass skirt, executes the same dance routine as "The Girl from Los Angeles" in Micheaux's film of that year. White producers had staged the play in 1930; the folk/biblical tale ran to rave reviews for five years before Hollywood made the film. As the stage reviewer for *Opportunity*, Brown most likely went to see the staged version when it first came out in 1930 before he crafted his apocryphal verse. In his review, Brown praised the play, calling it "movingly true to folk life."[21] Cultural workers, as those in the WPA projects of the 1930s, were intent on restoring a heartland to black culture, to the staging of southern black folkways. Such sentiment made plays like *Green Pastures* incredibly popular, and Hollywood's film version was also a hit when it came out in 1936.[22]

Despite the ways they were figured as symbols of urban decadence, the sleek-haired girls of the chorus line remained public figures of black mobility, "by way of Atlanta, Louisville, Washington, Yonkers / With stop-overs they've used all their lives." Many black performers were happy to get out of the states, and many established themselves in Europe, where they could be loved by their U.S. constituents from afar. They provided the black world a language of the resilient modern body constituted betwixt and between nation-states and their colonial outposts.

NOTES

1. J. Brown, *Babylon Girls*.

2. Stowe, *Uncle Tom's Cabin*, 204.

3. According to W. T. Lhamon, "Stowe's relation to the minstrel show was an intervention that went both ways. . . . She sluiced into abolitionist tableaus some of the power of minstrel conventions. . . . Minstrel material profoundly shaped her writing; and her writing, in turn, bequeathed figures to the working-class stage." See Lhamon, *Raising Cain*, 97.

4. After successfully staging a version of his show at the small theater they managed in Troy, New York, the show opened in 1852 at the National Theatre in New York City. Aiken played George Harris, George Howard played St. Clare, their small daughter, Cordelia, played Eva, and Caroline played Topsy. See Birdoff, *World's Greatest Hit*, 49.

5. Spillers, "Changing the Letter," 545.

6. Stampp, *Peculiar Institution*, 250.

7. Quoted in W. King, *Stolen Childhood*, 3.

8. McLaughlin, *Jefferson and Monticello*, 7.

9. Agamben, *Homo Sacer*, 4.

10. Sundquist, *To Wake the Nations*, 287.

11. Emery, *Black Dance*, 132–33, 164–71.

12. Rampersad, *Life of Langston Hughes*, 71; Lewis, *When Harlem Was in Vogue*, 81, 85.

13. Barnes, "Negro Art and America," 21.

14. Floyd, *Black Music in the Harlem Renaissance*.

15. Chapter 8 of her autobiography, *Dust Tracks on a Road*, is entitled "Backstage and the Railroad." See Zora Neale Hurston, *Hurston: Folklore, Memoirs, and Other Writings*, 635–65.

16. See "Chronology" in Hurston, *Hurston: Folklore, Memoirs and Other Writings*, and Hurston, *Dust Tracks on the Road.*

17. Sterling Brown, "Memphis Blues," in his *Southern Road*, 59.

18. Sterling Brown, "Tin Roof Blues," in his *Southern Road*, 105.

19. Sterling Brown, "Ma Rainey," in his *Southern Road*, 62.

20. Sterling Brown, "Cabaret (1927, Black & Tan Chicago)," in his *Southern Road*, 117. All further quotations from "Cabaret" are from *Southern Road*, 115–18.

21. The January 1931 review is collected in S. Brown, *Negro Poetry and Drama*, 119–20.

22. Rex Ingram played "De Lawd" and Ida Forsyne made a cameo appearance as Mrs. Noah.

SUGGESTIONS FOR FURTHER READING

Batiste, Stephanie Leigh. *Darkening Mirrors: Imperial Representation in Depression-Era African American Performance.* Durham, N.C.: Duke University Press, 2011.

Colbert, Soyica. *The African American Theatrical Body: Reception, Performance and the Stage.* Cambridge: Cambridge University Press, 2011.

Munoz, Jose. *Disidentifications: Queers of Color and the Performance of Politics.* Minneapolis: University of Minnesota Press, 1999.

Phelan, Peggy. *Unmarked: The Politics of Performance.* London: Routledge, 1993.

Roach, Joseph. *Cities of the Dead: Circum-Atlantic Performance.* New York: Columbia University Press, 1996.

Taylor, Diana. *The Archive and the Repertoire: Performing Cultural Memory in the Americas.* Durham, N.C.: Duke University Press, 2003.

COLEMAN HUTCHISON

Book History

In recent years book history has garnered a great deal of attention both within and without the academy. As a particularly "hot" or "sexy" field of inquiry, it has also garnered a number of alternative monikers: *histoire du livre*, the history of the book, the history of books, the sociology of texts, print culture studies, and textual studies, among others. One leading light in the field, David Scott Kastan, prefers a more descriptive title: "the new boredom." The fact that there is still an ongoing debate about what to call the damn thing speaks volumes about its often-contentious status as both an emergent discipline and a multi- and interdisciplinary endeavor. Book history sits—or, better, happens—at the interstices of several adjacent disciplines, including literary studies, history, bibliography, anthropology, sociology, journalism, communication, business and economic history, and library and information sciences. As a result, it draws on an impossibly diverse set of methodological tools, including those of analytical bibliography, textual criticism, printing history, and new media studies, to name only the most obvious. Such diversity led Robert Darnton to argue, in his field-defining 1982 essay "What Is the History of Books?," that book history might be fairly characterized as "interdisciplinarity run riot."[1]

So what, then, *is* "book history"? As luck would have it, both parts of the term are misnomers. Book history is by no means limited to the study of printed books, since book historians also discuss manuscripts, newspapers, periodicals, ephemera, and, increasingly, digital media. Moreover, many book historians want to imagine the future of human communication, not just illuminate its past. Nonetheless, as the editors of the discipline's flagship, titular journal note, "book history" is the "least unsatisfactory name for this scholarly frontier."[2]

With that faint praise in place, let's define the term for the purposes of this essay. At base, book history is concerned with both the materiality of texts and the material conditions by which those texts are produced, disseminated, and consumed. Its emphasis is on processes of communication usually but not always mediated by print—thus the ubiquitous term of art, "print culture." Book history is invested in all aspects and in every phase of the "life cycle" of a text: from author to agent, manuscript to page proof, cover design to marketing plan, hardcover to download, foreign edition to pirated copy, book tour to reading group. It is also open to all forms of print culture, be they high, low, polite, popular, or somewhere in between.

Although book historians have generally resisted monolithic or programmatic models, there is broad agreement that books and print culture can be best understood in terms of a "communications circuit," one that intersects a number of social, cultural, economic, and political matrices, and does so both in time and across space.[3] The emphasis, then, is on the role that print culture had, has, and will have in the lives of people and society writ large. In this regard, book history is profoundly invested in the social. Whether as function of what Jerome McGann calls the "socialization of texts" or what D. F. McKenzie has dubbed the "sociology of texts," book history argues that texts are always in and of the world.[4]

In making that argument, book historians tend to focus on specific parts of the communications circuit. Take, for example, *Uncle Tom's Cabin*. One book historian might examine the textual differences between its serial and book publications; another might study southern responses to Stowe; still another might focus on the novel's republication in foreign markets or its many stage adaptations. Book history promises to draw such disparate contributions into a more coherent critical conversation through its acknowledgment of the dynamism and totality of a given text's life cycle or circuit. Put simply, we can't hope to understand a novel like *Uncle Tom's Cabin* unless we reckon the complex interplay of *all* its social agents: author, editor, publisher, illustrator, designer, printer, supplier, distributor, bookseller, and reader. This means that the topics addressed in book historical scholarship are as varied as the names used to describe the field. A given collection of book historical essays might include pieces on author-agent relationships, publishing agreements, printing house practices, book design and manufacture, copyright and intellectual property, distribution and sales, and reader response and reviews. Needless to say, such a collection could also easily span five hundred years and several continents.

Despite its characteristic and steadfast diffuseness, book history does espouse several articles of faith: First, that material texts matter—that is, that the physical features of a given text influence the ways it is interpreted and received in a given historical context. Second, that texts suggest material histories—that is, that all texts are the product of historicizable processes of production and consumption. Third, that books (and indeed all forms of print culture) are profoundly collaborative endeavors that involve multiple agents working with diverse interests and agendas. Finally, that readers and reading are dynamic and fundamental parts of any communications circuit.

Thus, book history is committed to the proposition that, in the words of David D. Hall, "the better we understand the production and consumption of books, the closer we come to a social history of culture."[5] Put another way, at stake here is the entire history of human communication and meaning making. Given the end of the culture and theory wars, an increasingly corporate academy (with its demands for more efficient, interdisciplinary inquiry), and the ongoing "information revolution," is it any wonder that book history has emerged over the past two decades as an uncommon intellectual force?

Of course the study of print culture has a much longer history, dating to at least the Renaissance and the work of scholars, librarians, collectors, and printers. But book history as currently practiced took root in mid-twentieth-century Europe, following the publication of *L'apparition du livre* (1958) by the French *Annales* school historians Lucien Febvre and Henri-Jean Martin. At the same time, scholars in Britain and Germany were producing innovative work on printing history and reception studies, respectively. By the late 1970s—following the publication of an English translation of Febvre and Martin's opus, *The Coming of the Book: The Impact of Printing, 1450–1800* (1976)—these separate strands were beginning to rise and converge. The year 1979 proved something of an *annus mirabilis* for book history, with the publication of major studies by Elizabeth Eisenstein (*The Printing Press as an Agent of Change*) and Robert Darnton (*The Business of Enlightenment*).

In the 1980s, the "New Bibliography" (as embodied by R. B. McKerrow, W. W. Greg, and Fredson Bowers) also came under significant fire. Jerome McGann argued vociferously for new forms of textual and editorial theory, and D. F. McKenzie used his 1985 Panizzi Lectures at the British Library to expand both the purview of bibliography and definitions of "the text" (see his *Bibliography and the Sociology of Texts*). Meanwhile, Roger Chartier's research on a number of bookish topics—especially circulation, authorship, and appropriation—meshed well with that of theorists like Benedict Anderson, who continued to tout the relations between print and social cohesion. By the early 1990s, book history was booming: literary critics were talking more and more about the "materiality of the text," a number of national histories of the book were well under way, and scholars in various disciplines were beginning to consider innovations like the CD-ROM, hypertext, and digital edition. Book history even had its very own international scholarly organization, the Society for the History of Authorship, Reading, and Publishing (SHARP).

As this brief overview suggests, book history's origins had a strongly Eurocentric cast and character, but Americanists quickly took up its methodologies and lines of inquiry. Colonial New England was a particularly rich field for early American book historians like David D. Hall and Hugh Amory. In the early national period, Cathy Davidson's research on the rise of the novel in America (*Revolution and the Word* [1986]) and Michael Warner's Habermasian study of the print public sphere (*Letters of the Republic* [1990]) proved hugely influential. In turn, scholars working in the later nineteenth and twentieth centuries drew on a number of extant sources—especially William Charvat's pioneering research on the profession of authorship and Janice Radway's studies of popular readership—to challenge long-held assumptions about the production and consumption of American texts.

By far the most important institutional setting for work on the history of the book in America was—and continues to be—the American Antiquarian Society (AAS) in Worcester, Massachusetts. In 1983 the AAS founded a program called the History of the Book in American Culture, which has since hosted a number of major conferences, summer seminars, and the annual James Russell Wiggins Lecture. Most urgently, the program also oversaw the publication of the collaborative, five-volume *A History of the Book in America* (2000–10), which covers more than four hundred years and includes contributions from several dozen distinguished scholars.

One underrepresented topic in those volumes, and indeed in book history more generally, is the southern United States. Put simply, the print culture of the South remains frustratingly at the margins of American book history. More to the point, southern studies seems largely uninterested in book history per se. There are, perhaps, good reasons for such marginality and lack of interest. First, American book history is still a relatively new discipline; as with all new disciplines, its development has been uneven and uncoordinated. Second, the lack of commerce between southern studies and book history is not singular. As Leon Jackson has recently argued, African American studies and book history show a similar "failure to communicate."[6] Given that African American studies is a crucial disciplinary partner to southern studies, such failures may well be related. Third, print culture tends to be promiscuous. No matter where or how they are produced, texts often circulate beyond lines of region and nation. Thus, regional and national interpretive frames tend to distort the complexity of textual production and consumption; as a result, book historians largely resist such geographical principles.[7] Finally, there is a problem of definition: What *is* southern print culture? If defined strictly as texts produced in the U.S. South, then one might argue (a bit disingenuously) that there isn't enough of the stuff to justify extensive study.

In his inaugural James Russell Wiggins Lecture at the AAS, David D. Hall voiced an important theoretical caution: "A history of the book in America is not a history of *American* books. Quite the contrary. Ours was persistently a provincial culture dependent for its modes on a distant cosmopolitan center, be it London or some other central place."[8] Southern studies would do well to translate and then heed Hall's caution. A history of the book in the U.S. South need not be a history of southern books, especially in light of the rather vexed history of southern publishing industries. While southern book history might continue to emphasize familiar "southern writers"—many of whom, let's be clear, were published in the North—it might also take up novel topics, including the reception of foreign works in the South, the relations between religious and lay publishers, interracial reading communities, and independent bookstores, among many other topics. Suffice it to say, there are ample needs and opportunities in the history of the southern book.

A case study will help us to gauge some of those needs and opportunities; it will also highlight the sorts of questions that book history might ask of southern texts. Rather than take up a familiar or well-criticized text, I want to consider an obscure early southern novel, Nathaniel Beverley Tucker's *The Partisan Leader; A Tale of the Future*. As I have argued elsewhere, Tucker's novel is among the most confounding literary curios of the nineteenth century. Published in 1836, *The Partisan Leader* offers a history of the future, one in which Virginia struggles to free itself of the burden of federal occupation and oppression. I say "history" because Tucker insists that he is offering a historical account of 1848–49.

In Tucker's 1848, the tyrannical Martin Van Buren has just secured a fourth term as president of the United States. In response to his draconian rule, the lower southern states have seceded from the Union and formed a league of independent states—a hugely prosperous league of independent states due to a commercial treaty with England. Poor Virginia has been kept from joining its seceding "sister states" by Van Buren's "henchmen," and the Commonwealth is embroiled in brutal guerrilla conflict with federal troops. Against this backdrop, Tucker tells the tortured tale of the Trevor family, an august and noble clan of Virginians whose allegiances are spread thin among nation, region, and state. By the end of the bewildering narrative, the Trevor family is in fact a house divided, with one of its sons, Owen, fighting steadfastly for Van Buren's henchmen, and another, Douglas, fighting for

Virginian independence. The latter is a disgraced U.S. Army officer who, emboldened by the encouragement of his uncle, Bernard Trevor, and the mysterious separatist leader "B——," becomes the titular hero of the novel, "The Partisan Leader."

Along the way, the novel's thin plot provides a backdrop for Tucker's digressions on a number of political issues, including a national banking system, free trade, and states' rights constitutionalism. Tellingly, it is the tariff, not slavery, that leads to the secession of the southern states and the birth of a confederacy. This is not to say that Tucker avoids the issue of slavery; far from it, in fact. The novel makes a number of direct defenses of the peculiar institution and touts the steadfast loyalty of southern slaves.[9]

The novel was written in February, March, and April 1836 and rushed to print that summer in the dim hopes of influencing the outcome of the presidential election. Initially Senator William C. Preston of South Carolina arranged a clandestine publication with A. S. Johnston, proprietor of the *Columbia Telescope*, but Tucker was impatient for its publication and went instead went with Duff Green, a political ally and editor in Washington, D.C. By September of that year, 1,900 copies of the two-volume novel were in print. Despite the tight turnaround, Tucker hoped that the novel would circulate both nationally and internationally, helping readers throughout the United States and England to see the folly of supporting Van Buren. Much to Tucker's chagrin, Martin Van Buren was elected the eighth president of the United States just a few weeks after *The Partisan Leader* hit the streets.

Book historians would take great interest in the story of how this novel came to print. First, we can see in Tucker's allegiance with Preston and Green the shadowy relations between politics and prose. That both a sitting U.S. senator and a onetime member of Andrew Jackson's "Kitchen Cabinet" would offer to help get the novel published speaks to the ways that patronage and political power intersect worlds of print. Similarly, book historians might be interested in Tucker's decision to bypass a southern publisher in favor of a more efficient northern one. Finally, the author's desire to have the book read both throughout the country and across the Atlantic speaks once again to the promiscuity of print culture. As is often the case, this text moved fluidly across lines of region and nation, and in doing so called into question the rigidity of those lines.

Another aspect of *The Partisan Leader* worthy of book historical attention is its materiality, in particular its paratextual features (to crib a term from Gérard Genette). For instance, the novel's title page reveals a great deal about both its politics and its aims: "THE/PARTISAN LEADER; / A TALE OF THE FUTURE./ BY / EDWARD WILLIAM SIDNEY. / "SIC SEMPER TYRANNIS." / The Motto of Virginia. / "PARS FUI.". . . . .Virgil. / IN TWO VOLUMES. / VOL. I. / PRINTED/FOR THE PUBLISHERS, BY JAMES CAXTON. / 1856." This bibliographical information is, of course, fabulated. In an attempt to obscure the origins of the novel—and no doubt to escape responsibility for its radical politics—Tucker assumes the pseudonym "Sidney," a likely nod to the British poet and author of the *Old Arcadia*. Similarly, printer Green becomes "Caxton," seemingly a reference to William Caxton, the father of the English press and book trades. The two Latin epigraphs, "Thus always to tyrants" and "Play a part," respectively, acknowledge the ambitious cultural work that the novel undertakes. But most remarkable is the novel's publication date, "1856." Tucker violates convention and postdates *The Partisan Leader* by some twenty years.

The book's publication information is complemented by a dedicatory epistle, which employs the rhetoric of historicity and retrospection. "E.W.S." speaks of his "admiration of the gallant people, whose struggle for freedom [he] witnessed and partook," suggesting both that the fictional author was present for the events being described and that those events are long since passed. He goes on to describe a future present in which Virginia "honors with high places in her councils . . . the names of many with whom [he] once stood, shoulder to shoulder, in the eye of danger. . . . The record of their praise, and the reward of their glorious deeds, is on the page of history."[10] This remarkable claim suggests that in 1856 Virginia has not only "achieved her independence; lifted the soiled banner of her sovereignty from the dust" but also set up a government and begun writing histories of its genesis.[11] Tucker is insistent about the veracity of the tale he is telling; E.W.S. feels keenly a "duty to testify of what [he has] witnessed." Lest one miss the point, E.W.S. even appends a postscript to his dedication: "P.S. My date reminds me that this is the anniversary of that glorious day, on which Virginia first declared herself an independent State. May its auspicious return ever find you FREE, HAPPY, and GLORIOUS!"[12]

Book history's emphasis on the materiality of the text is occasionally derided as making too much of too little, of privileging minute or seemingly insignificant textual details such as title pages or dedications. In this case, however, Tucker's prefatory materials are crucial elements of the novel. (Indeed, it might not be too much to suggest that Tucker spent more time on his opening pages than he did the remainder of the novel, which is hampered by several inept shifts in narrative perspective and a confusing chronology.)

For instance, Tucker and Green's pseudonyms remind us how high the stakes could be for authorship and publication during this period. More to the point, the novel's prefatory paratexts work stubbornly to root the novel in time—1856 to be exact. There is little indication of an outside to the novel; its subtitle, "A Tale of the Future," offers the only winking acknowledgment of its artifice. As a result, these paratexts condition readerly responses to the novel's hybrid genre.

The Partisan Leader is less a prophecy than an odd melding of speculative, dystopian, and alternate-historical fiction. Above all else, Tucker's novel was aimed at influencing contemporary opinion and events in order to avert the future he projects. While some critics have read the novel as a resolutely occasional text—a strident campaign document and nothing more—such an interpretation leaves open the question, Why did Tucker use the novel form to make his partisan case? In contrast, book historians would likely focus on *The Partisan Leader*'s genre(s) and form, locating it in a field of cultural production and in relation to other works of political persuasion from the early national period.

Were they to take such a tack, book historians might also account for the novel's reception, which was exceedingly complex. Tucker intentionally left his novel unfinished, wanting to gauge public interest before continuing the story of Douglas Trevor. Yet additional parts of Tucker's "history" were never published, since there was little to no public interest in the first two volumes. (The *Southern Literary Messenger* did offer a long, laudatory review in its January 1837 issue; then again, Tucker was a close associate of the review's author, Abel P. Upshur, and publisher, Thomas W. White.) But reception takes place over time. Two Civil War–era republications of the novel suggest that *The Partisan Leader* found eager audiences long after its initial publication and the death of its author.

Perhaps predictably, the novel was reprinted during the Civil War in the South as *The Partisan Leader: A Novel, and an Apocalypse of the Origin and Struggles of the Southern Confederacy* (Richmond: West and Johnston, 1862). As its subtitle suggests, this Confederate edition emphasizes Tucker's purported powers of prophecy. Tucker's latter-day editor, the Reverend Thomas A. Ware, calls the novel a "great prophetic story, whose thrilling events have been essentially fulfilled." Ware also sees in the republication of the novel an opportunity "to illustrate the necessity of our position, to vindicate the justice of our cause, and to intensify Southern patriotism."[13] In making Tucker's "Tale of the Future" available to the inhabitants of that future, Ware hopes to shore up nationalist feeling and allow Confederate readers to locate their struggles within a historical context.

But West and Johnston's 1862 edition was not the first wartime reprinting of Tucker's novel. In 1861 Rudd and Carleton published a northern edition, which publically identified "Beverley Tucker of Virginia" as its author. Retitled *A Key to the Disunion Conspiracy*, the edition frames the novel not as prophecy or "Apocalypse" but as proof positive that the South had long been gunning for civil war. The edition opens with an "Explanatory Introduction": "The reader will learn from the following pages that the fratricidal contest into which our country has been led is not a thing of chance, but of deliberate design, and that it has been gradually preparing for almost thirty years." The anonymous editor sees the "dark plotters of South Carolina and Virginia" at every stop on the road to disunion, from the annexation of Texas to the repeal of the Missouri Compromise and the "crowning derelictions and treason of the Buchanan administration." Tucker's novel is, the northern editor avers, something of a how-to guide for secessionists: "Indeed, the Jeff. Davises, Yanceys, Pryors, Rhetts, Letchers, etc., seem to have done little else than servilely to follow out the programme sketched for them in this remarkable book." As such, the publishers promise a "Fac-Simile" of the 1836 edition; however, they also take care to italicize those portions of Tucker's original that seem suggestive of a vast southern conspiracy.[14]

247

These warring editions capture the competing cultures of print that distinguished the United and the Confederate States of America. In doing so, they also underscore the uses of print culture in times of conflict and the relations between literature and nationalism. Finally, these two editions speak profoundly to how different interpretative communities might regard and respond to the same text. As C. Hugh Holman notes, "It is, in a sense, a tribute to the accuracy with which Tucker expressed the issues of the antebellum political struggle that both sides should see his arguments as contributing to the righteousness of their causes."[15] Indeed, both editions sold reasonably well during the war.

Of course the novel's reception did not end with the cessation of Civil War hostilities. Following its first two republications, Vernon Parrington devoted a remarkable five-plus pages to *The Partisan Leader* in the second volume of his *Main Currents in American Thought* (1927). The novel was then republished by Knopf in 1933 as part of Bernard DeVoto's Americana Deserta series, with an introduction by colonial American historian Carl Bridenbaugh. The inclusion of *The Partisan Leader* in DeVoto's series put Tucker in heady company: Americana Deserta also reprinted James Fenimore Cooper's *The American Democrat* and Herman Melville's *Pierre; or The Ambiguities*.

More than thirty years later, in 1968, the Gregg Press produced yet another edition of this novel, this time as part of its American Novels of Muckraking,

Propaganda, and Social Protest series. Now Tucker was keeping company with Rebecca Harding Davis, Albion W. Tourgée, Charles W. Chesnutt, and Upton Sinclair. As these things go, a scholarly edition of the novel followed shortly thereafter. C. Hugh Holman's 1971 Southern Literary Classics edition was based, ironically enough, on the 1861 Rudd and Carleton text.

And this is to say nothing of non- or extra-print editions of the novel. In 1978 an original copy of the 1836 edition was photoduplicated and made available via microfilm (as part of the Wright American Fiction series). Another copy appeared online in 2000 as part of the University of Virginia's Early American Fiction Database. Finally, the 1862 Confederate version of the novel has been available since 1999 via the University of North Carolina's Documenting the American South project.

Book historians would find much of interest in the publication history I have just limned. Again, if book history concerns itself with the materiality of texts and the material conditions by which those texts are produced, disseminated, and consumed, then *The Partisan Leader* is a particularly compelling piece of print culture. The complexity of its 175-year life cycle and its various editions and material forms would allow book historians to engage a wealth of topics related to authorship, reading, and publishing. As the novel moves in and out of literary canons, among regions, and across media, it offers us an uncommon opportunity to see the social life of a print object, how it shapes and is shaped by various cultural, economic, and political realities.

Yet, despite the promise of such a case study, we lack a proper history of this strange book. *The Partisan Leader* remains a woefully understudied text in southern studies and a more or less complete absence in American book history. I read this as indicative of the ways the two fields have to date talked past each other. The time is ripe for southern studies to take up the tools of book history in earnest. Although major southern figures like Edgar Allan Poe, William Faulkner, Flannery O'Connor, and Eudora Welty have received book historical treatment, there remains much work to be done on southern print cultures. Fortunately, southernists may not be alone in these efforts. American book historians are increasingly turning their attention south. (For example, in 2010 the AAS hosted a summer seminar led by Jeannine DeLombard and Lloyd Pratt called "The Global American South and Early American Print Culture.") Call it what you will, the history of the southern book could be a key part of both "the New Southern Studies" and "the new boredom" in the years to come.

NOTES

1. Darnton, *Case for Books*, 179.
2. Greenspan and Rose, "Introduction to *Book History*," ix.
3. Darnton, *Case for Books*, 179–80.
4. See McGann, *Textual Condition*, 69–87; McKenzie, *Bibliography*, 13–17.
5. D. D. Hall, *Cultures of Print*, 1.
6. Jackson, "Talking Book," 252.
7. See D. D. Hall, *Cultures of Print*, 29.
8. Ibid., 27.
9. See Hutchison, *Apples and Ashes*, esp. 58–62 and 66–67.
10. N. B. Tucker, *Partisan Leader* (1856 [1836]), 1:iii, iv.
11. Ibid., 2:201.
12. Ibid., 1:v.
13. N. B. Tucker, *Partisan Leader* (1862), vii, viii.
14. N. B. Tucker, *Key to the Disunion Conspiracy*, i, iii, vi, iv, ix.
15. Holman, introduction, xx.

SUGGESTIONS FOR FURTHER READING

Casper, Scott E., Joanne D. Chaison, and Jeffrey D. Groves, eds. *Perspectives on American Book History: Artifacts and Commentary*. Amherst: University of Massachusetts Press, 2002.

Fink, Steven, and Susan S. Williams, eds. *Reciprocal Influences: Literary Production, Distribution, and Consumption in America*. Columbus: Ohio State University Press, 1999.

Finkelstein, David, and Alistair McCleery, eds. *The Book History Reader*. 2nd ed. New York: Routledge, 2006.

Gruesz, Kirsten Silva. *Ambassadors of Culture: The Transamerican Origins of Latino Writing*. Princeton, N.J.: Princeton University Press, 2002.

Hall, David D., ed. *A History of the Book in America*. 5 vols. Chapel Hill: University of North Carolina Press, 2010.

McHenry, Elizabeth. *Forgotten Readers: Recovering the Lost History of African-American Literary Societies*. Durham, N.C.: Duke University Press, 2002.

McKenzie, D. F. *Bibliography and the Sociology of Texts*. New York: Cambridge University Press, 1999.

Polk, Noel. *Children of the Dark House: Text and Context in Faulkner*. Jackson: University Press of Mississippi, 1996.

Literature

THOMAS F. HADDOX

Fifteen years into the twenty-first century, the term "southern literature" frequently seems to have less content among those who study it for a living than the scare quotes that often enclose it. This does not mean that the term lacks resonance: no doubt it continues to conjure up images of decaying plantation houses, lynched black bodies, still moments in piney woods, Confederate battle flags flying in front of mobile homes, congregations contorting in religious ecstasy, and sit-ins at lunch counters—with William Faulkner's blandly amiable face looming over it all. Yet despite this instant flow of association, "southern literature" without scare quotes won't do: one doesn't want to come off as privileging "literature" as something definable according to its own intrinsic properties and merits, nor does one want to convey so breezily that one knows just what "the South" and "southern" signify (that would be reification), approves of those who think that they do know, or (worst of all) wishes to affirm the constellation of conservative (and often racialized white) values that these terms still evoke in many quarters. The scare quotes serve the same function as what Heidegger and Derrida called reading "under erasure": Faulkner and all the rest still spring up upon command, but we emphasize the contingency of the relation between them and "southern literature" and thus preclude the accusation that we naively believe in the term's "real" content. If we decide to drop the scare quotes, we might resort to a judicious use of the plural—speaking, for instance, of southern literatures or of Souths—and never stop underscoring the always-contested nature of these terms. Such moves suggest that we can avoid identification with any "South" in particular. They also gesture toward a definition of "southern literature" capacious enough for critics so wary of entanglement: those bodies of texts that have at any time been claimed as "southern" by different groups of readers, with a variety of ends in mind.[1]

If we accept this definition, it becomes possible to identify, without committing oneself to any of them, all sorts of competing, partial accounts of when "southern literature" began and what its first texts might be, according to different criteria that reveal different commitments. First recorded oral narratives? The surviving myths and histories of Native American peoples, which predate European settlement of the New World. First texts written by people about what would become the South by people who had visited it? Depending on which geographical "South" you have in mind, possible candidates might include Christopher Columbus's journal (1492), Álvar Núñez Cabeza da Vaca's *Relación* (1542), or Arthur Barlow's exploration narrative (1584). First significant text that dwells on African slavery and indicates how central it and its legacy would become to defining the South? Possibly Robert Beverley's *History and Present State of Virginia* (1705). First example of a self-consciously "southern" literary genre, such as the slave narrative or the plantation novel? For the former, Olaudah Equiano's *Interesting Narrative* (1789) or Frederick Douglass's *Narrative of the Life of Frederick Douglass* (1845) (again, depending on your geographical South); for the latter, George Tucker's *The Valley of Shenandoah* (1824) claims temporal precedence, but John Pendleton Kennedy's *Swallow Barn* (1832) looms larger. First southern texts with avowedly nationalist aspirations? Take your pick, but the decades just before the Civil War would be the relevant period. First of many testimonies to the existence of this or that "New South"? Henry W. Grady's essay of that title (1886) is iconic. First attempt to establish a definitive and comprehensive southern canon? *The Library of Southern Literature* (1908–13). First glimpses of the emergence of the modern field of southern studies, some of whose institutions survive today? The writings of the Agrarians in the 1930s, with H. L. Mencken's essay "The Sahara of the Bozart" (1917) often cited as the grain of sand around which the pearl subsequently formed. First proofs of the consolidation of said field? Probably the landmark anthology *The Literature of the South* (1952), edited by Richmond Croom Beatty, Floyd C. Watkins, and Thomas Daniel Young, and the collection of essays coedited by Louis D. Rubin Jr. and Robert D. Jacobs, *Southern Renascence* (1953). The possibilities could be multiplied: any text that has ever been called "southern" could arguably serve as the point of departure for a new genealogy of southern literature. And within any of these genealogies, southern subregions (Appalachia, Tidewater, Piedmont, southern Louisiana, southern Florida) and minority populations (Vietnamese immigrants in New Orleans, Melungeons in eastern Tennessee, Cuban Americans in Miami, transplanted Yankees in the Atlanta suburbs) can assert their own historical and cultural particularity.

As Scott Romine has observed in his ironically titled *The Real South: Southern Narrative in the Age of Cultural Reproduction*, a critical practice that attends to such possibilities would "foreground the internal logics of reproductive modalities in an effort to situate them pragmatically within some

251

context of 'human practices' that renders them both legible and meaning-ful." It would refrain from asking about the "authenticity" of any conception of southern literature, bracketing or calling into question the relationship between texts and their putative referents, and would instead investigate the uses to which these conceptions are put. Its overarching assumption, in Romine's words, would be that "the 'real South' often turns out to be the one I desire, and the practice is not infrequently coercive: a matter of getting *you* to accept my South, my heritage, my culture, and so forth *as authentic*."[2] Since we are all presumably against coercion, the primary motive for study-ing southern literature must be to teach us to be on our guard against any claims to southern authenticity. We might enjoy this or that "southern" text or product, but we should never, so to speak, believe in it.

I will return to this matter of coercion and belief, but for now I would observe that Romine's lucid, elegant, and savvy account characterizes what has come to be called "the New Southern Studies"—the dominant paradigm in southern studies today—quite precisely. It derives considerable force from the fact that from the 1950s through much of the 1980s, most southernists, working in the tradition pioneered by the Agrarians and institutionalized by Rubin and like-minded critics (Cleanth Brooks, Thomas Daniel Young) *did* seem to believe unproblematically in a "real" South and in a correspondingly "authentic" southern literature that reflected it. Barbara Ladd summarizes their common assumptions:

> The traditional definition . . . goes like this: southern literature is characterized by a strong sense of place, based on memory, insularity, and a tragic history of defeat in the Civil War (the South was taken to be white); southern literature expresses the "universal" values of honor, chivalry toward women, gentleness with subordinates (the South was taken to be male and privileged); concrete, enmeshed in all the particularities of place and lived history, southern litera-ture is not reductive or abstract (for some, *reductive* and *abstract* are synonyms); southern literature reflects the southern belief in evil, in the Fall, and in the limited efficacy of any progressivist or reform agenda; southern literature, shaped by oral traditions, is as present to the reader as if it were spoken—it demands to be read aloud. Add the social categories (family, community, place), and you have a picture that is as much as anything else a late-modernist critique of modernity.[3]

The fissures and omissions in such a conception of southern literature should have been evident from the very beginning, even without the pres-sures of the Civil Rights Movement and of what John Egerton once called "the Americanization of Dixie"—but it was not until the 1980s and 1990s that forerunners of today's New Southernists, such as Anne Goodwyn Jones, Jefferson Humphries, and Michael Kreyling, began to chip away at the edifice. Today, the field looks quite different. In particular, southernists have become increasingly suspicious of arguments that do not at least gesture toward the totality of global capitalism—perhaps the only frame large enough to include all the struggles over the historical and present meaning of "the South."[4]

This emphasis on capitalism, however, does not necessarily imply a Marxist or even materialist orientation. In many respects, the New Southern Studies can be seen as a subfield of the broader movement once called "New Historicism," which has achieved disciplinary hegemony in English departments to such a degree that its assumptions and characteristic moves now often go without saying. Influenced by the "thick description" of anthropologist Clifford Geertz and the "genealogical" historical researches of Michel Foucault, New Historicists and their New Southern counterparts are attentive to historical details but wary of the metanarratives within which historians have generally made sense of them. The (New Southern) insight, for instance, that the U.S South is historically and economically linked to Latin American and Caribbean societies because of its legacy of racialized slavery, plantation agriculture, underdevelopment, and exploitation by industrial capitalism is emphasized primarily to critique claims of southern exceptionalism and to reveal the omnipresence of power struggles within any deployment of this or that "southern" text. It is not typically used (as a traditional Marxist might use it) to illustrate the contradictions that will one day bring down capitalism or to serve (as a liberal humanist might use it) as the kernel for a new, utopian southern order that might succeed in integrating everyone with some investment in the South, irrespective of race, gender, social class, or other identitarian axis. Such uses would, after all, betray metanarrative commitments.

Indeed, from the point of view of the New Southern Studies, the chief problem with any given conception of southern literature is precisely that some people *will* believe in it, usually because (as Romine suggests) they love or desire it and want it to survive and prevail. Inevitably, there will be a phenomenological gap between the critical distance required by New Historicism in general and the self-understanding of many southern writers and readers alike—who, contrary to critical expectation, can be found all across the political spectrum. Mythic intonations about southern community, after all, however constructed by an intellectual elite they might have been, often *did* resonate with lived experience (in Walter Benjamin's sense of *Erfahrung*)—because many southerners understood themselves to be living in small, deeply rooted, and relatively isolated communities, and because their art depicted such communities with only passing reference to the global capitalist context within which they were embedded.[5] In much contemporary southern literature, conscious awareness of such a context is difficult to find and often limited to a vague unease at the transformation of southern landscapes into strip malls and McMansions, or at the disappearance of familiar points of ideological reference, as the Civil War and the Civil Rights Movement no longer seem to mean what they once did. And yet southern writers from Tony Earley to Lee Smith to Cynthia Shearer continue to exploit this vein of unease and nostalgia, often achieving popular success.[6]

Critics who find all of this boring or retrograde have, to be sure, ways of dealing with such texts. They can be dismissed as signs of ideological confusion and their popularity as a reflection of false consciousness or narcissism—though the question of how we critics have managed to escape such false consciousness always lurks in the wings. Alternatively, we might try to recuperate such texts by reading them (so to speak) against their emotional grain or by multiplying distinctions, at the possible risk of proposing distinctions without differences. We might propose, for instance—as Michael Kreyling does in *Inventing Southern Literature*—that even if Lee Smith or Jill McCorkle depicts something like a community, it must be a different phenomenon from what Louis Rubin had in mind when he so reverently intoned that word, because it consists primarily of women, whose necessary exclusion from Rubin's community can be taken for granted.[7] Or we might point to Lewis Nordan's debt to magical realism in *Wolf Whistle* to suggest the continuity between his fictive Mississippians and real people in similar places in, say, northeastern Brazil. But such moves are dodges, because while they appear to challenge the fundamental grounding term—in this case, "community," endowed with its quasi-theological aura—they merely redefine it, locate it elsewhere, or seek to strip it of power by emphasizing the selfish, personal investments associated with it.

No one is really fooled. As anyone who has taught such texts knows, the first response on the part of students is usually the thrill of recognition, of personal experiences and obsessions certified by their presence in a novel. We might urge students to rise above such pettiness, but there's nothing to suggest that we critics of southern literature are any more immune to it, though we look for such certification in theories—or, perhaps more accurately, in what we perceive to be the critical cutting edge—as often as we do in novels. Jon Smith, one of the leading advocates of the New Southern Studies, puts it well: "The best and most revisionary theories of an entire regional literature that we have seen in 70 years . . . derive, like all meaning, in part from personal, unconscious fantasy. But—more than most of us would like to admit—such derivation is, quite inevitably, what the imagining of imagined communities is all about."[8] Scratch the surface of the discourse that justifies what we as southernist scholars do, and whether we realize it or not, the justification usually becomes: because it's what people like us do. Few of us, however, are as honest about this as Smith.[9]

Is it possible to bridge this gap between lived experience and theory without simply proposing our interpretations as personal expressions of this or that identification with a community (even, perhaps, a community as narrow as "southernist scholars")? I have no definite answer to propose here, but I would like to turn now toward one of the first important critical texts in southern studies to address this gap, Michael Kreyling's *Inventing Southern Literature* (1998). An acknowledged precursor to many of the most influential works in the New Southern Studies, Kreyling's text nevertheless diverges from them in its understated but abiding claim that belief—and all the potentially messy complications that flow from it—is unavoidable, however we may strive to suspend it out of a fear of being thought naive or unethical. Simply put, I can think of no other critical text that compels us to consider so forthrightly what we talk about when we talk about southern literature— and that does so without either denying the personal investments entailed by such talk (such as wanting certain texts to survive and others to become neglected) or reducing them to a merely narcissistic drama.

As its title implies, Kreyling's book argues that "southern literature," as traditionally understood, has been not the organic reflection of a monolithic culture but rather the achievement of a small group of intellectuals and writers with very particular goals in mind. When it first appeared, many readers, already familiar with "constructivist" arguments of this kind, suggested that Kreyling had gone either too far or not far enough. Readers friendlier to (but not uncritical of) the Agrarian tradition, such as Fred Hobson and Ernest Suarez, accused Kreyling of distorting their views and the views of the dominant tradition of southern literature, often in the service of a predictable reduction of literature to politics.[10] On the other hand, Kreyling's claim that the book was "not a counternarrative that seeks to dynamite the rails on which the official narrative runs" but rather "a metanarrative, touching upon crucial moments when and where the official narrative is made or problematically redirected" seemed to some readers far too accommodating to southern conservatism—Patricia Yaeger, for instance, quoted this passage in *Dirt and Desire* and then reached immediately for the dynamite.[11] What often went overlooked in these responses was Kreyling's own understanding of Benedict Anderson's notion of the imagined community—which doesn't lend itself so easily to such explosive intentions.[12] The thesis that communities are imagined is not, as Kreyling pointed out, "a breath-taking insight; contemporary literary critics and historians are weaned on the idea of the constructedness of meanings." But as Stanley Fish had emphasized some years before—and as too many critics still have not learned—"it can hardly be a criticism of something that it is socially constructed if everything is." Nor does an awareness of social construction make one more able to revise it, for "the impulse to revise has been experienced and acted upon long before social constructionism was ever thought up; and, moreover, those who have been persuaded to the social constructedness thesis are in no better position to revise than anyone else since the work of revision isn't furthered a whit by declaring it to be possible."[13]

In other words, the obvious application of Anderson's theory to the study of southern literature—something along the lines of "We must never forget that the South is a historically contingent entity whose meaning is contested"—tells us nothing about what attitude we should take toward the South or these contestations. What therefore prevents Anderson's thesis of the imagined community from becoming a mere tautology, a claim that historically specific cultural artifacts are made by historically specific cultures? Kreyling perceptively locates the thesis's value in the fact that it resists itself, that its conviction about the arbitrariness of meaning operates in a dialectical tension with beliefs that precede and always already shape whatever constructions we encounter. As he puts it,

> Anderson gives reverent place for "nonartefactual" values and realities: "love" (141), self-sacrifice (7, 144), and the possibility of a "metaphysical conception of man" (11, n.3). *Imagined Communities* oscillates between a skeptical pole— history (sometimes *history*)—and a kind of melancholy acknowledgment of what must not be thought in a post-Foucault age, that there is substance in concepts that have resisted and continue to resist our will to believe in their constructedness.

The issue, it would seem, is not whether we believe in the "constructedness" of southern culture or literature but whether acknowledging that constructedness means that we believe in its "reality" any less—or, perhaps even more acutely, whether we can engage with cultural texts in good faith without taking seriously (if not necessarily accepting) their claims to reflect *some* "reality." The wry but now dated phrase "what must not be thought in a post-Foucault age" (Why not? Has Foucault really made certain thoughts impossible?) suggests that even the "community" of southernist scholars exerts its own pressures to orthodoxy, its own a priori belief that there is nothing in which one can (or should) believe—against which even the most skeptical readers sometimes struggle. Kreyling describes his own project in similar terms: "The following argument concerning southernness in literature and literary history, using mostly prose fiction as 'cultural products,' should be understood within the arc described by Anderson's extremes of skepticism and love."[14]

Kreyling's argument here should not be taken to mean that the only two possible stances toward southern literature are skepticism and love, and that our first duty when we enter the fray is to declare our allegiance to one or the other. Nor does it mean that we are always both skeptical and loving toward the same objects—Kreyling makes it clear that he has little love for the Agrarian position and much skepticism toward it. It does mean, however, that we are always skeptical or loving toward *something*—and that our initial stance of skepticism or love toward that thing will have much to do with how we approach other things. There are indeed, as the New Southern Studies demonstrates, any number of attitudes to strike toward southern literature in general or southern texts in particular—but these attitudes, however varied, derive their meaning from a prior Yes or No to some value or felt imperative. It means, in short, that Kreyling's application of Anderson foregrounds the irreducibility of belief in a way that tends to be obscured in much of the work that has followed. Even a belief that "belief" must be interrogated is, after all, a belief—and if we are to persuade others of it, then we too might be accused of coercion.

Consider, for instance, Randall Kenan's novel *A Visitation of Spirits* (1989). In the broadest sense, it might be described as a "postsouthern" text—that is, a text about what happens when belief in "traditional" southern ways and possibly even in the reality of "the South" begins to wane.[15] Set in the rural, African American community of Tims Creek, North Carolina, in the years 1984–85, the novel's central event is the suicide of Horace Cross—young scion of the community's most respected family, the "Chosen Nigger" destined for greatness and chafing under the burden of his family's expectations.[16] In Tims Creek, the Crosses have been good farmers, (mostly) good Christians, and pillars of strength for generations, enduring and even thriving despite white racism and attaining a measure of real civic power in the wake of the Civil Rights Movement. And yet, as Horace's cousin Jimmy (whose own first-person "Confessions" interrupt the account of Horace's life and comment on it) points out, none of the lessons provided by this heritage can prevent Horace from killing himself: "I guess [Horace's family] didn't reckon the world they were sending him into was different from the world they had conquered, a world peopled with new and hateful monsters that exacted a different price" (188).

The easiest explanation for why Horace kills himself is that he is gay and knows that his family and community will never tolerate his sexuality. The appearance of a gay Cross, however, appears not as Horace's sole problem but rather as one of many fundamental social changes that Tims Creek finds difficult to accept. (Indeed, Horace tells Jimmy about his sexual acts with men and is not rejected or condemned—which itself suggests that the intensity of the community's homophobia is exaggerated.) Horace's own crisis is precipitated not by the discovery of his sexuality but by his family's reaction when they learn that he has pierced his ear because his new circle of white friends has done so. The possibility that the hope of the Crosses might be gay is inseparable from the possibility that he might form sincere friendships across racial lines—a point underscored when Horace imagines being called both "Cocksucker" and "Oreo" by the congregation of his church (87). Moreover, because the novel begins with a nostalgic description of a hog killing and ends with a "Requiem for Tobacco," the largest and most comprehensive frame for understanding Horace's suicide might be the demise of the traditionally agrarian economy of Tims Creek.

How, then, are we to read Kenan's novel? Certainly this framing of Horace's story within economic changes aligns with the emphasis of the New Southern Studies on the vicissitudes of global capitalism. It might suggest that we should read Tims Creek not as the locus of some authentic African American rural South but rather as a place whose racial, cultural, and economic characteristics are analogous with those of other places also caught up in the global and impersonal process of capitalist transformation and traditionally stratified along racial or ethnic divides. To identify with a place like Tims Creek, to dare to label it "authentic," would thus entail not only the misrecognition of how little place counts for under capitalism but also the violent exclusion of anything that might threaten this authenticity—most obviously, racial and sexual difference. That the novel ironically racializes this conservatism as black instead of white merely demonstrates all the more forcefully that any kind of exclusion is violence, that positive belief in southernness risks (as Romine suggests) becoming coercive.

And yet such a reading, though undoubtedly compelling, is itself dependent on belief, itself predicated on certain exclusions—as, in practice, any reading of any text will be. Not only does such a reading tend to view the "conservative" denizens of Tims Creek either as manifestations of structural evil or as objects of pity or contempt who cannot overcome their own culturally conditioned blindnesses, it cannot easily account for the novel's reverent dwelling on (to invoke Anderson and Kreyling again) "'non-artefactual' values and realities"—the social bonds created by the material processes of nonindustrial farming, the need for racial solidarity against white supremacy, and the belief of the community as a whole in Christianity. It is quite possible to acknowledge the tragedy of Horace and yet to believe that even though Tims Creek's "traditional" society could not easily accommodate him, it is nonetheless a better place than the world of supermarkets and video games that is replacing it. The novel's final paragraph (in the "Requiem for Tobacco") evokes such a possibility without unambiguously endorsing it:

> But it is good to remember that once upon a time hands, human hands, plucked ripe leaves from stalks and hands, human hands, wrapped them with twine and sent them to the fire. And it is good to remember that people were bound by this strange activity, this activity that put food on their tables and clothes on their backs and sent their young ones to school, bound by the necessity, the responsibility, the humanity. It is good to remember, for too many forget. (257)

An "Agrarian" reading of this passage—and of the novel as a whole—is certainly plausible. It is also certainly contestable, and any effort to persuade readers either of it or to put us on guard against it through a hermeneutics of suspicion will be equally committed, equally determined to see its reading prevail.

I want to suggest that such contestation is always with us, and that our own involvement in it cannot be elided simply by declining to take a stand, or to regard all other contestations as grabs for power while our own critical interventions remain securely aloof. After all, we perpetuate "southern literature" and all its accumulated baggage in the very act of taking it as an object of study. We cannot invoke the term without referring, however reluctantly, to the Agrarians and their attempts to define it, because to omit such reference would be ahistorical. Moreover, adopting a strict comparativist approach, insisting that there are and have always been multiple and contested Souths with multiple and contested histories, places us in a kind of performative contradiction: we deny the coherence of "southern literature," for fear of raising the ghosts of those privileged white men from Vanderbilt, but not to the point of actually rejecting the label "southernist" or eschewing meetings of the Society for the Study of Southern Literature. We may choose to attack the traces of neo-Agrarian nostalgia present in Kenan's novel, but in doing so, we ensure that people will read it—and thus run the risk that others might find this nostalgia attractive. What Kreyling calls "the Quentin thesis" has not, despite his ardent hope, gone away; it has merely assumed a different form.[17] Every act of critique, of demystification, amounts to the same cry: "I don't love it! I don't love it! I don't love it!" Because even if we don't love it, the results may prove to be much the same as if we did.

260

Perhaps, then, the most responsible attitude whenever we talk about southern literature would not be to cover our asses with scare quotes or to point out how every definition, no matter what it may be, is "constructed" (surely *this* claim, at this late date, can go without saying), but rather to declare ourselves forthrightly, to participate in the rough-and-tumble of contestation, knowing that we will probably not succeed in making our own idiosyncratic commitment prevail but fighting the good fight nevertheless, and doing so in the knowledge that this is precisely what binds us as a community of scholars. I will invoke Kreyling once more, for his remarkable vision of just what is at stake:

> My narrative of the invention of southern identity in the literary record moves to no happy ending. I have neither reassuring news that despite the appearance of discontinuity and confusion all will go on as before, the same yet different; nor do I have the proclamation of a new southern canon to replace the old one and inevitably to repeat the errors of the old one in the very act of believing itself to be a canon. What I have found in this study of literary maneuverings and reinventions—and have striven to explain in the book—is that "the South" is the richest site yet discovered in the U.S. cultural terrain for the study of and participation in the reinvention of culture. We should not wish this activity shut down; the process is our collective life.[18]

Even if we cannot escape the subjectivity of our judgments, cannot hide behind the apparent rigor of our analyses, and cannot overcome the suspicion that our readings may produce none of the political consequences that we would like, we can still see the value of our "collective life"—and we move to no "happy ending" because we move to no ending at all. Everything is grist for the mill—our loves and our suspicions, our personal experience and our intellectual commitments, even, perhaps, our performative contradictions. The work of reinvention in defense of what we believe to be true goes on, and it never ceases.

NOTES

1. Note that geographical criteria do not necessarily determine the boundaries of southern literature(s) according to this definition. Most "southern" texts will, predictably enough, be produced by people who lived in and wrote about the South. But not only does reliance on such a criterion beg the question of defining the South—the former Confederacy? all places in the U.S. where slavery existed legally after the ratification of the Constitution? all places in the New World where plantation agriculture established itself? perhaps even what Paul Gilroy dubbed "the black Atlantic?" or, as John Shelton Reed has proposed, all places where at least 35 percent of listings in urban telephone directories are "Southern"?—it ignores the fact that writers who exist outside these places have produced important work that engages with and betrays an investment in the South (Russell Banks, Toni Morrison, and V. S. Naipaul all come to mind). See J. S. Reed, *My Tears Spoiled My Aim*, 27.

2. Romine, *Real South*, 13, 14.

3. Ladd, "Literary Studies," 1629.

4. Excellent representative works include Smith and Cohn's edited volume, *Look Away!*; Bone's *Postsouthern Sense of Place*; Duck's *Nation's Region*; Benson's *Disturbing Calculations*; and, with a broader focus on culture, Peacock's *Grounded Globalism*.

5. Both *Erfahrung* and *Erlebnis* translate as "experience," but the former has connotations of "genuine" experience, richly felt and intellectually understood, while the latter remains, in Benjamin's words, "in the sphere of a certain hour in one's life." To mark an experience as "a precise point in time in consciousness"—that is, as *Erlebnis*—comes "at the cost of the integrity of its contents." See Benjamin, *Illuminations*, 163.

6. I do not mean to imply that Earley, Smith, and Shearer are all (or all equally) "conservative," or that there is nothing "critical" about their portrayals of the South. Nor are they all (or all equally) indifferent to the realities of global capitalism—Shearer's *The Celestial Jukebox*, in fact, is one of the most remarkable portraits of how global flows or people and capital have transformed the contemporary South. I do maintain, however, that all of them portray certain features of the South as lovable, embattled, and yet undeniably "southern"—and that arguably, this is enough to open them to the suspicion of metaphysical thinking.

7. Kreyling, *Inventing Southern Literature*, 123–24.

8. J. Smith, "Postcolonial, Black, and Nobody's Margin," 159.

9. In his more recent work, Smith seems to backtrack somewhat from the claim that "all meaning" is derived in part from fantasy. In *Finding Purple America*, he distinguishes between critical positions in southern studies that are grounded in a melancholic narcissism—which he defines in Lacanian terms as the desire to go on "getting all worked up about our desire" instead of attaining its object—and those positions grounded in rationality and informed by "ethical aspiration and the embrace of 'the other.'" I find the earlier Smith more persuasive, or at least more consistent, because I doubt that this distinction can really be maintained in the terms that the later Smith proposes. We can argue, of course, about the scope and meaning of "rationality," but it seems suspiciously easy to attribute failures of rationality to narcissism when narcissism for Lacan is well-nigh ubiquitous. Lacan cuts both ways, and Smith's own dwelling on his personal enthusiasms, from gardening in Birmingham to Neko Case's recent music, invites the same speculative diagnosis of narcissism that he levels against the work of many southernist scholars. Smith complains of those who ask "whether, as a result of modernity's instability, we have not Lost Something Very Important," but such a complaint

is easily reversed: why do not dual commitments to modernity and to antagonism similarly express a fear (or, in Lacanian terms, a desire to go on desiring) that we are in danger of Losing Something Very Important if we do not make similar commitments? See J. Smith, *Finding Purple America*, 3, 110, 6.

10. See F. Hobson, contribution to "A Symposium," 659–87; Suarez, "Writing Southern Literary History," 881–92.

11. Kreyling, *Inventing Southern Literature*, ix; Yaeger, *Dirt and Desire*, 34.

12. According to Benedict Anderson's immensely influential definition, a nation is "an imagined political community" because "the members of even the smallest nation will never know most of their fellow-members, meet them, or even hear of them, yet in the minds of each lives the image of their communion." Yet though his emphasis is on the nation-state, Anderson makes clear that "all communities larger than primordial villages of face-to-face contact (and perhaps even these) are imagined." It follows that almost any imaginable "South" would count as an imagined community. See B. Anderson, *Imagined Communities*, 6.

13. Kreyling, *Inventing Southern Literature*, ix; Fish, *Professional Correctness*, ix.

14. Kreyling, *Inventing Southern Literature*, x. Internal quotations from B. Anderson, *Imagined Communities*.

15. Important works on the notion of the "postsouthern" include Simpson's "What Survivors Do," collected in his *The Brazen Face of History*; F. Hobson's *Southern Writer in the Postmodern World*; and Bone's *Postsouthern Sense of Place*. I have suggested elsewhere that while the "postsouthern" does have considerable descriptive and analytical value when applied to certain texts, it is neither—as Kreyling puts it—"an emergency of the highest seriousness" nor "a relief" (*Inventing Southern Literature*, 148), precisely because it preserves earlier notions of the South in the very act of calling them into question. See my "Elizabeth Spencer"; see also Martyn Bone's essay in this volume.

16. Kenan, *Visitation of Spirits*, 13; text hereafter cited parenthetically.

17. Kreyling, *Inventing Southern Literature*, 106. Kreyling complains: "It is next to impossible to avoid [Quentin Compson] in any study of southernness. Quentin is the major life-support system in southern cultural discourse. As the agonized voice of its center, his remarks about the South echo in books and essays, introductions and epigraphs. Although I agree with Michael O'Brien that Quentin's usefulness has been exhausted, and that he and his words 'should be sealed up in concrete and deposited in the Tombigbee River' [O'Brien, *Rethinking the South*, 163–64], I want to postpone the moratorium just long enough to use Quentin against himself" (105). The move here is characteristic: I don't want to hear any more about Quentin, but I'll go on talking about him anyway, because even a "postsouthern" approach can't seem to do without him. This is, if you like, Kreyling's own performative contradiction. Jon Smith is correct to note that this particular contradiction continues in Kreyling's more recent work—see, for instance, his comments on *The South That Wasn't There* in *Finding Purple America*, 33–34. Internal quotation from O'Brien, *Rethinking the South*.

18. Kreyling, *Inventing Southern Literature*, 182.

SUGGESTIONS FOR FURTHER READING

Bone, Martyn. *The Postsouthern Sense of Place in Contemporary Fiction*. Baton Rouge: Louisiana State University Press, 2005.

Kreyling, Michael. *Inventing Southern Literature*. Jackson: University Press of Mississippi, 1998.

Romine, Scott. *The Real South: Southern Narrative in the Age of Cultural Reproduction*. Baton Rouge: Louisiana State University Press, 2008.

Smith, Jon. "Postcolonial, Black, and Nobody's Margin: The U.S. South and New World Studies." *American Literary History* 16, no. 1 (2004): 144–61.

Yaeger, Patricia. *Dirt and Desire: Reconstructing Southern Women's Writing, 1930–1990*. Chicago: University of Chicago Press, 2000.

STEVEN E. KNEPPER

Ecology/Environment

To study the southern states ecologically is to challenge the myth of a unified, organic South. While their climes are generally warm and wet, the southern states are ecologically diverse, ranging from the hardwood forests of Appalachia to the great swamps of Florida, the Outer Banks of North Carolina to the barrier islands of Louisiana. In his 1932 classic *Human Geography of the South*, sociologist Rupert Vance refers to "the South of Many Regions." It contains at least seven "physiographic regions," and "within these main divisions there are many subdivisions of soil and topography."[1] Though he never fully dispenses with the concept of the South, Vance qualifies it with attention to data and detail, with a schema of what we might today call southern "bioregions," defined not in terms of political boundaries but in terms of environmental factors and of human interaction with the environment.

Likewise, to study the environmental history of the southern states is to challenge the myth of a bucolic agrarian South. Their history, like that of the United States generally, is one of environmental degradation, from widespread deforestation to surface mining to the Deepwater Horizon oil spill. Perhaps the environmental crisis that most directly counters the myth of an idyllic agrarian South, however, is that of soil depletion and erosion, which plagued southern fields from the colonial period onward. Thomas Jefferson worried about the deleterious effects of corn and tobacco on the soil. He advocated a diversified, soil-conserving agriculture rather than economically lucrative but environmentally degrading cash-crop monocultures. As Donald Worster has explained, though, "the capitalistic agroecosystem shows one clear tendency over the span of modern history: a movement toward the radical simplification of the natural ecological order in the number of species found in an area and the intricacy of their interconnections."[2] Cash-crop monocultures, and especially monocultures of cotton, rather than diversified scientific farming, would exert the greater influence on southern economies, societies, and landscapes.

According to Worster, monocultures are one of the key transformations of modernity, fueling economic growth and producing copious amounts of food and fiber. But since monocultures do not occur naturally, they are plagued by a host of problems, including soil depletion and erosion in the case of many cash crops. And, indeed, cotton monocultures left severe levels of soil erosion and sterility, even gullies and trenches, in their wake as they moved across the Carolinas into Alabama and Mississippi and on into Arkansas and Texas. As Jack Temple Kirby has pointed out, the exotic species kudzu eventually played a key role as a "bandage over wounded ground," even though its introduction led to new environmental problems.[3]

265

The crisis of soil erosion came to a head in the "dirty thirties." In 1928 the U.S. Department of Agriculture published a short but influential document titled *Soil Erosion a National Menace.* Coauthors Hugh Hammond Bennett and W. R. Chapline identify what would become a major environmental factor in the Great Depression: the United States was losing its soil at an alarming rate. From the Mississippi alone, 428,715,000 tons of sediment flowed each year into the Gulf of Mexico. Much once-fertile land now lay in ruin. Writing before the recognized onset of the Depression in 1929, Bennett and Chapline issued a warning that American agriculture was already in dire shape and that the full effects of erosion were yet to be felt. "To visualize the full enormity of land impairment and devastation brought about by this ruthless agent is beyond the possibility of the mind," Bennett and Chapline claim. "An era of land wreckage destined to weigh heavily upon the welfare of the next generation is at hand."[4] Bennett and Chapline's words seem especially prophetic in light of the incipient dust bowl of the American West, but their primary concern in this document is the ravaged fields of the American South.

In 1936, Walker Evans toured the Cotton South, documenting the crisis of soil erosion. A photograph taken near Jackson, Mississippi, offers a dramatic perspective on the South's land abuse. A single tree represents the now-denuded vegetation that once secured the soil, while the long, rutted slopes of the ridge represent the scale of the crisis, the vast waste of the land. Of course, cash-crop monocultures, which were a primary cause of erosion, did not instrumentalize and exploit the soil alone. They did the same to laborers, first slaves and then sharecroppers. As ecocritic Paul Lindholdt writes, "Just as subjugation of nature involves the domination of people, subjugation of peoples involves domination of nature."[5] The history of slavery in the Americas is inseparable from the history of plantation monocultures. The human and environmental damage done by these monocultures should not be considered separately, for they are tightly interconnected. Arthur Raper, a colleague of Rupert Vance, demonstrated this in his 1937 essay "Gullies and

What They Mean," which describes the scars of soil erosion as "physical facts with social backgrounds and consequences." Raper argues that "the decisions to plant cotton and corn and to use hand processes and one-horse plows on Southern plantations are not made by [the tenant]. They are made for him by the system under which he lives, a system rooted in the philosophy of exploitation—of man through slavery and tenant farming, of land through clean-culture crops and shallow plowing."[6] By linking soil erosion and racial exploitation, Raper describes what we might today call a form of environmental racism. Black sharecroppers, who are held in poverty by a racist system, are forced to live amid—and indeed to contribute to—environmental degradation.

To study the southern United States ecologically, then, is to study its amazing biodiversity. To study the environmental history of the southern states is to study a problematic past. But what of the ecological study of literary and cultural representations of the South? This is a trickier matter, in large part because much writing about the South is overtly pastoral. In *The Country and the City* (1973), Raymond Williams examines how the pastoral mode, by idealizing the countryside, often veils rural work. Furthermore, it tends to obscure environmental degradation in the countryside. A sensitive critic, Williams holds that the traditional pastoral at times mourns real losses and conveys a legitimate sense of alienation, and it is important for how it conceptualizes nature, but in the end it can veil more than it reveals. Such veiling is often at work in the traditional canon of nineteenth- and early twentieth-century southern literature, obscuring both social injustice and ecological degradation. Despite important differences and intricacies, works of antebellum writers like John Pendleton Kennedy and William Gilmore Simms and postbellum writers like Thomas Nelson Page and Joel Chandler Harris all pastoralize the plantation, holding it up as an idyllic alternative to northern industrialism. For these writers, the plantation is not the site of the quite modern practice of exploiting land and labor in the production of cash-crop monocultures. It is instead paternalistic, premodern, rooted—a bastion against the very ills of modernity.

Perhaps the most important work in this vein is the 1930 polemic *I'll Take My Stand*, in which twelve intellectuals—many of whom were affiliated with Vanderbilt University—defend a besieged and beneficent agrarian South against an encroaching and insidious industrial North. As John Crowe Ransom explains in the opening "Statement of Principles," the essays of *I'll Take My Stand* "all tend to support a Southern way of life against what may be called the American or prevailing way; and all as much as agree that the best terms in which to represent the distinction are contained in the phrase, Agrarian *versus* Industrial."[7] This pastoral opposition is quite misleading. (Indeed, all simple comparisons of an agrarian South and an industrial North require scrutiny.) It obscures the fact that southern plantations and cash-crop monocultures were fundamental to industrial modernity—that, as Jack Temple Kirby asserts, "plantations resemble modern factories"—and it neglects the ills that result from them.[8] Indeed, there are few references to cash crops, sharecroppers, or soil erosion in *I'll Take My Stand*. Slavery is depicted as benignly paternalistic and economically inconsequential. Ransom and company thus idealize an abstract and idyllic agrarian South, rather than one embedded in a global economy and in the midst of environmental and social crisis.

267

This makes *I'll Take My Stand* a paradoxical and frustrating volume. Many of its critiques of industrialism are cogent. In his essay, Donald Davidson holds that industrialism is "dirtying up the landscape and rendering human life generally dull, mechanical, standardized, and mean."[9] Although he does not address the same tendency in cash-crop monocultures, Ransom critiques the modern instrumentalization of the natural world: "Man is boastfully declared to be a natural scientist essentially, whose strength is capable of crushing and making over to his own desires the brute materiality which is nature."[10] There is a nascent ecological sensibility in *I'll Take My Stand*. But the pastoral veil that the Southern Agrarians draw over the rural South hides the environmental degradation and social injustices exposed by Raper. In effect, the pastoral opposition at the core of this volume purportedly dedicated to defending the southern countryside actually forecloses any grappling with its most pressing problems.

Important departure points for an ecologically informed southern studies, then, are a suspicion of what the pastoral might hide and an acknowledgment of how environmental and social ills are often tightly interconnected. As Jay Watson rightly argues, "The region's long, highly visible history of poverty and its rich and troubled history of land use intertwine to foreground poverty itself as an environmental issue."[11] These may at first seem like odd starting points, though. In literary and cultural studies broadly, early ecocriticism centered on nature writing, wilderness, preservation, and the pastoral mode. This remains essential work, and these concerns are important for "green" southern studies. Yet there have been important efforts to widen the focus of ecocriticism, and it is now a broad and even eclectic field. In "The Trouble with Wilderness; or, Getting Back to the Wrong Nature" (1995), William Cronon warns that an excessive focus on wilderness reinforces a misleading pastoral opposition between nature and society, which in turn leads to a neglect of the fact that humans are a part of and constantly surrounded by the "wild."[12]

In the *Environmental Justice Reader* (2002), T. V. Reed offers another important, and in some ways complementary, critique of early ecocriticism. Reed holds that it has often neglected pressing questions of race, class, and gender. It particularly neglects the "crucial connections between environmental concerns and social justice."[13] Reed argues for an ecocriticism informed by environmental justice, a concept and a cause that has roots in the southern United States. In 1990 sociologist Robert Bullard published *Dumping in Dixie: Race, Class, and Environmental Quality*, a landmark environmental justice study. Bullard documents how "African American communities in the South—the nation's third world—because of their economic and political vulnerabilities, have been routinely targeted for the siting of noxious facilities; locally unwanted land uses, or LULUs; and environmental hazards."[14] Bullard studied African American communities in Texas, Louisiana, Alabama, and West Virginia that had been targeted for dump sites. He discovered a pattern of environmental racism that resulted in such communities bearing a disproportionate share of the nation's environmental hazards. Scholars following his lead have examined how minority communities and economically depressed areas suffer from similarly unequal burdens. They have joined grassroots activists in calling for a more equitable distribution—and significant reduction—of waste, toxicity, and degradation. One of the greatest strengths of the environmental justice movement is this close integration of activism, advocacy, and scholarly inquiry. This integration has drawn many scholars to environmental justice ecocriticism, and it has now become one of the most important ecological approaches to literary texts.

Because of the South's environmental history and its current environmental challenges, southern studies can contribute to the move beyond wilderness and nature writing to a wider reckoning with the problems of humans' interaction with nonhuman nature. It can also participate in deliberations on and calls for environmental justice. This requires an ecological rewriting of southern literary history, though, a thorough reconsideration of the southern canon that brings ecological concerns to the fore. Two important works that have helped launch this project are Jack Temple Kirby's *Mockingbird Song: Ecological Landscapes of the South* (2006) and Christopher Rieger's *Clear-Cutting Eden: Ecology and the Pastoral in Southern Literature* (2009). Both of these studies give close attention to southern literature and social thought of the 1920s, 1930s, and 1940s, a period that has often been called the Southern Renaissance. Both view this period as an ecological renaissance, not just a literary one, in which writers try to come to grips with the environmental crises of the Depression era. As my earlier examples of Vance, Bennett, Chapline, Evans, and Raper suggest, part of what makes this project so important is that it involves recovering important sources that are pertinent to ecological discussions today.

As Michael Kreyling has shown in *Inventing Southern History* (1998), southern literary history of the mid- to late twentieth century was highly influenced by the Southern Agrarians and their students. It tends to interpret the Southern Renaissance through the lens of *I'll Take My Stand*, emphasizing peculiarly southern values of community and place. Rieger rightly challenges the notion of a unified renaissance, maintaining that many writers and scholars of this period are actually reacting against the pastoral tradition of which *I'll Take My Stand* is a part. For Rieger, "the Southern Renaissance is a time of critically interrogating and demythologizing the past." The environmental crisis of the rural South is a key reason for this reaction against pastoral depictions of the southern past, for during the Depression "the ecological destruction wrought by the South's historical abuse of the land reaches a point where it can no longer be masked by moonlight and magnolias."[15]

It is hardly surprising, then, that one of the most prevalent literary modes of the Southern Renaissance is the antipastoral, which explicitly challenges the myth of a bucolic South of wholesome communities and healthy connections to place. Erskine Caldwell produced the most popular—and sensationalist—antipastoral depictions of the southern countryside. In *Tobacco Road* (1932), Caldwell depicts a family of impoverished sharecroppers living in a scarred and depleted Georgia countryside, one that—as the title suggests—has been ravaged by monocultures of first tobacco and then cotton. Caldwell paints a vivid picture of this decline and its effect on both the soil and its poorest tillers: "By the time Jeeter was old enough to work in the fields, the land had become such a great item of expense that most of it was allowed to grow up into pines. The soil had become depleted by the constant raising of cotton year after year, and it was impossible to secure a yield of more than a quarter of a bale to the acre. More and more guano was poured into the fields, and faster and faster was it washed away through the loose sandy soil before the cotton plants were able to reach it."[16] Caldwell's novels are set after cotton cultivation has largely moved west, leaving a wasteland behind, one which is now being overrun by invasive species of grass and pines. Both the croppers and their land have been instrumentalized and exploited.

The reaction against the southern pastoral tradition and its plantation myth does not, however, entail a rejection of the pastoral mode altogether. Rieger draws a useful distinction between traditional pastoral and "ecopastoral." Many writers of the Southern Renaissance rejected the traditional pastoral with its "over romanticizing of the past and propagandizing for racial hierarchy." They instead adopted a more ecological pastoral, one that "brings the natural world from the background to the foreground, making nature a presence in its own right, a force that influences humans rather than simply a passive entity to be acted upon."[17] Rather than idealizing the domesticated landscapes of the countryside—which in the South, as we have seen, are often the site of significant ecological degradation and social injustice— writers like Marjorie Kinnan Rawlings, Zora Neale Hurston, and William Faulkner tend to guardedly idealize wilderness. Rather than opposing country and city, then, or agrarian South and industrial North, ecopastorals such as Faulkner's *Go Down, Moses* tend to oppose wilderness and human civilization.

In Faulkner's novel, it is not the plantation that is under siege by industrialism but the "Big Woods" of the Yazoo-Mississippi Delta, which is being "punily and terrifically" attacked by "axe and saw." Indeed, protagonist Ike McCaslin repudiates his plantation inheritance and its legacy of exploitation, living for his yearly pilgrimages to the "Big Woods." In his character, the southern pastoral migrates from plantation to wilderness. Faulkner depicts this wilderness as having agency—it is "profound, sentient, gigantic and brooding"—but by the end of the novel most of it has been "deswamped and denuded and delivered," turned into "land across which there now came no scream of panther but instead the long hooting of locomotives."[18] *Go Down, Moses* is a poignant elegy for this lost wilderness, but it also exposes the dangers of the ecopastoral. McCaslin treats the "Big Woods" as an escape from the evils of society. He accepts the ecopastoral opposition of wilderness and human society. Yet in "Delta Autumn," when he is an old man, these evils find him even in the wilderness, when his young cousin's black mistress and their illegitimate son arrive in his tent. The arrogant and narcissistic Roth has recently abandoned them. Immediately after they leave, we learn that Roth has shot a doe out of season. Along with Ike, we must recognize that the wilderness offers no true refuge from the problems of society. An escape into the "Big Woods" offers no solutions to the problems of the plantation.

Rieger notes that in many of these ecological texts there "is a pronounced emphasis on labor in nature."[19] He is right, but this calls for another distinction beyond that of traditional pastoral and ecopastoral, one that does not rely on an opposition of nature and human society. In an important study of the "economy and the environment in early American writing," Timothy Sweet argues for the recovery of the Virgilian distinction between the pastoral and the georgic. According to Sweet, these literary modes both depict the countryside and the possibility of good rural living. They both tend to value the natural world. Resultantly, the distinction between them has been lost in most criticism—pastoralism has tended to subsume the georgic. But Sweet argues that there is a key difference, one that is especially relevant to contemporary ecological concerns: these two modes focus on two different types of human interaction with the natural world. "Where in the *Eclogues* Virgil understands the natural world as a site of leisure," Sweet explains, "in the *Georgics* he understands it primarily as a site of labor." The pastoral focuses on leisure in an idealized countryside—*I'll Take My Stand*, for instance, emphasizes leisure far more than labor—while the georgic focuses on work in a more realistic rural setting. At its root, the georgic confronts a serious ethical, economic, and ecological question that the pastoral does not directly address: it asks how humans can best find their place in and draw their living from nature. In doing so, it often confronts the very issues that Raymond Williams criticizes the pastoral for obscuring. The georgic, therefore, does not necessarily involve an opposition of country and city, nature and society. It tends to move past such oppositions altogether, focusing instead on how human society is itself a part of nature and dependent on it, on how nonhuman nature actively shapes human activity just as human activity shapes nature. Sweet defines the modern georgic as any work—poetry or prose, essay or fiction—that struggles with "defining the basic terms of the human community's relationship to the natural environment."[20]

The georgic is an important category for the ecological study of the Southern Renaissance, complementing and clarifying Rieger's ecopastoralism. The ecopastoral opposes wilderness and human civilization, while the georgic focuses on negotiating humans' economic relationship with nonhuman nature. As Rieger's study suggests, works such as Rawlings's *Cross Creek* contain both ecopastoral and georgic elements. The distinction is important, though, because pastoral and georgic can also stand alone as independent literary modes. It is especially useful to approach the work of progressive sociologists such as Vance, Raper, and Howard Odum as modern georgics. Jack Temple Kirby surveys the ecological thinking of these "Regionalists" in *Mockingbird Song*. He argues that they were key figures who "helped invent and embraced a particular reformist version of scientific ecology whose thesis and goals centered upon nature's own system of self-correction, equilibrium, and human emulation of nature's harmony."[21] Kirby suggests that their work in some ways culminates in that of Odum's sons, Howard T. and Eugene, who helped found ecosystem ecology.

In their "regional planning," the Regionalists envision southern economies that are far less environmentally destructive, that seek to conserve rather than rapaciously exploit. In *Human Geography*, Vance draws a distinction between "destructive exploitation" and "constructive exploitation." "The distinction," he explains, "is based on the difference between mining an irreplaceable store and reaping an annual 'flow' of resources." Farming and lumbering, for instance, can be classified as either destructive or constructive exploitation depending on the method used by the farmer or the forester. Soil mining and clear-cutting, which were prevalent methods of the late nineteenth- and early twentieth-century South, are clear examples of destructive exploitation, of "mining" rather than "cropping." "One of the highest forms of regional planning," according to Vance, "consists of the transference of resources from the mining to the cropping economy accompanied by the orderly conservation of stored resources where this is not possible."[22] This was the conceptual foundation of his georgic vision for the South.

Agricultural reform was of course central to the regional planning of Vance, Raper, and Odum. In order to counter the social injustices and ecological degradation of plantation monocultures, they advocated for more widespread landownership, greater racial equality, tenancy reforms, and for scientific, diversified agriculture that explicitly sought to preserve the integrity of the soil. In *Southern Regions of the United States*, Odum sounds like a present-day local foods advocate, pointing out that many of the South's needs for foodstuffs and agricultural products are met by shipping them in from outside the South: peas, carrots, spinach, rutabagas, milk, cheese, butter, even Christmas trees.[23] According to Odum, a better southern economy would be one in which the region's farmers met these needs. This would allow farmers to make more money by selling their products directly to consumers, and it would encourage diversification and therefore a reduction in soil-degrading cash crops. The Regionalists sought to balance the well-being of the land, the farmer, and the wider society, moving their studies clearly into the realm of the georgic.

It is important to note that while the Regionalists advocated a diversified agriculture for the South, theirs is not the backward-looking Agrarianism of *I'll Take My Stand*. It is progressive, seeking a better future rather than a simple return to the past. They are in fact proposing a new narrative of progress, one in which social and ecological health, rather than economic expansion, is the measuring stick. Of course, one could argue that such a project is just as romantic as that of the Southern Agrarians. The Regionalists' georgic visions were, after all, never realized. Small farmers continued to disappear from the South, and industrial agriculture took their place. Yet Kirby argues that this is a too-simple conclusion:

> The great wave of "big ag" across the South since World War II—southern farms are now second in scale only to the West's—may render hopelessly quaint the Regionalists' dream of a landscape of small proprietorships managed by prudent, soil-conserving men and women. Quaint is not the equivalent of wrong, however, and industrial gigantism was by no means inevitable. Big ag was engineered politically by representatives of machinery manufacturers, chemical producers, fiber and food processors and shippers, and many institutional economists and agronomists.[24]

This "engineering" of big agriculture, far from discrediting the georgics of the Regionalists, makes them all the more important. The Regionalists' particular reforms matter less than does their claim that a different economy is possible, practicable, and necessary. For the most cogent of georgics asserts the plausibility of a different outcome, cutting through any false sense of inevitability. They encourage us to abandon the sort of complacent logic that accepts the status quo and dismisses visions of change as romantic. Such thinking not only enables the continuation of serious environmental degradation and social injustice; it also helps generate them. Writing about modern industrial agriculture, the Indian activist and scientist Vandana Shiva argues, "Monocultures first inhabit the mind, and are then transferred to the ground. Monocultures of the mind generate models of production which destroy diversity and legitimise that destruction as progress, growth and improvement."[25] Monocultures—and many other environmentally degrading practices—are sustained by a way of thinking that treats them as inevitable or necessary, even if regrettable.

Another important departure point for a green southern studies, then, is a resistance of such legitimizing logic, a belief that different, less exploitative realities are possible. This allows for a southern studies that involves both theory and praxis. For the South today faces new forms of many of the same environmentally degrading and socially unjust practices that have shaped its past. As the recent documentary *Food, Inc.* (2008) testifies, monocultures, environmental injustice, and environmental racism have not left southern agriculture. The film highlights factory poultry farms in Kentucky, where genetic monocultures of chickens are raised in ethically questionable and ecologically degrading confinement and where "owners" themselves are held in a sort of vassalage to megacompanies that can revoke contracts on a whim, leaving farmers neck-deep in debt. The documentary also exposes the exploitation of immigrant workers at a Smithfield Hams North Carolina processing plant, where labor conditions are uncannily similar to those of the turn-of-the-century meatpacking industry depicted (and supposedly changed forever) by Upton Sinclair's 1906 classic, *The Jungle*.

Another pressing practice is that of mountaintop-removal coal mining, an environmentally devastating form of surface mining that involves leveling mountains to get at the coal seams below. Much of the rubble produced by mountaintop removal is pushed into surrounding valleys, devastating waterways. There is a long tradition of Appalachian literature protesting the environmental injustice of coal mining in Appalachia, stretching back to James Still's novel *River of Earth* (1940). Contemporary writers have responded to mountaintop removal as well, perhaps most notably in Silas House and Jason Howard's collection of oral histories, *Something's Rising: Appalachians Fighting Mountaintop Removal* (2011), which includes an interview with novelist and activist Denise Giardina and a foreword by writer Lee Smith.

Scholars of the U.S. South have not been silent about either industrial agriculture or mountaintop-removal mining, but they have had too little to say. Perhaps the greatest benefit of a greener southern studies, then, is that it would encourage scholars to become more engaged with environmental struggles on the ground. The scope of this essay is not exhaustive— it is meant to be suggestive, rather than comprehensive. But I do hope that it has shown that the intertwined environmental and literary histories of the southern states have important resources to offer, ones that allow scholars to craft their own georgics and thus to speak to our own great environmental crisis.

NOTES

1. Vance, *Human Geography of the South*, 20, 23.
2. Worster, *Wealth of Nature*, 58.
3. Kirby, *Mockingbird Song*, 112.
4. Bennett and Chapline, *Soil Erosion*, 17, 22.
5. Lindholdt, "Literary Activism," 247.
6. A. Raper, "Gullies and What They Mean," 201, 203.
7. Twelve Southerners, "Introduction," xxxvii.
8. Kirby, *Mockingbird Song*, 77.
9. D. Davidson, "Mirror for Artists," 28.

10. Ransom, "Reconstructed but Unregenerate," 8.
11. Watson, "Economics of a Cracker Landscape," 497.
12. See Cronon, "Trouble with Wilderness," 69–90.
13. T. V. Reed, "Toward an Environmental Justice Ecocriticism," 145.
14. Bullard, *Dumping in Dixie*, xv.
15. Rieger, *Clear-Cutting Eden*, 4, 5.
16. Caldwell, *Tobacco Road*, 85.
17. Rieger, *Clear-Cutting Eden*, 5, 5.
18. Faulkner, *Go Down, Moses*, 325, 169, 347, 325.
19. Rieger, *Clear-Cutting Eden*, 16.
20. Sweet, *American Georgics*, 2.
21. Kirby, *Mockingbird Song*, xiv.
22. Vance, *Human Geography*, 482.
23. Odum, *Southern Regions*, 45.
24. Kirby, *Mockingbird Song*, 250.
25. Shiva, *Monocultures of the Mind*, 7.

SUGGESTIONS FOR FURTHER READING

Bullard, Robert. *Dumping in Dixie: Race, Class, and Environmental Quality*. Boulder, Colo.: Westview Press, 1990.
Cowdrey, Albert E. *This Land, This South: An Environmental History*. Lexington: University of Kentucky Press, 1983.
House, Silas, and Jason Howard, eds. *Something's Rising: Appalachians Fighting Mountaintop Removal*. Lexington: University Press of Kentucky, 2009.
Kirby, Jack Temple. *Mockingbird Song: Ecological Landscapes of the South*. Chapel Hill: University of North Carolina Press, 2006.
Rieger, Christopher. *Clear-Cutting Eden: Ecology and the Pastoral in Southern Literature*. Birmingham: University of Alabama Press, 2009.
Sutter, Paul S., and Christopher J. Manganiello. *Environmental History and the American South: A Reader*. Athens: University of Georgia Press, 2009.

PART V

Structures of Feeling

JOHN T. MATTHEWS

Twice each year, the Louisiana State Penitentiary at Angola invites the public to Rodeo Day. Visitors pay admission to watch inmates compete in steer wrestling, bull riding, and other more "gladiatorial" contests; spectators may also browse booths that sell arts and crafts made by the convicts. Jessica Adams describes this event in *Wounds of Returning*, her book on the persistence of plantation mentalities in the modern South. Staged by a prison population that has been "segregated" as a labor force (in Louisiana making license places, elsewhere doing data entry, small manufacturing, and service industry tasks), the spectacle both reveals and disguises the state's historical reliance on invisible coerced labor. The penitentiary rodeo evokes the Deep South's slave-worked plantation system that propelled expansion into the Southwest; the crafts fair makes minimally visible the work performed for centuries by chattel, leased convicts, and present-day inmates, though the prisoners' expropriated labor hides within the displays of "hobbies" done on their "own" time. Items offered for sale include elaborate handmade decorative objects—jewelry boxes made of crushed cigarette boxes, cabinets ornamented with thousands of burnt match stubs. As spectators negotiate prices with prisoners through chain-link barriers, Adams observes, "the multiple stages of Marx's commodity fetish come to life." This is not some universal example of commodity fetishism, to be clear; Adams notes the specific conditions that index the southern plantation: commandeered labor enforced by the state; the reduction of human beings to "animate [state] property"; and the reenactment of personal combat honed on "southern frontiers." Adams summarizes, quoting first from Joan Dayan: "'[The] practice of rendering certain groups of people as "dead in law"' in the United States originated in 'the "black codes" of the Caribbean and the American South'; thus the segregation of prisoners on a plantation would identify all inmates, whatever their racial history, with slaves restrained within a circum-Caribbean system. Inmates at Angola, as they live and work on a plantation, are heirs of slaves."[1] Angola Rodeo Day addresses the realities of southern-inspired state violence by presenting them fetishistically, binding them to nostalgia for the Wild West and staging an artificial exhibition of free-market relations. Unwanted knowledge is displayed so openly that it goes into hiding as spectacle.

Unlike most of the critical terms covered in this collection, fetish is not a standard topic in the study of southern literature. Nor is it a prominent idea in literary studies, despite having a central place in many other analytic disciplines, from anthropology and religious studies to psychoanalysis, Marxist theory, film studies, and theories of ideology. In this chapter, I shall examine some of the varieties of fetishism that readers may find useful in trying to understand how literature about the South often resorted to ways of disguising or silencing the most disquieting features of, say, plantation slaveholding or rural poverty. Any effort to discuss the usefulness of the concept of fetishism to southern (or any) literary study must acknowledge that what is meant by fetish varies from discipline to discipline, and reflects the long history of the term (from at least the Middle Ages, when the Catholic Church began to use the Latin word *facticium*, meaning "artificial," to condemn witchcraft).

Lorraine Gamman and Merja Makinen distinguish three major understandings of fetishism: anthropological, economic, and psychoanalytical. Freud used "fetishism" as the term for an abnormal sexual fixation that impedes psychological development. Afflicted patients seemed to be sexually aroused more by the properties of objects than by human characteristics. At its most extreme, such behavior manifests as pathological; associated stimuli substitute altogether for a sex partner. The fetish can play a crucial role in the formation of heterosexual identity for the male child. According to Freud's model, boys enjoy so intense a feeling for their mothers that they wish subconsciously to bring about the death of the father. The child's fear that the father knows of such murderous intent and might punish the child with castration coincides with the child's realization that the mother "lacks" a penis. Freud proposes that the boy associates this condition with his own fear of castration, interpreting the mother's lack as a loss. A solution to this tangle of fear and desire comes in the form of the phantasm of the mother's phallus, a thing that must have existed yet does not. Some children, according to the model, handle the anxiety caused by the notion of the mother's castration by finding some consoling object metonymically suggestive of the mother's "lost" sexual parts, for example, a slipper or a fur garment. The pathological fetishist fails to surrender this substitutionary solution and becomes arrested in a form of juvenile sexuality.

Whatever the arguable plausibility of this account for psychoanalytic purposes, the subtlety of Freud's model remains compelling as a description of how unwanted knowledge may be both acknowledged and disavowed through the mediation of a fantasy object. Such objects "know" that they cannot restore wholeness, yet they substitute for it as if they could. What distinguishes the function of fetish—and this is what makes it so useful a concept in other disciplines too—is that fetish operates as a form of conscious (or open) disavowal (or hiding). "Disavowal, unlike displacement or sublimation," Gamman and Makinen summarize, "is not a total denial of the desire experienced, which is subsequently repressed into another sphere. . . . Through the use of the fetish, the practitioner is able to continue to believe the false, while also knowing that it cannot be true."[2]

Needless to say, the masculinist hetero-normative bias of Freud's model limits its usefulness, despite his efforts to retool it to the development of girls. However, Freud's hypotheses have been defended by some feminists as *historically* accurate descriptions of the nineteenth century's bourgeois sex-gender system. Anne McClintock has returned Freud's theories of fetishization to their nineteenth-century contexts in both Victorian domestic labor arrangements and European imperialism; her critique suggests the two other realms of the fetish that Gamman and Makinen identify, the economic and the anthropological.

McClintock argues that Freud's theory of fetishization functions ironically as a kind of fetishization itself, since it elides the role of an important female worker in most bourgeois households, Freud's included. According to McClintock, the scenes Freud posits as introducing boys to sexual difference and mediating paternal rivalry fantasize the presence of the mother, since the person actually involved in such psychic and physical transactions was typically a nursemaid.[3] Freud himself recounts how his sexual education was conducted by such a young woman. We can use McClintock's critique here to represent the way the fetish functions in Marx's theory of the commodity to "forget" labor's social origins. Marx argues that goods for purchase under market capitalism have their value determined by their relation to one another; intrinsically incommensurable items must be equated in abstract units (perfected in the money form itself). In a necessary sleight of hand, we treat commodities as if their value inhered in the goods themselves, as if they possessed a kind of life of their own, on the order of the animate fetishistic object. Gamman and Makinen describe this process as "a disavowal of human labour, a displacement of value from the people who produce things onto the things themselves."[4] Both Freud and Marx gravitate to the notion of the fetish because of its explicit association with the magical thinking of primitive animism.

Marx's recourse to fetishism reflects its earliest appearance as a construct used by European merchants to facilitate commerce with West African tribes as early as the fifteenth century. William Pietz has documented the utility of the concept in "the abrupt encounter of radically heterogeneous worlds." The Portuguese hoping to trade with tribes on the Guinea coast applied their word *feitiço* (already used to designate and demean witchcraft and the licentious female sexuality associated with it) to the inexplicable social and natural order seemingly responsible for setting the values of objects that the natives were willing to trade and accept in exchange. The strange objects that natives revered, held to be worthless by traders, came to symbolize the alternative ontology and economy of an alien people. The fetish in Pietz's account served to mediate incommensurable value systems: "The fetish could originate only in conjunction with the emergent articulation of the ideology of the commodity form that defined itself within and against the social values and religious ideologies of two radically different types of noncapitalist society, as they encountered each other in an ongoing cross-cultural situation."[5] The association of fetish with the contact between European traders and African coastal tribes suggests the term's pertinence to the precapitalist commercial ventures in the Atlantic that eventually led to New World plantation colonialism and the perverse form of commodity fetishism embodied in the African slave trade. The anthropological "concept of the fetish emerged alongside that of the commodity form in the sixteenth and seventeenth centuries."[6]

As a contact-zone term, "fetish" implied pejorative judgments of the racial and cultural inferiority of primitives, as it dismissed the worth of any deeper knowledge about the social worlds out of which trade partners materialized. In this way, objects taken as fetishes already performed the sort of acknowledgment-as-disavowal that Marx came to identify as the enabling feature of capitalist exchange.[7] This anthropological function of the fetish as the marker of cross-cultural in/comprehension shows up after centuries of New World colonialism in George Washington Cable's novel *The Grandissimes*, published in 1880 and set in New Orleans in the years immediately following the Louisiana Purchase in 1803. The novel describes the murky, volatile scene of racial and economic striving in Creole society, as it follows the fortunes of the black and white sides of the prominent Grandissime family. At one point, an insulted quadroon woman plans the murder of a white man and sends her slave to perform it. The would-be assassin, Clemence, is detected before she can act, however, and she is lynched by a white Grandissime who suspects her of ties to voodoo. At Clemence's capture, a strange object falls from her clothing: a miniature coffin containing the wax effigy of a human arm. The figure proves to be a voodoo charm, fashioned in reference to the historical personage Bras-Coupé (French for "severed arm"), whose resistance to the death against slavery made him legendary. The slave's fetish (Cable uses the word) signifies the violent history of New World slavery and the measures forged to throw it off (suicidal rebellion but also tactics of resistance such as voodoo).[8] Jenny Franchot has interpreted the fetish in Cable's scene as "the materialization of the colonized Other as both individual and alternative religious tradition." Franchot points out that *The Grandissimes* ultimately discredits voodoo and that the fetish object is misinterpreted to alleviate anxieties about the colonized Other. But the fetishistic object does possess power, if only temporarily, to challenge the prevailing romance of national greatness:

> We struggle both to find out the story of Bras-Coupé and the story of America's relationship to France, Spain, Germany, England, Africa, and the West Indies. We resist the knowledge that America has indeed a past whose regional truths are not cut off from the national one but intrinsic to it. Imperial formation and bodily dismemberment or disfigurement are linked narratives. Not only are the wages of imperialism violence, but also the imperial nation is formed through severing parts of the national body or history.[9]

In a similar way, fetish objects appear at several moments in Faulkner's fiction to contest the confidence of elites in the plantation ethos. In *Absalom, Absalom!*, a Virginian overseer on a Haitian sugar plantation discovers an enigmatic object one morning—a pig bone, some chicken feathers, and a rag with pebbles tied in a sack. Knowing but overlooking the slaves' discontentment, Sutpen soon finds himself subduing a revolt by the plantation's blacks. Faulkner alludes here to the well-known role that voodoo played in the Haitian Revolution, in which Toussaint-Louverture's mustering of slave resistance relied on the common mystical faith of otherwise isolated blacks. The fetish object in *Absalom* signifies a long history of human slaughter, debasement, forced labor, and retaliatory bloodletting, but it functions in the usual way to proclaim the unwanted knowledge of black hostility while remaining largely incomprehensible to whites. Sutpen knows that he is inserting himself into a brutal colonial history, but he acts as if he does not, disavowing the reality that the "sheen on the dollars was not from gold but from blood."[10]

Such diegetic examples of the fetish point to a primordial piece of knowledge that the romance of national greatness finds unbearable: Until well into the nineteenth century, the U.S. South was as much a part of the colonial Caribbean plantation world as it was of the U.S. republic, and the republic itself was dependent on the commerce of plantation agriculture. That "the South" actually belonged to a pan-Caribbean colonial world, as Édouard Glissant suggests, or even more broadly to a hemispheric plantation order, as Antonio Benítez-Rojo proposes, means that a freestanding U.S. South, understood as a distinct region of the nation, was an artificial construct, a kind of fetishistic fantasy.[11] The broadly schizoid mentality that characterizes national attitudes toward the American South descends from the earliest efforts of the republic to make sense of its dependence on actual ways of life that fundamentally contradicted its ideals. Jennifer Rae Greeson has traced the projection of otherness onto the South back to the crucible of national origins. From the outset, it seemed incumbent on those describing the new republic to suppress the seeming violations of liberty, individualism, self-ownership, and enlightened reason being committed in the feudal, slaveholding South.

The Haitian historian Michel-Rolph Trouillot complains that accounts of the Haitian Revolution have tended to "silence" the significance of successful black rebellion against French rule. Trouillot notes how elites involved in the revolution devised methods of representation to neutralize challenges to legitimacy. Although he does not use the terminology of the fetish, his account of how a physical site of national memory functions both to acknowledge and disavow contradictions in Haiti's revolutionary history illustrates the logic of cultural fetishism. Trouillot considers the example of Sans Souci, a palace built in the mountains of northern Haiti by Henri Christophe (a black rebel leader himself who, as Henry I, became the infamous first "king" of the republic). Henri's spectacular royal residence was meant to demonstrate how free blacks could equal the greatest of European accomplishments. Henri erected his palace on the site of Millot, a former colonial plantation that as a slave he had once managed. As king, however, Henri became notorious for his reimposition of regulations that all but re-enslaved the *noirs*, darker Haitians of more immediate African descent who had been field hands before independence. Many believe Henri betrayed his own class in deciding that the colonial sugar economy, with its vast slave-worked plantations, had to be perpetuated to guarantee the new republic's prosperity. Sans Souci itself exemplified the rule of neo-slavery since many forced workers died in its construction. Nonetheless, Trouillot observes, the ruins of Sans Souci stand even today in Haiti as a popular memorial to Afrocentrism and the nation's revolutionary triumph.

In order for Sans Souci to signify this way, however, it must function as a site of forgetting as well as commemoration. Haitians who take pride in Sans Souci as a monument to the overthrow of colonial rule must overlook the extent to which the early republic replicated the colonial slave-run plantation system. Such equivocation at the core of the republic's anticolonial history resonates in the suppressions and outright misrepresentations to which *white* elites resorted elsewhere in the Americas and Europe to quell the fear of slave revolt and black self-governance. According to Trouillot, Henri tellingly inscribes anxieties about his own compromised legitimacy and violent African resistance to it in his very naming of the residence "Sans Souci" (French for "carefree"). Almost entirely forgotten in popular knowledge of the revolution is the murder, close to the eventual site of the palace, of one of Henri Christophe's principal rivals, an ex-slave from the Congo named Jean-Baptiste Sans Souci, who had accused Henri of a traitorous realliance with the French. Trouillot speculates that Henri mindfully planted Sans Souci's name on the palace as an act of hiding the African's story in plain sight. "The king," Trouillot summarizes suggestively, "was engaged in a transformative ritual to absorb his old enemy."[12] The royal residence both designates and overwrites the problems posed by Jean-Baptiste's Africanist revolt within revolt.

285

Trouillot finds one more meaning hidden in "Sans Souci": this was also the name of the Prussian king Frederick the Great's royal residence in Potsdam. Although Trouillot finds no evidence proving Henri's familiarity with the imperial monarch, there is a record of the presence of German colonists in Haiti, including a few engineers, at the time of the palace's construction. Trouillot concludes that "it is more than probable that [Henri] was aware of Potsdam's existence and that he knew what it looked like." Such legible but undocumented European connections resemble the difficulties Franchot cites in excavating "the story of America's relationship to France, Spain, Germany, England, Africa, and the West Indies."[13]

One of the most potent legacies of fetishistic thinking in New World plantation contexts came to be the artifice of race that evolved to justify European imperial domination of darker peoples around the world, including the enslavement of Africans. Racial stereotype operates as a kind of fetish, Homi Bhabha has theorized, because it assuages the anxious suspicion of those in power that their subjects are actually fully human but different, rather than damaged or inferior versions of themselves. Bhabha extrapolates the Freudian model of sexual difference to the circumstances of racial difference. He identifies a "*functional* link between the fixation of the fetish and the stereotype (or the stereotype as fetish)": "For fetishism is always a 'play' or vacillation between the archaic affirmation of wholeness/similarity—in Freud's terms: 'All men have penises'; in ours: 'All men have the same skin/race/culture'—and the anxiety associated with lack and difference—again, for Freud 'Some do not have penises'; for us 'Some do not have the same skin/race/culture.'"[14] Bhabha's formulations have been highly influential, and for the purpose of gaining a sense of the wide range of potential applications of the concept of the fetish to topics associated with southern literature—notably the history of colonial plantation society and economy, slavery and ideologies of race, and the overvaluation of some forms of sexual taboo—Bhabha's theoretical apparatus can be provocative.[15]

Think of Faulkner's portrayal of the power of racial, sexual, and even regional stereotype to organize Joe Christmas's romantic encounter with Joanna Burden in *Light in August*. The characters come together as fantasies of stereotype to each other, Joe pretending to break into the plantation mistress's house like a cabin slave, Joanna discovering her sexual passion as a ravishing by a "Negro." Racial stereotype is bound to sexual stereotype as the lovers play out various roles assigned to blacks and whites, men and women, southerners and New Englanders, as Faulkner exposes the artifices of a dominant mentality. Ralph Ellison cites such fetishistic stereotypes when he has the black protagonist of *Invisible Man* summoned by a wealthy white philanthropist, who wishes him to indulge her fantasy of being raped by a "black beast." Such works show the noxious persistence of stereotype as fetish in American culture—"fetish," precisely because stereotype is a form of disavowed knowledge, an unseen seen (like Ellison's physically visible but socially invisible man). Glenda Carpio has argued that a somewhat later American novel, Ishmael Reed's *Flight to Canada* (1976), challenges such persistence by incorporating "aspects of postmodernism to show the connections between chattel slavery's reification of people and bodies and the fetishistic notions of race and sexuality it has produced." In Carpio's analysis, Reed draws on imaginative modes associated with voodoo as a way of "breathing life into stereotypes" in order to show that, like zombies, "they are inert in essence but alive in their effects." While Reed understands stereotypes as products of slavery and racism that memorialize the past, he also wishes to "defetishize" stereotype in order to break its hold.[16] Let me note that Reed's imaginative challenge to stereotype depends on the fact that fetish is a form of disavowal that keeps what is suppressed in *conspicuous* hiding and hence available to notice and confrontation.

Another familiar mode of fetishism represented in southern literature involves the traditional South's hypervaluation of female sexual purity.

Explanations for the plantation world's insistence on women's absolute chastity may be found readily enough in the economic and social requirements of landed gentry everywhere: the patrimonial transmission of land and wealth had to be safeguarded by unimpeachable paternity. There could be no question of wives bearing illegitimate heirs. Nor could daughters be allowed to "ruin" their value as future wives by losing their virtue before marriage. Such social fantasies project a kind of reality that leads to the fetishization of the female body as at once spiritually pure and sexually reproductive; at once the necessary guarantor of dynasty and the greatest threat to it; the schizoid fusion of sisterly innocence and maternal reproductivity; the essence of virtue and the embodiment of fungible property. One solution to such tensions is the equivocation offered by the logic of fetishization. An example would be Poe's "The Fall of the House of Usher," in which the virginal Madeline Usher is a fetishized form of a vaguely aristocratic (and hence plausibly southern plantation) ethos. Living, Madeline embodies purity, robed in white, her cloistered innocence guarded by her brother. But her disinterred body bears ambiguous wounds of defloration, childbearing, murder. As a ghostly figure, Madeline functions like a fetish object, allowing the planter world to acknowledge the violence done to the socially dead like her (and all its other actual casualties like slaves)—"*We have put her living in the tomb!*" Usher exclaims—and at the same time to disavow its import, since the entire house collapses silently, and the visiting narrator escapes with an enigmatic tale.[17]

One of the most influential contemporary reconsiderations of ideology has been Slavoj Žižek's effort to describe social imaginative forms as fetishistic techniques for concealing the antagonisms and inequities that structure "the real" of Western capitalism. The enabling move for Žižek is his attempt to synthesize Freud's and Marx's versions of fetish in order to articulate the intersections of individual and collective fantasy. In *The Sublime Object of Ideology*, Žižek argues that social reality is a question less of what social actors *know* than of what they actually *do*. It is that feature of acknowledgment and disavowal that attracts Žižek to the fetish form in Freud and Marx. Ideology is not bad faith, or some conscious deception of self or others about the way things are, but instead a suppression that structures and produces reality: "Ideology is not a dreamlike illusion that we build to escape insupportable reality; in its basic dimension it is a fantasy-construction which serves as a support for our 'reality' itself: an 'illusion' which structures our effective, real social relations and thereby masks some insupportable, real, impossible kernel." That kernel may be "conceptualized" as "antagonism," "a traumatic social division which cannot be symbolized."[18]

Compare Quentin Compson's extreme valuation of his sister's sexual purity in *The Sound and the Fury*. Like Madeline Usher, Caddy is held to signify an aristocratic ethos as a fetishized figure of the purity, leisure, and refinement that masks a bloody traumatic social division hidden in plain

288 sight. That the Compsons' plantation world is ending, however, exposes the artifice of that fetishistic ideology. As Quentin broods on Caddy's fall, he keeps encountering the social material that has been released by the corresponding fall of the planter South: blacks whose indignities and ambitions suddenly become noticeable; women whose complaints about their trivialized or violated lives become audible; immigrants whose homes are also to be found now in America. The novel formulates Quentin's state of mind by creating a narrative discourse that exhibits the characteristics of at once knowing and disavowing the condition of loss. Eric Santner has extended the idea of fetishism into the domain of narrative analysis by suggesting that certain works of fiction fetishize the circumstances of traumatic events:

> By narrative fetishism I mean the construction and deployment of a narrative consciously or unconsciously designed to expunge the traces of the trauma or loss that called that narrative into being in the first place. The use of narrative as fetish may be contrasted with that rather different mode of symbolic behavior that Freud called *Trauerarbeit* or the "work of mourning." Both narrative fetishism and mourning are responses to loss, to a past that refuses to go away due to its traumatic impact. The work of mourning is a process of elaborating and integrating the reality of loss or traumatic shock by remembering and repeating it in symbolically and dialogically mediated doses; it is a process of translating, troping, and figuring loss. . . . Narrative fetishism, by contrast, is the way an inability or refusal to mourn emplots traumatic events, it is a strategy of undoing, in fantasy, the need for mourning by simulating a condition of intactness, typically by situating the site and origin of loss elsewhere.[19]

What Quentin must deal with is not finally the loss of his privilege and prosperity but his apprehension that they were illegitimate from the outset—an insight to be drawn from the story of plantation "design" in *Absalom, Absalom!* Whatever tricks Quentin resorts to, he cannot shake the shadow of melancholic repetition. Quentin has no story to tell, only a trauma experienced over and over. His death by melancholia in *The Sound and the Fury* ensues after he rejects the opportunity to mourn offered to him in *Absalom, Absalom!* by Shreve, who tries to draw his suicidal roommate toward the working through that "translating, troping, and figuring loss" might enable. The Compsons do not mourn: Benjy's domain is a set of fetishistic souvenirs meant to deny Caddy's loss even as they substitute for it, a discourse arrested melancholically in the antechambers of narrative. Jason's monologue resorts to narrative fetishism as he scorns any inclination to engage the past and instead produces a fantastic tale by, as Santner says, "simulating a condition of intactness."

Let me conclude with another illustration of narrative fetishism in a southern novel, Julia Peterkin's *Black April*. The story of a foreman who directs a 1920s Georgia sea-island cotton plantation run by free blacks (but still owned by absentee northern whites), Peterkin's work was praised widely for its well-informed descriptions of Gullah culture, including the reproduction of its distinctive dialect. Peterkin had grown up in Georgia as the daughter of a physician and later married a man who owned a working plantation. As the mistress of Lang Syne, she studied the culture of its black labor force. *Black April* recounts the eponymous protagonist's magnetic personality, his determination to modernize agriculture at Blue Brook, and his tragic end as the victim of betrayal in love and a physical affliction that takes his life.

April's demise results from his poisoning by a chemical used to combat boll weevils. Overexposed to it, April loses feeling in his feet. The course of the disease climaxes in a gruesome scene in which he soaks his legs in a medicinal solution, only to discover his rotted toes have floated to the surface. April gets treatment at a clinic, but he returns a double amputee, and he dies not long after, the wreck of a former colossus. Most critics note that the episode involving April's toes resembles an awful event in Peterkin's own years as mistress of Lang Syne. The father of one of her black employees suffered from gangrenous feet. Julia bathed his feet one day with warm water, to which a drop of harmless carbolic acid had been added. Horribly, the man's toes fell off, and though Julia understood she had not caused the damage, she suffered the victim's complaints for long afterward.

Peterkin's fictionalization produces effects of disavowal suggestive of narrative fetishism. Throughout the novel, the narrator insulates herself from the traumatic events reported: all the violence is black on black, all the culpability for misfortune laid to blacks, and all the scenes of horrific recognition narrated from a safe distance. When April suffers the loss of his toes, the narrator postpones its direct representation, describing the news passing among the group but not saying what it is until the end of the scene. When a child is forced to look on his dead mother's body, the trauma shatters each one's mental and bodily intactness: both dead mother and seeing son come apart—she is chin, hands, feet, lips, teeth, and half-lidded eyes; he is floating eyeballs.[20] But the narrator preserves her discursive intactness by confining all the horror to the boy's reaction alone; when the child finally passes out, the narrator has nothing of her own to say about the confrontation with black morbidity on the plantation.

One of the most prominent stylistic traits of the novel also contributes to what Santner describes as the "situating [of] the site and origin of loss elsewhere." Peterkin's descriptions of the natural world create the sensation of free-floating grief: "The darkness of the night was terrible as Breeze ran through it toward the Quarters. A cedar limb creaked mournfully as the wind wrung it back and forth. Its crying was like sorrowful calls for aid."[21] Nature itself is desolate, but whether at the prospect of the demise of a way of life, or at the suffering embedded in its history and perpetuation, or something else, is impossible to say. This sense of fetishistic concealment indicates a misrecognition of the original trauma of New World plantation slaveholding. As in *The Sound and the Fury*, the event that seems to structure the drama of the novel is modernization, experienced as a loss. From this standpoint, April's descent epitomizes modernization as a narrative of decline: he is unmanned by his imposition of modern ways, deceived by a modern, educated woman, and buried in a full-sized coffin that takes the measure of his diminishment. Yet the novel uncovers complicating evidence that the plantation is not *to be* ruined by new elements of modernity but rather was corrupted from the outset by versions of those very elements. April's assumption of mastery in the absence of the plantation's actual landlords serves to renew a system of domination, peonage, exploitation of the land for profit, labor violence, sexism, and so on that characterized the New World settler plantation from the beginning.

NOTES

1. J. Adams, *Wounds of Returning*, 151, 145, 10, 153–54. Quotation from J. Dayan, "From the Plantation," 194–96.

2. Gamman and Makinen, *Female Fetishism*, 45–46.

3. See McClintock, *Imperial Leather*, 87–95.

4. Gamman and Makinen, *Female Fetishism*, 28.

5. Pietz, "Problem of the Fetish," 6, 7.

6. Gamman and Makinen, *Female Fetishism*, 28.

7. McClintock discusses extensively the way foreign lands were described by European explorers in a vocabulary and imagery suggestive of fetishistic sexual objects.

8. Cable represents the scorn accorded voodoo practitioners like Clemence and her mistress Palmyre: "But the feelings handed down to Clemence had come through ages of African savagery; through fires that do not refine, but that blunt and blast and blacken and char; starvation, gluttony, drunkenness, thirst, drowning, nakedness, dirt, fetichism [*sic*], debauchery,

slaughter, pestilence and the rest—she was their heiress; they left her the cinders of human feelings." See Cable, *Grandissimes*, 331.

9. Franchot, "Unseemly Commemoration," 514, 515.

10. Faulkner, *Absalom, Absalom!*, 201–2.

11. See Glissant, *Faulkner, Mississippi*, and Benítez-Rojo, *Repeating Island*.

12. Trouillot, *Silencing the Past*, 65.

13. Ibid., 62.

14. Bhabha, *Location of Culture*, 106–7.

15. For a critique of Bhabha's model of fetish in a debate about Toni Morrison's *Beloved*, see Krips, *Fetish*, 45–56.

16. Carpio, "Conjuring the Mysteries of Slavery," 563, 565, 567.

17. Poe, *Complete Tales and Poems*, 245.

18. Žižek, *Sublime Object of Ideology*, 45.

19. Santner, "History beyond the Pleasure Principle," 144.

20. Peterkin, *Black April*, 278–79, 222–23.

21. Ibid., 178.

SUGGESTIONS FOR FURTHER READING

Bhabha, Homi K. *The Location of Culture*. New York: Routledge, 2004.

Gamman, Lorrain, and Merja Makinen. *Female Fetishism*. New York: New York University Press, 1994.

Krips, Henry. *Fetish: An Erotics of Culture*. Ithaca, N.Y.: Cornell University Press, 1999.

Matthews, John T. *William Faulkner: Seeing through the South*. Chichester, England: Wiley-Blackwell, 2009.

Pietz, William. "The Problem of the Fetish, I." *RES: Anthropology and Aesthetics* 9 (Spring 1985): 5–17.

Santner, Eric L. "History beyond the Pleasure Principle: Some Thoughts on the Representation of Trauma." In *Probing the Limits of Representation: Nazism and the "Final Solution,"* edited by Saul Friedlander, 143–54. Cambridge, Mass.: Harvard University Press, 1992.

Žižek, Slavoj. *The Sublime Object of Ideology*. New York: Verso, 1997.

BRIALLEN HOPPER

Fundamentalism

"Fundamentalism" is a fighting word. Born during the culture wars of the 1920s while creationism and evolution battled it out in a hot Tennessee courtroom, it is something between a technical term and an insult. It denotes the faith of Protestants who believe in the divine inspiration of the Bible and in the divinity, virgin birth, saving power, resurrection, and second coming of Jesus—a group that includes approximately a third of all Americans, though they are more likely to refer to themselves in less loaded terms, as "saved," "evangelical," "born-again," "Bible-believing," or just "Christian." It evokes pulpit-pounding preachers, right-wing politicians, and (more recently) Muslim terrorists. Among skeptics, it refers to the religion of a place trapped in a premodern past. And in the United States, it is short-hand for a Bible Belt culture famously described by Baltimore journalist H. L. Mencken in 1917 as "Baptist and Methodist barbarism."[1]

Mencken was one of the most influential journalists of his era, and he used white southern Christians to represent everything that threatened America's aspirations to artistic, intellectual, and cultural progress. He reported on the 1925 Scopes trial, in which a Tennessee high school teacher was convicted of illegally teaching evolution in schools. The trial drew national attention by dramatizing the conflict between fundamentalists (traditional Christians who believed in a literal interpretation of the creation narratives found in the biblical book of Genesis) and "modernists" (liberal Christians, agnostics, or atheists who were willing to be guided by scientific evidence, and who read scripture figuratively or not at all). Mencken's scathing articles about what he called "the Monkey Trial" helped to fix fundamentalism in the national imagination as incorrigibly antimodern, conservative, white, and southern. In his account, believers were sub-human: possessed of "so-called minds" and wallowing in "theological bilge," they were "poor white trash" or "primates." Mencken's story of southern religion has proved durable and continues to dominate many twenty-first-century critiques of religion and American culture. To name only one of countless examples, humorist Bill Maher relied heavily on Mencken-style caricature in his documentary *Religulous* (2008), visiting a Kentucky "Creation Museum" and talking to local believers in his quest to prove that all religion is "ridiculous."

Mencken's (and Maher's) dismissal of southern belief is undeniably classist. But its dehumanizing tendencies pale in comparison to the lethally dehumanizing racism that was at the heart of much white southern Christianity. As Mencken wrote, "The most booming sort of piety, in the South, is not incompatible with the theory that lynching is a benign institution. Two generations ago it was not incompatible with an ardent belief in slavery."[2] Here Mencken is understating the case: rather than simply lacking incompatibility, American religion and racism were always inescapably bound together. It is no coincidence that white Christians' militant legal and cultural battles for doctrinal purity in the early twentieth century raged alongside a revitalized obsession with race purity, a lynching epidemic, and the resurgence of the Ku Klux Klan. White southern Protestants cared about the literal interpretation of the Bible partly because they read the Bible as a literal and irrefutable defense of slavery and segregation. To quote Frederick Douglass's devastating analysis of southern religion from his 1845 *Narrative of the Life of Frederick Douglass, an American Slave*: "The slave auctioneer's bell and the church-going bell chime in with each other, and the bitter cries of the heart-broken slave are drowned in the religious shouts of his pious master. Revivals of religion and revivals in the slave-trade go hand in hand together."[3]

But the same religion that denied the humanity of African Americans also gave them the means to escape, withstand, recover, and resist. This is the ironic crux of southern Christianity. The "lynching bees" that brought white southerners together in a travesty of Christian communion created a different kind of sacred ground for black Christians, as each lynched black body became a new incarnation of Christ, an unbearable and sacred symbol of black life and black overcoming. At least that is the argument of black liberation theologian James Cone, who grew up in Jim Crow Arkansas and came of age in the Civil Rights and Black Power Movements. Cone argues that "until we can see the cross and the lynching tree together, until we can identify Christ with a 'recrucified' black body hanging from a lynching tree, there can be no genuine understanding of Christian identity in America, and no deliverance from the brutal legacy of slavery and white supremacy."[4]

Partly in spite of this terrible history, partly because of it, the old-time religion of the South has a redemptive resonance beyond the boundaries of region and belief. The sweet sound of spirituals and black and white southern gospel has long been the soundtrack of America's spiritual strivings, and even outsiders who are at odds with the practices and politics of fundamentalism have embraced its music. A primary example is New England intellectual W. E. B. Du Bois, who was made uneasy by some southern forms of black Christianity. He was alienated by the seemingly "grotesque" quality of black vernacular worship—"the mad abandon of physical fervor,—the stamping, shrieking, and shouting, the rushing to and fro and wild waving of arms, the weeping and laughing, the vision and the trance"—and he was wary of the fatalistic and inward-looking elements of traditional black faith.

294   But he built *The Souls of Black Folk* (1903) around the music that the faithful made, beginning each chapter with a musical epigraph. As he wrote: "The Music of Negro religion . . . still remains the most original and beautiful expression of human life and longing yet born on American soil. Sprung from African forests, where its counterpart can still be heard, it was adapted, changed, and intensified by the tragic soul-life of the slave, until, under the stress of law and whip, it became the one true expression of a people's sorrow, despair, and hope." On the basis of this traditional and deeply religious southern art, Du Bois placed his hope in "the deep religious feeling of the real Negro heart," which would someday lead to a political revival: "Some day the Awakening will come, when the pent-up vigor of ten million souls shall sweep irresistibly toward the Goal, out of the Valley of the Shadow of Death, where all that makes life worth living—Liberty, Justice, and Right— is marked 'For White People Only.'"[5]

Most listeners are not as attuned as Du Bois was to the revolutionary (or resurrectionary) political potential of southern Christian music. But from the formerly enslaved Jubilee singers to the Sam Cooke–fronted Soul Stirrers, from the Carter family to Carrie Underwood, southern gospel and Christian country continue to signify an instant authenticity capable of stirring the faithful while cutting through secular defenses of irony and unbelief. No other form of religion brings together sacred and secular reverence in quite the same way. This convergence can be seen in the diverse audiences of New Orleans–born gospel singer Mahalia Jackson and Arkansan country singer Johnny Cash, who each thrilled true believers, critics, and an international public, and it was spectacularly demonstrated when the octuple-platinum soundtrack to the Coen brothers' *O Brother Where Art Thou?* (2000) made temporary superstars of a homeschooled gospel girl group and an Appalachian dirge singer, and went on to win the Grammy for Album of the Year. Southern gospel is arguably the closest thing America has to a spiritual common denominator, traveling across decades and state lines with shifts in meaning but no loss in power. An exemplary case in point: The camp-meeting classic "Amazing Grace" was first published with its popular tune in *The Southern Harmony, and Musical Companion* in 1847. Popularized during nineteenth-century revivals, it was sung at secular funerals from San Francisco to New York during the AIDS epidemic of the 1980s, because it was the only song everyone knew.

Beyond the music, classic images and narratives of southern Protestantism serve a host of aesthetic and political purposes in secular contexts, adding authenticity, warmth, or heat. Georgia writer Flannery O'Connor was famously a Catholic, but her fiction uses fundamentalist Protestants (who seem at first just a few steps removed from Mencken's caricatures or Du Bois's grotesques) as a starting point for shattering explorations of race and grace. Robert Duvall's Oscar-nominated *The Apostle* (1997) redeemed and deepened the figure of the flawed southern preacher for believers and nonbelievers alike. Born-again redemption narratives undergird the career arcs and durable political personae of southern politicians Jimmy Carter and Bill Clinton. And the fleeting images of a clapping choir, a neon cross, "the laying on of hands," "getting filled with the spirit," a church sign, and a river baptism in the opening credits of HBO's *True Blood* give an extra frisson to televised Louisianan vampire sex.

For outsiders to fundamentalist faith, the continuing cultural resonance of southern religion depends on a dynamic of disgust and desire caught up in century-old classism and centuries-old racism and reinforced by more-recent red state/blue state mythologies. But these strong associations with primitivism, racism, freedom, and folk authenticity can be as limiting as they are illuminating. Many truisms about fundamentalism are far too simple.

First, as George Marsden and other historians of American religion have shown, fundamentalism has never been the exclusive domain of less educated southerners, even at its moment of origin.[6] In the 1920s, around the same time as the Scopes trial, the fundamentalist/modernist battle was being just as fiercely fought in bastions of the northeastern elite. In 1922, the famous liberal preacher Harry Emerson Fosdick preached a sermon titled "Shall the Fundamentalists Win?," an antifundamentalist manifesto that cost him his job at New York City's fashionable First Presbyterian Church. Fosdick's battle cry was promptly rebutted by J. Gresham Machen, a professor of the New Testament at Princeton Theological Seminary. Mencken liked to caricature fundamentalist Christians as uneducated denizens of a cultural desert, but Machen was a brilliant Johns Hopkins– and Princeton-educated scholar who had also done graduate work in Germany. His critique of modernist approaches to the Bible, *Christianity and Liberalism* (1923), succeeded in giving fundamentalist ideas a measure of intellectual legitimacy. Both Machen and Fosdick lost their jobs as a result of the controversy (Fosdick was too liberal for his institution, Machen too conservative for his), but each ultimately landed on his feet—Fosdick leading the newly formed Riverside Church in New York, and Machen founding the brand-new Philadelphia-based Westminster Theological Seminary.

The skirmish ended, but the struggle for the soul of Protestantism was far from over. Within and beyond the South, battles over fundamentalism dominated both national theological debates and mainstream church politics and resulted in the formation of new religious alliances and institutions throughout the country. Evangelicals developed a strong institutional infrastructure of their own, and they also sought to pursue their mission in secular contexts. Sarah Hammond has shown how powerful twentieth-century businessmen blended evangelicalism and entrepreneurship in their efforts to influence the culture for God, adapting the techniques of marketing to save souls, and pouring their wealth into evangelical colleges and nonprofits. Today, as Michael Lindsay demonstrates in *Faith in the Halls of Power* (2008), evangelicals are present and influential in all areas of American life, from the Ivy League to Wall Street to Hollywood. According to Lindsay, these "cosmopolitan evangelicals" are makers and shapers of mainstream and elite American culture, not exiles from it.[7]

Beyond the halls of power, popular fundamentalist Protestantism has also had a more complicated national geography than regional stereotypes would suggest. Pentecostalism is a telling example. The Pentecostal movement, which emphasizes modern miracles and speaking in tongues, may have roots in southern camp meetings, but it traces its beginning to the Azusa Street Revival in Los Angeles in 1906. A decade later, California Pentecostalism gave the United States its first modern mass-media superstar, revivalist preacher and faith healer Aimee Semple McPherson. Though McPherson famously toured the South in a "Gospel Car," she was a Canadian based in Los Angeles, and during the 1920s and 1930s she enjoyed vast success and influence. McPherson used brand-new mass media to preach traditional faith from a young city that was fast becoming the entertainment capital of the world. She was the second woman to have a broadcast license, and she ministered nationally over the radio. In the words of contemporary writer Carey McWilliams, McPherson was "more than just a household word: she was a folk hero and a civic institution; an honorary member of the police and fire departments; a patron saint of the service clubs; an official spokesman for the community on problems grave and frivolous."[8] Even H. L. Mencken sought her out.

Pentecostalism vividly illustrates the way southern modes of religious expression are often popularized, reproduced, and circulated elsewhere, but it is far from the only example. As Darren Dochuk argues in *From Bible Belt to Sunbelt* (2011), twentieth-century migration patterns led to a southern-inflected western evangelicalism that has profoundly shaped national politics and culture.[9] Today, a hybrid form of evangelicalism is a dominant culture in many parts of the country, not just in the traditional "Bible Belt," and evangelicalism's recent and current superstars are predominantly based not in the Old South but in the West and the Southwest. T. D. Jakes, an African American multimedia minister and spiritual advisor to George W. Bush, has a flourishing megachurch in Dallas. Joel Osteen, a televangelist and proponent of the "prosperity gospel" (a belief that Christian faith is the way to achieve material success), preaches to a television audience of seven million people in one hundred countries from his church in Houston. And Rick Warren, the Hawaiian-shirt-wearing author of *The Purpose Driven Life* (over thirty million copies have been sold), who prayed at the 2009 inauguration of Barack Obama, is the pastor of the Saddleback Church in Southern California. Meanwhile, the current capital of evangelicalism is arguably Colorado Springs, sometimes called "the Evangelical Mecca" or the "Evangelical Vatican," which is home to approximately eighty evangelical organizations.

The past century of Christian media stars demonstrates evangelicalism's geographical reach. It also illustrates another surprising aspect of fundamentalism: its love of the new. Aimee Semple McPherson's eagerness to embrace the medium of radio broadcasting anticipates the fervor with which later fundamentalist leaders have taken to television and the Internet. For all their supposed antipathy to modernity, when it comes to spreading the Word, fundamentalists have often been in the technological vanguard. In *Heaven Below: Early Pentecostals and American Culture* (2003), Grant Wacker describes the way American fundamentalist subcultures have been characterized by both "primitivism" and "pragmatism"—maintaining a belief in unchanging and otherworldly truth while resourcefully adapting both their message and its media to modern life.[10] This embrace of popular culture means that evangelical culture simultaneously functions as an alternative to and a microcosm of the broader culture.

Kentucky-born essayist John Jeremiah Sullivan, editor of the *Paris Review* and a self-described former evangelical, explores both of these impulses and functions in "Upon This Rock," an essay about a Christian rock festival held in Pennsylvania. Sullivan starts by satirizing evangelical culture's status as a mostly modern American microcosm:

> The Evangelical strata were more or less recognizable from my high school days. . . . Lots were dressed like skate punks or in last season's East Village couture (nondenominationals); others were fairly trailer (rural Baptists or Church of God); there were preps (Young Life, Fellowship of Christian Athletes—these were the ones who'd have the pot). You could spot the stricter sectarians right away, their unchanging antifashion and pale glum faces.

Unlike Wacker, who celebrates fundamentalists' adaptability and innovation, Sullivan initially dismisses Christian pop culture as a kind of pragmatic "parasitism" designed to keep Christians safe from the world and/or to lure unsuspecting non-Christians into the fold—a cheap knock-off of mainstream popular culture: "Remember those perfume dispensers they used to have in pharmacies—'If you like Drakkar Noir, you'll love Sexy Musk'? Well, Christian rock works like that. Every successful crappy secular group has its Christian off-brand." Later, this regionless off-brand culture is contrasted with a deeply real regional religion from below the Mason-Dixon line. When Sullivan meets some Appalachian backwoods believers at the festival, men who speak anachronistic "Chaucerian" English, "lived off game," and "knew all the plants of the forest, which were edible, which cured what," he falls into a moving if somewhat stereotypical meditation on timeless Appalachian authenticity and the beauty of primitive faith.[11]

Sullivan's analysis of evangelical culture reproduces some familiar and potentially reductive hierarchies in writing about the South. In particular, it seems to privilege an imagined rural purity over a supposedly debased mass culture. But Sullivan's perspective is different partly because he is interested in how intertwined these two cultures are: his "timeless" true believers express their faith not through folksy gospel or shape-note singing but through contemporary mass-produced Christian rock. And ultimately his story is a reversal of the usual script. Most outsiders want to appropriate the music and leave the religion; instead, Sullivan dismisses the music and then wistfully, lovingly describes the faith.

Sullivan's work is a corrective to nostalgic accounts of fundamentalist religion that ignore or dismiss the new. It is also a corrective to the vast body of writing on evangelicalism that sees it primarily or exclusively through the lens of conservative politics. Of course it would be impossible to write a history of southern fundamentalism without acknowledging its immense influence on modern conservatism. The decades-long resistance to enforced racial integration and affirmative action, the defeat of the feminist Equal Rights Amendment in the 1970s, the rise of anti-gay-rights and antiabortion movements in the 1970s and 1980s, and the conservative coalition that produced the Reagan and Bush presidencies and various iterations of a conservative Congress: all these have depended heavily on the support of white southern Christians. In the wake of the Civil Rights Act of 1964 and the Voting Rights Act of 1965, Richard Nixon's race-baiting "southern strategy" mobilized millions of alienated white southerners to move to the Republican Party, shaking up the long-Democratic "Solid South" and setting the stage for the rise of the Reagan-era religious right. But the alliance between southern fundamentalism and the Republican Party was not inevitable, and the familiar narrative of religion and reactionary politics obscures the more complicated role that southern evangelicalism has played in American political culture apart from the polarizing "culture wars." Since the 1980s, it's true, fundamentalism has tended to act within and upon politics in a manner reminiscent of the Scopes trial, with its strict binaries of believer and unbeliever, liberal and conservative. But the intervening decades played host to a more unpredictable version of evangelical culture, one that offered itself as a kind of national religiosity whose tropes and commitments had value even for those who rejected its creed.

Consider the career of North Carolinian revivalist Billy Graham. Deeply rooted in the southern camp-meeting tradition, Graham preached a gospel of personal salvation that allowed him to maintain alliances across the political and religious spectrum. Graham was nonpartisan, not apolitical. He gained a national reputation in 1949 when conservative media magnate William Randolph Hearst decided to publicize his Los Angeles revival meetings or "crusades." The not-particularly-religious Hearst saw Graham's message as a means to unify Americans against godless Communism. With Hearst's help, Graham quickly became a popular celebrity with unprecedented political access, praying with and counseling both Democratic Truman and Republican Eisenhower (and all subsequent presidents) and appearing on the cover of Henry Luce's *Time* magazine in 1954.

Graham's connection with the conservative Hearst and Luce media empires might make him seem embedded in the conservative establishment, and he certainly shared both men's passionately anti-Communist views. But Graham is a registered Democrat, and he steadfastly refused to endorse a presidential candidate until 2012. Furthermore, long before most white clergy North or South were willing to advocate for integration, Graham spoke openly against racial segregation as a sin. He invited Martin Luther King Jr. to share the pulpit with him at a 1957 crusade at Madison Square Garden, and for decades he worked closely with African American singer Ethel Waters. Later Graham took his antiracist crusade global, preaching against apartheid to an integrated crowd of South Africans in 1973.

Throughout the culture wars of the late twentieth century, Graham mostly focused on political commitments that both parties ostensibly shared (anti-Communism, racial equality) while largely avoiding issues that divided them (abortion, sexuality). He carefully distanced himself from the overt partisanship represented by his fellow southern fundamentalists Jerry Falwell and Pat Robertson, instead maintaining his own unique form of political access and influence. Graham's gospel was light on brimstone and bright with the promise of being born again—an all-American gospel of forgiveness and second chances. During the long decades between Scopes and Reagan, he helped to make southern-style revivalist faith into a mainstream, media-friendly, nonpartisan, and sometimes even prophetic civic religion.

At the same time that Graham was popularizing southern fundamental-ism as a kind of de facto national faith, some black political leaders were wielding it as a fundamental political critique of America itself. The Civil Rights Movement of the 1950s and 60s was created by an unlikely coali-tion—fundamentalists, liberal Protestants, Catholics, Jews, agnostics, athe-ists—but the movement's public language (whether it was used and under-stood literally or metaphorically) was often a Bible-based black vernacular infused with the same songs that W. E. B. Du Bois had celebrated half a century earlier. The Reverend Martin Luther King Jr. was not a fundamen-talist by belief or training, but he perfected traditional southern black faith as a homiletic mode, lifting familiar religious language into soaring new flights of rhetoric that resounded in America's living rooms on the evening news. Like the righteousness he preached about, King's language "rolled down like waters." It powerfully pulled together the King James Bible, spirituals and gospel music, traditional call-and-response refrains of the black church, per-sonal testimony, history, philosophy, psychology, social theory, and modern theology. King was profoundly critical of the American Christianity of his time and of the complacent American exceptionalism that undergirded it, but ironically his version of southern faith has subsequently become canon-ized as a high point of religion and politics in the United States, more nec-essary and more durable than Graham's. Reduced to sound bites, King's ser-mons, speeches, and epistles have become a new brand of endlessly malleable civic religion—a legacy that is continuously appropriated by politicians with widely divergent political and religious commitments.

Some forms of movement faith have proved much harder for the nation to assimilate. For many leaders and foot soldiers of the Civil Rights Movement, fundamentalist faith was simple truth and fuel: they believed that Jesus would go before them, that he was with them in their cells. No one was bet-ter at preaching this literal, visceral message than Fannie Lou Hamer, a for-mer sharecropper and a legendary organizer and visionary of the Mississippi movement. Hamer's testimony was rooted in her experiences of enduring exploited labor, forced sterilization, sexual assault, and brutal beatings, a sur-vival story she narrated as an authoritative foundation for her faith and politics.

Hamer interpreted the Bible by asserting an absolute one-to-one equivalence between scriptural stories and the present-day struggle (a centuries-old mode of Biblical interpretation called "typology" that is still familiar from Puritan images like the "City on a Hill"). Like the Puritan preacher John Winthrop, Hamer placed herself and her friends directly into the biblical narrative. Scorning Christians who saw the church as a social club and mocking traditionally sacrosanct male ministers, among many other targets, Hamer argued that the Bible was coming dramatically to life right then and there in Mississippi. In one of her speeches, she and her coworkers re-embody the Old Testament story of the Hebrew children in the fiery furnace:

> Now you can't tell me you trust God and come out to a church every Sunday with a bunch of stupid hats on seeing what the other one have on and paving the preacher's way to hell and yours too. Preachers is really shocking to find them out. You know they like to rear back in the corners and over the rostrum and said, "What God has done for Meshach, Shadrach, and Abednego." But what he didn't know, God has done the same thing for Fannie Lou Hamer, Annell Ponder, and Lawrence Guyot.[12]

Hamer's obstinate faith gave her the courage to preach searing, scathing jeremiads against inequality to diverse audiences, including at one point to a national television audience at the 1964 Democratic National Convention, in defiance of then-president Johnson (the jeremiad, a denunciation of national sin and call to repentance, is another classic Puritan religious genre). As Hamer once said: "One day America will crumble. Because God is not pleased."[13]

Southern evangelical faith is language, culture, performance, and politics, but it can't be reduced to any or all of these things. In Hamer's hands, it was a source of an otherwise unthinkable strength and glory, but it has also been a source of well-earned shame. At once elite and everyday, regional and national and global, cutting-edge and preserved in amber, southern Protestantism simultaneously unites and divides the United States and prophesies its bitter end. In the second decade of the twenty-first century, the coalition between U.S. fundamentalists and political conservatives appears to be crumbling; young evangelicals are increasingly uninterested in the culture wars of their parents' generation, and "social issues" are beginning to cost conservatives votes. The South, like the nation, is becoming more religiously diverse, and more and more Americans (including many former fundamentalists) are identifying their religion as "none." It is not clear what new forms of faith the next generation will bring. What is clear is that despite Mencken's critique, southern fundamentalism has always provided an incredibly rich legacy for people within and outside the fold—even, arguably, an intellectual legacy. As the former fundamentalist Christine Rosen writes,

> My fundamentalist education gave me a profound respect for my fellow human beings; it taught me the dangers of pride and the joys of helping others; it gave me a love of the Bible and a lifelong devotion to language and music. It left my mind open to entertaining and eventually experiencing a great many un-orthodox ideas, including the many insights I gained from science and from history. It taught me the value of reading, the usefulness of memorization, and the importance of speaking and writing clearly. Its insistence on the careful study of Scripture gave me an appreciation for what the theologian Reinhold Niebuhr once described as "the ambiguity of human virtue."[14]

Or, in the words of the former Pentecostal proselytizer and current atheist intellectual Michael Warner: "Curiously enough, given that fundamentalism is almost universally regarded as the stronghold and dungeon-keep of American anti-intellectualism, religious culture gave me a passionate intellectual life of which universities are only a pale ivory shadow."[15]

In the end, it might even be this common intellectual heritage that unites the otherwise extraordinarily diverse people of southern fundamentalism past and present and future: a shared sense that the stakes are high, that beliefs matter, that words can change the world; that there is a book of life, and that anyone who speaks its words can make themselves and the world anew.

NOTES

1. Mencken, "Sahara of the Bozart," 137. The widely circulated 1920 version of the essay was preceded by a shorter version published in 1917 in the *New York Evening Mail*.

2. Ibid., 147.

3. Douglass, *Narrative of the Life*, 105.

4. Cone, *Cross and the Lynching Tree*, xv.

5. Du Bois, *Souls of Black Folk*, 116, 125.

6. See Marsden, *Fundamentalism and American Culture*.

7. See Hammond, "God Is My Partner," and Lindsay, *Faith in the Halls of Power*.

8. Quoted in Sutton, *Aimee Semple McPherson*, 88.

9. See Dochuk, *From Bible Belt to Sunbelt*.

10. Wacker, *Heaven Below*, 12–14.

11. J. J. Sullivan, "Upon This Rock."

12. Hamer, *Speeches of Fannie Lou Hamer*, 50.

13. Ibid., 52.

14. Rosen, *My Fundamentalist Education*, 227.

15. Warner, "Tongues Untied," 216.

SUGGESTIONS FOR FURTHER READING

Bendroth, Margaret Lamberts. *Fundamentalism and Gender, 1875 to the Present.* New Haven, Conn.: Yale University Press, 1996.

Griffith, R. Marie. *God's Daughters: Evangelical Women and the Power of Submission.* Berkeley: University of California Press, 2000.

Marsden, George. *Fundamentalism and American Culture.* Rev. ed. New York: Oxford University Press, 2006.

Raboteau, Albert J. *Slave Religion: The Invisible Institution in the Antebellum South.* New York: Oxford University Press, 1978.

Schweiger, Beth Barton, and Donald G. Mathews, eds. *Religion in the American South: Protestants and Others in History and Culture.* Chapel Hill: University of North Carolina Press, 2004.

303

Exceptionalism

SYLVIA SHIN HUEY CHONG

With the election of Barack Obama to the U.S. presidency in 2008, many commentators saw the twilight of two forms of exceptionalism—American and southern—that had dominated U.S. political and popular rhetoric in recent decades. After all, the historic election of the first African American president, swept into office with the help of former Republican-dominated states Virginia, North Carolina, and Florida, seemed to signal the waning of a form of racialized electoral politics dating from the Nixon era deemed the "southern strategy." Here was the dawn of a new postracial society, destroying the myth that southern voters were somehow locked into a post-civil-rights antiblack resentment that served the domination of the Republican Party in that region. And when Obama received the 2009 Nobel Peace Prize less than a year after his election, it spoke to international hopes of a sea change from the post-9/11 foreign policy of George W. Bush's administration, with its planks of strong interventionism and unilateral military action reviving fears of American exceptionalism run amok.

How sadly those hopes have dissipated, as the last six years have shown how many aspects of southern and of American exceptionalism have remained intact. Far from eradicating race-baiting in politics, Obama's election has rejuvenated a slice of the Far Right in the United States under the unruly banner of a revived Tea Party. While adopting the symbolism of colonial-era Yankee rebellion, these new American revolutionaries are concentrated in the South and the Midwest, and their cries against tyranny are against not the British Crown but an American government viewed as corrupted by a black Muslim dictator-elect hiding his origins as a Nigerian prince beneath a supposed birth certificate from, of all places, Hawai'i. One of Obama's greatest crimes, according to these critics, is that he and his family renounce the greatness of the American nation. Alarmed that the first lady, Michelle Obama, announced during the 2008 campaign, "For the first time in my adult lifetime, I'm proud of my country," conservatives such as Obama's opponent in 2012, Mitt Romney, rebuked Obama on the campaign trail: "Our president doesn't have the same feelings about American exceptionalism that we do."[1] The recent excesses of political rhetoric, which have labeled the president every-thing from a terrorist to a Nazi to an antebellum slave owner, have prompted one commentator, *Washington Post* columnist Kathleen Parker, to write that "the GOP is fast becoming regionalized below the Mason-Dixon line and increasingly associated with some of the South's worst ideas. . . . Southern Republicans, it seems, have seceded from sanity."[2]

Likewise, the continuation of Bush-era policies under the Obama admin-istration, from the extraterritorial military prisons at Guantanamo Bay to the use of drones to wage the war on terror in Afghanistan and Pakistan, has brought back the specter of the United States as the Lone Ranger of international relations, forging its own righteous path without care for mul-tinational coalitions or United Nations approval. Perhaps in overcompensa-tion for attacks on his patriotism, President Obama argued for intervention in the Syrian civil war in a speech in September 2013 to the UN General Assembly, stating as justification, "Some may disagree, but I believe America is exceptional, in part because we have shown a willingness, to the sacrifice of blood and treasure to stand up, not only for our own interests, but for the interests of all."[3] In an uncanny echo of Joseph Stalin's 1929 reproach to the U.S. Communist Party, it fell to, of all people, Russian president Vladimir Putin to chastise Obama in the opinion pages of the *New York Times* for resurrecting American exceptionalism to justify this use of military force. Sounding a surprisingly sober "plea of caution from Russia" that hid his own nation's interests in Syria, Putin gave the lie to Obama's claim to moral high ground, asserting, "Millions around the world increasingly see America not as a model of democracy but as relying solely on brute force, cobbling coalitions together under the slogan 'you're either with us or against us.'"[4] It is as if the violent rhetoric of southern exceptionalism—as seen in Parker's invocation of Civil War references to castigate the New Right as a premod-ern aberration in our postracial utopia—has returned with a vengeance in the latest rebirth of American exceptionalism as global blood debt, offering "blood and treasure" in return for moral and geopolitical fealty.

The tangled fate of these two exceptionalisms, American and southern, may have been brought to the fore by the contradictions of these recent events, but they have been linked since their first appearance during the birth of the U.S. nation-state. According to the *Oxford English Dictionary*, the noun "exceptionalism," naming an ideology in which the United States constitutes an exception to the general historical, social, and economic laws that seemed to have governed national development in European nation-states, is itself of fairly recent coinage. It arises from a 1929 dispute between

Stalin and U.S. Communist Party leader Jay Lovestone about whether the U.S. working class, at the cusp of the Great Depression, was ready for revolution, or whether "the specific peculiarities of American capitalism" stood in the way of revolutionary consciousness.[5] For Stalin, Lovestone's claims, denounced as the "heresy of American exceptionalism," were far from a sign of the United States' superiority, as the adjective "exceptional" might suggest; rather, it marked the United States as an aberration, monstrously exempt from the march of history in the rest of the world toward capitalist decline and Communist revolution. Later rearing its head as the "Negro question" within the American "national question," a version of southern exceptionalism also emerges out of these Marxist debates. Even as Stalin was expelling the Lovestonites, the Communist International (Comintern) Sixth Congress in 1928 elevated the struggle of American Negroes within the party's agenda, helping to mobilize national and international Communist support for the Scottsboro Boys in Alabama in 1931. In the "Black Belt thesis," the South contained the "necessary conditions for a national revolutionary movement among the Negroes," countering Lovestone's pessimism about the complacency of the American working class at large.[6] However, in practice these efforts often floundered on the residual racism of white Communist organizers, and even non-Communist black activism was persecuted by the U.S. government under the cover of the Red scare.

It is ironic, given the original negative connotations of the term, that American exceptionalism would be subsequently taken up by U.S. intellectuals and politicians as a positive attribute. In Louis Hartz's *The Liberal Tradition in America* (1955), a paradigmatic example of the Cold War era's "consensus history," the failures mourned by the Lovestonites become celebrated as accomplishments: "European liberalism, because it was cursed with feudalism, was forced to create the mentality of socialism, and thus was twice cursed. American liberalism, freed of the one, was freed of the other, and hence was twice blessed."[7] Hartz's invocation of divine blessings harkens back to one of the earliest strains of American exceptionalist thought, found among the Puritan settlers of the New England region. En route to what would become the Massachusetts Bay Colony, John Winthrop set out the idea of the New World as not merely another refuge for his persecuted religious sect but as a "city upon a hill," a chosen land for a chosen people to enact God's kingdom on earth.[8] Here, the Puritan vision of being "elect" forms the basis for their exceptionalism—a dream that the new American colonies will succeed where the corrupt Old World has failed, which retroactively remakes the New World from a conquered territory into the predestined location for such redemption. This New England strain of exceptionalism mobilizes the sacred to justify the protonational, thus marrying a universal logic to a historical particularity.

Later New England elites helped to enshrine this regional history as a national origin story. In 1820, on the bicentennial of the Pilgrim landing at Plymouth Rock, Massachusetts, Daniel Webster famously celebrated Plymouth as the place where "Christianity, and civilization, and letters made their first lodgement, in a vast extent of country, covered with a wilderness, and peopled by roving barbarians."[9] Echoing themes and comparisons that would later appear in Alexis de Tocqueville's *Democracy in America* (1835, 1840), Webster extols the legacy of "free and popular government," which the Pilgrims supposedly bequeathed to us, rejecting the "unequal" and "feudal" systems that continued to dominate the European nations. The ritual of celebrating Thanksgiving along the pattern of the first New England settlers also began in this period, popularized by magazine editor Sarah Josepha Hale in the 1830s–1840s and institutionalized by Abraham Lincoln after the Union victory at Gettysburg in 1863. After the Civil War, Progressive Era educators seized on the holiday as an object lesson in nationalism and assimilation, helping to conflate the more egalitarian Pilgrims with their theocratic Puritan neighbors as well as to romanticize early contact between the settler colonists and Native Americans. Later scholars such as Perry Miller and Sacvan Bercovitch have reaffirmed the centrality of Puritan ideas within American culture, even as their work has enabled critiques of the exceptionalism that such ideas inspired. More recently, the allure of New England colonial-era references in our contemporary politics reflects the attractiveness of this marriage of religion and nationalism, as witnessed not only in the "Tea Party" moniker but also in the title of a 2011 documentary, *A City upon a Hill: The Spirit of American Exceptionalism*, produced by the conservative nonprofit Citizens United and narrated by former Georgia congressman Newt Gingrich.

Interestingly, Webster's explanation of American exceptionalism also tangentially evoked that other exceptionalism, southern. For a brief paragraph, the specter of the "African slave-trade" invades his Plymouth Rock Oration, as an "odious and abominable" phenomenon that is not "fit" for the "land of the Pilgrims."[10] Although unnamed, the South stands here in contrast to New England, a site of uncivilized "misery and torture" unbefitting a nation representing the "blessings of good government and religious liberty." As Jennifer Rae Greeson has argued, the region has played a significant role in the political imaginary of the early U.S. nation, almost a century before the infamous "lost cause" of the Civil War that is usually touted as central to the idea of southern exceptionalism. By Greeson's reckoning, the South functioned as an "internal other for the nation," symbolizing during the early years of the republic a colonial, decadent, tropical outpost marked by its reliance on both agricultural production and black chattel slavery.[11] This allowed the Northeast to differentiate itself as the metropolitan and modernizing center of the nation, disavowing its own reliance on the products as well as the modes of production of the South. Contemporary conservative politics has also found it necessary to sever its celebrated colonial and revolutionary precursors from the plantation-and-slave South, which threaten to taint Virginian founding fathers such as Thomas Jefferson, George Washington, and James Madison. Tea Party activists agitated for history textbooks in Tennessee to remove references to founding fathers as slave owners, and in 2011 the Republican majority in the House of Representatives led a reading of the text of the U.S. Constitution into the Congressional Record that notably omitted the section regarding the three-fifths compromise, among other passages. Together, these incidents underscore not only the disconnect between the triumphant narratives of national beginnings in American exceptionalism and the legacy of slavery as the dark mark of southern exceptionalism, but also the dependency of the national ideal on its abjected and repressed internal other. In other words, southern exceptionalism becomes the "exception to the exception" that ratifies the *rule* of American exceptionalism, in the double sense of both *norm* and *hegemony*.

This early separation of the "South" from the national explains the power of the Plymouth Rock origin myth against the messier story told by another, more southerly candidate for birthplace of the nation: Jamestown (in present-day Virginia), the first permanent English settlement in the Americas, established in 1607 and best known for the tale of Pocahontas, the Powhatan Indian princess who saved the life of Jamestown leader John Smith and later married tobacco planter John Rolfe. However, Anna Brickhouse's work on "hemispheric Jamestown" highlights the Spanish presence in Virginia in the late 1500s, through Jesuit accounts of a failed settlement ended by the violent rebellion of another young Powhatan named Don Luis, who had been raised by Spaniards but later betrayed them.[12] This counternarrative opposes the Puritan origin myth in multiple ways: not only does it tie the pre–U.S. South as much to Latin America and the Caribbean as to New England, showing the presence of multiple and competing colonial empires in the Americas, but it also presents different models for conceptualizing the interaction between indigenous peoples and European colonists beyond myths of naive Native generosity. But even cleansed of its Spanish and Native prehistory, Jamestown still troubles the triumphant teleology of American exceptionalism, in particular because it is the site where African slaves were first brought to colonial America in 1619, leading back to the shameful story previously relegated to the South. Perhaps placing the United States' birth in Jamestown would mean accepting the "exception" of slavery as part of the nation's foundation and open the door to wider discussions of the importance of chattel slavery and the plantation economy even in the Northeast and the Mid-Atlantic colonies.

Although this negative vision of southern exceptionalism allows American exceptionalism to export, as it were, its unwanted characteristics to its outcast region, a critique of both exceptionalisms must start with the fact that these "exceptions" were wholly unexceptional. The Cold War era heightened the ideological stakes of the American exceptionalist argument, as the moral high ground outlined in publisher Henry Luce's essay "The American Century" (1941) before World War II was threatened by the hypocrisies of America's treatment of its racial minorities. Under scrutiny not only by the Soviet bloc but by the "nonaligned" Third World nations, whose allegiances were up for grab, the United States attempted to explain its "Negro problem" as a momentary misstep in its larger commitment to democracy. Thus, what Gunnar Myrdal named the "American dilemma" in the title of his 1944 Carnegie Corporation study was precisely this preservation of American exceptionalism—a celebration of "liberty, equality and justice" deemed the "American Creed"—from the challenge posed by antiblack racism, which was localized to a recalcitrant South. Even the Civil Rights Movement, celebrated as a national triumph, is viewed as a "southern" phenomenon, ignoring the entrenched nature of de facto segregation and continued discrimination taking place in other regions. As chronicled by the contributors to the recent essay collection *The Myth of Southern Exceptionalism* (2010), the "South" has been made to stand in for all manner of social and political problems, from the normalization of segregation to the brutality of the modern prison system, thus drawing attention away from the presence of similar issues in Detroit, New York, or Los Angeles. Even the recent rise of the religious Right and neoconservative retooling of racial tropes in electoral politics has been characterized by pundits as a "southernization" of American politics, rather than acknowledging the national roots of these conservative trends. After all, Richard Nixon, widely seen as the first Republican president to deploy the "southern strategy" to turn Democratic strongholds into GOP stalwarts in the late 1960s, had his start in California—a hotbed of postwar suburban white *ressentiment*—as did later Republican icon Ronald Reagan. If the South is the sole exception to the greatness of American exceptionalism, then the myth of national greatness can be perpetuated; however, if the exception turns out to be the rule, the entire nationalist enterprise becomes suspect.

But lest we dwell on the North-South (as well as the black-white) binary as the main opposition within American exceptionalism, there is another axis, East-West, that runs influentially throughout its history. The westward expansion of U.S. territories—sacralized as Manifest Destiny—not only brought an influx of new land and resources to exploit but also introduced additional ideological oppositions and tensions. Through a series of Indian wars and violent removals, Native groups on the East Coast were sequestered into reservations that nominally preserved their sovereignty but more importantly neutralized their claims to land and resources desired by white settlers. By the time Fredrick Jackson Turner celebrated the western frontier in 1893 as the true birthplace of America—the "crucible" in which European immigrants were finally "Americanized"—not only had the actual frontier, in turns of "unclaimed" land, disappeared, but so had the "Indians" on those lands with whom earlier settlers had clashed. Turner's "frontier thesis" was not a claim of chronological priority over Plymouth or Jamestown but rather an attempt to establish the psychological uniqueness of a kind of "American character," and it has been spread not only through the popularity of the "western" in film and literature but also by scholars such as Henry Nash Smith and Richard Slotkin. Turner's newly minted "Americans" not only displaced Natives on their land but literally *took their place*—the frontier takes the European immigrant "from the railroad car and puts him in the birch canoe . . . strips off the garments of civilization, and arrays him in the hunting shirt and the moccasin."[13] This symbolic redface minstrelsy is echoed in both the original Tea Party of 1773, when American colonists donned Indian disguises to dump British tea into Boston Harbor, and the current reincarnation of the Tea Party, where a new "nativism" defends a narrow vision of the real America against the incursions of immigrants, blacks, and liberals. While acts of epistemological violence, these appropriations of the position of the "first" Americans hide an even more brutal history of conflict between European settlers and Native tribes, where Indians did not simply vanish but were killed, driven off, or forcibly assimilated. The Indian removals and Indian wars are forgotten as exceptions to American exceptionalism, but the symbolic primacy of Native Americans shows how intrinsic this history is to the development of the nation.

The nineteenth-century westward expansion of the U.S. also brought two other racial groups within American borders and into the symbolic orbit of American exceptionalism: Asians and Latinos/as. The end of the Mexican-American War (1846–48) not only affirmed the U.S. annexation of Texas but also brought a wide swath of populated territory into U.S. possession; subsequent wars and military coups at the turn of the nineteenth century also incorporated the Philippines, Puerto Rico, Guam, and Hawai'i as U.S. territories. Despite the exceptionalist claim that America never had imperial aspirations like the British or the Spanish, these colonial acquisitions, along with American military and economic activity throughout the Pacific Rim and Latin America, inaugurated a period of American empire that would have ramifications for the rest of the twentieth century and well into the twenty-first—as witnessed in the current use of Cuban territory at Guantanamo Bay as a military prison. While the United States divested itself of many of these territorial possessions, either through political incorporation or ostensible independence, these territories have left a legacy not only of racialized migrants but also of military exploitation and political exclusion. The treatment of these latecomer colonies, as opposed to the original thirteen, would give the lie to American exceptionalism but would be managed through a different logic of exception than the South—by outright exclusion rather than internal quarantine. As debated by a series of early twentieth-century Supreme Court decisions known as the Insular Cases, the liminal status of these U.S. territories would be marked by the notion that they were a part of, yet apart from, the rest of the nation—affirming U.S. sovereignty over the territories but denying rights to their residents. While this form of second-class citizenship would remain a sore point in territories such as Puerto Rico and Guam, even residents of areas that achieved statehood found themselves subordinated to incoming white settlers, leading some Chicano/a and Native Hawai'ian activists to levy charges of internal colonization stemming from the initial military conquest of their homelands in the nineteenth century. As Chicano author Américo Paredes has pointed out, "The border moved—we didn't."[14]

The history of Asians, Latinos/as, and Native tribes in the United States thus complicates not only the *exceptionalness* but also the *Americanness* of American exceptionalism, by tying the United States inextricably to a global history as well as forming undigested pockets of otherness within the nation-state itself—in the words of filmmaker Trinh T. Minh-ha, the "Third World within the First."[15] One intellectual consequence of this interpenetration of the foreign within the national has been the application of postcolonial theory to American studies, which has allowed scholars to consider the United

States' imperial and settler colonialist past in relation to other areas such as South Africa, Indonesia, India, and Vietnam. The transnational and hemispheric turn in American studies of the last few decades has also redefined the regional and geographic frameworks in which the United States has been situated as a unit of study. More than simply enabling comparative work, these frameworks encourage viewing the United States as a dependent node in a larger network, whether that be the Black Atlantic, Aztlán, the Global South, the Pacific Rim, the Fourth World, or the Americas writ large. The dispersed structure of contemporary economies, transportation, and communications means that these networks do not even need to be thought of as geographically adjacent or coherent, making Cambodia-Detroit as logical a unit as El Paso-Ciudad Juárez. These same critiques of American exceptionalism may well apply also to southern exceptionalism, which in recent years has made a comeback in popular as well as political culture as an erstwhile form of white "ethnicity." Battling for attention in a cosmopolitan marketplace of images and tastes, celebrities such as the chef Paula Deen and the reality show stars of *Duck Dynasty* peddle a version of southern culture that attempts to shed the historical baggage of the Lost Cause and Jim Crow in favor of a nostalgic construction of premodern rural hospitality and regional particularity. However, as with the Confederate flag, recurrent racial controversies trouble the message that these assertions of cultural identity are merely "heritage, not hatred." What is commonly recognized as southern "culture" was never racially or ethnically pure; it is a product of cultural miscegenation between whites and blacks during a *longue durée* of unequal relations, and it now finds itself, like "American identity," under pressure by migration, globalization, and hybridization.

Further diluting the regional-racial specificity of southern identity is the ability of "outsiders" to claim membership in the New South, from foreign interlopers in the country music scene such as Keith Urban (Australia) or Shania Twain (Canada), to new Latino/a and Asian urban enclaves in iconic southern cities. For example, in the wake of Hurricane Katrina, New Orleans turned out to be not just a "chocolate city" but also the home of one of the largest Vietnamese American communities in the South, in the suburb of Versailles, part of a larger Vietnamese diaspora reaching to Washington, D.C., Atlanta, and Houston. And Latinos/as, the fastest-growing minority group in the United States, are also finding a foothold in the South, concentrating around Atlanta as well as in the Raleigh-Durham-Chapel Hill triangle. While the presence of Asians and Latinos/as in the South is far from new— there have been Hispanics along the Gulf Coast since the era of Spanish colonialism, small pockets of Filipinos known as the "Manilamen" have occupied an island outside New Orleans since the 1700s, and Chinese were brought into Mississippi soon after the Civil War—these contemporary communities underscore the similarity between the South and other U.S. regions undergoing dramatic demographic change since the immigration reforms of the 1960s. But the increasing racial diversity of the New South is not itself sufficient to undo the political ideologies underlying the exceptionalism of the Old South. That the first two South Asian governors in the United States, Bobby Jindal of Louisiana and Nikki Haley of South Carolina, were elected in southern states is not a sign of growing acceptance of new minorities in the South but rather the utility of Asian American model minorities as "exceptions" that prove the old racial politics of the "southern strategy": of the "Negro problem," recoded as crime and welfare, as drains on the libertarian utopia imagined by the new Republican Party. And battles over immigration have crept eastward from the Southwest to the Southeast, emerging as hot-button issues in unlikely locales like Manassas, Virginia, as seen in Eric Byler and Annabel Park's documentary, *9500 Liberty* (2009). The Southern Poverty Law Center has dubbed the exploitation of immigrant labor through guest-worker programs as a new form of "slavery," casting the shadow of the Old South over the ills of the new globalization.[16]

Thus, far from dismantling exceptionalism on its own, the transnational turn has also enabled the return of American exceptionalism from its Cold War ashes, although now it defends the United States not from its Communist bloc Other but from the dispersed threats of "terror" emanating globally from both state and nonstate actors. According to the political theorist Giorgio Agamben, the "state of exception" names the contradiction of a legalized suspension of the rule of law, supposedly justified by the extraordinary circumstances of a state of siege or war but often a bald defense of state sovereignty and power.[17] Ironically, it is modern democracies like postrevolutionary France and the United States, rather than dictatorships such as Nazi Germany or the Stalinist USSR, that tend to invoke such states of exception, validating what seem to be authoritarian moves as necessary to preserving the essence of democracy. The link between American exceptionalism—the assertion of the United States's unique responsibility to defend democracy and freedom throughout the world—and the state of exception—resulting in the suspension of civil liberties within the United States to wage this war "for democracy"—is tangled indeed, as the state of exception appears to violate the principles of exceptionalism that generate that state in the first place. But ultimately this "new" crisis harkens back to the previous dialectic between American and southern exceptionalisms, not least of which is the precedent of Lincoln's own invocation of emergency powers, including his unilateral suspension of the writ of habeas corpus as well as his Emancipation Proclamation, during the Civil War. The exception to the exception—the South—generates the state of exception that allows for the reassertion of the rule of national sovereignty—the Union at large—under a benevolent guise. 9/11 also recalls other, more recent states of exception that have produced historical exceptions to the rule of American democracy, most notably 12/7—Pearl Harbor, that other day of infamy—and the subsequent segregation and incarceration of over 120,000 Japanese Americans for the sake of national security. And let us not forget the current president, Obama, himself a seeming exception to a line of white heads of state, who has nonetheless continued to carry the mantle for American exceptionalism in his foreign and domestic policies. These examples remind us that the interrogation of exceptionalisms cannot stop at simply expanding the subject through diversifying its contents, crossing its borders, or atoning for its historical sins. The proliferation of exceptions to exceptionalism shows the protean power of the concept, morphing to respond to its critics without ceding any of its monopoly on violence, both real and epistemic. Perhaps the most useful response to exceptionalism's logic is to forgo the framework of the nation or region altogether. Riffing on Janice Radway's 1998 modest proposal for American studies, what might it mean to stop taking either "America" or "the South" as the object of our studies?[18] To stop thinking about American or Southern literature, culture, politics, identity completely? The loss of one horizon of intelligibility might open our vision to another world, that wholly unexceptional one that we are already living in.

NOTES

1. Frederick, "Michelle Obama's 'Proud' Remarks;" Philip Rucker, "Romney Questions Obama's Commitment."

2. Parker, "Tip for the GOP."

3. Eilperin, "Obama Tells Other World Leaders."

4. Putin, "Plea for Caution from Russia."

5. Morgan, *Covert Life*, 91.

6. Berland, "Emergence of the Communist Perspective," 203.

7. Hartz, *Liberal Tradition in America*, 78.

8. See Winthrop, "Model of Christian Charity."

9. Shewmaker, *Daniel Webster*, 95.

10. Ibid., 97–98.

11. Greeson, *Our South*, 1.

12. See Brickhouse, "Hemispheric Jamestown," 18–35.
13. F. J. Turner, "Significance of the Frontier," 76, 61.
14. Quoted in Saldívar-Hull, *Feminism on the Border*, 21.
15. Trinh, *Woman, Native, Other*, 98.
16. See *Close to Slavery*.
17. See Agamben, *State of Exception*.
18. See Radway, "What's in a Name?," 1–32.

SUGGESTIONS FOR FURTHER READING

Edwards, Brian T., and Dilip Parameshwar Gaonkar, eds. *Globalizing American Studies*. Chicago: University of Chicago Press, 2010.

Greeson, Jennifer Rae. *Our South: Geographical Fantasy and the Rise of National Literature*. Cambridge, Mass.: Harvard University Press, 2010.

Joshi, Khyati Y., and Jigna Desai, eds. *Asian Americans in Dixie: Race and Migration in the South*. Urbana-Champaign: University of Illinois Press, 2013.

Lassiter, Matthew D., and Joseph Crespino, eds. *The Myth of Southern Exceptionalism*. Oxford: Oxford University Press, 2010.

Noble, David W. *Death of a Nation: American Culture and the End of Exceptionalism*. Minneapolis: University of Minnesota Press, 2002.

Romance/Abjection

RICHÉ RICHARDSON

If average American citizens had to think of the region with which the nation has conventionally sustained a love/hate relationship, or indeed, that the nation has sometimes loved to hate, then the one that would most readily come to mind for many is the U.S. South. The region has maintained a central role within this national melodrama and elicited visceral affective responses in light of a perceived conservatism regarding politics, religion, and race, on the one hand, and a perceived excessiveness in areas such as sports and food cultures, on the other. Emotions about the region have typically been mixed, a dance of sorts from romance to nostalgia to downright disdain. There is a curious paradox in how the region defines so much of the national agenda, on the one hand, and remains so irrelevant and expendable to it, on the other. This expendability has been most poignantly dramatized in recent years, for instance, in the benign governmental neglect of New Orleans that perhaps made the aftereffects of Hurricane Katrina far more devastating in 2005. To be sure, even the U.S. South's geographical positioning in the nation as a space that one must go down to (i.e., as in "down South") invokes notions of lowering and descent, at worst a descent into a symbolic hell.

Nostalgic representations of the South in the United States as "romantic" are epitomized within the mythology of the Old South in literature and culture. Film has played a role in the nationalization of such romantic myths of the region from the early days of the medium in the twentieth century in productions such as D. W. Griffith's *Birth of a Nation*, the 1915 epic film based on Thomas Dixon's *The Leopard's Spots* (1902) and *The Clansman* (1905). David O. Selznick's 1939 film *Gone with the Wind*, based on Margaret Mitchell's 1936 novel, immortalized these narratives of the region on screen by visually representing characters such as Scarlett O'Hara as a southern belle festooned in lavish gowns and tended by Mammy against the backdrop of expansive plantations such as Tara and Twelve Oaks in all their splendor before the Civil War. Over time, some of the historical scholarship on the region has also played a primary role in reinforcing the mythic glorification of the region or in meditating on what is at stake in this ideology, which has been grounded in notions of southern exceptionalism. Furthermore, the U.S. South has also been characterized as a pariah region and represented as a "problem" in the nation, a representation linked to its history of slavery, secession, and segregation. These representations, including significations of the U.S. South as a racist, rebel, reactionary, and redneck region, have made it a fecund site for discussion within discourses of psychoanalysis from object relations theory and ego psychology to definitions of "abjection" that have been classically outlined by Julia Kristeva in *Powers of Horror: An Essay on Abjection*. In her words,

> the abject has only one quality of the object—that of being opposed to *I*. If the object, however, through its opposition, settles me within the fragile texture of a desire for meaning, which, as a matter of fact, makes me ceaselessly and infinitely homologous to it, what is *abject*, on the contrary, the jettisoned object, is radically excluded and draws me toward the place where meaning collapses. . . . It lies outside, beyond the set, and does not seem to agree on the rules of the game. And yet, from its place of banishment, the abject does not cease challenging its master.[1]

Karen Shimakawa builds on Kristeva's discourse on abjection by relating the notion of "national abjection" to definitions of Americanness that are contingent on the othering of Asian Americans variably portrayed as foreigners in a symbolic sense or as honorary whites.[2] The notion of "national abjection" is highly translatable and usable for pondering mechanisms of othering across a range of racial and ethnic categories in the United States. During an era when racial profiling has intensified in light of the panic over illegal immigration and new nativist ideologies have resurfaced in the public sphere of politics, it seems especially indispensable, and its manifestations in constituting racial and ethnic identity formations in the nation belie widespread perceptions of the nation as postracial and colorblind that have expanded in the wake of its election of Barack Obama as the first African American president of the United States. This is a reactionary political climate that states in the U.S. South historically associated with the "southern strategy," which advanced the neoconservative movement in the United States over the past several decades, have been salient in fomenting in recent years.

Numerous epistemologies on the U.S. South also implicitly and explicitly bespeak the region's status as a site of national abjection and frame it in relation to romance and abjection. Contemporary perspectives in southern studies that examine the U.S. South in light of postcolonial, New World, and hemispheric studies perspectives that allow us to recognize continuities in forms of southern subjection in relation to the U.S. North can help us to understand the relevance of an interpretive paradigm such as national abjection for this region. Just a few of the books published over the years that seem indispensable for studying the mythical character of the U.S. South and to draw on for thinking about the abjection/romance problematic related to the region include W. J. Cash's *The Mind of the South*; Patrick Gerster and Nicholas Cords's two-volume *Myth and Southern History*, which focuses on the Old and the New South; W. Fitzhugh Brundage's edited collection *Where These Memories Grow: History, Memory, and Southern Identity*; Bertram Wyatt-Brown's *Southern Honor: Ethics and Behavior in the Old South*; C. Vann Woodward's *The Burden of Southern History*; Larry J. Griffin and Don H. Doyle's *The South as an American Problem*; and David Goldfield's *Still Fighting the Civil War: The American South and Southern History*, along with more-recent titles such as Suzanne Jones and Sharon Monteith's edited volume titled *South to a New Place: Region, Literature, Culture*; Jon Smith and Deborah Cohn's anthology *Look Away!: The U.S. South in New World Studies*; Leigh Anne Duck's *The Nation's Region: Southern Modernism, Segregation, and U.S. Nationalism*; and Matthew D. Lassiter and Joseph Crespino's *The Myth of Southern Exceptionalism*. The field of cultural geography has produced valuable epistemologies for addressing difference and otherness in the U.S. South, among them David Sibley's *Geographies of Exclusion: Society and Difference in the West* and Tim Cresswell's *In Place/Out of Place: Geography, Ideology and Transgression*.

Southern romance is one vital context in which discourses of romance have been developed in southern literary history. Furthermore, contemporary popular novels that foreground plot elements related to southern romance (i.e., by best-selling authors such as Nora Roberts) literalize the genre most saliently in the contemporary literary marketplace and build on the genre of romance novels that Janice A. Radway discusses in *Reading the Romance: Women, Patriarchy and Popular Literature*. According to Radway, "The contemporary romance's prose is dominated by cliché, simple vocabulary, standard syntax, and the most common techniques associated with the nineteenth-century realist novel."[3] Radway's analytical emphasis on a cohort of women in a midwestern setting invites us to think about how southern female audiences in all their race, class, and sexual diversity consume the general romance genre, including any novels with southern specificity, and how they engage popular television shows such as *Designing Women* and films such as *Steel Magnolias*. Furthermore, such interpretive contexts invite us to consider how ideologies of race and southern masculinity and femininity impact the narrative logic of such works, along with the long history of sentimental writings aimed at northern female audiences during the nineteenth century that thematize the U.S. South and slavery, such as *Uncle Tom's Cabin* and a litany of slave narratives. Even an organization such as the Ku Klux Klan has been rendered heroically when depicted as chivalrous and protective of southern womanhood and has thus helped to constitute narratives of romance in southern history.

Notably, Scott Donaldson describes F. Scott Fitzgerald's relationship with the U.S. South as a romance and mentions the author's tendency to "glamourize the region" in light of his wife, Zelda Sayre's, southern background. In southern studies, the "family romance" has been a salient mode in southern literary history as developed under the heading of a variety of authors. It has been synonymous with the literary repertoire of William Faulkner and evident in the repertoires of other southern authors ranging from Robert Penn Warren to Lillian Smith.[4]

It is useful to pause and overview several recent perspectives that explicitly or implicitly invoke the concept of abjection, and that seem to be particularly useful within discourses of abjection related to the U.S. South in the contemporary era. In recent years, some of the most compelling dialogues in the field of southern studies have focused on topics such as race, gender, and the body and from a psychoanalytic perspective have drawn on the concept of abjection. As they have helped to revolutionize southern studies, these critical dialogues have also made valuable contributions to fields such as feminist and gender studies, including femininities and masculinities. Patricia Yaeger's *Dirt and Desire: Reconstructing Southern Women's Writing, 1930–1990* is one notable contribution along these lines. This study examines the U.S. South and femininity by looking at southern narratives by women that highlight the grotesque and the monstrous as opposed to the beautiful and feminine bodies that epitomize conventional notions of the southern lady. According to Yaeger, in such literary works, "anomaly gets figured as monstrosity, and monstrosity itself becomes a way of casting out or expelling the new." While anthropological work, especially Mary Douglas's *Purity and Danger*, is essential to Yaeger's analysis of dirt as a metaphor in southern literature, discussion of topics such as trauma and racial melancholy ground this study in the discourses of Freudian psychoanalysis. Furthermore, her discussion of dirt, decadence, and the body lends it profound implications for discourses of abjection within the multifaceted and diverse critical realm of psychoanalysis. In introducing this important study, Yaeger writes:

> [I will explore] the prevalence in southern women's writing of flesh that has been ruptured or riven by violence, of fractured, excessive bodies telling us something that diverse southern cultures don't want us to say. That is, instead of the grotesque as decadent southern form, I want to examine the importance

of irregular models of the body within an extremely regulated society and to focus on figures of damaged, incomplete, or extravagant characters described under rubrics peculiarly suited to southern histories in which the body is simultaneously fractioned and overwhelmed.[5]

320

In the popular arena, the idea of abjection has also been profoundly evident in southern rap discourse, particularly among artists identifying with the "dirty South." This theme in music resonates with the recurrent invocation of dirt in relation to southern identity that Yeager has identified. It evokes the burden of the region's racial history, on the one hand, and the material conditions of grappling with poverty and surviving in the region, on the other. At another level, it addresses sex and sexuality in keeping with the masculine bravado of hip-hop.

The special issue of the journal *American Literature* in 2001, "Violence, the Body and 'The South,'" coedited by Houston A. Baker Jr. and Dana D. Nelson, which famously issued the call for "a new Southern studies," has been a catalyzing force that has helped to revolutionize the field over the past decade. It is notable that in their critical introduction, the editors refer to the U.S. South as "America's abjected regional other."[6] This volume's very premise is grounded in part in theories of abjection. The idea of abjection has organically informed the shape of the paradigm of the New Southern Studies itself. The clarion call for a centering of the South in American cultural studies has attempted to remedy the benign critical neglect of the South in a range of academic fields, while at the same time divesting the conventional approaches that have stifled more innovative critical dialogue about the region. The issue's unsettling of a host of contemporary binaries in the field, from "North" and "South" to schisms between "pleasure" and "violence," suggests that even concepts such as "abjection" and "romance" are intertwined and are irreducible to the U.S. South. Notably, Baker sustains his investment in the discourse of psychoanalysis in his compelling study titled *Turning South Again: Rethinking Modernism, Re-Reading Booker T.*[7]

Joel Peckham's "Eudora Welty's *The Golden Apples*: Abjection and the Maternal South" also contributes valuably to discourses on gender through a grounding in abjection as an apparatus to consider the role of southern patriarchy in constituting divisions between men and women in the South and sheltering the latter category because of the long-standing panic related to miscegenation. As Peckham observes,

The gaze, especially in Welty's work, is often more complicit than anything Foucauldian power dynamics can account for—and the object of the gaze, is therefore, more threatening than the observer can anticipate. To see a thing is to acknowledge its existence. And to acknowledge the abject as such is to give it viability and infectious force—so that a cold stare almost inevitably leads to fascination, the observer becomes the voyeur. When the gaze is returned the dynamics of power transference become even more complex and the coherency of the carceral network fractures, its borders blur.[8]

Sabrina Boyer's "'Thou Shalt Not Crave Thy Neighbor': *True Blood*, Abjection, and Otherness" examines the popular HBO series *True Blood*, "southern vampire mysteries" based on Charlaine Harris's Sookie Stackhouse series, which is set in the town of Bon Temps in Louisiana. In this essay, Boyer engages the vampire as an outside and other figure and examines the impact of a southern setting on this figure, beginning with an overview of representations of the vampire in television and film. Boyer concludes that "despite the thoughtful use of the vampire archetype to explore notions of difference and otherness surrounding race and sexuality, the *True Blood* series ultimately fails to redefine, disrupt and upset the historical racist, sexist and homophobic ideologies of the South." Boyer goes on to note that "despite its representation of women who wield power and break taboos, of vampires who fight for their own equality; despite its exploration into individual vs. collective responsibility and into difference surrounding vampires as a form of hopeful change, the disruption only goes so far."[9]

In my own work, as elaborated in 2007 in the study *Black Masculinity and the U.S. South: From Uncle Tom to Gangsta*, the methodology highlights theories of abjection within psychoanalysis in examining the othering of black male southerners within the African American category and discussing strategies of characterization that prioritize urban masculine identity in Charles Fuller's *A Soldier's Play* and that preclude subjectivity for the main southern black male character. The study suggests that comparative work is useful for fields such as black studies and southern studies because blackness is serviceable in facilitating a range of cultural flows and identity formations in national and global contexts, while the invisibility and abjection of black bodies parallel processes whereby the U.S. South, in spite of its historical abjection in this nation, "is nevertheless serviceable as a paradigm for processing cultural formations within a global context." Similarly, the study argues that abjection conditions how the U.S. South is approached and engaged as an academic topic: "The historical status of the South as an 'abject' region also impacts somewhat the extent to which the region is viewed in academia as a legitimate object of study. The region has therefore remained excluded or marginal as a topic of discussion in scholarly dialogues at times."[10]

The history of poor whites and poor rural blacks reaches back to the era of slavery and should be studied comparatively in pondering the raced, classed, and gendered system of racial distinction that emerged in the antebellum South based on purist and superior notions of whiteness. Similar perceptions of black rural southerners as inferior and pathological do not typically register in dialogues on poor whites and the profusion of stereotypes routinely related to this category, which obscures the role of blacks in helping to constitute perceptions of abjection in the nation. Indeed, histories related to the Civil War, Reconstruction, Jim Crow, and civil rights have positioned blacks in the United States at the center in constituting the southern problem. On the other hand, the plantation myth of the antebellum South, whose signal narratives included the casting of black women as naturally nurturing mammy figures, has played a salient ideological role in constituting blackness and notions of southern romance.

As the profusion of contemporary scholarship reveals, gender and race have been key frameworks for thinking about notions of abjection in contemporary southern studies. At this point, I want to turn to a brief consideration of Kathryn Stockett's 2009 novel, *The Help*, which, I would suggest, saliently foregrounds the abjection/romance nexus. The novel manifests dimensions related to race, gender, class, the body, and a curious "toilet" metaphor that are useful to think about in light of theories of abjection, and specifically following Kristeva's elaboration on notions of the improper and uncleanness, excrement, and (building on the work of Mary Douglas) defilement; similarly, the relationship between its character Eugenia "Skeeter" Phelan and her family's black maid, Constantine Bates, rehearses classic aspects of southern romance. Such thematics are also discernible in the 2011 film *The Help*, directed by Tate Taylor.

The best-selling novel by Stockett has garnered controversy in part because of the allegation that Stockett appropriated the story of its primary character, Aibileen Clark (Viola Davis), including her name, from Stockett's brother's maid Ableen Cooper, whose lawsuit against the author was dismissed in Jackson, Mississippi, in 2010 on the basis that the statutes of limitation were up. Similarly, while the film has been widely popular, to the point of being collectively screened by numerous black women's book clubs and sororities and being featured in a screening at the White House organized by first lady Michelle Obama, it has also been critiqued in part for a representation of black southerners that some regard as unrealistic and stereotypical. As Patricia A. Turner notes in a *New York Times* opinion piece, "This movie deploys the standard formula. With one possible exception, the

322

white women are remarkably unlikable, and not just because of their racism. Like the housewives portrayed in reality television shows, the housewives of Jackson treat each other, their parents and their husbands with total callousness. In short, they are bad people, therefore they are racists."[11] The term "the help" is a complicated signifier in the film, and if it most directly describes the domestic service of black women in white households, it also speaks to the support that Skeeter provides them and the ways in which they support her by claiming their voices and sharing their subversive domestic work narratives. *The Help*, whose embedded fictive novel mirrors the novel by Stockett, is very much a performative novel on writing about writing.

The time that the novel begins—on the toddler Mae Mobley's August birthday—is noteworthy when considering that Aibileen's mourning of her son Treelore ended with the birth of the baby, even as Mrs. Leefolt suffers from "baby blues," or what is known now as postpartum depression. In Aibileen's interactions with the toddler Mae Mobley, the novel mentions toilet training among primary skills to teach at its beginning. Aibileen teaches Mae Mobley such skills as much as imparting lessons in self-esteem and racial tolerance.

Early in the novel, the only option for a worker at the Leefolt home who needs to go to the bathroom is to find a private place outside. Aibileen muses, "Here we is with two [bathrooms] in the house and one being built and they still ain't no place for this man to do his business" (23). Similarly, Aibileen's only option is to give him a paper cup to drink from when he asks for a drink of water. The toilet recurs as a motif throughout the narrative economy of the novel and in a way even feels awkward to discuss, notwithstanding its most famous (indeed, *infamous* in the eyes of many critics) aestheticization in Marcel Duchamp's provocative 1917 art piece titled *Fountain*, a urinal marked as "R. Mutt" that heralded a new modern turn in twentieth-century art.

The bathroom is the primary signifier of private domestic space in the novel, and through it we can understand how much the politics of segregation, which polarized public spaces on the basis of race in the Jim Crow South, had their parallel in private home settings. Early on, the character Aibileen alludes to the unspeakability of the politics related to separate bathrooms for black workers when she comments, "The bathroom situation, it just ain't something I really want to discuss" in pondering dialogues with Skeeter about experiences as a maid.[12]

Hilly Holbrook's Home Help Sanitation Initiative, a proposition that she shares at bridge club, proposes to institutionalize this segregation by calling

for whites to install bathrooms in their garages for their black maids to prevent them from using the facilities in white homes. "In the mornings, that
bathroom seat get cold out there, give me a little start when I set down.
It's just a little room they built inside the carport. Inside is a toilet and a
little sink attached to the wall. A pull cord for the lightbulb. Paper have to
set on the floor" (105). Skeeter offers a similar description of Constantine's
bathroom in the novel, though Skeeter admits to never having been inside.
Hilly bills the bathroom initiative as "a disease-preventative measure" on the
premise that blacks carry diseases. The perception that blacks are diseased
exists in the minds of white characters such as Hilly alongside the stereotype
that blacks steal. The pathology of blacks as diseased is iterated by Elizabeth
Leefolt in scolding Mae Mobley about exposing herself to diseases when she
uses the bathroom built outside especially for Aibileen. Through its thick
symbolic economy of toilets and thematic content related to segregation in
private spaces, *The Help* demonstrates how black bodies are pathologized,
spatially marginalized, and marked as abject.

Hilly further degrades Aibileen by asking her how she likes having her
own new separate bathroom, an exchange reminiscent of a scene in Richard
Wright's "The Ethics of Living Jim Crow" in which the young Wright is
forced to say that he likes seeing a white man hit a black woman's behind.[13]
Aibileen is also prohibited from leaving her lunch in the refrigerator.
Aibileen's acknowledgment of the expectation that she will go outside to
the bathroom in inclement weather is reminiscent of the situation related to
black sanitation workers that led Dr. Martin Luther King Jr. to Memphis,
Tennessee, where two black sanitation workers, because they were prohibited
from coming inside along with white workers, had died trying to shelter
themselves from rain on the back of a garbage truck when its compactor was
activated. Michael Honey's examination of racist signage and iconography of
the civil rights era, such as small sinks marked as "colored" juxtaposed with
a standard-sized one marked as "white," poignantly suggests that the goal
of Jim Crow was to subordinate blacks and to keep them in their perceived
"place." The externality of this bathroom space is a telling illustration of
the Jim Crow South's positioning the black subject as inferior, subordinate,
apart, unequal, other and as the primary point of contrast with those in the
category white. Significantly, Minny is forced to hide in the bathroom once
when "Mister Johnny," her employer, Celia's husband, returns home unexpectedly, a situation that calls to mind how antebellum slaves such as Harriet
Jacobs retreated to the garret to find safety. The novel's penultimate scene,
which features toilets littering the character Hilly Holbrook's yard when

Skeeter deliberately includes a misprint in the Junior League's newsletter requesting that people deliver their old toilets to Hilly, takes this toilet metaphor to the absolute extreme. It links her with waste, impurity, and defilement as much as her ingestion of the pie that contains Minny's excrement, retaliation over having been fired for attempting to use the bathroom as the maid at Hilly's home. This scene in the novel violates a major taboo and is so unspeakable that it is reducible to the sound bite "the terrible awful." While she is most aggressive in marking blacks as abject, in an ironic turn, Hilly becomes the ultimate signifier of abjection by the novel's end.

The novel offers a further discourse on abjection when it constructs the character Celia Foote as a Marilyn Monroe look-alike, but portrays her as a white woman who is not a "lady," who is "lazy," and who is marked as "white trash" due to her background in Sugarditch, Mississippi, and for having gotten pregnant out of wedlock and marrying Johnny Foote, Hilly's former beau. While opulent, her home is described as being covered with dust, a description reminiscent of Yeager's description of a major motif linked to some grotesque southern feminine types. In this characterization, the novel speaks well to Tara McPherson's insights related to how notions of the southern lady have been contingent on race and class.[14] Some of the literal work of the maids in the novel involves removing dirt and dust, as much as the column that Skeeter writes for the newspaper speaks to cleaning and housekeeping. Skeeter is also linked to this imagery, for example, as dust covers her as she rides to town in her car, as well as to a death motif in the novel. However, Celia is the novel's ultimate pariah. She is literally avoided by the other white women in town and excluded from all social activities, a marginality that reaches its extreme at the Children's Benefit sponsored by the Junior League, where she shows up in a tight-fitting dress, becomes a spectacle for guests, and ends up vomiting, another important marker of her abjection. Noteworthy, too, is the novel's recurrent imagery related to emaciated bodies or bodies marked by difference. Hilly's mother, Mrs. Walters, is described by Hilly as being "skinny as a telephone pole" (7). Mrs. Leefolt is also linked to thinness. Skeeter is described as being "painfully tall" (67).

The romance element of the novel is more marginal but evident nonetheless. For example, the relationship of the black maid Aibileen with Mae Mobley is steeped in the mythology of mammy at some levels, as is the relationship between Skeeter and Constantine. Several flashbacks to the past feature loving exchanges between these two characters in scenes depicting Constantine, portrayed by the veteran actress Cicely Tyson, combing Skeeter's hair in childhood or reminding her of her beauty as a young woman. (The film plays up this dimension of her character and fails to follow the novel in depicting her as mixed-race and the mother of a mixed-race, white-looking daughter named Lulabelle, who is also possibly the product of an incestuous relationship.) Significantly, these scenes typically occur in a picturesque outdoor clearing on the Phelan land on a bench under a tree. This is precisely the spot where the ill-fated romance between Skeeter and Stuart Whitmore begins, which culminates in a marriage proposal. The letters exchanged between Skeeter and Constantine anticipate the exchange between Aibileen and Skeeter and the work of Aibileen as the new writer for the newspaper column "Miss Myrna" at the *Jackson Journal*, which the novel promises in its closing pages. As Stockett's postscript to the novel, titled "Too Little, Too Late," recalls, the novel was in part inspired by her fond memories of her family's maid Demetrie while growing up. The novel offers a backhanded but nevertheless romantic glorification of southern social life, the propertied elite, and notions of aristocracy.

The novel's dialect language forms for black characters seem designed to mark its time period. That it flouts, say, black middle-class societies that existed in Jackson at the time, and that were linked to institutions in the city such as Jackson State and Tougaloo, suggests this novel's investments in aspects of southern nostalgia. Aspects of the novel's linguistic economy in effect exoticize and romanticize blackness. Similarly, passages that describe Skeeter's hair as being "kinky, more pubic than cranial" (66), that describe the Phelan maid Pascagoula as being "black as night" (67), and that describe Minny as having skin "blacker than Aibileen's by ten shades, and shiny and taut, like a pair of new patent shoes" (191) seem retrograde and come across as linguistically careless and naive. They make one wonder how far we have come from references to blacks as "darkies" in novels such as Margaret Mitchell's *Gone with the Wind*. The reality is that there is a thin line between uses of the word "black" as an epithet and as a mere descriptor; such language is touchy at best, even in black communities, and potentially offensive, regardless of the shade of a person's skin complexion. For some, being *called* "black," even if they are, has been grounds for fighting in the most extreme and violent reactions to this terminology; in this sense, it registers with the fury of "yo' mama" in the dozens game.

This new novel, whatever its shortcomings, will help to feed conversations in southern literature in the years to come. It provides one poignant illustration of how much "abjection" and "romance" still figure in shaping discourses on the U.S. South and demonstrates the continuing utility and relevance of these two terms for critical and theoretical work in southern studies. As interesting as it has been to look at where they have been and where they seem to be now, it will be interesting indeed to see where these dialogues will go as so much exciting new southern scholarship continues to develop, a contemporary southern scholarship at a crossroads and not so eager to rest in the interpretive paradigms for the U.S. South that have been salient or accessible in the past. In this sense, it is pleasing, and indeed liberating and empowering, that the jury is still out on how we will think with these words as time goes on.

NOTES

1. Kristeva, *Powers of Horror*, 1–2.
2. See Shimakawa, *National Abjection*.
3. Radway, *Reading the Romance*, 189.
4. See Donaldson, "Scott Fitzgerald's Romance"; see also R. H. King, *Southern Renaissance*.
5. Yaeger, *Dirt and Desire*, 7, xiii. See also A. G. Jones and Donaldson, *Haunted Bodies*.
6. H. Baker and Nelson, "Violence, the Body, and 'The South,'" 231–44.
7. See H. A. Baker, *Turning South Again*.
8. Peckham, "Eudora Welty's *The Golden Apples*," 195–96.
9. Boyer "'Thou Shalt Not Crave Thy Neighbor,'" 38.
10. Richardson, *Black Masculinity and the U.S. South*, 14, 13.
11. P. Turner, "Dangerous White Stereotypes."
12. Stockett, *Help*, 27. Text hereafter cited parenthetically.
13. R. Wright, *Uncle Tom's Children*.
14. See McPherson, *Reconstructing Dixie*.

SUGGESTIONS FOR FURTHER READING

Baker, Houston A., Jr., and Dana D. Nelson. "Violence, the Body, and 'The South.'" *American Literature* 73 (2001): 231–44.

Kristeva, Julia. *Powers of Horror: An Essay on Abjection*. New York: Columbia University Press, 1982.

McPherson, Tara. *Reconstructing Dixie: Race, Gender, and Nostalgia in the Imagined South*. Durham, N.C.: Duke University Press, 2003.

Shimakawa, Karen. *National Abjection: The Asian American Body Onstage*. Durham, N.C.: Duke University Press, 2002.

Sibley, David. *Geographies of Exclusion: Society and Difference in the West*. New York: Routledge, 1995.

Yaeger, Patricia. *Dirt and Desire: Reconstructing Southern Women's Writing, 1930–1990*. Chicago: University of Chicago Press, 2000.

Modernism/Modernity

MELANIE BENSON TAYLOR

It has become almost a cliché to begin any discussion of the modern South by invoking H. L. Mencken's 1917 "The Sahara of the Bozart," the scathing essay in which he derides the region as "almost as sterile, artistically, intellectually, culturally as the Sahara Desert." In literature, music, painting, theology, education, and science, Mencken avers, the region had produced only "an awe-inspiring blank" since the Civil War.[1] While the famously dyspeptic critic had little more regard for the "tawdry and tacky" Yankee by contrast, he was particularly repulsed by the South's postemancipation erosion of racial purity and natural aristocracy, and along with it, the evacuation of regional culture. In many ways, the southern literary renaissance that flourished in the 1920s and 1930s arose directly out of catalytic sentiments like Mencken's, which were hardly atypical. While critics have labored long and variously to contextualize the South's sudden intellectual explosion onto the broader landscape of transnational literary modernism, nearly all agree that the movement was at least partly inspired by a zealous desire to both defend and escape the aura of the South's intractable "backwardness" with what Fred Hobson has deemed "a mixture of pride and shame."[2] Such understandings are rooted in the not-so-tacit assumption that modernity constituted a radical rupture in southern history, inciting an ideological and aesthetic crisis for the artists and intellectuals struggling to reconcile its disorienting temporalities. Reconsidered in the wake of the New Southern Studies' progressive critical methodologies, however, the character of the modernist movement in the U.S. South—and even Mencken's own critique of the region—reveals a much more complicated, expansive picture not just of parochial insularity but also of incipient and unsettling globalization, and with it, a protracted reckoning with notions of "authenticity" and humanism that has only intensified with the progress of the new century.

Early commentaries on southern modernism incompletely explicated the South's long delay and abrupt entry onto the modernist stage. Some critics have credited World War I for compelling among southern intellectuals the same cataclysmic reexaminations and crises of faith occurring elsewhere and prompting the international literary

Modernist movement. Consonantly, the exponential growth of industry and capitalist development spurred widespread anxiety, defensiveness, and introspection that filtered eventually and more dramatically into the sluggishly modernizing region. Writers such as William Faulkner, Allen Tate, Robert Penn Warren, and Tennessee Williams were seen as ambivalently negotiating the collision of an idealized plantation past and an encroaching modernity that threatened to annihilate any remaining vestiges of a distinctive and grander culture. Scholars assumed that the South's writers came to such material consciousness belatedly simply because regional development itself was deferred; however, such views failed to consider the structural conditions that precipitated this radically uneven development in ways that could not be overcome simply by reason or prosperity. Indeed, more-recent scholarship on southern "progress" builds on Immanuel Wallerstein's foundational world-systems theory, which posits that modern economic development relies on a core-periphery model of production and exploitation. Seen through this global-comparative lens, the seemingly unique conditions and frustrations of the post-Reconstruction South are placed in the instructive context of similar Third World and decolonizing geographies.[3] Readers have thus become better equipped to see the South not as an inexplicable anomaly but rather as a tactically underdeveloped periphery, as well as a container for the fears and anxieties of a nation in the grip of rapid social change and economic turmoil, as foundational works by Jennifer Rae Greeson, Tara McPherson, and Leigh Anne Duck have averred.

Appreciating the complex colonial etiologies of the South's ideological production changes fundamentally our appraisal of its modern ambivalence and strenuous singularity. We know now that these uncanny retreats to the local, regional, and traditional are primarily a function of materiality: labored constructions of cultural authenticity emerge with a vengeance to buttress an endangered matrix of perceived racial, cultural, and aristocratic preeminence. Even Mencken's vitriol thinly disguises his investment in a culture more familiar and dear than he admits, as a native southerner (born in Baltimore) himself. In his somewhat hyperbolic elision of class with culture, he appeals directly to fellow southerners similarly vexed by the ascendant "trash," both white and black, that was driving down the region's intellectual property values, as it were. At the heart of these anxieties, as Mencken's critique betrays, is a terror over position, purity, and prosperity often mischaracterized as a peculiar southern pathology rather than the deepening national and global crisis of humanism and hierarchy that it was. In the process of recognizing the South's extreme iterations of this phenomenon, critical trends have urged us to reevaluate similar permutations in national and global environments throughout the twentieth and twenty-first centuries.

What appears at first glance to be a belated emergence from nostalgia and an entry into cautious liberalism instead belies a distinct fear that the world's "trash" might multiply and litter our own manicured lawns. Such distress is rarely as candid as Mencken's, but that is precisely the obfuscation at work in southern modernism's efforts: it lurches forward with one eye trained obstinately on a past being endlessly reconstructed in retrospect. While earlier critical conversations diagnosed this trend as one of "alienation," most scholars were willing to credit the well-meaning if stunted progressivism evinced by Faulkner and others. Increased attention to the period's female and minority writers (such as Eudora Welty, Flannery O'Connor, and Richard Wright) has further expanded our purview to include marginalized perspectives more patently hostile to—but not necessarily immune from— the region's retrograde amnesia. Such developments alter fundamentally the ways we now frame even the apparently "enlightened" works of the modern South, particularly those that seem poised to subvert the strictures of southern benightedness.

In *The Real South* (2008), Scott Romine delineates the process by which the epic "South" now instantiated as legend was produced in antiphonal response to "contemporary economic pressures and to flows of culture that are increasingly global and dispersed in nature." Drawing on Fredric Jameson, Slavoj Žižek, and Walter Benjamin's critiques of cultural production under capitalism, Romine uncovers the paradoxical revivification of local and regional "authenticity" as a stay against the discomposing mobility and anonymity of transnational and corporate culture. Yet, as he points out, the "double-bind of the word, which is at its core an advertising word, is that it cannot properly refer to anything: once something is called 'authentic,' it already isn't. More precisely, authenticity articulates a structure of desire and hence of absence." Romine demonstrates the South's canny turn toward a sanitized version of its own distinguishing and distinguished past as a means of managing the encroaching ills of finance capitalism; yet he astutely demonstrates that the very projects most hostile to capitalism are often the ones most susceptible to its offerings and influence. The circular effect conceals itself in delusions of linearity and rupture: that is, "tradition requires a narrative apparatus or sequence (tradition → modernity) that conceals modernity's actual status as tradition's constitutive underside."[4]

Works like Romine's make it easier to disentangle the mystifications of southern nostalgia from the brutal truths of its antebellum idylls; more than that, though, they shatter earlier critical apologias that explained southern modernism's vexations as true crises of rupture, belatedness, and loss. The anxiety and "backwardness" induced by progress are unveiled not as linear regressions but as integral fractures in the dangerous mystifications of capitalism's ahistorical logic and linearity. Conceiving of southern culture as an antidote to modern materialism was the primary project of the Nashville Agrarians who penned *I'll Take My Stand* as a manifesto against industrial-capitalism and in tribute to the South's proprietary claim to a fundamentally humanist alternative. While these positions have been roundly deconstructed for their discomposing nostalgia and racism, they nonetheless continue to haunt the margins of the field and culture in nagging ways. As Romine shrewdly hypothesizes, "Southern studies has never quite been able to get over the Agrarians, despite their retrograde politics and numerous overt attempts at academic assassination . . . [because] their localized culture war predicted the broader forms that cultural warfare would assume over the course of their century and into the next."[5] One of these "broader forms" has been the battle waged by American Indians against a colonial-capitalist assault on Indigenous culture and a subsequent recuperation of tribal nations in radical—and often hyperbolic and mythical—contradistinction to Western culture and values, particularly economic. Dismantling the fraudulent cultural reproductions by which the South redressed its losses requires us to reckon soberly with the more sympathetic efforts of Native American communities to remake their own communities in fictional ways.

Aided explicitly and indispensably by the critical deconstructions of the southern culture industry, new examinations of Native literary culture are performing similar work.[6] Concomitantly, southern scholars have been instrumental in delineating just how and why the myth of the anticapitalist, anti-industrial Native American became so fixed in the American imagination—helped along by southerners, cloaked in ideological redface, who usurped the Native experience to lend credence to their own dispossession, align themselves against the industrial-capitalist North, and cleverly establish their own "nativist" claims to southern lands.[7] Of course, this process of genealogical obfuscation necessarily entailed repressing the muddying details of colonial extirpation and extermination by which the South not only participated in but in many ways actually spearheaded and invigorated national projects of Indian removal and resettlement. Nonetheless, enfolding Indians as kindred allies and easy allegories in the larger vision of southern exceptionalism becomes a key strategy for southern modernists as various as Faulkner, Ransom, Warren, Caroline Gordon, and others; only recently have our critical conversations begun to unravel the reactionary logic and destructive legacies of such fictions for southerners and Native Americans alike.

These new frames cohere to radically revise our appreciation for a work like *Ship of Fools*, which long posed a critical problem for scholars struggling to reconcile the novel's seemingly hysterical bleakness with Katherine Anne Porter's earlier and more mannered, principled, and poetic works of individual autonomy, ethical probity, and historical consciousness. Affected deeply by the mounting horrors of Fascism, Nazism, and Communism in the decades following World War I, Porter's once fervent liberal-democratic ideologies became increasingly and emphatically conservative; by 1944, as Robert Brinkmeyer chronicles, Porter was casting herself "as a distinguished southern lady from the aristocratic South" in essays such as "Portrait: Old South." Perhaps unexpectedly, the "independent, aristocratic southerner" became an ideal stronghold from which to critique "modern authoritarianism and its diminishment of the individual." Porter's defense against totalitarian incursions peaked with *Ship of Fools*, which Brinkmeyer reads as a "sad conclusion to Porter's career," which had become infected by the "extreme thinking" provoked by international crises, reactionary southern nostalgia, and the "virulent racism that was now surfacing (a dark underside of her unreconstructed southernness)."[8] Brinkmeyer's work in defining Porter's complicated global consciousness, paired with Romine's rethinking of southern identity formation under the pressures of external rather than insular crises and models, helps us to reread Porter's darkest and most troubling work as a logical—if "extreme"—conclusion to a career trained consistently on rescuing the individual artist and the South from the terrible tyranny of cultural and economic change on a global scale.

The genesis for *Ship of Fools* began with a similar voyage Porter herself made in 1931, from Veracruz, Mexico, to Bremerhaven. Along the way, she grew intimate with a number of Germans who initially charmed her with their "soft voices and good manners" and only later surprised and betrayed her with their chilling manifestations of the country's extreme social and economic turmoil.[9] It took more than three subsequent decades for the novel to be completed, and its final form bears the imprint of her increasingly agonized disillusionment with an age that seemed to corrupt pervasively and indiscriminately. The infectious global catastrophe of authoritarianism and capitalism is made emphatic in her deliberately international cast of characters, all thoroughly unlikable, narcissistic individuals dramatizing her bleak notion that "none of us has any real alibi in this world."[10] She begins the novel with a list of characters segregated by nationality, underscoring her efforts to posit each as an allegorical proxy for his or her country of origin. There are only four Americans on board, while the rest are from Germany, Switzerland, Sweden, Spain, and Mexico. On this decidedly "second-class" ship, the passengers are not aristocratic but anxiously striving elite: they are merchants, manufacturers, oil investors, professors, and artists whose fragile class, national, or racial superiority rests in uncertain economic measures and scales. The passengers panic incoherently when separated briefly from their possessions, but in the restoration of their baggage "each discovered again what it was he had believed lost for a while though he could not name it—his identity. Bit by bit it emerged, travel-worn, half-hearted but still breathing, from a piece of luggage or some familiar possession in which he had once invested his pride of ownership, and which, seen again in strange, perhaps unfriendly surroundings, assured the owner that he had not always been a harassed stranger, a number, an unknown name and a caricature on a passport. Soothed by this restoration of their self-esteem, the passengers looked at themselves in mirrors with dawning recognition."[11] More a critique of authoritarianism than capitalism, Porter's narrative tacitly affirms the buying power of individual authority and possession; it separates the anonymous workers in steerage from the fledgling, self-possessed individuals in the ascendant decks. What is less certain to this later Porter is whether anyone can afford the privilege of the ticket.

At the end of her list of "Characters," Porter identifies en masse the 876 "souls" in steerage: "Spaniards, men, women, children, workers in the sugar fields of Cuba, being deported back to the Canaries and to various parts of Spain (wherever they came from) after the failure of the sugar market." Porter shrewdly substitutes national affiliation here with the borders of the market, which is the only identifying principle for these adrift laborers. From their upper berths, the other passengers very literally look down on the workers whose strife mimics that of the slaves undergoing the Middle Passage: "It was plain they were there by no will or plan of their own," the narrator observes, "and in the helpless humility of enslavement they were waiting for whatever would be done to them next" (57). They are packed in cruelly like animals, "wallowing on the floor, being sick" (72), and constantly threatened with being "[laid] in irons" if they refuse to submit like docile creatures (159). Early in the journey, two devilish twins, Ric and Rac, hurl a shoe down at a worker who has fallen over into his own vomit but instead hit a young woman and her baby. The act is not mere juvenile mischievousness but a harbinger for Ric and Rac's cruel antics throughout the text and the adults' professed outrage over their "inhuman" behavior; yet it is increasingly obvious that they simply fail to recognize the new generation of redoubled brutality that they themselves have spawned. One passenger gleefully imagines his own solution to the workers' pestilence: "I would put them all in a big oven and turn on the gas," he declares, at which his female companion exclaims, "'Oh,' . . . doubling over with laughter, 'isn't that the most original idea you've ever heard?'" (59). Nothing "original" is produced in such solutions, Porter conveys in the brutal irony of hindsight; the evil twins receive the inheritance of the modern world's endless capacity for reproducing evil in strikingly redundant ways, whether in the exploitation of workers and slaves or the extermination of "lesser" humans.

Indeed, catastrophic historical events like the Nazi Holocaust forced many Americans—and particularly southerners—to peer more critically at the humanitarian outrages tainting U.S. history, as Brinkmeyer demonstrates comprehensively in *The Fourth Ghost: White Southern Writers and European Fascism, 1930–1950* (2009). For Porter, it had the opposite effect of strengthening her appraisal of American exceptionalism generally, and southern exceptionalism in particular. While none of her characters in *Ship of Fools* can rightly be identified as sympathetic, the ones who come closest are U.S. citizens. One of the Americans, a starry-eyed young artist named Jenny, seems patently a stand-in for a youthful Porter, prior to the annihilation of her wistful dreams and independent spirit (expressed most poignantly in the Miranda stories of the 1930s and 1940s). Jenny hails from a "midsouthern state," adores workers, Mexicans, and Indians, and likes to join in labor strikes and revolutions wherever she finds them; in short, as several critics have noted, she seems to be the one who "suffers all the personal anxiety and social adversity that Porter herself endured" as a female artist.[12] She is also the only character capable of recognizing the humanity of those in steerage; when a Basque peasant dies after leaping overboard to save a rich German couple's dog, Jenny is the only passenger from the upper decks to attend his funeral, much to the bafflement of her fellow passengers. "You know how these Americans are," a European woman explains to the captain. "They worship primitive things because they cannot understand better. They are corrupted by the Negro, of course—what can we expect?" (175). By echoing the American crime of slavery, Porter allows Jenny the role of ambassador of American reform and moral cleansing—at the very moment when Germany is just beginning to succumb to its own humanitarian disease, Jenny reminds us that America's errors are past anterior.

And yet the past has an unnerving way of refusing to stay put. Jenny's easy identification with the drowned peasant is less a celebration of American exceptionalism than an indictment of its tendency to reproduce infectiously in the delusions of modernity's progressive, liberal ideologies. Her ability to empathize with the plight of these neo-slaves seems to derive explicitly not just from the South's moral transgressions but also from its delusions of transcendence. At the core of her integrative vision, the lesson of indigeneity looms large: "I love the Indians," Jenny says. "I've got a weakness for them. I feel certain I learned something from them, even if I don't know what it is yet" (56). At this point, she has already scandalized the rest of the passengers by arriving on board in an authentic native Mexican worker's pantsuit. Porter herself remarked on the allure of the Natives in Veracruz, where she found among "the shrillness and meanness of Mexico" that "only the Indian gives any charm of being."[13] Elsewhere in Mexico, she often expressed her disgust over the way Indian goods and art forms were blatantly commodified, transformed into replica statues for rich families' gardens, and provided the fodder for "make-believe primitives" to adopt and pervert for market purposes.[14] Jenny's naive appropriation of Indian garb allows Porter some distance perhaps from her well-intentioned former self, prior to a deeper understanding of the market's ability to devour culture. Yet that very recognition is what seemingly invigorates her own conviction of an inviolable spirit of "being" within the Indian type, one capable of providing lessons for the rest of humanity—even if we "don't know what it is yet." The opening scenes of *Ship of Fools* perpetuate this logic by featuring a small Indian man who placidly surveys a scene of grotesque corruption: seamy prostitutes, graphically disfigured beggars, striking workers, and the anxious, harried tourists awaiting embarkation. Only the Indian appears repulsed, transcendent, mythical: he "sat motionless, looking away" at a world no one else can see (15).

This mysterious transubstantiation of indigenous authenticity, humanity, and being becomes the functional stand-in for worldly asceticism, racial tolerance, ethical deliverance, and communal empathy in a modern world increasingly stripped of such possibilities and eroded by market relations and priorities. For this reason, Jenny's role in the novel is a flimsy and tragic one, overridden sometimes viciously by the racist and sexist behaviors of her fellow passengers. Jenny is seen secretly by her own boyfriend, David, as the "nameless, faceless, cureless pestilence of man's existence, the chattering grievance-bearing accusing female Higher Primate" (397). In blatantly Faulknerian prose, David undermines Jenny's moral pretensions and, in turn, steadily assaults her confidence in her painting; he even convinces her to stop using the bold colors she loves, leaving her with black and white, pen and ink. Jenny becomes literally more palatable in the cleansing of her artist's palette, particularly for a man who considers women mere objects for consumption. He recalls meticulously cleaning an American Indian prostitute back home in Colorado, scrubbing lice out of her hair and bathing her body from head to toe, but "after having prepared the dish so carefully, found his appetite gone" (377). David's revulsion stands in direct counterpoise to Jenny's seductive internalization of the Indian, which David implicitly banishes along with his exorcism of color from her artistic consciousness. Jenny seems to acquiesce, knowing that "men love to eat themselves sick and then call their upchuck by high-sounding names." "Oh," she tells David, "I do hope you won't ever make yourself sick on me!" (281). Her jarringly gleeful tone belies the extent to which she resists, via Porter's wizened detachment, the very notion of being evacuated, devoured, and regurgitated—color, Indian, and all—by the gluttonous, "high-sounding" appetite of the white male elite.

It is not difficult to read the "black and white" art consigned to Jenny as Porter's own lament for the black-and-white tones of modern southern writing, one fixated irremediably on a biracial past that exceeded such simplistic, reductive lines. Porter parodies such stark racism most strikingly in the character of Denny, another American southerner. In his small Texas border town where his father was mayor and "rich from local real estate," he had never had to "prove his own importance" over the Mexicans and Negroes in his midst (24): "A man knew who he was and what was what, and niggers, crazy Swedes, Jews, greasers, bone-headed micks, polacks, wops, Guineas, and damn Yankees knew their place and stayed in it" (334). So do women: Denny spends much of the voyage failing to seduce one of the Spanish prostitutes on board, complaining bitterly: "She'll put out all right or it'll be the last white man she'll ever gyp" (280). Throughout the novel, wives and prostitutes alike are routinely slapped, kicked, punched, ridiculed, silenced, and disciplined. More horrifying than the casual pervasiveness of this violence is its explicit internalization and even endorsement by the women themselves. One of the German widows perversely acknowledges with a "positive thrill of sensual excitement" that "the crown of womanhood was suffering for the sake of love" (155). One can't read these scathing depictions without reference to Porter's own biography: as a young woman, she had married a well-to-do Texas rancher's son (much like Denny) who beat her mercilessly, once even tossing her down a flight of stairs and breaking her ankle, and another time, stunning her unconscious with a hairbrush.

Only one woman on board seems to fight back against the abuses that Porter and her women share: a forty-six-year-old divorcée named Mrs.

Treadwell, another of Porter's obvious alter egos, this time for the aging, bitter, disillusioned woman she knew she was becoming. Before Mrs. Treadwell boards the ship at Veracruz, a beggar woman on the streets asks her for money; refused, she leaves a vindictive and bruising pinch on Mrs. Treadwell's arm. "This is surely not a thing that really happens, is it?" Mrs. Treadwell wonders (14). The bruise clearly reifies the repressed gulf between rich and poor, an awareness that comes in a shock of pain and disbelief, but it is also a more personal revelation for Mrs. Treadwell, one that merges gender and economic exploitation at once. Later, she wonders: "Was I ever really married to a man so jealous he beat me until I bled at the nose? I don't believe it. . . . It's something I read about in a newspaper . . . but I still bleed at the nose if I am frightened enough at anything" (208). For women in Porter's world, violence is ordinary, just, and encompassing; more chilling, though, is its ability to be repressed to the point of complete disbelief and detachment, despite the body's stubborn ability to continue bruising and bleeding. This seems Porter's most apt and revealing metaphor for the process by which social and racial crises and collisions affect us: only by activating the personal, private reservoirs of trauma that prevent us from truly communal acts of justice and humanity. The array of differently wounded and wounding characters on board Porter's *Ship of Fools* underscores repeatedly that global interconnections, mobility, and expanding class and moral consciousness were only pushing individuals further into their own violent, self-protective solipsisms.

Near the end of the novel, a sexually frustrated and intoxicated Denny decides he'll finally have his way with that Spanish prostitute; he staggers off in search of his prey but mistakenly ends up knocking on Mrs. Treadwell's cabin instead. She opens the door to Denny's threats and proceeds immediately to beat him, the proxy for her abusive first husband (and perhaps Porter's own, reportedly the inspiration for Denny), attacking first with her fists, "sharply, again and again, in the mouth, on the cheek, on the nose," and then, with her spangled high-heeled shoe held

> firmly by the sole [she] beat him in the face and head with the heel, breathlessly, rising on her knees and coming nearer, her lips drawn back and her teeth set. She beat him with such furious pleasure a sharp pain started up in her right wrist and shot to her shoulder and neck. The sharp metal-capped high heels at every blow broke the skin in small half moons that slowly turned scarlet, and as they multiplied on his forehead, cheeks, chin, lips, Mrs. Treadwell grew cold with fright at what she was doing, yet she could not for her life stop herself. (465)

When she does eventually stop, she promptly tosses her shoe overboard, washes the makeup off her face, takes a few sleeping pills, and quickly forgets her hideously satisfying crime.

The moment of savagery ends as quickly as it begins and is as efficiently washed away and tamped down—as are all our most simple and abominable acts of cruelty, whether a single high-heel bludgeoning by an abused woman, a lone sandal hurtled at a beggar by mindless children already conditioned into a culture of cruelty, or a massive extermination of a race of people in a Holocaust, an Indian genocide, or a system of chattel slavery. No sooner have we lived through such acts, Porter intimates, than we find some way to purge them. As her name none too subtly implies, Mrs. Treadwell does "tread well"—both in her prim, mannered elitism and in her perverse "tread" all over Denny's rabid face—and such characterizations remind us that the heart of the well-heeled aristocracy conceals a terrible sense of victimization, vengeance, and repression at its core. For all the desire to move forward represented by Mrs. Treadwell's explosion of rage, Porter's characters spend vast amounts of time trying to go backward—back home, back to Paris, back to youth. Even young, wistful, headstrong Jenny, so much a vision of what Porter once knew herself to be, ends the book painting without color and declaring, "David, darling . . . I could creep back inside and be your rib again!" There, she imagines, she will remain "like a petrified fetus for the rest of [her] life" (212).

It is an apt simile for this allegory about southern modernity's frustrated hopes, petrified humanism, and cyclical returns to home harbors and haunting, repetitive histories. In many ways, the novel's Jenny Brown/Mrs. Treadwell dyad tracks neatly with Porter's own backpedaling attitudes in the face of modernity's terrible disenchantments. What *Ship of Fools* intimates, however, is Porter's dreadful recognition that such horrors cannot be evaded, that in fact, they have always lurked beneath the veneer of society's labored graces. Read in the wake of new critical trends in both southern and American studies, works like Porter's ask us to engage in a difficult reckoning: What modernity spawns is neither new nor original, and no plantation idyll or mythical indigene can save us from humankind's innate and insular hungers.

NOTES

1. Mencken, "Sahara of the Bozart," 136, 139.

2. F. Hobson, "New South," 249.

3. Building on foundational world systems theories advanced by Immanuel Wallerstein, a number of scholars have reexamined the South's role as colonial periphery for the industrial-capitalist North. See, for instance, Persky, *Burden of Dependency*; G. Wright, *Old South, New South*; and Woodward, *Origins of the New South*, especially his chapter titled "The Colonial Economy."

4. Romine, *Real South*, 3, 4, 6.

5. Ibid., 4.

6. See M. B. Taylor, *Reconstructing the Native South*.

7. As Annette Trefzer explains in her pivotal *Disturbing Indians*, modern southern fiction returned obsessively to archaeological sites and themes to contemplate what southerners of the period were actively excavating: their ancestral and ideological connections to the indigenous forebears that lent historicity, longevity, and proprietary claims to their unsettled region.

8. Brinkmeyer, *Fourth Ghost*, 226.

9. Ibid., 204–7.

10. Titus, *Ambivalent Art of Katherine Anne Porter*, 199.

11. Porter, *Ship of Fools*, 21. Text hereafter cited parenthetically.

12. Titus, *Ambivalent Art*, 12.

13. Porter, *Letters*, 60.

14. Ibid., 24–25.

SUGGESTIONS FOR FURTHER READING

Brinkmeyer, Robert H. *The Fourth Ghost: White Southern Writers and European Fascism, 1930–1950*. Baton Rouge: Louisiana State University Press, 2009.

Duck, Leigh Anne. *The Nation's Region: Southern Modernism, Segregation, and U.S. Nationalism*. Athens: University of Georgia Press, 2006.

Greeson, Jennifer Rae. *Our South: Geographic Fantasy and the Rise of National Literature*. Cambridge, Mass.: Harvard University Press, 2010.

Singal, Daniel Joseph. *The War Within: From Victorian to Modernist Thought in the South, 1919–1945*. Chapel Hill: University of North Carolina Press, 1982.

Smith, Jon, and Deborah Cohn, eds. *Look Away! The U.S. South in New World Studies*. Durham, N.C.: Duke University Press, 2004.

Trefzer, Annette. *Disturbing Indians: The Archaeology of Southern Fiction*. Tuscaloosa: University of Alabama Press, 2007.

MARTYN BONE

Postsouthern

Lewis P. Simpson coined the term "postsouthern" in his 1980 essay "The Closure of History in a Postsouthern America." In doing so, Simpson sought to delineate a new and distinctive literary moment in which "the history of the literary mind of the South seeking to become aware of itself," which Simpson took to be a defining aspect of Southern Renaissance writing, no longer seemed to operate. Simpson's was essentially a narrative of decline: there is an elegiac tone to the statement that "the epiphany of the southern literary artist will not be repeated. The Southern Renascence will not come again."[1] His ambivalent vision of a "postsouthern America" had both temporal and spatial dimensions: the phrase denoted not only the end of a distinctive southern (literary) history but also the incorporation of regional identity into a supposedly homogenized nation. Here Simpson echoed journalist John Egerton's claim in *The Americanization of Dixie* (1974) that "the South is just about over as a separate and distinct place."[2] But while Simpson worried about the death of southern distinctiveness, he allowed that the fiction of Walker Percy might yet yield "a return to a participation in the mystery of history."[3]

If Simpson valued Percy's fiction because it seemed to retain a residual sense of the "historical consciousness" that Allen Tate saw as central to Renaissance-era southern literature, he also suggested that Percy's novel *The Last Gentleman* (1966) operates at the hinge between the modernism of the Southern Renaissance and southern literature's postsouthern turn. This view of Percy would be echoed by later critics such as Philip E. Simmons, who argued that Percy's 1961 novel "*The Moviegoer* is a transitional text, treating postmodern themes in a late modernist mode" because "Percy's history of the suburbanization of the South" still "attaches to a larger mythic history" associated with "the values of the aristocratic, agrarian South."[4] *The Moviegoer* opens with its narrator and protagonist, Binx Bolling, having escaped his wealthy family's history by leaving New Orleans's Garden District for an "ordinary life" as a moviegoer and stockbroker in suburban Gentilly, but ends with Binx back in the Garden District and uneasily reconciled with his aristocratic aunt Emily. Thus Percy's debut novel explores new postsouthern landscapes but ultimately returns to more familiar southern (literary) territory.

Simpson's neologism was not immediately influential: it would be more than a decade before other critics began to explore and extend the potential of "postsouthern" as, in Michael Kreyling's phrase, "an enabling word" for southern literary studies.[5] Kreyling himself took the lead in adopting and adapting the term. As its title suggests, Kreyling's essay "Fee Fie Faux Faulkner: Parody and Postmodernism in Southern Literature" (1993) yokes the postsouthern to the postmodern much more explicitly (and enthusiastically) than did Simpson. Whereas Simpson worried about "the closure of history" and Fred Hobson in *The Southern Writer in the Postmodern World* (1991) fretted that Bobbie Ann Mason's characters "are products of a *society* that disregards history," Kreyling insists that "history still exists" in the South, but that "we now acknowledge that we know it through a system of representations rather than in an unmediated, direct way."[6] For Kreyling, then, the South's encounter with postmodernism entailed not a loss of historical consciousness but rather a heightened awareness of how history itself is subject to representation. Exhibiting a much more positive view of postmodernism than Simpson, Hobson, and the Marxist critic Fredric Jameson, who diagnosed "the waning of our historicity" as a debilitating symptom of postmodern life, Kreyling insists that "the postmodernist does not erase the past, she rethinks it under the destabilizing condition of irony."[7] By declaring that in the postmodern world there can be "no recourse to the totalizing and totally authoritative referent: capitalism, patriarchy, the novel, the South," Kreyling also departs from Jameson's negative view of postmodernism as the "cultural logic" of a totalized, globalized form of capitalism. Instead, he echoes Jean-François Lyotard's claim that "the postmodern condition" is characterized by "incredulity toward metanarratives."[8] The master narrative or "totally authoritative referent" subjected to Kreyling's own incredulous scrutiny is the neo-Agrarian model of southern literary history that he would critique more extensively in *Inventing Southern Literature* (1998).

Drawing on Linda Hutcheon's model of postmodern literary parody as a strategy through which contemporary writers liberate themselves from the influence of their literary predecessors, "Fee Fie Faux Faulkner" formulates a theory of postsouthern parody. Kreyling proposes that writers such as Reynolds Price, Harry Crews, and Barry Hannah make intertextual, parodic reference to the work of William Faulkner, Flannery O'Connor, and other Renaissance-era figures as a way of negotiating the burden of southern literary history. "Assessing parody is where the postmodern southern literary critic must start": not only a logical move in a "postmodern-postsouthern condition" characterized by the precession of representations but also a way of recognizing that "the South" was always a complex of ideas, images, and narratives that may have had little reference to empirical reality.[9] In "The Practice of Place in a Postsouthern Age" (2000), Scott Romine observes that Kreyling's advocacy of the postsouthern marked a conceptual break with neo-Agrarian southern literary studies by emphasizing and even embracing the notion that literature does not primarily relate to a "real South"—that is, the material, regional geography to which "southern literature" was traditionally understood to refer, so much so that such literature has routinely been lauded for its "sense of place." The postsouthern text turns away from the real South to parody "previous imitations of place"—most notably, the postage stamp of native soil depicted throughout Faulkner's Yoknapatawpha saga. Romine concludes by wondering if "southern literature . . . might, in fact, dispense with reality altogether," with writers like Hannah and Lewis Nordan "generat[ing] their own worlds without especially borrowing from ours."[10]

Along with Percy and Richard Ford, Hannah is the author whose work has attracted most critical attention as emblematic of the postsouthern turn. In an essay for *Perspectives on Barry Hannah* (2007), I argue that Hannah uses postsouthern parody in *Airships* (1978) and *Ray* (1980) both to revise Faulkner's representation of southern military heroism in *Sartoris* (1929) and to critique a broader "neo-Confederate" master narrative in which Civil War generals such as J. E. B. Stuart and Nathan Bedford Forrest have been figured as the great men of southern history. Yet in the essay that precedes mine in *Perspectives*, James B. Potts portrays Hannah, along with Charles Frazier and Cormac McCarthy, as sustaining rather than breaking from the Southern Renaissance tradition of Faulkner and Tate. In Potts's view, Hannah's adherence to myth and "the desire for transcendence" distinguishes his work from postsouthern fiction that "while decrying the 'nostalgia' of the southern past . . . directs attention away from the idealized best to the realized worst." For Potts, postsouthernism's conscious puncturing of mythology and transcendence merely reduced southern literature to the "redneck grotesques" of Crews and Larry Brown.[11]

Though rather less pessimistic than Potts, Romine too has raised some issues regarding the potential limitations of postsouthern literature and criticism. He notes that the contemporary southern writer may not be freed by the postmodern turn to a nonreferential, intertextual, and parodic mode, because "even without a mimetic South to imitate, the South remains as an absent cause, an imperative (implicit on Kreyling's part) for Barry Hannah to parody Faulkner and not Ernest Hemingway; postsouthern literature can be delineated . . . only by its relationship to earlier writing that could image itself as Southern (capital S, no quotation marks)."[12] In "Elizabeth Spencer, the White Civil Rights Novel, and the Postsouthern" (2004), Thomas F. Haddox echoes and extends Romine's ruminations about the "parasitic, parodic" nature of postsouthern literature. Haddox notes the "paradox" that "a postsouthern critic who wishes to reject the metaphysical claims of the southern literary past can only do so by recycling the content of the past, by redeploying all of its familiar tropes"; as such, "the postsouthern cannot simply be a leaving behind of southern literature." Here both Romine and Haddox have identified a phenomenon that we might term the sub-postsouthern persistence of the "southern." However, where Romine remains relatively positive about postsouthernism's move away from mimesis to intertextual parody, Haddox supports the view that postsouthern "recycling" amounts to a "falling off" from the Southern Renaissance. Indeed, Haddox identifies the ominous "symptoms of the postsouthern" as emerging already in 1956 with Elizabeth Spencer's *Voice at the Back Door*, a "white civil rights novel" featuring "characters who are formulaic, predictable, and often laughable."[13] Such an assessment dovetails with Potts's view that in postsouthern fiction "the magnificent intensity of southern literature . . . seems to have dissipated in favor of cartoonish reductions."[14] By connecting postsouthernism to the emergence of the white civil rights novel, Haddox also reanimates Floyd C. Watkins's 1970 argument that southern writers' attempts to address race relations had resulted in "the death of art."[15] With qualifications, Haddox reaffirms Watkins's bleak take on the parlous state of post-Renaissance southern literature and renames it "postsouthern."

Despite varying degrees of critical enthusiasm, the postsouthern has often been figured as a distinctive break—be it positive or negative—from what went before. A problem here may be that sometimes critics have been too inclined to look for breaks (or at least distinctive periodizations) between the modern and the postmodern, the southern and the postsouthern, or the Renaissance and the post-Renaissance. Jon Smith has caustically observed, in a review of my book *The Postsouthern Sense of Place in Contemporary Fiction* (2005), that "there's only a 'break' if, like [Lewis] Simpson, you're a neoagrarian fantasist, or like Jameson, you're overinvested in postmodern exceptionalism."[16] Romine has remarked that "an overdeveloped eschatological sense is one of the more enduring characteristics of the southern literary tradition," and it may be that both champions and critics of postsouthernism have followed in this tradition by foregrounding apparent breaks in southern literary history, rather than mapping its more complicated continuities and contradictions.[17] Having said that, Haddox and Romine have suggested that postsouthern parody was not really much of a break after all, given its parasitic relationship to the Renaissance-era host texts. More recently, Smith has argued that even putatively revisionist, postsouthernist scholarship recurs to traditional models of southern literature (and southern literary studies), noting that both Romine and I "have spent quite a lot of time arguing with the agrarians."[18] In other words, critics keep raising Agrarianism by trying to bury it—another manifestation of the sub-postsouthern persistence of the "southern."

It may be too that there is a bigger quandary to consider. If postsouthern literature—or perhaps more pointedly, postsouthern literary criticism—is concerned primarily with intertextuality, parody, and hyperrealist invention, has it "dispense[d] with reality altogether," become totally detached from the "real South"? Probably not: even Haddox, who has lamented the "replacement of symbolic depth with simulacra" in postsouthern literature, allows that it still engages with social reality (his bone of contention was that such literature, in the form of white civil rights fiction, does so with disastrous aesthetic consequences).[19] In *The Postsouthern Sense of Place in Contemporary Fiction*, I seek to recast the definition of postsouthern literature so that it might refer to and interrogate the changing social and economic geography of the South. I draw on (then) recent work by postmodern geographers like David Harvey and Edward Soja to propose that the application of a "simultaneously historical and geographical materialism" to postsouthernism could help account for contemporary capitalism's tremendous impact on southern "place."[20] I argue too that a revised definition of "postsouthern" retains critical use value because, while the term *may* signify a break with familiar ideas of "the South" and "southern literature," the etymological retention of "southern" helps remind us of historical continuities with earlier forms of uneven development and exploitation in the region.[21]

The Postsouthern Sense of Place applies this historical-geographical materialist version of postsouthernism to a range of literary texts, beginning with Percy's *The Moviegoer* and concluding with Toni Cade Bambara's *Those Bones Are Not My Child* (1999). Richard Ford emerges as the single most significant exponent of postsouthern fiction. In *A Piece of My Heart* (1976) and the first two installments of the Frank Bascombe trilogy—*The Sportswriter* (1986) and *Independence Day* (1995)—Mississippi-born Ford develops the most impressively sustained and subtle critique of established notions of "the South," "southern literature," and its supposed "sense of place." I was not the first critic to figure Ford's fiction as postsouthern: in 1991, Hobson broached the possibility that *The Sportswriter* was postsouthern, while Matthew Guinn's *After Southern Modernism* (2000) interprets Frank Bascombe as a "postsouthern expatriate." However, whereas Hobson concluded that *The Sportswriter* is in fact "a southern novel in a southern tradition" and that Frank remains residually "southern" because he is "keenly attuned to place," I insisted that in the Bascombe novels "such 'southern' metaconcepts as 'place' and 'community' . . . are contingent upon land speculation and development."[22] In *Independence Day*, Frank's new job as a realtor helps him come to a more sophisticated understanding of capitalist property relations in postsouthern America, especially the fetishization of "place" as a commodity.

My materialist approach culminated with a case study of Atlanta as a postsouthern "international city" (the sobriquet applied to Atlanta by its civic-corporate boosters since the early 1970s). However, this global capital of capital still exhibits historical continuities with familiar southern places, especially in the form of racial segregation and uneven development. For example, Tom Wolfe's mammoth novel *A Man in Full* (1998) both critiques the ways in which global capitalism has produced a "sense of placelessness" in downtown Atlanta and depicts those less glamorous loci, often populated by immigrants, that exist within or on the borders of the "international city." But it is Bambara's book that most thoroughly maps the tensions between Atlanta's global economic status and enduring local realities of spatial and racial inequality; *Those Bones* does so through its detailed attention to black working-class life in the wake of the Atlanta child murders of 1979–81, with their grim echoes of earlier violence against black southern bodies.

As should be evident from the foregoing discussion, the theory and practice of postsouthernism since 1980 has occurred primarily within literary studies. It is important to note, then, that some of the earliest and most recent approaches to postsouthernism have concentrated on other art forms. One of the first discussions of "Post-Southernism" can be found in Stephen Flinn Young's 1989 essay on postmodern sculpture. Showcasing once more the critical concern with the nature of the relationship between the postsouthern and the South's assumed "sense of place," Young begins by pondering whether "we may have even become prisoners of our own fascination" with sense of place, "for when change overtakes us and place, even the place we call the South, is not the place it used to be, anxiety strikes."[23] Yet whereas Romine and Julius Rowan Raper have suggested that contemporary nonrealist literature might help liberate southerners from a suffocating adherence to an "extraordinary sense of place" that (as Raper puts it) "is a mainstay still of Modern Southern Fiction—but, less and less, of modern Southern life," ultimately Young expresses a yearning for art that retains the "pre-postmodern . . . sense of place."[24] He finds it in contemporary sculpture that, for all its formal innovation, focuses its representative attention on familiar rural figures and landscapes. Thus Young's otherwise valuable early analysis ends up folding the postsouthern back into familiar ideas of southernness.

A more recent and persuasive attempt to extend postsouthern theory beyond literary studies is Jay Watson's 2011 essay "Mapping Out a Postsouthern Cinema." Noting that "the concept [postsouthern] has been slow to make its way into the burgeoning field of southern film studies," Watson identifies three very different movies as contributions to an inchoate "postsouthern film canon." The first of those films is the Burt Reynolds vehicle *Sharky's Machine* (1981), which Watson reads as a film that depicts Atlanta as an increasingly international city. Watson too is concerned to reconnect postsouthern art (though he notes wryly that *Sharky's Machine* "is no cinematic masterpiece") to a contemporary socioeconomic geography that is less regionally distinctive than defined by the intensification of global capitalism. In particular, Watson unpacks the film's almost fetishistic focus on developer John Portman's Peachtree Center in downtown Atlanta—an analog to Portman's Bonaventure Hotel in Los Angeles, the case study for Jameson's reading of postmodern architecture—as a location that departs from its regional-southern surroundings to become "what Jameson calls 'the hyperspace' of multinational capitalism."[25]

For Watson, *Sharky's Machine* is, like *The Moviegoer* for other critics, a transitional text that "hints at the postsouthern without embracing it." By contrast, Richard Linklater's debut film *Slacker* (1991) features a vast cast of characters who become "the new cartographers of the postsouthern era." Watson argues that *Slacker* treats such "traditionally 'southern' themes [as] family, storytelling, community, history and place" in postsouthern parodic fashion, while the depiction of Austin, Texas, as a "decentered neighborhood landscape" devoid of distinctive urban markers is "disorienting." Yet the film's "slacker" characters counter any resulting sense of placelessness through a contingent, everyday form of Jameson's "cognitive mapping"; in doing so they "are also performing a preliminary, provisional mapping of the contemporary post-South." Watson's third and final example of postsouthern cinema is perhaps the most intriguing, as it diverges strikingly from existing definitions of postsouthernism: Mira Nair's *Mississippi Masala* (1991) "gets at the postsouthern by way of the postcolonial."[26] By focusing on the encounter between immigrant Ugandan Indians and native African

Americans in Greenwood, Mississippi, the film emphasizes that the experience of economic globalization and the related influx of immigrants are not confined to major metropolitan centers. If Gerald Creed and Barbara Ching are correct in saying that, in the "postmodern social theory" of Jameson, Soja, and others, the "stable reference point has been the city" at the almost total expense of the country, then Watson's reading of *Mississippi Masala* provides a timely check on postsouthernism's tendency to look away from the rural South to urban centers such as Atlanta and Austin. Furthermore, Nair's film (like Bambara's novel) foregrounds regional-historical continuities of inequality and prejudice: "*Mississippi Masala* attests to the persistence, even into the postsouthern era, of older structures of consciousness, rooted in slavery and segregation, which work within the black community to keep black people down."[27]

Watson's formative canon of postsouthern cinema could be extended to include Ross McElwee's *Sherman's March* (1986) and Kevin Willmott's *C.S.A.* (2004). McElwee's movie is set up as a documentary-style exploration of the lingering impact on the South of General Sherman's infamous march to the sea. Though the film does loosely follow the trajectory of Sherman's march, its chronology and geography are increasingly oriented around the lovelorn McElwee's interactions with various (white) southern women. In postmodern fashion, the film foregrounds its own production and how the distinctions between reality and simulation, history and performance, become ever more blurred: during a visit to the ruins of a church torched by Sherman's soldiers, McElwee reflects, "It seems I'm filming my life in order to have a life to film. . . . I ponder the possibility that [his friend] Charlene is right that filming is the only way I can relate to women." Yet it is precisely through this self-reflexive focus on simulation and performance that *Sherman's March*, in Tara McPherson's words, "manages to reveal the artifice of southern femininity," while also interrogating mythic notions of southern masculinity.[28] Burt Reynolds recurs in McElwee's film as a reference point for a performative, mediated form of white masculinity in the postsouthern era. McElwee declares early on, "Sherman aside, I'm disconcerted to find myself in competition with the likes of Burt Reynolds"; later, he states his desire to discuss with Reynolds "his views on such topics as concepts of masculinity and romance in the South." However, on the one occasion he does get to speak to Reynolds, it turns out to be a look-alike who is lurking outside the star's hotel in search of work as a body double.

Like *Sherman's March*, *C.S.A.* formally and thematically taps into Americans' enduring fascination with the Civil War only to subvert it. A counterfactual "mockumentary" by the African American director and professor of film studies Kevin Willmott, *C.S.A.* uses a parodic, satirical take on the Confederacy to make more-serious points about contemporary issues—but in this case, with a concerted focus on race. Like Hannah's Jeb Stuart stories, *C.S.A.* constructs a sly alternative history of the Confederacy: the film is built around a supposed British documentary about the Confederate States of America since the South's victory in 1865, including the maintenance of slavery into the present. The documentary, shown by public demand on a San Francisco channel of the Confederate television network, is interspersed with commercials for such products as the Shackle (an electronic device to prevent slaves escaping), Darkie toothpaste, and Niggerhair cigarettes, as well as promotional spots for such regular series as *Runaway* (a reality show about police efforts to apprehend runaway slaves). The British documentary, replete with stentorian voice-over and talking-head historians, is clearly a parody of Ken Burns's PBS *Civil War* series. Yet if the film's use of parody and counterfactual history makes it conspicuously postmodern or postsouthern—Kreyling observes in *The South That Wasn't There* (2010) that in the age of postmodern simulation we are "inundated by the power of otherwise" as "technologies (especially visual) became available for the creation of the illusion of historicity"—the commercial products have real historical reference points (Darkie Toothpaste and Niggerhair tobacco were actual products), while *Runaway* recalls the frequent focus on black criminality in reality shows like *Cops*.[29] As Leigh Anne Duck has remarked, "[*C.S.A.*'s] dystopian Confederate States . . . resemble the actual United States so closely as to constitute, in Willmott's words, a 'metaphor' for the dualities in a purportedly democratic but palpably inequitable nation."[30] If Willmott's C.S.A./U.S.A. is a different kind of postsouthern America than that adumbrated by Simpson, it serves to remind us that a truly "postracial" society remains elusive, and that the color line remains not merely a regional but a national problem.

This brings me to the most conspicuous lacuna in existing definitions and discussions of postsouthernism: the failure to attend to literary and other cultural texts by and about black southerners. For all its emphasis on interrogating earlier master narratives of "the South" and "southern literature," postsouthern literary criticism has tended to recapitulate a version of southern literary history that, even with the turn to parody, remains glaringly white. This may have something to do with Romine's point that "postsouthern literature can be delineated . . . only by its relationship to earlier writing that could imagine itself as Southern." So, because earlier scholars defined the Southern Renaissance almost exclusively as the cultural expression of white southerners, even contemporary critics otherwise sympathetic to an expansion of the southern literary canon have read postsouthern literature along white lines: Hannah parodying Faulkner, Ford interrogating Percy, or (in Guinn's *After Southern Modernism*) Mason taking her stand against the Agrarians. Haddox goes so far as to suggest that the "emergence of the postsouthern" is suspiciously coterminous with the increase in black southern agency and activism during the Civil Rights Movement: "Just when African Americans begin to challenge, in a highly visible and overtly political way, the hegemonic narratives of the white South, white southerners conclude, whether reluctantly or joyfully, that these narratives are dead or at least evacuated of efficacy."[31] Though one might well question Haddox's implication that there is a causal relationship between white southern reaction to the Civil Rights Movement and the rise of postsouthernism, it is true that postsouthern theory and criticism have marginalized black southern writing and too often occluded racial concerns. When African American authors have been included in debates about postmodernism and southern literature, they have sometimes been figured as the last, best hope that redeems the traditional southern literary dispensation. Hobson's *The Southern Writer in the Postmodern World* concludes by invoking Ernest Gaines as the writer who sustains the established vision of southern literature as defined by "place, community, man's ties to the natural world" even as white counterparts like Hannah, Ford, and Mason seemed to be breaking definitively from it.[32] A decade later, Guinn read Randall Kenan's early fiction primarily as a "postmodern reinterpretation within the black literary tradition," and only secondarily as suggesting "the possibility of a nexus between [the African American literary tradition of] Signifying . . . and the mythoclastic tendencies common to postmodern white fiction."[33] The Kenan chapter is the only one of seven in *After Southern Modernism* devoted to a black southern writer. Similarly, my study of Bambara's *Those Bones* was the only one of *The Postsouthern Sense of Place*'s ten chapters that focused on an African American author.

One relatively recent novel by a black southern writer that seems ripe for reading as postsouthern is *The Wind Done Gone* (2001), Alice Randall's much discussed "unauthorized parody" of Margaret Mitchell's *Gone with the Wind* (1936). Cleaving as closely as it does to Mitchell's novel, *The Wind Done Gone* exemplifies both the possibilities and liabilities of postsouthern parody. In *The Real South* (2009), Romine remarks that like earlier southern literary parodies of *Gone with the Wind* by O'Connor and Percy, *The Wind Done Gone* "must resuscitate Tara in order to kill it off"; in other words, here we have another striking example of the paradoxical sub-postsouthern persistence of the "southern."[34] Yet, as Kreyling notes, *The Wind Done Gone*'s textual play also makes the serious point that Mitchell's novel was hardly "original" either, drawing as it did on preexisting southern mythologies. By foregrounding the story of Scarlett O'Hara's biracial half sister Cynara and fleshing out black characters who feature in Mitchell's novel, "*The Wind Done Gone* gives the stereotyped and silenced their proper voices and subjectivities."[35] Haddox, however, is less persuaded by *The Wind Done Gone*'s claims to "speak for the Negro," insisting that the novel's "utopian potential, instead of resting on a materialist understanding of history, sees historical change entirely as a matter of discursive redescription." For Haddox, Randall's text is entirely too intertextual and ahistorical to give the "silenced their proper voices"; instead, it exemplifies a "ludic postmodernism" that (in Teresa L. Ebert's words) "substitutes a politics of representation for radical social transformation."[36] It is notable that neither Haddox, Romine, nor Kreyling explicitly defines or discusses Randall's novel as "postsouthern." Nor do they consider the possibility that Randall's novel achieves a relative autonomy from Mitchell's host text, either by extending its intertextual range from *Othello* via Frederick Douglass's 1845 *Narrative* and Faulkner's *Light in August* to Billie Holiday's rendition of "Strange Fruit," or through its increasing emphasis on Cynara's life story as separate from *Gone with the Wind*'s white characters (Scarlett/Other dies halfway through the novel; Cynara subsequently marries and then divorces Rhett Butler/R.) and its narrative geography (Cynara moves to Washington D.C., where she becomes romantically involved with a black Reconstruction congressman from Alabama).

Critics might also consider in what ways Jesmyn Ward's National Book Award–winning *Salvage the Bones* (2011), about a poor black Mississippi family confronting Hurricane Katrina, signifies in postsouthern fashion on Faulkner's *As I Lay Dying* (1930). Then there are the numerous allusions to Zora Neale Hurston's life and work in *Louisiana* (1994), by the Jamaican novelist and sociologist Erna Brodber: Do they constitute a simultaneously postsouthern and circum-Caribbean intertextuality? Here though we might note a final problem with existing discussions of postsouthernism: the failure to incorporate insights from postcolonial theory and to fully account for the ligatures (literary, historical, economic, demographic) between the U.S. South and other parts of the world, especially the Caribbean, Latin America, and Africa. It may in fact be that the postsouthern moment has passed, peripheral to and superseded by the hemispheric and transnational turns in (new) southern studies. Perhaps postsouthernism as it was defined between 1980 and 2005 became too entrenched in postmodern ideas of literary parody, or too heavily invested in how contemporary white southern writers negotiate their relationship to the Agrarians or Faulkner, to be of much use to the New Southern Studies. Jon Smith and Deborah Cohn term the title of *Look Away! The U.S. South in New World Studies* (2004) a "postsouthernist gesture" because it knowingly references yet refutes "the paradigm of white southern nativism, *I'll Take My Stand*"; otherwise, however, postsouthernism is conspicuous by its absence from this and other key works in the New Southern Studies.[37] Still, to the degree that postsouthern theory and criticism has engaged with economic globalization and the transnational migration of Asian, African, Latin American, and Caribbean peoples to the South—as in my assessment of immigrant populations in Wolfe's *A Man in Full* or Watson's reading of *Mississippi Masala*—there may yet be scope for recasting "the postsouthern by way of the postcolonial" and the Global South.

There are some tentative signs that the more materialist wing of postsouthernist scholarship is developing in a direction that intersects with ecocriticism. In a recent essay, Michael P. Bibler offers a sobering check on postmodern deconstructions of the "real South" by emphasizing the threat that ecological catastrophe poses to the region's material geography. Bibler "stress[es] the urgency of confronting the real, material threats to southern nature that the critical discourse of postsouthernism has so far tended to ignore: environmental degradation and climate change."[38] He suggests that a combination of postsouthern and environmental criticism can help us confront the ways in which "the physical, economic, and material actualities of the southern landscape" are threatened by devastation, as so acutely demonstrated by Hurricane Katrina's impact on New Orleans and the Gulf Coast in 2005 or the tornadoes that devastated Tuscaloosa in 2011. Bibler himself offers a postsouthernist *and* environmentalist reading of Scott Elliott's 2003 novel *Coiled in the Heart*, which depicts both the economic and the ecological transformation of rural southern landscapes in dystopian, even apocalyptic terms. This kind of postsouthern-materialist approach may well prove more useful than an emphasis on parody to an emerging, ecocritically informed branch of the New Southern Studies. Whether critics will still call it postsouthernism is another matter. Musing on future directions for Hannah scholarship in the wake of the New Southern Studies, Mark Graybill anticipates "new, post-postsouthern methodologies." For Graybill, this double post designation is necessary to distinguish the "more materialist ... orientation" of "the next wave of Hannah criticism," which he identifies with the New Southern Studies, from postsouthernism's earlier overdetermined association with parody and textuality.[39]

NOTES

1. Simpson, *Brazen Face of History*, 268–69.
2. Egerton, *Americanization of Dixie*, xxi.
3. Simpson, *Brazen Face of History*, 269.
4. Simmons, "Toward the Postmodern Historical Imagination," 621, 603.
5. Kreyling, *"Fathers,"* 186.
6. F. Hobson, *Southern Writer*, 18; Kreyling, "Fee Fie Faux Faulkner," 3.
7. Jameson, *Postmodernism*, 21; Kreyling, "Fee Fie Faux Faulkner," 6.
8. Kreyling, "Fee Fie Faux Faulkner," 3; Lyotard, *Postmodern Condition*, xxiv.
9. Kreyling, "Fee Fie Faux Faulkner," 7.
10. Romine, "Where Is Southern Literature?," 22, 25.
11. Potts, "Shade of Faulkner's Horse," 79–80.
12. Romine, "Where is Southern Literature?," 22.
13. Haddox, "Elizabeth Spencer," 567–68, 562, 568.
14. Potts, "Shade of Faulkner's Horse," 80.
15. See Watkins, *Death of Art*.
16. J. Smith, review of *Postsouthern Sense of Place*, 373.
17. Romine, "Where is Southern Literature?," 9.
18. J. Smith, "Toward a Post-Postpolitical Southern Studies," 79.
19. Haddox, "Elizabeth Spencer," 566.
20. Soja, *Postmodern Geographies*, 12.
21. Bone, *Postsouthern Sense of Place*, 50–51.
22. F. Hobson, *Southern Writer*, 57, 50; Bone, *Postsouthern Sense of Place*, 134.
23. S. F. Young, "Post-Southernism," 41.
24. J. R. Raper, "Inventing Modern Southern Fiction," 9.
25. Watson, "Mapping Out a Postsouthern Cinema," 220, 242, 220, 224.
26. Ibid., 220, 232, 227, 226, 232, 220.
27. Creed and Ching, "Recognizing Rusticity," 244; Watson, "Mapping Out a Postsouthern Cinema," 239.
28. McPherson, *Reconstructing Dixie*, 135.
29. Kreyling, *South That Wasn't There*, 182.
30. Duck, "Plantation/Empire," 80–81.
31. Haddox, "Elizabeth Spencer," 579.
32. F. Hobson, *Southern Writer*, 92.
33. Guinn, *After Southern Modernism*, 139–40.
34. Romine, *Real South*, 55.
35. Kreyling, *South That Wasn't There*, 158.
36. Haddox, "Alice Randall's *The Wind Done Gone*," 130, 123.
37. J. Smith and Cohn, "Introduction," 13.
38. Bibler, "Serpents in the Garden," 119.
39. Graybill, "'I Am, Personally, the Fall of the West,'" 686.

SUGGESTIONS FOR FURTHER READING

Bone, Martyn. *The Postsouthern Sense of Place in Contemporary Fiction*. Baton Rouge: Louisiana State University Press, 2005.

Haddox, Thomas F.. "Elizabeth Spencer, the White Civil Rights Novel, and the Postsouthern." *Modern Language Quarterly* 65, no. 4 (December 2004): 561–81.

Kreyling, Michael. "Fee Fie Faux Faulkner: Parody and Postmodernism in Southern Literature." *Southern Review* 29 (1993): 1–15.

———. *The South That Wasn't There: Postsouthern Memory and History*. Baton Rouge: Louisiana State University Press, 2010.

Romine, Scott. "Where Is Southern Literature? The Practice of Place in a Postsouthern Age." In *South to a New Place*, edited by Suzanne Jones and Sharon Monteith, 23–43. Baton Rouge: Louisiana State University Press, 2002.

Watson, Jay. "Mapping Out a Postsouthern Cinema: Three Contemporary Films." In *American Cinema and the Southern Imaginary*, edited by Deborah E. Barker and Kathryn McKee, 219–52. Athens: University of Georgia Press, 2011.

Trauma

JON SMITH

All conservatism begins with loss.
—Andrew Sullivan, *The Conservative Soul*

In the summer of 2009, in anticipation of its upcoming biennial conference, the Society for the Study of Southern Literature issued a call for papers that sounded rather personally aggrieved. "In the southern United States," it began, "'hard times' seems redundant: the South has always been the bad news region of the country. We are the site of violence, poverty, despair, bigotry, and floods of biblical proportions, which makes us something to see. So we become a preferred destination: for tourists and carpetbaggers, entrepreneurs and retirees, historians and theorists, writers and readers. And hard times turn into good times, at least for some."[1] Pitting a unified southern "we" against an inspired roster of exploitive outsiders, the call takes its twenty-first-century stand by reiterating a mix of both reputable and disreputable accounts of "southern identity" as distinctively grounded in loss, abjection, and trauma. The still surprisingly reputable narrative is that of "the South" as the traumatized (invaded, defeated, colonized, and suitably chastened) exception to American exceptionalism. Usually traced to the historian C. Vann Woodward's 1953 essay "The Irony of Southern History," that vision of southern trauma was given new life nearly half a century later when the "hemispheric" turn in American and southern studies sought to tie the U.S. South to other postcolonial, postplantation New World regions farther south, from the Caribbean to Brazil. For Woodward, "the South" had learned "the taste left in the mouth by the swallowing of one's own words" from what he called "the experience of military defeat, occupation, and reconstruction"; hence, the region was less likely to buy into the U.S. "legend of irresistible progress, success, and victory." Woodward claimed this experience was something the U.S. South shared with "nearly all the peoples of Europe and Asia," but in 1999 Deborah Cohn, following the lead of not only Woodward but also the Latin American Boom writers, set the tone for the next decade's work in southern studies (and much work in hemispheric American studies) by redubbing this experience "the search for meaning in difficult pasts."[2] She called it a point of commonality specifically between what she dubbed "the two souths": the U.S. South and the hemispheric one.

The less reputable narrative, of course, is the bitter one of unashamed white grievance and victimhood, in which innocent southern whites suffer at the grasping hands, and are shamed by the judgmental yet voyeuristic gaze, of "carpetbaggers . . . historians and theorists." As Eudora Welty, a relatively liberal advocate of this view, defensively put it in 1965 in response to civil rights demonstrations in Jackson, "We [whites] in the South are a hated people these days; we were hated first for actual and particular reasons, and now we may be hated still more in some vast unparticularized way. I believe there must be such a thing as sentimental hate. Our people hate back."[3] Although the call for papers does gesture toward black southernness—"hardship," it proclaims, "inspires the creativity necessary . . . for the traditional activities of 'making a chicken stretch,' 'piecing a quilt,' or singing the blues"—markers of such a feminized, reactionary southern blackness find themselves subordinated to an essentialized and biracial southern poverty.[4] The role of white southerners, rich and poor, in producing and maintaining black southern poverty is played down (such poverty is instead naturalized alongside "floods of biblical proportions"); the role of outsiders in profiting off southern misery, however, is not. (Such anger at outside agitators is generally absent from black southern discourse; consider, for example, Dr. Martin Luther King Jr.'s dismissal of insider/outsider distinctions in the letter from Birmingham jail.) This long-standing story is one not of chastening and growth but of resentment; in the most basic Freudian terms, it is a tale of melancholia (in which one remains stuck in one's trauma), not mourning (in which one works through it).

It is becoming clear that we have long confused, even obscured, the nature of "southern trauma." If the call for papers can move so easily and unconsciously between a narrative of general southern trauma and one of traditionally white southern grievance and victimhood, it may be because, structurally and historically, the two are actually the same narrative. Over the past century, the reputable argument for a traumatized South has been gradually yet systematically abstracted from a decidedly less reputable airing of specifically white grievances. Far from originating with Woodward, the idea of a southern exceptionalism grounded in defeat was, in fact, a staple of the New South period that the Arkansas-born historian spent most of his career studying. In 1908, for example, Edwin Alderman, president of the University of Virginia and coeditor of the Library of Southern Literature, told a New

York audience that "the South was the overburdened section of America. No other Americans have ever known in its direst form, the discipline of war and defeat. No other region among the great culture nations, ever lost in less than a decade over one-tenth of its population, three and a half billions of its wealth, the form of its society and the very genius of its life, save a certain unconquerable courage and self-reliance. No other region except Poland ever knew such losses, and Poland ceased to exist." If "the form of its society and the very genius of its life" sounds like it might mean white supremacy, that's because it does. "Our poor human nature," Alderman declared,

> has never been put to a severer test than this enduring South, and our poor human nature has nowhere endured that test more finely. For the first time in history it was sought to put over a white race as their rulers a black race, recently held by them in slavery. Their sense of superiority to the race so set over them, and their extraordinary unity, welded still more firmly by the fires of war, alone enabled Southern whites to emerge whole from the ordeal. It was a sad time, and left behind a bitter deposit.[5]

Woodward's famous phrase "the experience of military defeat, occupation, and reconstruction" achieves its global resonance precisely by abstracting out the feature that mattered most to Alderman: the very specific loss of white supremacy—however temporary—caused by that defeat, occupation, and Reconstruction. Further abstraction is necessary if one is to make the next step with Fred Hobson, who in *South to the Future* (2002) argues, citing Woodward, that "poverty, frustration, failure, and a *felt* knowledge of history also apply, even more strongly if for quite different reasons, to black southerners."[6] In turn, Hobson's own abstraction is a prerequisite to an argument Deborah Cohn and I advance in our 2004 introduction to *Look Away! The U.S. South in New World Studies*. Citing Hobson, we write of "a different and more globally recognizable kind of defeat: the South's continuing experience of New World plantation colonialism, a system that, both before and after the war, most benefited white men in distant metropoles (something often complained of in white southern discourse) and most burdened black southerners (something almost never complained of in white southern discourse)."[7]

More recently, Melanie Benson Taylor, who in her 2011 book *Reconstructing the Native South* does much to set the terms for the current Native turn in southern studies, extends our postcolonial argument to the settler colonialism we generally overlooked: "The biracial U.S. South and its Native American survivors," she writes, "have far more in common than geographical proximity. . . . Both groups are haunted by their own private, separate histories of sweeping loss and crippling nostalgia."[8] Such investment of "southern identity" in abject, melancholic defeat is thus probably, and quite remarkably, the only idea that has survived in southern studies from at least the New South period through the agrarianism and neoagrarianism of the 1930s–1970s, the canon expansions of the 1980s and 1990s, the hemispheric or postcolonial turn of the 2000s, and the native turn of the 2010s. However uncharitably, one might even call it the oldest surviving Confederate idea.

For a number of reasons beyond its suspect origins, it is past time we reconsider this idea of a unified, distinctly traumatized South. To some degree, of course, southern historians have already done so. Woodward himself ultimately conceded in the early 1990s that his real purpose in writing "The Irony of Southern History" "lay more in supporting belief in the continuing distinctiveness of the South than in establishing the irony of its history."[9] Historians such as Gaines Foster, Michael O'Brien, and Carl Degler have noted, commonsensically enough, that the white South had not, in fact, necessarily learned what it was supposed to have learned from "defeat": indeed, from the 1898 war through the invasion of Iraq, white southerners have disproportionately celebrated the sort of self-righteous imperial interventions that Woodward supposed they had learned to resist.

Outside such historians' rather general assessments of Woodward's "thought," however, less has been said about the theoretical and, more properly, psychoanalytical shortcomings of Woodward's vaguely psychoanalytic theory. Of these, perhaps Woodward's greatest error lies in his use of the definite article: *the* experience. Of course, different people can, and daily do, subjectively experience what is objectively the same thing (a movie, a rappelling trip, an essay, an eclipse, a defeat) very differently. Less commonsensically, some responses to loss in particular are healthy, others less so: hence Freud's durable distinction between mourning and melancholia. From a psychoanalytic perspective, one great error of the past century's work in southern studies has surely been its tendency—mostly in the service first of "southern distinctiveness," later of "hemispheric studies"—to gloss over the differences not only among and within white, black, Native, Caribbean, Hispanic, and other experiences of trauma but also of the traumas themselves. Alderman's stunning failure of empathy in declaring Reconstruction no less a test of human nature than slavery itself emblematizes this problem but hardly exhausts it.

The loss of white supremacy, however, is not only qualitatively different from but also, until recently, much less studied in the U.S. context than the losses and defeats suffered by all the other groups listed above. This dearth of scholarship is unfortunate, for as a number of historians have now observed, most tenets of contemporary conservatism in the United States, as well as its heightened emotionalism, are traceable to the national loss of white supremacy in the postwar period. Rather than comparing the traumatic loss of white supremacy to the various traumas of that practice's victims (slaves, victims of the Monroe Doctrine, and so on), however, we might do better—if we are interested in understanding the conservatism that still drives much of American politics—to compare the traumatic loss of white supremacy in the United States to the negotiation of similar narcissistic wounds in places for which the theoretical model has been more fully developed. Paul Gilroy examines one such experience, that among white Britons in the wake of the British Empire, in his 2004 book *Postcolonial Melancholia*, but the fullest psychoanalytic treatment in the past half century surely comes from postwar Germany: Alexander and Margarete Mitscherlich's now-classic *Die Unfähigkeit zu trauern* (1967), translated into English in 1975 as *The Inability to Mourn*.

For the Mitscherlichs, decades after the fall of the "Thousand Year Reich" and all its gratifying master race rhetoric, Germans were still failing to mourn the narcissistic loss of their infantile fantasies of omnipotence. As with slavery and later with U.S. apartheid, "an epoch of maximum self-glorification now proved to be inextricably connected with the greatest crimes." Under normal or healthy circumstances, they write, "where there is guilt, we expect remorse and the need to make amends. Where loss has been suffered, mourning follows, and where an ideal has been tarnished, where face has been lost, the natural consequence is shame." Yet in postwar Germany, something very unhealthy took place instead: "the process of denial extended . . . to the occasions for guilt, mourning, and shame."[10] Of course, the Mitscherlichs' analysis does not transfer perfectly: the white South's ideals were not, for example, embodied in a single individual—not Robert E. Lee, much less Jefferson Davis—to anything like the extent that Germany's were in the Führer. Moreover, in failing to mourn their loss, Germans did not slip into melancholia but rather, in the Mitscherlichs' account, immersed themselves completely in the task of rebuilding the (West) German economy. (Germany became, to borrow from Atlanta's mayor William Hartsfield, "the country too busy to hate.") They withdrew—unconsciously—all interest from what had once been highly gratifying activities, and "this rejection of inner involvement in one's own behavior under the Third Reich prevented a loss of self-esteem that could hardly have been mastered, and a consequent outbreak of melancholia in innumerable cases."[11] The U.S. South, on the other hand, seems to have experienced a complicated mix of frenetic boosterism (especially during the New South period) and, more commonly, profound melancholia; the lost loved object became the "lost cause," a beautiful, lost sociopolitical dream to be savored melancholically rather as Poe savored the death of a beautiful woman. A psychoanalytic study of the tensions and synergies between these two forms of not mourning in the New South period would be a useful history indeed.

Despite the white South's arguably more complex response to losing its infantile fantasies, however, the basic psychic mechanisms of denial and what the Mitscherlichs' English translators call "identification with the victim" (not, in fact, a sense of empathy with their own victims but rather a strong sense of themselves *as* victims; see Alderman) offer a disturbing point of commonality. To see how, we might consider an example from southern sociologist John Shelton Reed's *My Tears Spoiled My Aim*. While in West Germany in the 1980s, Reed relates, he approached some Germans born well after the fall of the Reich. "I suggested that we had something in common: How did it feel to them, I asked, to have lost a war, to recognize that the world may [*sic*] be a better place for it, but nevertheless to know that you lost? They simply did not understand the question. They seemed to have no sense that *they* had lost a war, no sense of identification with the generation that had happened to. For some reason, I found that disturbing."[12]

For several reasons, the exchange is telling—and very strange. First, for most people the salient point about the Nazis, of course, is not that they "lost" but that they murdered six million Jews and tried to conquer the world, just as the salient point about the Confederacy is not that it "lost" but that it fought for slavery and tried to destroy the Union. Second is Reed's phrasing: he renders both Confederates and Nazis "the generation that had happened to": oddly passive victims, though perhaps less of the moral and military victors than of fate (which "happens"). Third, Reed not only identifies with Confederates but also cannot fathom why young Germans would not identify with Nazis (a move that is morally only possible, I think, if one sees those Nazis as passive). In wondering why Germans are not stuck in melancholy, Reed (as I have argued elsewhere) inverts Freud: in his imagination, melancholy is normal, and mourning is pathological. As Slavoj Žižek summarizes this inversion, "mourning is a kind of betrayal, the 'second killing' of the (lost) object, while the melancholic subject remains faithful to the lost object." Weirdly enough, Reed's kind of southern conservatism actually maps precisely onto what Žižek goes on to lambaste as the present-day Left's "politically correct" treatment of ethnicity and postcoloniality: the presumption that "when ethnic groups enter capitalist modernization . . . they should not renounce their tradition through mourning but retain their melancholic attachment to their lost roots."[13] It is precisely this structural similarity, however—the fact that for the past decade or more melancholy has been considered "cool" in cultural studies—that has made possible the South's role in the hemispheric turn (and perhaps other turns as well): abstract out the racism, and "the South" becomes yet another sympathetically melancholy victim in an academic regime that loves professing its sympathies with melancholy victims.

Once again, however, things are more interesting if we do not abstract out the racism. In *White Flight: Atlanta and the Making of Modern Conservatism*, historian Kevin Kruse makes two linked arguments. First, southern whites saw themselves not as oppressors, as historians have commonly imagined them, but as victims: "In their own minds, segregationists were instead fighting *for* rights of their own—such as the 'right' to select their neighbors, their employees, and their children's classmates, the 'right' to do as they pleased with their private property and personal businesses, and, perhaps most important, the 'right' to remain free from what they saw as dangerous encroachments by the federal government."

Second, that attitude had national, not just local or southern, ramifications:

> The issues that stood at the center of [Atlanta's] struggle also stood at the center of the postwar national debate: the demise of white supremacy and the rise of white suburbia; the fragmentation of old liberal coalitions and the construction of new conservative ones; the contested relationship between the federal government and state and local entities; the debates over the public realm and the private; the struggle over the distribution of money and the sharing of power; the competing claims to basic rights and responsibilities of citizenship; and, of course, conflicts rooted in divisions of generation, class, and, above all, race. All these issues spread far beyond the city limits of Atlanta and into every corner of the country.[14]

Many American whites, in Kruse's view, saw the loss of white supremacy as a loss of their own "rights," and many of the tenets of American conservatism derive from this perceived loss. Such conservatism fits the model advanced by Corey Robin in *The Reactionary Mind*: "Historically, the conservative has favored liberty for the higher orders and constraint for the lower orders. What the conservative sees and dislikes in equality, in other words, is not a threat to freedom but its extension. For in that extension, he sees a loss of his own freedom." Or, as Robin puts it elsewhere, "far from being an invention of the politically correct, victimhood has been a talking point of the Right ever since Burke decried the mob's treatment of Marie Antoinette."[15]

It seems that in history and political science, at least, we may be at the beginning of a paradigm shift. In the emerging model (as advanced in history not only by Kruse but by Matthew Lassiter, Joseph Crespino, and other younger historians of conservatism), white southern trauma is important to American cultural studies not because it echoes Latin American trauma, black southern trauma, Native southern trauma, and so on, as much of the New Southern Studies and American studies has been telling us, but because it offers a case study in the roots of American conservatism. What literary and cultural studies can add to this paradigm shift is, I will argue in the remainder of this essay, an explanation of two features of this conservatism: first, the persistence of a sense of grievance long after the grievance itself has vanished, and, second, conservatism's eerie ability to shift the object of its anxiety—from, say, the Negro who wants to marry your daughter to the homosexual who wants to convert your son—so thoroughly that it forgets the original object ever existed.

The chief term to be introduced into this discussion is *enjoyment*. At the most basic level, people continue to maintain a sense of righteous grievance because, however perversely, it feels enjoyable to do so: it is simply much more fun to be all worked up over something, even something unpleasant, than to feel nothing at all. This is a commonsensical enough point, perhaps, but it possesses a powerful intellectual lineage. In his famous essay "Mourning and Melancholia," Freud notes that "the self-tormenting in melancholia . . . is without doubt enjoyable." He also describes cases in which "the patient cannot consciously perceive what he has lost. . . . This, indeed, might be so even if the patient is aware of the loss which has given rise to his melancholia, but only in the sense that he knows *whom* he has lost but not *what* he has lost in him."[16] It is from both clinical observation and a very close reading of Freud's essay—and from other essays Freud published in the second decade of the twentieth century, such as "The Drive and Its Vicissitudes" (1915)—that Lacan worked out his own theory of the drives. (Scholars in other disciplines baffled by the famously difficult French analyst's appeal to many literary critics might start with the simple fact that Lacan is an incredibly attentive close reader, and not just of Freud.) At its most basic, that theory is this: We need to shift our attention from questions of desire to questions of drive. In desire, we love somebody or something. But that's too simple. As Freud noted, we often do not know what it is we desire in that somebody or something. This object is what Lacan names the *objet petit a.* Desire is about attaining somebody or something. But drive is what underlies all desire, and drives are by definition insatiable. This does not mean for Lacan what it does for "common sense" and much romantic plotting: that as soon as one obtains one object of desire one wants a different one. Rather, it is that drives derive satisfaction not from obtaining an object but from endlessly circling it: the pleasure derives from the agitation, not the satisfaction.

Melancholy, in Lacan's account as in Freud's, is inexplicable without an understanding of drives, for in melancholy the "lost loved object" is, in its very painful absence, perpetually *overpresent* to the melancholic's imagination. In the southern context, we might consider a remark of John Shelton Reed's on the Public Radio International show *Whad'Ya Know?* with Michael Feldman. In an episode broadcast from Chapel Hill in 2002, Feldman asks Reed whether the Civil War is still an issue in the South. Reed quips, "Among some it is. . . . I always tell people, 'Bring the spoons back and we'll forget all about it.'" Set aside for a moment the salient question of who most deserves reparations after 1865. Reed's is a deceptively simple formula for the healing of this alleged 140-year-old traumatic wound. His request appears reasonable enough, even comically so, but it enables the spoons to be perpetually present precisely because *the spoons are never coming back*. It is a license for infinite melancholy.

We should also note that for Lacan as for Freud, "*as far as the object in the drive is concerned, let it be clear that it is, strictly speaking, of no importance. It is a matter of total indifference.*"[17] If it weren't the spoons, it would be something else, and something else, and something else. As historian Ted Ownby shrewdly observes, "Writers do not seem to tire of asking whether a South still exists. Perhaps the time has come that we should. The question tends to construe a few key elements in a regional past as the essence of the South and then judges whether industrialization or agricultural mechanization or the Sun Belt economy or migration or the civil rights movement or two-party politics or something else has challenged, eroded, or overcome these essential elements."[18] In Ownby's account, what matters to a common sort of southern historian is not the particular lost loved object (hence his "or something else") but the untiring circling of the question—precisely the function of the drive.

And what has continued down through generations in southern studies, the white South, and U.S. conservatism more broadly has been attention not to a specific loss or trauma but a particularly addictive, unacknowledged, and prerational disposition toward endlessly circling loss itself. On his blog at *The*

Daily Beast, Andrew Sullivan has called Žižek a "pseud" and "over-rated," but it may be not only because Sullivan does not appear to have read much Žižek but also because Žižek has Sullivan's number. In *The Conservative Soul*, Sullivan writes movingly of ideas well known to those who have studied stand-taking white southern fantasy from the Agrarians to no small number of contemporary "southernists":

363

> In America, the future is always more important than the past. But the past lingers; and America, for all its restlessness, or perhaps because of its restlessness, is a deeply conservative place. The regret you feel in your life at the kindness not done, the person unthanked, the opportunity missed, the custom unobserved, is a form of conservatism. The same goes for the lost love or the missed opportunity: these experiences teach us the fragility of the moment, and that fragility is what, in part, defines us. . . .
>
> These little griefs are what build a conservative temperament.[19]

Žižek (writing some years earlier) is unsatisfied with this sort of explanation:

> A person who has lived all his life in a certain city, and is finally compelled to move elsewhere, is, of course, saddened by the prospect of being thrown into a new environment—what is it, however, that actually makes him sad? It is not the prospect of leaving the place which was his home for long years, but the much more subtle fear of losing his very attachment to this place. What makes me sad is the fact that I am aware that, sooner or later—sooner than I am ready to admit—I will integrate myself into a new community, forgetting the place which now means so much to me. In short, what makes me sad is the awareness that I will lose my desire for (what is now) my home.[20]

For a Lacanian, what we learn from Sullivan's "little griefs" is not that the conservative appreciates the fragility of the moment but that the conservative fears the fragility, the inevitable diminution, of his or her own desire.

What Lacanian theory thus helps us understand is a fundamental structure of feeling. In much U.S. popular culture, that structure informs the endless irrational, even antirational, circling of contemporary conservatism, the deep pleasure millions of Americans, nearly all of them older and white, derive from the upsetting "news" presented to them daily on *Fox and Friends*, the alternate reality where Barack Obama is a Kenya-born Muslim socialist. When one can no longer publicly nurse a sense of grievance over the loss of white supremacy, "this is a white man's country" morphs into "this is a Christian nation," and conservatives stop abhorring Dr. Martin Luther King Jr. and begin trying to adopt him. (The same thing has happened with Bill Clinton and may well happen again with Obama himself.) It doesn't matter if the threat is the Negro who wants to marry your daughter or the homosexual who wants to convert your son: what matters is having the threat—or, more precisely, the fear—of a life without the fantasy threat to structure it, to keep the drive in motion.

And in much traditional southern studies, the same structure of feeling applies. Traditional southern studies has never been about the "presence of the past" but rather about the *over*presence of the past. It doesn't matter what the "spoons" are—the loss of white supremacy or changes wrought by "industrialization or the Sun Belt economy or migration or the civil rights movement"—it just matters whether one feels sufficiently melancholy about them. (Asking the question keeps the circling open; really answering it, closing it down, is the last thing the traditional southernist wants.) The mid-2000s, for example, saw white southernists suddenly weeping over civil rights figures—Medgar Evers, Emmett Till—who had died half a century earlier. What matters is not the object of the melancholy but what we might call the structure of feeling that informs it, a structure erected a century earlier by the United Daughters of the Confederacy.

Of course, *all* scholarship is structured at some level by fantasy. But southernist fantasy, like conservative fantasy, has been peculiarly narcissistic, and peculiarly infantile, for at least a century, and more likely a century and a half. Luckily, the nation—and the field—seem finally to be outgrowing their peculiar institutions.

NOTES

1. "Call for Papers," Society for the Study of Southern Literature.
2. Woodward, *Burden of Southern History*, 190; Cohn, *History and Memory*, 1.
3. Welty, "Must the Novelist Crusade?," 155.
4. "Call for Papers," Society for the Study of Southern Literature.
5. Alderman, "Growing South," 6201, 6200.
6. F. Hobson, *South to the Future*, 2.
7. J. Smith and Cohn, "Introduction," 2.
8. M. B. Taylor, *Reconstructing the Native South*, 1.
9. Woodward, *Burden of Southern History*, 236.
10. Mitscherlich and Mitscherlich, *Inability to Mourn*, 24, 25.
11. Ibid., 26.
12. J. S. Reed, *My Tears Spoiled My Aim*, 48.
13. Žižek, "Melancholy and the Act," 141, 142.
14. Kruse, *White Flight*, 9, 15.
15. Robin, *Reactionary Mind*, 8; Robin, "Conservatism and Counterrevolution," 15.
16. Freud, "Mourning and Melancholia," 250, 244.

17. Lacan, *Four* Fundamental *Concepts of Psychoanalysis*, 168.
18. Ownby, *American Dreams in Mississippi*, 159.
19. Sullivan, *Conservative Soul*, 9.
20. Žižek, "Melancholy and the Act," 149.

SUGGESTIONS FOR FURTHER READING

Freud, Sigmund. "Mourning and Melancholia." In *The Standard Edition of the Complete Psychological Works of Sigmund Freud*, vol. 14, *On the History of the Psycho-Analytic Movement, Papers on Metapsychology and Other Works (1914–1916)*, 237–58. London: Hogarth Press, 1957.

Lacan, Jacques. *The Four Fundamental Concepts of Psycho-Analysis*. New York: W. W. Norton, 1981.

Mitscherlich, Alexander, and Margarete Mitscherlich. *The Inability to Mourn: Principles of Collective Behavior*. New York: Grove Press, 1975.

Robin, Corey. *The Reactionary Mind: Conservatism from Edmund Burke to Sarah Palin*. New York: Oxford University Press, 2011.

Santner, Eric. *Stranded Objects: Mourning, Memory, and Film in Postwar Germany*. Ithaca, N.Y.: Cornell University Press, 1993.

Smith, Jon. *Finding Purple America: The South and the Future of American Cultural Studies*. Athens: University of Georgia Press, 2013.

Žižek, Slavoj. "Melancholy and the Act." In *Did Somebody Say Totalitarianism? Five Interventions in the (Mis)use of a Notion*. New York: Verso, 2001.

Works Cited

Abbot, Andrew. "Transcending General Linear Reality." *Sociological Theory* 6 (1988): 169–86.

Abel, Elizabeth. *Signs of the Times: The Visual Politics of Jim Crow.* Berkeley: University of California Press, 2010.

"About Husk." Husk Restaurant. Accessed November 15, 2012. http://www.huskrestaurant .com/about/.

"About Us." The Old Mill. Accessed March 13, 2013. http://www.old-mill.com/aboutus.

Achebe, Chinua. *Things Fall Apart.* 1959. New York: Anchor, 1994.

Adams, Jessica. *Wounds of Returning: Race, Memory and Property on the Postslavery Plantation.* Chapel Hill: University of North Carolina Press, 2007.

Adams, Rachel. *Continental Divides: Remapping the Cultures of North America.* Chicago: University of Chicago Press, 2009.

Adorno, Theodor. "A Social Critique of Radio Music." *Kenyon Review* 7, no. 2 (1945): 208–17.

Agamben, Giorgio. *Homo Sacer: Sovereign Power and Bare Life.* Stanford, Calif.: Stanford University Press, 1998.

———. *State of Exception.* Translated by Kevin Attell. Chicago: University of Chicago Press, 2005.

Alderman, Edwin. "The Growing South." In vol. 14 of *The Library of Southern Literature,* edited by C. Alphonso Smith, 6197–219. Atlanta: Martin and Hoyt, 1910.

Alexander, Michelle. *The New Jim Crow: Mass Incarceration in the Age of Colorblindness.* New York: New Press, 2010.

Amende, Kathaleen E. *Desire and the Divine: Feminine Identity in White Southern Women's Writing.* Baton Rouge: Louisiana State University Press, 2013.

"The American Society of Tropical Medicine." Editorial. *Southern Medical Journal* 4 (February 1911): 175–76.

Anderson, Benedict. *Imagined Communities: Reflections on the Origin and Spread of Nationalism.* Rev. ed. London: Verso, 1991.

Anderson, Eric Gary. "Native American Literature, Ecocriticism, and the South: The Inaccessible Worlds of Linda Hogan's *Power.*" In Jones and Monteith, *South to a New Place,* 165–83.

———. "On Native Ground: Indigenous Presences and Countercolonial Strategies in Southern Narratives of Captivity, Removal, and Repossession." *Southern Spaces,* August 9, 2007. Accessed February 4, 2015. http://www.southernspaces.org/2007/native-ground -indigenous-presences-and-countercolonial-strategies-southern-narratives-captivity.

———. "Red Crosscurrents: Performative Spaces and Indian Cultural Authority in the Florida Atlantic Captivity Narrative of Jonathan Dickinson." *Mississippi Quarterly* 65, no. 1 (2012): 17–32.

———. "South to a Red Place: Contemporary American Indian Literature and the Problem of Native/Southern Studies." *Mississippi Quarterly* 60, no. 1 (Winter 2006–7): 5–32.

Anderson, Warwick. "Pacific Crossings: Imperial Logics in United States' Public Health Programs." In *Colonial Crucible: Empire in the Making of the Modern American State*, edited by Alfred W. McCoy and Francisco A. Scarano, 277–87. Madison: University of Wisconsin Press, 2009.

Andrews, William L., Minrose C. Gwin, Trudier Harris, and Fred Hobson, eds. *The Literature of the American South*. New York: W. W. Norton, 1998.

"Antebellum Coarse White Grits." Anson Mills. Accessed March 11, 2013. http://ansonmills.com/products/8.

Anzaldúa, Gloria. "To(o) Queer the Writer: *Loca, escrita y chicana*." In *Inversions: Writing by Dykes and Lesbians*, edited by Betsy Warland, 249–63. Vancouver, B.C.: Press Gang, 1991.

Appiah, Kwame Anthony. "The Conservation of 'Race.'" *Black American Literature Forum* 23, no. 1 (1989): 37–60.

———. "The Uncompleted Argument: Du Bois and the Illusion of Race." *Critical Inquiry* 12, no. 1 (1985): 21–37.

Arnold, David. "'Illusory Riches': Representations of the Tropical World, 1840–1950." *Singapore Journal of Tropical Geography* 21, no. 1 (2000): 6–18.

———. "Inventing Tropicality." In *The Problem of Nature: Environment, Culture, and European Expansion*, 141–68. Oxford: Blackwell, 1996.

———. *The Tropics and the Traveling Gaze: India, Landscape, and Science, 1880–1858*. Seattle: University of Washington Press, 2006.

Baker, Houston A., Jr. "Caliban's Triple Play." *Critical Inquiry* 13, no. 1 (1986): 182–96.

———. *Turning South Again: Re-Thinking Modernism/Re-Reading Booker T.* Durham, N.C.: Duke University Press, 2001.

Baker, Houston A., Jr., and Dana D. Nelson. "Violence, the Body, and 'The South.'" *American Literature* 73 (2001): 231–44.

Baker, Philip, and Peter Mühlhäusler. "Creole Linguistics from Its Beginnings, through Schuchardt to the Present Day." In Stewart, *Creolization*, 84–107.

Balibar, Étienne, and Immanuel Wallerstein. *Race, Nation, Class: Ambiguous Identities*. London: Verso, 1991.

Bambara, Toni Cade. *Those Bones Are Not My Child*. New York: Pantheon, 1999.

Bancroft, Hubert Howe. *History of California*. Vol. 7, *1860–1890*. San Francisco: History Company, 1890.

Baptist, Edward E. *The Half Has Never Been Told: Slavery and the Making of American Capitalism*. New York: Basic Books, 2014.

Barnard, Rita. "Of Riots and Rainbows: South Africa, the U.S., and the Pitfalls of Comparison." *American Literary History* 17, no. 2 (2005): 399–416.

Barnes, Albert C. "Negro Art and America." In *The New Negro: Voices of the Harlem Renaissance*, edited by Alain Locke, 19–25. New York: Simon and Schuster, 1997.

Bascom, William. *Ifa Divination: Communication between Gods and Men in West Africa*. Bloomington: Indiana University Press, 1969.

Batiste, Stephanie Leigh. *Darkening Mirrors: Imperial Representation in Depression-Era African American Performance*. Durham, N.C.: Duke University Press, 2011.

Beatty, Richmond Croom, Floyd C. Watkins, and Thomas Daniel Young, eds. *The Literature of the South*. 1952. Glenview: Scott Foresman, 1968.

Beaumont, Gustave de, and Alexis de Tocqueville. *On the Penitentiary System in the United States and Its Application in France*. 1833. Chicago: Vail-Ballou Press, 1964.

Bell, Madison Smartt. *Soldier's Joy*. New York: Ticknor and Fields, 1989.

Belnap, Jeffrey, and Raúl Fernández. "Introduction: The Architechtonics of José Martí's 'Our Americanism.'" In *José Martí's "Our America": From National to Hemispheric Cultural Studies*, edited by Jeffrey Belnap and Raúl Fernández, 1–24. Durham, N.C.: Duke University Press, 1998.

Bendroth, Margaret Lamberts. *Fundamentalism and Gender, 1875 to the Present*. New Haven, Conn.: Yale University Press, 1996.

Benítez-Rojo, Antonio. *The Repeating Island: The Caribbean and the Postmodern Perspective*. 2nd ed. Translated by James E. Maraniss. Durham, N.C.: Duke University Press, 1995.

Benjamin, Walter. *Illuminations: Essays and Reflections*. Edited by Hannah Arendt. Translated by Harry Zorn. New York: Schocken, 1968.

Bennett, H. H., and W. R. Chapline. *Soil Erosion a National Menace*. United States Department of Agriculture Circular No. 33. Washington, D.C.: United States Government Printing Office, 1928.

Benson, Melanie R. *Disturbing Calculations: The Economics of Identity in Postcolonial Southern Literature, 1912–2002*. Athens: University of Georgia Press, 2008.

Berland, Oscar. "The Emergence of the Communist Perspective on the 'Negro Question' in America: 1919–1931, Part Two." *Science and Society* 64, no. 2 (Summer 2000): 194–217.

Berrey, Stephen A. *The Jim Crow Routine: Everyday Performances of Race, Civil Rights, and Segregation in Mississippi*. Chapel Hill: University of North Carolina Press, 2015.

Bérubé, Michael. "American Studies without Exceptions." *PMLA* 118, no. 1 (January 2003): 103–13.

Bhabha, Homi K. *The Location of Culture*. New York: Routledge, 2004.

———. *Nation and Narration*. Hove, England: Psychology Press, 1990.

Bibler, Michael P. *Cotton's Queer Relations: Same-Sex Intimacy and the Literature of the Southern Plantation, 1936–1968*. Charlottesville: University of Virginia Press, 2009.

———. "Serpents in the Garden: Historic Preservation, Climate Change, and the Postsouthern Plantation." In Bone, Ward, and Link, *Creating and Consuming the U.S. South*, 117–38.

Birdoff, Harry. *The World's Greatest Hit*. New York: S. F. Vanni, 1947.

Blackmon, Douglas A. *Slavery by Another Name: The Re-enslavement of Black Americans from the Civil War to World War II*. New York: Anchor, 2009.

Bone, Martyn, ed. *Perspectives on Barry Hannah*. Jackson: University Press of Mississippi, 2007.

———. *The Postsouthern Sense of Place in Contemporary Fiction*. Baton Rouge: Louisiana State University Press, 2005.

Bone, Martyn, Brian Ward, and William A. Link, eds. *Creating and Consuming the American South*. Gainesville: University of Florida Press, 2015.

Bonilla-Silva, Eduardo. *Racism without Racists: Color-Blind Racism and the Persistence of Racial Inequality in the United States*. 2nd ed. Lanham, Md.: Rowman and Littlefield, 2006.

Bordonaro, Cory. "Shop Local: Jack Rudy Tonic." *Southern Living*, November 2012, NC10.

Bourdieu, Pierre. *The Field of Cultural Production*. New York: Columbia University Press, 1993.

Bow, Leslie. *Partly Colored: Asian Americans and Racial Anomaly in the Segregated South*. New York: New York University Press, 2010.

Boles, John B., ed. *A Companion to the American South*. Oxford: Blackwell, 2002.

369

Boyer, Sabrina. "'Thou Shalt Not Crave Thy Neighbor': *True Blood*, Abjection, and Otherness." *Studies in Popular Culture* 33, no. 2 (2011): 21–41.

Branch, Michael P., and Scott Slovic, eds. *The ISLE Reader: Ecocriticism, 1993–2003*. Athens: University of Georgia Press, 2003.

Brasell, R. Bruce. "'The Degeneration of Nationalism': Colonialism, Perversion, and the American South." *Mississippi Quarterly* 56, no. 1 (Winter 2002–3): 33–54.

Brattain, Michelle. "The Pursuits of Post-Exceptionalism: Race, Class, and Politics in the New Southern Labor History." In *Labor in the Modern South*, edited by Glenn T. Eskew, 1–46. Athens: University of Georgia Press, 2001.

Brickhouse, Anna. "Hemispheric Jamestown." In *Hemispheric American Studies*, edited by Caroline F. Levander and Robert S. Levine, 18–35. New Brunswick, N.J.: Rutgers University Press, 2008.

Brinkmeyer, Robert H., Jr. *The Fourth Ghost: White Southern Writers and European Fascism, 1930–1950*. Baton Rouge: Louisiana State University Press, 2009.

———. *Remapping Southern Literature: Contemporary Southern Writers and the West*. Athens: University of Georgia Press, 2000.

Brodber, Erna. *Louisiana*. London: New Beacon Books, 1994.

Brodie, Fawn M. *Thomas Jefferson: An Intimate History*. New York: W. W. Norton, 1974.

Brown, Charles Brockden. *Edgar Huntly; or, Memoirs of a Sleep-Walker*. Edited by Norman S. Grabo. New York: Penguin, 1988.

Brown, Jayna. *Babylon Girls: Black Women Performers and the Shaping of the Modern*. Durham, N.C.: Duke University Press, 2008.

Brown, Rosellen. *Half a Heart*. New York: Farrar, Straus, and Giroux, 2000.

Brown, Sterling. *Negro Poetry and Drama and The Negro in American Fiction*. New York: Atheneum, 1969.

———. *Southern Road*. New York: Harper and Row, 1980.

Broyard, Bliss. *One-Drop: My Father's Hidden Life—A Story of Race and Family Secrets*. New York: Little Brown, 2007.

Brundage, W. Fitzhugh, ed. *Where These Memories Grow: History, Memory, and Southern Identity*. Chapel Hill, N.C.: University of North Carolina Press, 2000.

Buck-Morss, Susan. *Hegel, Haiti, and Universal History*. Pittsburgh: University of Pittsburgh Press, 2009.

Bullard, Robert. *Dumping in Dixie: Race, Class, and Environmental Quality*. Boulder, Colo.: Westview Press, 1990.

Burden of Dreams. Directed by Les Blank with Maureen Gosling. Flower Films, 1982. DVD.

Burgett, Bruce, and Glenn Hendler, eds. *Keywords for American Cultural Studies*. New York: New York University Press, 2007.

Burgett, Paul. "Vindication as a Thematic Principle in the Writings of Alain Locke on the Music of Black Americans." In *Black Music in the Harlem Renaissance*, edited by Samuel A. Floyd Jr., 29–40. Knoxville: University of Tennessee Press, 1990.

Buring, Daneel. *Lesbian and Gay Memphis: Building Communities behind the Magnolia Curtain*. New York: Routledge, 1997.

Butler, Judith. *Bodies That Matter: On the Discursive Limits of "Sex."* New York: Routledge, 1993.

Cable, George Washington. *The Grandissimes: A Story of Creole Life*. New York: Charles Scribner's Sons, 1880.

Cabrera, Lydia. *Afro-Cuban Tales.* Translated by Alberto Hernandez-Chiroldes and Lauren Yoder. Lincoln: University of Nebraska Press, 2004.

———. *Ayapá: Cuentos de Jicotea.* 1971. Miami: Ediciones Universal, 2006.

Caldwell, Erskine. *Tobacco Road.* New York: Charles Scribner's Sons, 1932.

"Call for Papers, 2010 Biennial Conference." Society for the Study of Southern Literature. Accessed October 8, 2012. http://h-net.msu.edu/cgi-bin/logbrowse.pl?trx=vx&list=h -louisiana&month=0906&week=b&msg=OHd2anThgavVx1%2BOwPu3HA&user=&pw=.

Calloway, Colin G. *First Peoples: A Documentary Survey of American Indian History.* Boston: Bedford/St. Martin's, 2012.

Campbell, James T. *Songs of Zion: The African Methodist Episcopal Church in the United States and South Africa.* Chapel Hill: University of North Carolina Press, 1998.

Capote, Truman. "Children on Their Birthdays." In *The Complete Stories of Truman Capote,* 135–54. New York: Vintage International, 2005.

Caramanica, Jon. "Hip-Hop Traditionalism in Two Variations." *New York Times,* July 2, 2010. Accessed September 19, 2014. http://www.nytimes.com/2010/07/03/arts/music/03krit .html?_r=0.

Carby, Hazel V. "'On the Threshold of Woman's Era': Lynching, Empire, and Sexuality in Black Feminist Theory." *Critical Inquiry* 12, no. 1 (1985): 262–77.

Carpio, Glenda R. "Conjuring the Mysteries of Slavery: Voodoo, Fetishism, and Stereotype in Ishmael Reed's *Flight to Canada.*" *American Literature* 77, no. 3 (2005): 563–89.

Cartwright, Keith. *Sacral Grooves, Limbo Gateways: Travels in Deep Southern Time, Circum-Caribbean Space, Afro-creole Authority.* Athens: University of Georgia Press, 2013.

Carter, Dan T. *Scottsboro: A Tragedy of the American South.* Baton Rouge: Louisiana State University Press, 1969.

Cash, W. J. *The Mind of the South.* 1941. New York: Vintage, 1991.

Casper, Scott E., Joanne D. Chaison, and Jeffrey D. Groves, eds. *Perspectives on American Book History: Artifacts and Commentary.* Amherst: University of Massachusetts Press, 2002.

Cast Away. Directed by Robert Zemeckis. Twentieth-Century Fox, 2000. DVD.

Castillo, Debra. *Redreaming America: Toward a Bilingual American Culture.* Albany: State University of New York Press, 2004.

Cell, John W. *The Highest Stage of White Supremacy: The Origins of Segregation in South Africa and the American South.* Cambridge: Cambridge University Press, 1982.

Césaire, Aimé. *Discourse on Colonialism.* 1955. New York: Monthly Review Press, 1972.

Chafe, William H., Raymond Gavins, and Robert Korstad, eds. *Remembering Jim Crow: African Americans Tell about Life in the Segregated South.* New York: New Press, 2001.

Chapman, Peter. *Bananas: How the United Fruit Company Shaped the World.* Edinburgh: Canongate Books, 2007.

Chase, Leah. *The Dooky Chase Cookbook.* Gretna, La.: Pelican, 2004.

Chase-Riboud, Barbara. *Sally Hemings: A Novel.* New York: Viking Press, 1979.

Chenault, Wesley, and Stacy Braukman. *Gay and Lesbian Atlanta.* Charleston, S.C.: Arcadia, 2008.

A City upon a Hill: The Spirit of American Exceptionalism. Directed by Kevin Knoblock. CU Productions, 2011. DVD.

Claiborne, Craig. "For a Carolina Chef, Helpings of History." *New York Times,* July 10, 1985, C1, C6.

Clifford, James. *The Predicament of Culture: Twentieth-Century Ethnography, Literature, and Art*. Cambridge, Mass.: Harvard University Press, 1988.

Close to Slavery: Guestworker Programs in the United States. Montgomery, Ala.: Southern Poverty Law Center, 2013.

Cobb, James C. *Away Down South: A History of Southern Identity*. New York: Oxford University Press, 2005.

Cocks, Catherine. *Tropical Whites: The Rise of the Tourist South in the Americas*. Philadelphia: University of Pennsylvania Press, 2013.

Cohen, Robin, and Paola Toninato, eds. *The Creolization Reader: Studies in Mixed Identities and Cultures*. London: Routledge, 2009.

Cohn, Deborah N. *History and Memory in the Two Souths*. Nashville: Vanderbilt University Press, 1999.

———. "U.S. Southern and Latin American Studies: Postcolonial and Inter-American Approaches." *Global South* 1 (2007): 38–44.

Colbert, Soyica. *The African American Theatrical Body: Reception, Performance and the Stage*. Cambridge: Cambridge University Press, 2011.

Cone, James. *The Cross and the Lynching Tree*. Maryknoll, N.Y.: Orbis Books, 2011.

Cowdrey, Albert E. *This Land, This South: An Environmental History*. Lexington: University of Kentucky Press, 1983.

Cox, Karen. *Dreaming of Dixie: How the American South Was Created in American Popular Culture*. Chapel Hill: University of North Carolina Press, 2011.

Creed, Gerald W., and Barbara Ching. "Recognizing Rusticity: Identity and the Power of Place." In *Knowing Your Place: Rural Identity and Cultural Hierarchy*, edited by Gerald W. Creed and Barbara Ching, 1–38. New York: Routledge, 1997.

Cresswell, Tim. *In Place/Out of Place: Geography, Ideology and Transgression*. Minneapolis: University of Minnesota Press, 1996.

Cronon, William. "The Trouble with Wilderness; or, Getting Back to the Wrong Nature." In *Uncommon Ground: Rethinking the Human Place in Nature*, edited by William Cronon, 69–90. New York: W. W. Norton, 1995.

Cruz, Jon. *Culture on the Margins: The Black Spiritual and the Rise of American Cultural Interpretation*. Princeton, N.J.: Princeton University Press, 1999.

C.S.A.: The Confederate States of America. Directed by Kevin Willmott. 2004. IFC Films, 2006. DVD.

Curtin, Philip D. *Death by Migration: Europe's Encounter with the Tropical World in the Nineteenth Century*. New York: Cambridge University Press, 1989.

———. *The Rise and Fall of the Plantation Complex: Essays in Atlantic History*. Cambridge: Cambridge University Press, 1998.

Dailey, Jane, ed. *The Age of Jim Crow*. New York: W. W. Norton, 2008.

Darnton, Robert. *The Business of Enlightenment: A Publishing History of the Encyclopédie, 1775–1800*. Cambridge, Mass.: Harvard University Press, 1979.

———. *The Case for Books: Past, Present, Future*. New York: PublicAffairs, 2009.

Dash, J. Michael. *Haiti and the United States: National Stereotypes and the Literary Imagination*. New York: Palgrave McMillan, 1997.

———. *The Other America: Caribbean Literature in a New World Context*. Charlottesville: University of Virginia Press, 1998.

Davidson, Cathy N. *Revolution and the Word: The Rise of the Novel in America*. Expanded ed. New York: Oxford University Press, 2004.

Davidson, Donald. "A Mirror for Artists." In Twelve Southerners, *I'll Take My Stand*, 28–60.

Davis, Thadious M. "Expanding the Limits: The Intersection of Race and Region." *Southern Literary Journal* 20, no. 2 (Spring 1988): 3–11.

———. *Southscapes: Geographies of Race, Region, and Literature*. Chapel Hill: University of North Carolina Press, 2011.

Davis, Thulani. *My Confederate Kinfolk: A Twenty-First Century Freedwoman Discovers Her Roots*. New York: Basic Books, 2006.

Dayan, Colin. *The Law Is a White Dog: How Legal Rituals Make and Unmake Persons*. Princeton, N.J.: Princeton University Press, 2011.

———. "Servile Law." In *Cities without Citizens*, edited by Eduardo Cadava and Aaron Levy, 87–119. Philadelphia: Slought Foundation, 2003.

Dayan, Joan. "From the Plantation to the Penitentiary: Chain, Classification, and Codes of Deterrence." In *Slavery in the Caribbean Francophone World: Distant Voices, Forgotten Acts, Forged Identities*, edited by Doris Y. Kadish, 191–210. Athens: University Georgia Press, 2000.

Deane, Seamus. "Imperialism/Nationalism." In *Critical Terms for Literary Study*, 2nd ed., edited by Frank Lentricchia and Thomas McLaughlin, 354–68. Chicago: University of Chicago Press, 1995.

Delgado, Grace. *Making the Chinese Mexican: Global Migration, Localism, and Exclusion in the U.S.-Mexico Borderlands*. Palo Alto, Calif.: Stanford University Press, 2012.

Deloria, Philip J. *Playing Indian*. New Haven, Conn.: Yale University Press, 1998.

Deloria, Vine, Jr. *Red Earth, White Lies: Native Americans and the Myth of Scientific Fact*. Golden, Colo.: Fulcrum, 1997.

Derrida, Jacques. "But, beyond . . . (Open Letter to Anne McClintock and Rob Nixon)." Translated by Peggy Kamuf. *Critical Inquiry* 13, no. 1 (1986): 155–70.

———. "Racism's Last Word." Translated by Peggy Kamuf. *Critical Inquiry* 12, no. 1 (1985): 290–99.

Dews, Carlos L., and Carolyn Leste Law, eds. *Out in the South*. Philadelphia: Temple University Press, 2001.

Dickey, James. *Deliverance*. New York: Laurel, 1970.

Dimock, Wai Chee. *Empire for Liberty: Melville and the Poetics of Individualism*. Princeton, N.J.: Princeton University Press, 1989.

Dochuk, Darren. *From Bible Belt to Sunbelt: Plain-Folk Religion, Grassroots Politics, and the Rise of Evangelical Conservatism*. New York: W. W. Norton, 2011.

Dollard, John. *Caste and Class in a Southern Town*. 1937. New Haven, Conn.: Yale University Press: 1957.

Donaldson, Scott. "Scott Fitzgerald's Romance with the South." *Southern Literary Journal* 5 (Spring 1973): 3–17.

Douglass, Frederick. *Narrative of the Life of Frederick Douglass, an American Slave, Written by Himself*. Edited by David W. Blight. New York: Bedford Books, 1983.

Doyle, Michael. *Empires*. Ithaca, N.Y.: Cornell University Press, 1986.

Driskill, Qwo-Li. "Doubleweaving Two-Spirit Critiques: Building Alliances between Native and Queer Studies." *GLQ: A Journal of Lesbian and Gay Studies* 16, nos. 1–2 (2010): 69–92.

Driver, Felix. "Imagining the Tropics: Views and Visions of the Tropical World." *Singapore Journal of Tropical Geography* 25 (March 2004): 1–17.

Dubois, Laurent. *Avengers of the New World: The Story of the Haitian Revolution*. Cambridge, Mass.: Harvard University Press, 2005.

373

Du Bois, W. E. B. "The Color Line Belts the World." In *W. E. B. Du Bois: A Reader*, edited by David Levering Lewis, 42–43. New York: Henry Holt, 1995.

———. *The Souls of Black Folk: Essays and Sketches.* 1903; New York: Cosimo, 2007.

———. "The Souls of White Folk." *Independent*, August 18, 1910.

duCille, Ann. *The Coupling Convention: Sex, Text and Tradition in Black Women's Fiction.* New York: Oxford University Press, 1993.

Duck, Leigh Anne. *The Nation's Region: Southern Modernism, Segregation, and U.S. Nationalism.* Athens: University of Georgia Press, 2006.

———. "Plantation/Empire." *CR: New Centennial Review* 10, no. 1 (Spring 2010): 77–87.

———. "Southern Nonidentity." *Safundi: The Journal of South African and American Studies* 9, no. 3 (July 2008): 319–30.

Dunaway, Wilma. *The First American Frontier: Transition to Capitalism in Southern Appalachia, 1700–1860.* Chapel Hill: University of North Carolina Press, 1996.

———. *Women, Work and Family in the Antebellum Mountain South.* Cambridge: Cambridge University Press, 2008.

Dunn, Hampton. "Florida: Jewel of the Gilded Age." *Gulf Coast Historical Review* 10 (1994): 19–28.

Eagleton, Terry, Fredric Jameson, and Edward W. Said. *Nationalism, Colonialism, and Literature.* Minneapolis: University of Minnesota Press, 1990.

Eakin, Marshall C. "When South Is North: The U.S. South from the Perspective of a Brazilianist." Keynote address presented at symposium on "The U.S. South in Global Contexts," Oxford, Miss., February 14, 2003.

Edelman, Lee. *No Future: Queer Theory and the Death Drive.* Durham, N.C.: Duke University Press, 2004.

Edge, John T. Introduction to *The New Encyclopedia of Southern Culture*, Vol. 7, *Foodways*, edited by John T. Edge, xix–xx. Chapel Hill: University of North Carolina Press, 2007.

———. "Kiss My Grits." *Gourmet*, October 2000. Accessed November 11, 2012. http://www.gourmet.com/magazine/2000s/2000/10/grits.

Edwards, Brian T. and Dilip Parameshwar Gaonkar, eds. *Globalizing American Studies.* Chicago: University of Chicago Press, 2010.

Egerton, John. *The Americanization of Dixie: The Southernization of America.* New York: Harper's Magazine Press, 1974.

———. "Grits." In *Encyclopedia of Southern Culture*, vol. 2, edited by Charles Reagan Wilson and William Ferris, 495. New York: Doubleday, 1989.

Eilperin, Juliet. "Obama Tells Other World Leaders: 'I Believe America Is Exceptional.'" *Washington Post*, Post Politics blog, September 24, 2013. Accessed January 7, 2014. http://www.washingtonpost.com/blogs/post-politics/wp/2013/09/24/obama-tells-other-world-leaders-i-believe-america-is-exceptional/.

Eisenstein, Elizabeth. *The Printing Press as an Agent of Change.* Cambridge: Cambridge University Press, 1979.

Elliott, Scott. *Coiled in the Heart.* New York: Penguin, 2003.

Ely, Melvin Patrick. *Israel on the Appomattox.* New York: Knopf, 2005.

Emery, Leonore Lynn Fauley. *Black Dance in the United States from 1619 to 1970.* PhD diss., University of California, 1971. Ann Arbor: University Microfilms.

Equiano, Olaudah. *The Interesting Narrative of Olaudah Equiano or, Gustavus Vassa, the African.* Edited by Shelly Eversley. New York: Modern Library, 2004.

Eskew. Glenn T., ed. *Labor in the Modern South*. Athens: University of Georgia Press, 2001.

Espinosa, Mariola. *Epidemic Invasions: Yellow Fever and the Limits of Cuban Independence*. Chicago: University of Chicago Press, 2009.

Falk, William W. *Rooted in Place: Family and Belonging in a Southern Black Community*. Brunswick, N.J.: Rutgers University Press, 2004.

Falk, William W., Larry L. Hunt, and Matthew O. Hunt. "Return Migrations of African-Americans to the South: Reclaiming a Land of Promise, Going Home, or Both?" *Rural Sociology* 69, no. 4 (2004): 490–509.

Fanon, Frantz. *Black Skin, White Masks*. Translated by Charles Lam Markmann. 1952. New York: Grove, 1967.

Faulkner, William. *Absalom, Absalom!* 1936. New York: Vintage, 1990.

———. *As I Lay Dying*. New York: Jonathan Cape, Harrison Smith, 1930.

———. *Go Down, Moses*. 1942. New York: Vintage, 1990.

———. *Light in August*. 1932. New York: Vintage, 1997.

———. *The Sound and the Fury*. 1929. New York: W. W. Norton, 1997.

Faust, Drew Gilpin. *The Creation of Confederate Nationalism: Ideology and Identity in the Civil War South*. Baton Rouge: Louisiana State University Press, 1989.

Febvre, Lucien, and Henri-Jean Martin. *The Coming of the Book: The Impact of Printing, 1450–1800*. Translated by David Gerard. London: Verso, 1976.

Fichte, Johann Gottlieb. "Reden an die deutsche Nation." In vol. 2 of *Werke*, edited by Peter Lothar Oesterreich, 539–788. Frankfurt am Main: Deutsche Klassiker Verlag, 1997.

"55th Annual GRAMMY Awards Nominees." Accessed February 6, 2013. http://www.grammy.com/nominees.

Filene, Benjamin. *Romancing the Folk: Public Memory and American Roots Music*. Chapel Hill: University of North Carolina Press, 2000.

Fink, Leon. *The Maya of Morganton: Work and Community in the Nuevo New South*. Chapel Hill: University of North Carolina Press, 2007.

Fink, Steven, and Susan S. Williams, eds. *Reciprocal Influences: Literary Production, Distribution, and Consumption in America*. Columbus: Ohio State University Press, 1999.

Finkelstein, David, and Alistair McCleery, eds. *The Book History Reader*. 2nd ed. New York: Routledge, 2006.

Fischer, Sybille. *Modernity Disavowed: Haiti and the Cultures of Slavery in the Age of Revolution*. Durham, N.C.: Duke University Press, 2004.

Fish, Stanley. *Professional Correctness: Literary Studies and Political Change*. Oxford: Clarendon, 1995.

Fitzcarraldo. Directed by Werner Herzog. New World Pictures, 1982. DVD.

Fitzhugh, George. *Cannibals All! or, Slaves without Masters*. Edited by C. Vann Woodward. Cambridge, Mass.: Belknap Press, 1960.

Floyd, Samuel A., Jr., ed. *Black Music in the Harlem Renaissance*. Knoxville: University of Tennessee Press, 1990.

———. "Music in the Harlem Renaissance: An Overview." In Floyd, *Black Music in the Harlem Renaissance*, 1–27.

Foner, Eric. "The Master and His Mistress." *New York Times*, October 3, 2008. Accessed June 12, 2013. http://www.nytimes.com/2008/10/05/books/review/Foner-t.html?pagewanted=all&_r=0.

Food, Inc. Dir. Robert Kenner. Magnolia Pictures, 2008. DVD.

Ford, Richard. *Independence Day*. New York: Alfred A. Knopf, 1995.

———. *The Sportswriter*. New York: Vintage, 1986.

Forman, Jr., James. "Racial Critiques of Mass Incarceration: Beyond the New Jim Crow." *New York University Law Review* 87 (2012): 21–69.

Fortier, Alcée. *Louisiana Folk-Tales in French Dialect and English Translation*. New York: American Folklore Society, 1895.

Foucault, Michel. *The Birth of the Clinic: An Archaeology of Medical Perception*. New York: Pantheon Books, 1973.

———. *Discipline and Punishment: The Birth of the Prison*. New York: Vintage, 1995.

———. *Madness and Civilization: A History of Insanity in the Age of Reason*. New York: Vintage, 1988.

Franchot, Jenny. "Unseemly Commemoration: Religion, Fragments, and the Icon." *American Literary History* 9, no. 3 (1997): 502–21.

Frederick, Don. "Michelle Obama's 'Proud' Remarks Draw Conservative Fire." *Los Angeles Times*, Top of the Ticket blog, February 19, 2008. Accessed January 7, 2014. http://latimesblogs .latimes.com/washington/2008/02/michelle-obama.html.

Frenkel, Stephen. "Geographical Representations of the 'Other': The Landscape of the Panama Canal Zone." *Journal of Historical Geography* 28, no. 1 (2002): 85–99.

———. "Jungle Stories: North American Representations of Tropical Panama." *Geographical Review* 86, no. 3 (2002): 317–33.

Freud, Sigmund. "Mourning and Melancholia." In *The Standard Edition of the Complete Psychological Works of Sigmund Freud*, vol. 14, *On the History of the Psycho-Analytic Movement, Papers on Metapsychology and Other Works (1914–1916)*, 237–58. London: Hogarth Press, 1957.

Frey, William H. "The New Great Migration: Black Americans' Return to the South, 1965–2000." Brookings Institution, May 2004. Accessed June 13, 2013. http://www.brookings. edu/~/media/research/files/reports/2004/5/demographics%20frey/20040524_frey.pdf.

Friedman, Susan Stanford. "Why Not Compare?" *PMLA* 126, no. 3 (2011): 753–62.

Frost, William Goodell. "Our Contemporary Ancestors in the Southern Mountains." *Atlantic Monthly* 83, no. 497 (March 1899): 311–20.

Gamman, Lorraine, and Merja Makinen. *Female Fetishism*. New York: New York University Press, 1994.

García Márquez, Gabriel. *Leaf Storm, and Other Stories*. Translated by Gregory Rabassa. New York: Harper and Row, 1972.

Gates, Henry Louis, Jr. "Reading '*Race*,' Writing and Difference." *PMLA* 123, no. 5 (2008): 1534–39.

———. "Talkin' That Talk." *Critical Inquiry* 13, no. 1 (1986): 203–10.

———. "Writing 'Race' and the Difference It Makes." *Critical Inquiry* 12, no. 1 (1985): 1–20.

Gates, Henry Louis, Jr., and Gene Andrew Jarrett, eds. *The New Negro: Essays on Race, Representation, and African American Culture, 1892–1938*. Princeton, N.J.: Princeton University Press, 2007.

Gatewood, William B., Jr. *Black Americans and the White Man's Burden, 1898–1903*. Urbana: University of Illinois Press, 1975.

Gayarré, Charles. *The Creoles of History and the Creoles of Romance*. New Orleans: C. E. Hopkins, 1885.

Gerbi, Antonello. *The Dispute of the New World: The History of a Polemic, 1750–1900*. Translated by Jermey Moyle. Pittsburgh: University of Pittsburgh Press, 1973.

Gerster, Patrick, and Nicholas Cords, eds. *Myth and Southern History.* Vol. 1, *The Old South.* Carbondale: University of Illinois Press, 1989.

———, eds. *Myth and Southern History.* Vol. 2, *The New South.* Carbondale: University of Illinois Press, 1988.

Gieryn, Thomas F. "A Place for Space in Sociology." *Annual Review of Sociology* 26 (2000): 463–96.

Gilderbloom, John I. *Invisible City: Poverty, Housing and New Urbanism.* Austin: University of Texas Press, 2008.

Gillman, Susan. "The New, Newest Thing: Have American Studies Gone Imperial?" *American Literary History* 17, no. 1 (Spring 2005): 196–214.

Gilmore, Glenda Elizabeth. *Gender and Jim Crow: Women and the Politics of White Supremacy in North Carolina, 1896–1920.* Chapel Hill: University of North Carolina Press, 1996.

Gilpin, Patrick J., and Marybeth Gasman. *Charles S. Johnson: Leadership beyond the Veil in the Age of Jim Crow.* New York: State University of New York Press, 2003.

Gilroy, Paul. *The Black Atlantic: Modernity and Double Consciousness.* Cambridge, Mass.: Harvard University Press, 1993.

Glissant, Édouard. *Caribbean Discourse: Selected Essays.* Charlottesville: University of Virginia Press, 1992.

———. *Faulkner, Mississippi.* Translated by Barbara B. Lewis and Thomas C. Spear. Chicago: University Chicago Press, 2000.

———. *Poetics of Relation.* Translated by Betsy Wing. Ann Arbor: University of Michigan Press, 1997.

Godden, Richard. "*Absalom, Absalom!,* Haiti and Labor History: Reading Unreadable Revolutions." *ELH* 61, no. 3 (Fall 1994): 685–720.

Goldfield, David. *Region, Race, and Cities: Interpreting the Urban South.* Baton Rouge: Louisiana State University Press, 1997.

———. *Still Fighting the Civil War: The American South and Southern History.* Baton Rouge: Louisiana State University Press, 2004.

Goldman, Ruth. "Who Is That Queer Queer?: Exploring Norms around Sexuality, Race, and Class in Queer Theory." In *Queer Studies: A Lesbian, Gay, Bisexual, and Transgender Anthology,* edited by Brett Beemyn and Mickey Eliason, 169–82. New York: New York University Press, 1996.

Gómez, Nicolás Wey. *The Tropics of Empire: Why Columbus Sailed South to the Indies.* Cambridge, Mass.: MIT Press, 2008.

Gone with the Wind. Directed by Victor Fleming. Selznick International Pictures, 1939. DVD.

Gordon-Reed, Annette. *The Hemingses of Monticello: An American Family.* New York: W. W. Norton, 2008.

Gotham, Kevin Fox. *Authentic New Orleans: Tourism, Culture, and Race in the Big Easy.* New York: New York University Press.

Gotham, Kevin Fox, and M. Greenberg. "From 9/11 to 8/29: Post-Disaster Recovery and Rebuilding in New York and New Orleans." *Social Forces* 87, no. 2 (2008): 1039–62.

Gouge, Earnest. *Totkv Mocvse/New Fire: Creek Folktales by Earnest Gouge.* Norman: University of Oklahoma Press, 2004.

Graham, T. Austin. *The Great American Songbooks: Musical Texts, Modernism, and the Value of Popular Culture.* New York: Oxford University Press, 2013.

Gramsci, Antonio. "Some Aspects of the Southern Question." 1926. In *Pre-Prison Writings,* edited by Richard Bellamy, translated by Virginia Cox, 313–37. Cambridge: Cambridge University Press, 1994.

Grandin, Greg. *Empire of Necessity: Slavery, Freedom, and Deception in the New World*. New York: Metropolitan Books, 2014.

———. *Fordlandia: The Rise and Fall of Henry Ford's Forgotten Jungle City*. New York: Metropolitan Books, 2009.

Grant, Susan-Mary. *North over South: Northern Nationalism and American Identity in the Antebellum Era*. Lawrence: University of Kansas Press, 2000.

Grantham, Dewey W. *The South in Modern America: A Region at Odds*. Fayetteville: University of Arkansas Press, 2001.

Graybill, Mark. "'I Am, Personally, the Fall of the West': Postmodernism and the Critical Reception (and Legacy) of Barry Hannah's Fiction." *Literature Compass* 8, no. 10 (2011): 677–89.

Green, Chris, Rachel Rubin, and James Smethurst. "Radicalism in the South since Reconstruction: An Introduction." In *Radicalism in the South since Reconstruction*, edited by Chris Green, Rachel Rubin, and James Smethurst, 1–12. New York: Palgrave, 2006.

The Green Pastures. Directed by Marc Connelly and William Keighley. Warner Brothers, 1936. DVD.

Greenspan, Ezra, and Jonathan Rose. "An Introduction to *Book History*." *Book History* 1, no. 1 (1998): ix–xi.

Greeson, Jennifer Rae. *Our South: Geographic Fantasy and the Rise of National Literature*. Cambridge, Mass.: Harvard University Press, 2010.

Greider, William. *One World, Ready or Not: The Manic Logic of Global Capitalism*. New York: Touchstone, 1997.

Griffin, Farah Jasmine. " *'Race,' Writing and Difference*: A Meditation." *PMLA* 123, no. 5 (2008): 1516–21.

Griffin, Larry J. "The Promise of a Sociology of the South." *Southern Cultures* 7, no. 1 (2001): 50–75.

Griffin, Larry J., and Don H. Doyle, eds. *The South as an American Problem*. Athens: University of Georgia Press, 1995.

Griffith, R. Marie. *God's Daughters: Evangelical Women and the Power of Submission*. Berkeley: University of California Press, 2000.

Grillo, Evelio. *Black Cuban, Black American: A Memoir*. Houston: Arte Público Press, 2000.

Griswold, Wendy. *Regionalism and the Reading Class*. Chicago: University of Chicago Press, 2008.

Griswold, Wendy, and Nathan Wright. "Cowbirds, Locals, and the Dynamic Endurance of Regionalism." *American Journal of Sociology* 109, no. 6 (2004): 1411–1451.

"Grits—Gourmet Cheddar Cheese Grits." The Old Mill. Accessed March 13, 2013. http ://www.old-mill.com/product/1970/20.

"Grits—White Corn." The Old Mill. Accessed March 13, 2013. http://www.old-mill.com /product/665/20.

Grooms, Anthony. *Bombingham*. New York: Free Press, 2001.

Gruesz, Kirsten Silva. *Ambassadors of Culture: The Transamerican Origins of Latino Writing*. Princeton, N.J.: Princeton University Press, 2002.

———. "America." In Burgett and Hendler, *Keywords for American Cultural Studies*, 16–22.

———. "The Gulf of Mexico System and the 'Latinness' of New Orleans." *American Literary History* 18, no. 3 (Fall 2006): 468–95.

Grunwald, Michael. *The Swamp: The Everglades, Florida, and the Politics of Paradise*. New York: Simon and Schuster, 2007.

Guinn, Matthew. *After Southern Modernism: Fiction of the Contemporary South*. Jackson: University Press of Mississippi, 2000.

Gunning, Sandra. "Nancy Prince and the Politics of Mobility, Home and Diasporic (Mis) Identification." *American Quarterly* 53, no. 1 (2001): 32–69.

Guridy, Frank. *Forging Diaspora: Afro-Cubans and African Americans in a World of Empire and Jim Crow*. Chapel Hill: University of North Carolina Press, 2010.

Guterl, Matthew Pratt. "South." In Burgett and Hendler, *Keywords for American Cultural Studies*, 230–33.

Haddox, Thomas F. "Alice Randall's *The Wind Done Gone* and the Ludic in African American Historical Fiction." *Modern Fiction Studies* 53, no. 1 (Spring 2007): 120–39.

———. "Elizabeth Spencer, the White Civil Rights Novel, and the Postsouthern." *Modern Language Quarterly* 65, no. 4 (December 2004): 561–81.

Hagood, Taylor. *Faulkner's Imperialism: Space, Place, and the Materiality of Myth*. Baton Rouge: Louisiana State University Press, 2008.

Hahn, Stephen. *A Nation under Our Feet: Black Political Struggles in the Rural South*. Cambridge, Mass.: Harvard University Press, 2003.

Halberstam, Judith. *In a Queer Time and Place: Transgender Bodies, Subcultural Lives*. New York: New York University Press, 2005.

Hale, Grace Elizabeth. *Making Whiteness: The Culture of Segregation in the South, 1890–1940*. New York: Pantheon, 1998.

Hale, Grace Elizabeth, and Robert Jackson. "'We're Trying Hard as Hell to Free Ourselves': Southern History and Race in the Making of William Faulkner's Literary Terrain." In *A Companion to William Faulkner*, edited by Richard C. Moreland, 28–45. Malden, Mass.: Blackwell, 2007.

Hall, David D. *Cultures of Print: Essays in the History of the Book*. Amherst: University of Massachusetts Press, 1996.

———, ed. *A History of the Book in America*. 5 vols. Chapel Hill: University of North Carolina Press, 2010.

Hall, Jacquelyn Dowd. "The Long Civil Rights Movement and the Political Uses of the Past." *Journal of American History* 91, no. 4 (2005): 1233–63.

Hall, Jacquelyn Dowd, et al., eds. *Like a Family: The Making of a Southern Cotton Mill World*. 1982. Chapel Hill: University of North Carolina Press, 2000.

Hall, Stuart. "Créolité and the Process of Creolization." In Cohen and Toninato, *Creolization Reader*, 26–38.

Hallward, Peter. "Haitian Inspiration: On the Bicentenary of Haiti's Independence." *Radical Philosophy* 123 (2004): 2–7.

Hamer, Fannie Lou. *The Speeches of Fannie Lou Hamer: To Tell It Like It Is*. Edited by Maegan Parker Brooks and Davis W. Houck. Jackson: University Press of Mississippi, 2011.

Hammond, Sarah. "God Is My Partner: An Evangelical Businessman Confronts Depression and War." *Church History* 80, no. 3 (September 2011): 498–519.

Handley, George. *New World Poetics: Nature and the Adamic Imagination of Whitman, Neruda, and Walcott*. Athens: University of Georgia Press, 2007.

———. "Oedipus in the Americas: *Lone Star* and the Reinvention of American Studies." *Forum for Modern Language Studies* 40, no. 2 (Spring 2004): 160–81.

379

————. *Postslavery Literatures in the Americas: Family Portraits in Black and White*. Charlottesville: University Press of Virginia, 2000.

Hannerz, Ulf. "The World in Creolization." In *Readings in African Popular Culture*, edited by Karen Barber, 12–18. Bloomington: Indiana University Press, 1997.

Harkins, Anthony. *Hillbilly: A Cultural History of an American Icon*. New York: Oxford University Press, 2005.

Harris, Eddy L. *South of Haunted Dreams: A Ride through Slavery's Old Back Yard*. New York: Simon and Schuster, 1993.

Harris, Wilson. "History, Fable and Myth in the Caribbean and Guianas." In *Selected Essays of Wilson Harris: The Unfinished Genesis of the Imagination*, edited by Andrew Bundy, 152–66. New York: Routledge, 1999.

————. *The Womb of Space: The Cross-Cultural Imagination*. Westport, Conn.: Praeger, 1983.

Hartman, C., and G. D. Squires, eds. *There Is No Such Thing as a Natural Disaster: Race, Class and Hurricane Katrina*. New York: Routledge, 2006.

Hartz, Louis. *The Liberal Tradition in America*. New York: Harcourt, Brace and World, 1955.

Harvey, David. *Spaces of Hope*. Berkeley: University of California Press, 2000.

Hechter, Michael. *Internal Colonialism: The Celtic Fringe in British National Development*. Berkeley: University of California Press, 1975.

Herod, Andrew. *Labor Geographies: Workers and the Landscapes of Capitalism*. New York: Guilford, 2001.

Herring, Scott. *Another Country: Queer Anti-Urbanism*. New York: New York University Press, 2010.

Hesse, Barnor. "Symptomatically Black: A Creolization of the Political." In Lionnet and Shih, *Creolization of Theory*, 37–61.

Hinrichsen, Lisa. *Possessing the Past: Trauma, Imagination, and Memory in Post-Plantation Southern Literature*. Baton Rouge: Louisiana State University Press, 2015.

Hobsbawm, Eric J., and Terence O. Ranger. *The Invention of Tradition*. Cambridge: Cambridge University Press, 1983.

Hobson, Fred. Contribution to "A Symposium: The Business of Inventing the South." *Mississippi Quarterly* 52 (Fall 1999): 659–87.

————. Introduction to Hobson, *South to the Future*, 1–12.

————. "The New South, 1880–1940." In *The Literature of the American South: A Norton Anthology*, edited by William L. Andrews et al., 245–53. New York: W. W. Norton, 1998.

————. *The Southern Writer in the Postmodern World*. Athens: University of Georgia Press, 1991.

————, ed. *South to the Future: An American Region in the Twenty-First Century*. Baton Rouge: Louisiana State University Press, 2002.

Hobson, Geary, Janet McAdams, and Kathryn Walkiewicz. "Introduction: The South Seldom Seen." In Hobson, McAdams, and Walkiewicz, *People Who Stayed*, 1–22.

————, eds. *The People Who Stayed: Southeastern Indian Writing after Removal*. Norman: University of Oklahoma Press, 2010.

Holman, C. Hugh. Introduction to *The Partisan Leader: A Tale of the Future*, by Nathaniel Beverley Tucker, vii–xxiii. Chapel Hill: University of North Carolina Press, 1971.

hooks, bell. *Yearning: Race, Gender, and Cultural Politics*. Boston: South End Press, 1990.

House, Silas, and Jason Howard, eds. *Something's Rising: Appalachians Fighting Mountaintop Removal*. Lexington: University Press of Kentucky, 2009.

Howard, Gregory. *Life on the Color Line: The True Story of a White Boy Who Discovered He Was Black*. New York: Dutton, 1995.

Howard, John, ed. *Carryin' On in the Lesbian and Gay South*. New York: New York University Press, 1997.

———. "Introduction: Carryin' On in the Lesbian and Gay South." In Howard, *Carryin' On in the Lesbian and Gay South*, 1–14.

———. *Men Like That: A Southern Queer History*. Chicago: University of Chicago Press, 1999.

Howe, Stephen. *Empire: A Very Short Introduction*. New York: Oxford University Press, 2002.

Hughes, Langston. "The Negro Artist and the Racial Mountain," *Nation* 122, no. 3181 (June 23, 1926): 694.

Hume, David. *Hume: Political Essays*. Edited by Knud Haakonssen. Cambridge: Cambridge University Press, 1994.

Huntington, Ellsworth. *Civilization and Climate*. New Haven, Conn.: Yale University Press, 1915.

Hurston, Zora Neale. *Dust Tracks on a Road*. Philadelphia: J. B. Lippincott, 1942.

———. *Hurston: Folklore, Memoirs, and Other Writings*. Edited by Cheryl A. Wall. New York: Library of America, 1995.

———. *Tell My Horse: Voodoo and Life in Haiti and Jamaica*. 1938. New York: HarperPerennial, 2009.

———. *Their Eyes Were Watching God*. 1937. New York: Harper and Row, 1990.

Hutchison, Coleman. *Apples and Ashes: Literature, Nationalism, and the Confederate States of America*. Athens: University of Georgia Press, 2012.

Iannini, Christopher. "'The Itinerant Man': Crèvecoeur's Caribbean, Raynal's Revolution, and the Fate of Atlantic Cosmopolitanism." *William and Mary Quarterly* 61 (April 2004): 201–34.

Irwin, Robert. "¿Qué hacen los nuevos americanistas? Collaborative Strategies for a Post-nationalist American Studies." *Comparative American Studies* 2, no. 3 (2004): 303–23.

Jackson, Leon. "The Talking Book and the Talking Book Historian: African American Cultures of Print: The State of the Discipline." *Book History* 13 (2010): 251–308.

James, Allison. "Cooking the Books: Global or Local Identities in Contemporary British Food Cultures?" In *Cross-Cultural Consumption: Global Markets, Local Realities*, edited by David Howes, 77–92. London: Routledge, 1996.

James, C. L. R. *The Black Jacobins: Toussaint L'Ouverture and the San Domingo Revolution*. New York: Vintage, 1989.

Jameson, Fredric. *Postmodernism, or, the Cultural Logic of Late Capitalism*. London: Verso, 1991.

———. *Signatures of the Visible*. New York: Routledge, 1990.

Jefferson, Thomas. Letter to Marquis de Chastellux, September 2, 1785. The Letters of Thomas Jefferson, The Avalon Project at Yale Law School. Accessed February 5, 2015. http://avalon.law.yale.edu/18th_century/let34.asp.

———. Letter to Rufus King, 13 July 1802. In Vol. 9 of *The Works of Thomas Jefferson*, edited by Leicester Ford, 383. New York: G. P. Putnam's Sons, 1905.

———. *Notes on the State of Virginia*. Philadelphia: Prichard and Hall, 1788.

———. "Notes on the State of Virginia." In Thomas Jefferson, *Writings*, 288–90. New York: Library of America, 1984.

Jefferson in Paris. Directed by James Ivory. Touchstone Pictures, 1995. DVD.

Jenkins, McKay. *The South in Black and White: Race, Sex, and Literature in the 1940s.* Chapel Hill: University of North Carolina Press, 1999.

Johnson, Charles S. *Growing Up in the Black Belt: Negro Youth in the Rural South.* Washington, D.C.: American Council on Education, 1941.

———. *Shadow of the Plantation.* Chicago: University of Chicago Press, 1934.

Johnson, E. Patrick. "'Quare' Studies, or (Almost) Everything I Know about Queer Studies I Learned from My Grandmother." *Text and Performance Quarterly* 21, no. 1 (2001): 1–25.

———. *Sweet Tea: Black Gay Men of the South.* Chapel Hill: University of North Carolina Press, 2008.

Johnson, James Weldon. *Along This Way: The Autobiography of James Weldon Johnson.* New York: Da Capo Press, 2000.

———. *The Autobiography of An Ex-Coloured Man.* 1912. New York: Vintage, 1989.

Johnson, Walter. *River of Dark Dreams: Slavery and Empire in the Cotton Kingdom.* Cambridge, Mass.: Harvard University Press, 2013.

Jones, Anne Goodwyn, and Susan V. Donaldson, eds. *Haunted Bodies: Gender and Southern Texts.* Charlottesville: University of Virginia Press, 1997.

Jones, Gayl. *Mosquito.* Boston: Beacon Press, 1999.

Jones, Leroi (Amiri Baraka). *Cuba Libre.* New York: Fair Play for Cuba Committee, 1960.

Jones, Suzanne W. "Imagining Jefferson and Hemings in Paris." *Transatlantica: Revues d'études américains* 1 (2011). Accessed July 17, 2013. http://transatlantica.revues.org/5391.

———. *Race Mixing: Southern Fiction since the Sixties.* Baltimore: Johns Hopkins University Press, 2004.

———. "Who Is a Southern Writer?" *American Literature* 78, no. 4 (2006): 725–27.

Jones, Suzanne W., and Sharon Monteith, eds. *South to a New Place: Region, Literature, Culture.* Baton Rouge: Louisiana State University Press, 2002.

Joshi, Khyati Y., and Jigna Desai, eds. *Asian Americans in Dixie: Race and Migration in the South.* Urbana-Champaign: University of Illinois Press, 2013.

Justice, Daniel Heath. "Notes toward a Theory of Anomaly." *GLQ: A Journal of Lesbian and Gay Studies* 16, nos. 1–2 (2010): 207–42.

Kaplan, Amy. *The Anarchy of Empire in the Making of U.S. Culture.* Cambridge, Mass.: Harvard University Press, 2005.

Kaplan, Amy, and Donald E. Pease, eds. *Cultures of United States Imperialism.* Durham, N.C.: Duke University Press, 1993.

Kaplan, Justin. *Mr. Clemens and Mark Twain: A Biography.* 1966. New York: Simon and Schuster, 2006.

Kelley, Robin D. G. *Hammer and Hoe: Alabama Communists during the Great Depression.* Chapel Hill: University of North Carolina Press, 1990.

———. "Notes on Deconstructing 'The Folk.'" *American Historical Review* 97, no. 5 (1992): 1400–1408.

Kenan, Randall. *A Visitation of Spirits.* New York: Grove Press, 1989.

Key, V. O. *Southern Politics in State and Nation.* 1949. Knoxville: University of Tennessee Press, 1984.

Khan, Aisha. *Callaloo Nation: Metaphors of Race and Religious Identity among South Asians in Trinidad.* Durham, N.C.: Duke University Press, 2004.

———. "Creolization Moments." In Stewart, *Creolization,* 237–53.

———. "Good to Think? Creolization, Optimism, and Agency." *Current Anthropology* 48, no. 5 (2007): 653–73.

Killens, John Oliver. Introduction to Killens and Ward, *Black Southern Voices*, 1–4.

Killens, John Oliver, and Jerry W. Ward, Jr., eds. *Black Southern Voices: An Anthology of Fiction, Poetry, Drama, Nonfiction, and Critical Essays*. New York: Meridian, 1992.

Killian, Lewis. *White Southerners*. 1970. New York: Random House, 1987.

King, Richard H. *A Southern Renaissance: The Cultural Awakening of the American South, 1930–1955*. New York: Oxford University Press, 1980.

King, Wilma. *Stolen Childhood: Slave Youth in Nineteenth-Century America*. Indianapolis: University of Indiana Press, 2011.

Kirby, Jack Temple. *Mockingbird Song: Ecological Landscapes of the South*. Chapel Hill: University of North Carolina Press, 2006.

Kirshenblatt-Gimblett, Barbara. "Folklore's Crisis." *Journal of American Folklore* 111, no. 441 (Summer 2008): 281–327.

Klarman, Michael J. *From Jim Crow to Civil Rights: The Supreme Court and the Struggle for Racial Equality*. New York: Oxford University Press, 2004.

Krehbiel, Henry Edward, *Afro-American Folksongs: A Study in Racial and National Music*. New York: G. Schirmer, 1914.

Kreyling, Michael. "*The Fathers*: A Postsouthern Narrative Reading." In *Southern Literature and Literary Theory*, edited by Jefferson Humphries, 186–205.

———. "Fee Fie Faux Faulkner: Parody and Postmodernism in Southern Literature." *Southern Review* 29 (1993): 1–15.

———. *Inventing Southern Literature*. Jackson: University Press of Mississippi, 1998.

———. *The South That Wasn't There: Postsouthern Memory and History*. Baton Rouge: Louisiana State University Press, 2010.

Krips, Henry. *Fetish: An Erotics of Culture*. Ithaca, N.Y.: Cornell University Press, 1999.

Kristeva, Julia. *Powers of Horror: An Essay on Abjection*. New York: Columbia University Press, 1982.

Kruse, Kevin M. *White Flight: Atlanta and the Making of Modern Conservatism*. Princeton, N.J.: Princeton University Press, 2007.

Kupperman, Karen Ordahl. "Fear of Hot Climes in the Anglo-American Colonial Experience." *William and Mary Quarterly* 41 (April 1984): 213–40.

Lacan, Jacques. *The Four Fundamental Concepts of Psycho-Analysis*. New York: W. W. Norton, 1981.

Ladd, Barbara. "Faulkner's Paris: State and Metropole in a Fable." *Faulkner Journal* 26, no. 1 (Spring 2012): 115–28.

———. "Literary Studies: The Southern United States, 2005." *PMLA* 120, no. 5 (October 2005): 1628–35.

———. *Resisting History: Gender, Modernity, and Authorship in William Faulkner, Zora Neale Hurston, and Eudora Welty*. Baton Rouge: Louisiana State University Press, 2007.

Lassiter, Matthew D., and Joseph Crespino, eds. *The Myth of Southern Exceptionalism*. New York: Oxford University Press 2009.

Latins Anonymous. *Latins Anonymous: Plays*. Houston: Arte Público Press, 1996.

Lee, Felicia R. "Dark Tales Illuminate Haiti, before and after Quake." Review of *Haiti Noir*, edited by Edwidge Danticat. *New York Times*, January 9, 2011, C1.

Levander, Caroline. "Sutton Griggs and the Borderlands of Empire." *American Literary History* 22, no. 1 (Spring 2010): 57–84.

Levine, Lawrence. "The Folklore of Industrial Society: Popular Culture and Its Audiences." *American Historical Review* 97, no. 5 (1992): 1369–99.

383

Lewis, David Levering. *When Harlem Was in Vogue.* New York: Penguin, 1997.

Lhamon, W. T. *Raising Cain: Blackface Performance from Jim Crow to Hip-Hop.* Cambridge, Mass.: Harvard University Press, 1998.

Lichtenstein, Nelson, ed. *Wal-Mart: The Face of Twenty-First-Century Capitalism.* New York: New Press, 2006.

Limón, José E. *American Encounters: Greater Mexico, the United States, and the Erotics of Culture.* Boston: Beacon Press, 1998.

Lindholdt, Paul. "Literary Activism and the Bioregional Agenda." In *The ISLE Reader: Ecocriticism, 1993–2003,* edited by Michael P. Branch and Scott Slovic, 243–57. Athens: University of Georgia Press, 2003.

Lindsay, D. Michael. *Faith in the Halls of Power: How Evangelicals Joined the American Elite.* New York: Oxford University Press, 2008.

Linebaugh, Peter, and Marcus Rediker. *The Many-Headed Hydra: Sailors, Slaves, Commoners, and the Hidden History of the Revolutionary Atlantic.* Boston: Beacon, 2000.

Lionnet, Françoise, and Shu-mei Shih, eds. *The Creolization of Theory.* Durham, N.C.: Duke University Press, 2011.

Littlebear, Richard. "Just Speak Your Language: *Hena'haanehe.*" In *Native American Voices: A Reader,* edited by Susan Lobo, Steve Talbot, and Traci L. Morris, 90–92. Upper Saddle River, N.J.: Prentice Hall, 2010.

Littlefield, Daniel F., Jr., and James W. Parins. *Native American Writing in the Southeast: An Anthology, 1875–1935.* Jackson: University Press of Mississippi, 1995.

Litwack, Leon F. *How Free Is Free? The Long Death of Jim Crow.* Cambridge, Mass.: Harvard University Press, 2009.

Livingstone, David N. "Human Acclimatization: Perspectives on a Contested Field of Inquiry in Science, Medicine, and Geography." *History of Science* 25 (December 1987): 359–94.

———. "Race, Space and Moral Climatology: Notes toward a Genealogy. *Journal of Historical Geography* 28 (April 2002): 159–80.

Lloyd, David, and Peter O'Neill. *The Black and Green Atlantic: Cross-Currents of the African and Irish Diasporas.* Houndmills, England: Palgrave Macmillan, 2009.

Lloyd, Richard. "Urbanization and the Southern United States." *Annual Review of Sociology* 38, no. 24 (2012): 1–24.

Locke, Alain. *The Negro and His Music.* Washington, D.C.: Associates in Negro Folk Education, 1936.

———, ed. *The New Negro: An Interpretation.* New York: Albert and Charles Boni, 1925.

Lofgren, Charles A. *The Plessy Case: A Legal-Historical Interpretation.* New York: Oxford University Press, 1987.

Loichot, Valérie. *Orphan Narratives: The Postplantation Literature of Faulkner, Glissant, Morrison, and Saint-John Perse.* Charlottesville: University of Virginia Press, 2007.

Lomax, John A. *Cowboy Songs and Other Frontier Ballads.* New York: Sturgis and Walton, 1910.

———. *Cowboy Songs and Other Frontier Ballads.* Rev. ed. New York: Macmillan, 1938.

Long, Carolyn Morrow. *A New Orleans Voudou Priestess: The Legend and Reality of Marie Laveau.* Gainesville: University Press of Florida, 2006.

Lott, Eric. *Love and Theft: Blackface Minstrelsy and the American Working Class.* New York: Oxford University Press, 1993.

Lovato, Roberto. "Juan Crow in Georgia." *Nation,* May 26, 2008. Accessed October 18, 2013. http://www.thenation.com/article/juan-crow-georgia.

Lowe, Lisa. *The Intimacies of Four Continents.* Durham, N.C.: Duke University Press, 2015.

Luce, Henry R. "The American Century." *Life*, February 17, 1941, 62–65.

Lugo, Julia Cristina Ortiz. *De Arañas, Conejos y Tortugas: Presencia de África en la cuentística de tradición oral en Puerto Rico.* San Juan: Centro de Estudios Avanzados de Puerto Rico y el Caribe, 2004.

Lyons, Scott Richard. *X-Marks: Native Signatures of Assent.* Minneapolis: University of Minnesota Press, 2010.

Lyotard, Jean-François. *The Postmodern Condition: A Report on Knowledge.* Manchester, England: Manchester University Press, 1984.

Lytle, Andrew. "The Hind Tit." In Twelve Southerners, *I'll Take My Stand*, 201–45.

MacIntyre, Rebecca C. "Promoting the Gothic South." *Southern Cultures* 11 (Summer 2005): 33–61.

Mackie, John Milton. *From Cape Cod to Dixie and the Tropics.* New York: G. P. Putnam, 1864.

Malone, Bill C. *Singing Cowboys and Musical Mountaineers: Southern Culture and the Roots of Country Music.* Athens: University of Georgia Press, 1993.

Marsden, George. *Fundamentalism and American Culture.* Rev. ed. New York: Oxford University Press, 2006.

Marshall, F. Ray. *Labor in the South.* Cambridge, Mass.: Harvard University Press, 1967.

Martins, Luciana L. "A Naturalist's Vision of the Tropics: Charles Darwin and the Brazilian Landscape." *Singapore Journal of Tropical Geography* 21 (March 2000): 19–33.

Marx, Karl. *Capital: A Critique of Political Economy.* New York: Cosimo Books, 2007.

———. *The Poverty of Philosophy.* Translated by H. Quelch. 1913. Amherst, N.Y.: Prometheus Books, 1995.

Massey, Douglas S., and Nancy A. Denton. *American Apartheid: Segregation and the Making of the Underclass.* Cambridge, Mass.: Harvard University Press, 1993.

Massey, Douglas S., Jonathan Rothwell, and Thurston Domina. "The Changing Bases of Segregation in the United States." *Annals of the American Academy of Political and Social Science* 626 (2009): 74–90.

Matory, J. Lorand. *Black Atlantic Religion: Tradition, Transnationalism, and Matriarchy in the Afro-Brazilian Candomblé.* Princeton, N.J.: Princeton University Press, 2005.

Matthews, John T. "Recalling the West Indies: From Yoknapatawpha to Haiti and Back." *American Literary History* 16, no. 2 (2004): 238–62.

———. *William Faulkner: Seeing through the South.* Chichester, England: Wiley-Blackwell, 2009.

McAdams, Janet. Excerpt from "Betty Creek: Writing the Indigenous Deep South." In Hobson, McAdams, and Walkiewicz, *People Who Stayed*, 251–56.

McClennen, Sophia. "Inter-American Studies or Imperial American Studies?" *Comparative American Studies* 3, no. 4 (2005): 393–413.

McClintock, Anne. *Imperial Leather: Race, Gender, and Sexuality in the Imperial Contest.* New York: Routledge, 1995.

McClintock, Anne, and Rob Nixon. "No Names Apart: The Separation of Word and History in Derrida's 'Le Dernier Mot du Racisme.'" *Critical Inquiry* 13, no. 1 (1986): 140–54.

McCracken, Grant. *Culture and Consumption: New Approaches to the Symbolic Character of Consumer Goods and Activities.* Bloomington: Indiana University Press, 1988.

McGann, Jerome. *The Textual Condition.* Princeton, N.J.: Princeton University Press, 1991.

McGehee, Margaret T. "Disturbing the Peace: *Lost Boundaries, Pinky*, and Censorship in Atlanta, Georgia, 1949–1952." *Cinema Journal* 46, no. 1 (2006): 23–51.

McGuire, Danielle L. *At the Dark End of the Street: Black Women, Rape, and Resistance—A New History of the Civil Rights Movement from Rosa Parks to the Rise of Black Power.* New York: Vintage, 2011.

McHenry, Elizabeth. *Forgotten Readers: Recovering the Lost History of African-American Literary Societies.* Durham, N.C.: Duke University Press, 2002.

McKay, Claude. *Home to Harlem.* 1928. Boston: Northeastern University Press, 1987.

McKenzie, D. F. *Bibliography and the Sociology of Texts.* Cambridge: Cambridge University Press, 1999.

McLaughlin, Jack. *Jefferson and Monticello: The Biography of a Builder.* New York: Henry Holt, 1988.

McPherson, Tara. *Reconstructing Dixie: Race, Gender, and Nostalgia in the Imagined South.* Durham, N.C.: Duke University Press, 2003.

Melville, Herman. "Benito Cereno." In *Billy Budd and Other Stories,* 159–258. New York: Penguin, 1986.

———. *Pierre: or, The Ambiguities.* 1852. New York: Penguin, 1996.

Mencken, H. L. "The Sahara of the Bozart." In *Prejudices: Second Series,* 136–54. New York: Alfred A. Knopf, 1920.

Mendible, Myra. "Introduction: Embodying 'Latinidad'; An Overview." In *From Bananas to Buttocks: The Latina Body in Popular Film and Culture,* edited by Myra Mendible, 1–28. Austin: University of Texas Press, 2007.

"Menu." Café Amelie. Accessed March 13, 2013. http://www.cafeamelie.com/uploads/files/DINNER%202013.pdf.

"Menus." Bubba Gump Shrimp Company. Accessed February 12, 2013. http://www.bubba gump.com/assets/menus/new-orleans.pdf; http://www.bubbagump.com/assets/menus/new-york.pdf.

Metress, Christopher. "Fighting Battles One by One: Robert Penn Warren's *Segregation.*" *Southern Review* 32, no. 1 (1996): 166–71.

Mignolo, Walter D. *The Idea of Latin America.* Malden, Mass.: Blackwell, 2005.

Milian, Claudia. *Latining America: Black-Brown Passages and the Coloring of Latino/a Studies.* Athens: University of Georgia Press, 2013.

Miller, Karl Hagstrom. *Segregating Sound: Inventing Folk and Pop Music in the Age of Jim Crow.* Durham, N.C.: Duke University Press, 2010.

Minchin, Timothy J. *Fighting against the Odds: A History of Southern Labor since World War II.* Gainesville: University Press of Florida, 2005.

Mississippi Masala. Directed by Mira Nair. Los Angeles: Samuel Goldwyn Company, 1991. DVD.

Mitchell, Margaret. *Gone with the Wind.* New York: Macmillan, 1936.

Mitscherlich, Alexander, and Margarete Mitscherlich. *The Inability to Mourn: Principles of Collective Behavior.* New York: Grove Press, 1975.

Moltke-Hansen, David. "Intellectual and Cultural History of the Old South." In *A Companion to the American South,* edited by John B. Boles, 212–31. Oxford: Blackwell, 2002.

Monroe, Mina. *Bayou Ballads: Twelve Folk-Songs from Louisiana.* New York: G. Schirmer, 1921.

Moon, Michael, and Cathy N. Davidson, eds. *Subjects and Citizens: Nation, Race, and Gender from Oroonoko to Anita Hill.* Durham, N.C.: Duke University Press, 1995.

Moran, Michelle. *Colonizing Leprosy: Imperialism and the Politics of Public Health in the United States*. Chapel Hill: University of North Carolina Press, 2007.

Moreton, Bethany. *To Serve God and Wal-Mart: The Making of Christian Free Enterprise*. Cambridge, Mass.: Harvard University Press, 2009.

Morgan, Ted. *A Covert Life: Jay Lovestone, Communist, Anti-Communist, and Spymaster*. New York: Random House, 1999.

Morris, Aldon. *The Origins of the Civil Rights Movement*. New York: Free Press, 1984.

Munoz, Jose. *Disidentifications: Queers of Color and the Performance of Politics*. Minneapolis: University of Minnesota Press, 1999.

Murphy, Gretchen. *Hemispheric Imaginings: The Monroe Doctrine and Narratives of U.S. Empire*. Durham, N.C.: Duke University Press, 2005.

My Cousin Vinny. Directed by Jonathan Lynn. 1992. Twentieth Century Fox, 2000. DVD.

Myrdal, Gunnar. *An American Dilemma: The Negro Problem and Modern Democracy*. New York: Harper and Brothers, 1944.

Naipaul, V. S. *A Turn in the South*. New York: Vintage, 1990.

Nance, William L. *The Worlds of Truman Capote*. New York: Stein and Day, 1970.

Nightingale, Carl H. *Segregation: A Global History of Divided Cities*. Chicago: University of Chicago Press, 2012.

The 1928 and 1930 Comintern Resolutions on the Black National Question in the United States. Washington, D.C.: Revolutionary Review Press, 1975.

9500 Liberty. Directed by Annabel Park and Eric Byler. 2009. Team Marketing, 2011. DVD.

Nixon, Rob. *Homelands, Harlem, and Hollywood: South African Culture and the World Beyond*. New York: Routledge, 1994.

Noble, David W. *Death of a Nation: American Culture and the End of Exceptionalism*. Minneapolis: University of Minnesota Press, 2002.

Norman, Brian. *Neo-Segregation Narratives: Jim Crow in Post-Civil Rights American Literature*. Athens: University of Georgia Press, 2010.

North, Michael. *The Dialect of Modernism: Race, Language, and Twentieth-Century Literature*. New York: Oxford University Press, 1994.

Nunn, Erich. "American Balladry and the Anxiety of Ancestry." In *Transatlantic Roots Music: Folk, Blues, and National Identities*, edited by Jill Terry and Neil A. Wynn, 57–76. Jackson: University Press of Mississippi, 2012.

———. "Country Music and the Souls of White Folk." *Criticism: A Quarterly for Literature and the Arts* 51, no. 4 (Fall 2009): 623–49.

Nwankwo, Ifeoma. *Black Cosmopolitanism: Racial Consciousness and Transnational Identity in the Nineteenth-Century Americas*. Philadelphia: University of Pennsylvania Press, 2005.

Oakes, James. *The Ruling Race: A History of American Slaveholders*. New York: W. W. Norton, 1998.

O'Briant, Don. "Anger at Klan Fuels New Novel." *Atlanta Journal-Constitution*, June 12, 1989, B1.

O'Brien, Michael. *The Idea of the American South, 1920–1941*. Baltimore: Johns Hopkins University Press, 1979.

———. *Rethinking the South: Essays in Intellectual History*. Baltimore: Johns Hopkins University Press, 1988.

O'Connor, Flannery. *Mystery and Manners*. Edited by Sally and Robert Fitzgerald. New York: Farrar, Straus and Giroux, 1969.

387

Odum, Howard W. *Southern Regions of the United States*. Chapel Hill: University of North Carolina Press, 1936.

Oggel, Terry L. "Speaking Out about Race: 'The United States of Lyncherdom' Clemens Really Wrote." *Prospects: An Annual of American Cultural Studies* 25 (2000): 115–58.

Orfield, Gary. "Reviving the Goal of an Integrated Society: A 21st Century Challenge." UCLA: The Civil Rights Project/Proyecto Derechos Civiles, January 2009. Accessed June 7, 2012. http://civilrightsproject.ucla.edu/research/k-12-education/integration-and-diversity/reviving-the-goal-of-an-integrated-society-a-21st-century-challenge/orfield-reviving-the-goal-mlk-2009.pdf.

Oshinsky, David M. *Worse than Slavery: Parchman Farm and the Ordeal of Jim Crow*. New York: Free Press, 1997.

Ownby, Ted. *American Dreams in Mississippi: Consumers, Poverty, and Culture, 1830–1998*. Chapel Hill: University of North Carolina Press, 1999.

Owomoyela, Oyekan. *Yoruba Trickster Tales*. Lincoln: University of Nebraska Press, 1997.

Page, Walter Hines. "The Hookworm in Civilization." *World's Work* 24 (September 1912): 504.

Painter, Nell Irvin. "'The South' and 'The Negro': The Rhetoric of Race Relations and Real Life." In *The South for New Southerners*, edited by Paul D. Escott and David R. Goldfield, 42–66. Chapel Hill: University of North Carolina Press, 1991.

Palmié, Stephan. "Is There a Model in the Muddle? 'Creolization' in African Americanist History and Anthropology." In Stewart, *Creolization*, 178–200.

Paredes, Américo. *George Washington Gómez: A Mexicotexan Novel*. Houston: Arte Público Press, 1989.

Parker, Kathleen. "A Tip for the GOP: Look Away." *Washington Post*, August 5, 2009. Accessed January 7, 2014. http://articles.washingtonpost.com/2009-08-05/opinions/36804055_1_southern-republicans-gop-senators-republican-party.

Paterson, Mark. *Consumption and Everyday Life*. London: Routledge, 2006.

Pavlić, Edward. *Crossroads Modernism: Descent and Emergence in African-American Literary Culture*. Minneapolis: University of Minnesota Press, 2002.

Peacock, James L. *Grounded Globalism: How the U.S. South Embraces the World*. Athens: University of Georgia Press, 2007.

———. "The South and Grounded Globalism." In Peacock, Watson, and Matthews, *The American South in a Global World*, 265–76.

Peacock, James L., Harry L. Watson, and Carrie R. Matthews, eds. *The American South in a Global World*. Chapel Hill: University of North Carolina Press, 2005.

Pease, Donald. "New Perspectives on U.S. Culture and Imperialism." In Kaplan and Pease, *Cultures of United States Imperialism*, 22–37.

Peckham, Joel B. "Eudora Welty's *The Golden Apples*: Abjection and the Maternal South." *Texas Studies in Literature and Language* 43, no. 2 (2001): 194–217.

Pendergrass, Sabrina. "Routing Black Migration to the Urban U.S. South: Social Class and Sources of Social Capital in the Destination Selection Process." *Journal of Ethnic and Migration Studies* 39 (2013): 1441–59.

Percy, Walker. *The Moviegoer*. New York: Vintage, 1961.

Perdue, Theda, and Michael Green. *The Columbia Guide to American Indians of the Southeast*. New York: Columbia University Press, 2001.

Pérez Firmat, Gustavo. *The Havana Habit*. New Haven, Conn.: Yale University Press, 2010.

Pérez, Louis A., Jr. *The War of 1898: The United States and Cuba in History and Historiography*. Chapel Hill: University of North Carolina Press, 1998.

Persky, Joseph J. *The Burden of Dependency: Colonial Themes in Southern Economic Thought*. Baltimore: Johns Hopkins University Press, 1992.

Peterkin, Julia. *Black April*. Athens: University Georgia Press, 1998.

Phelan, Peggy. *Unmarked: The Politics of Performance*. London: Routledge, 1993.

Phillips, McCandlish. "Amid City's Hum, Poetry." *New York Times*, May 14, 1970. Accessed June 29, 2010. NYT ProQuest.

Phillips, Ulrich Bonnell. "The Central Theme of Southern History." *American Historical Review* 34 (1928): 30–43.

Pietz, William. "The Problem of the Fetish, I." *RES: Anthropology and Aesthetics* 9 (Spring 1985): 5–17.

Plaag, Eric W. "'There Is an Abundance of Those Which Are Genuine': Northern Travelers and Souvenirs in the Antebellum South." In Stanonis, *Dixie Emporium*, 24–49.

Poe, Edgar Allan. *The Complete Tales and Poems*. New York: Vintage, 1975.

———. *The Narrative of Arthur Gordon Pym*. London: Wiley and Putnam, 1838.

———. "Slavery." *Southern Literary Messenger* 2, no. 5 (April 1836): 336–39.

Polk, Noel. *Children of the Dark House: Text and Context in Faulkner*. Jackson: University Press of Mississippi, 1996.

Porter, Katherine Anne. *Letters of Katherine Anne Porter*. Edited by Isabel Bayley. New York: Atlantic Monthly Press, 1990.

———. *Ship of Fools*. New York: Little, Brown, 1962.

Poteet, William Mark. *Gay Men in Modern Southern Literature: Ritual, Initiation, and the Construction of Masculinity*. New York: Peter Lang, 2006.

Potts, James B., III. "The Shade of Faulkner's Horse: Cavalier Heroism and Archetypal Immortality in Barry Hannah's Postmodern South." In Bone, *Perspectives on Barry Hannah*, 65–84.

Powhatan, Rose. "Surviving Document Genocide." In Hobson, McAdams, and Walkiewicz, *People Who Stayed*, 23–28.

Prager, Jeffrey, Douglas Longshore, and Melvin Seeman, eds. *School Desegregation Research: New Directions in Situational Analysis*. New York: Plenum Press, 1986.

Prashad, Vijay. *The Darker Nations: A People's History of the Third World*. New York: New Press, 2007.

———. *The Poorer Nations: A Possible History of the Global South*. New York: Verso, 2013.

Pugh, Tison. *Queer Chivalry: Medievalism and the Myth of White Masculinity in Southern Literature*. Baton Rouge: Louisiana State University Press, 2013.

Putin, Vladimir V. "A Plea for Caution from Russia." *New York Times*, September 11, 2013. Accessed January 7, 2014. http://www.nytimes.com/2013/09/12/opinion/putin-plea-for-caution-from-russia-on-syria.html.

"Quar." In *Smokey Mountain Voices: A Lexicon of Southern Appalachian Speech*, edited by Harold F. Farwell, Jr., and J. Karl Nicholas, 130. Lexington: University Press of Kentucky, 1993.

Raboteau, Albert J. *Slave Religion: The Invisible Institution in the Antebellum South*. New York: Oxford University Press, 1978.

Radway, Janice A. *Reading the Romance: Women, Patriarchy and Popular Literature*. Chapel Hill: University of North Carolina Press, 1991.

———. "What's in a Name? Presidential Address to the American Studies Association, 20 November 1998." *American Quarterly* 51, no. 1 (March 1999): 1–32.

Ramírez, Mari Carmen, ed. *El Taller Torres-Garcia: The School of the South and Its Legacy.* Austin: University of Texas Press, 1992.

Ramírez Berg, Charles. *Latino Images in Film: Stereotypes, Subversion, and Resistance.* Austin: University of Texas Press, 2002.

Rampersad, Arnold. *The Life of Langston Hughes.* Vol. 1, *1902–1941, I, Too, Sing America.* New York: Oxford University Press, 2002.

Randall, Alice. *The Wind Done Gone.* Boston: Houghton Mifflin, 2001.

Ransom, John Crowe. "Reconstructed but Unregenerate." In Twelve Southerners, *I'll Take My Stand,* 1–27.

Raper, Arthur. "Gullies and What They Mean." *Social Forces* 16, no. 2 (1937): 201–7.

Raper, Julius Rowan. "Inventing Modern Southern Fiction: A Postmodern View." *Southern Literary Journal* 22, no. 2 (Spring 1990): 3–18.

Rawlings, Marjorie Kinnan. *Cross Creek.* New York: Scribner's, 1942.

Ray, Douglass, ed. *The Queer South: LGBTQ Writers on the American South.* Little Rock: Sibling Rivalry Press, 2014.

Rediker, Marcus. *The Slave Ship: A Human History.* New York: Penguin, 2007.

Reed, Ishmael. ¬*Flight to Canada.* New York: Random House, 1976.

———. *Mumbo Jumbo.* 1972. New York: Scribner's, 1996.

Reed, John Shelton. *My Tears Spoiled My Aim: Reflections on Southern Culture.* Columbia: University of Missouri Press, 1993.

———. *One South: An Ethnic Approach to Regional Culture.* Baton Rouge: Louisiana State University Press, 1982.

———. "On Narrative and Sociology." *Social Forces* 68, no. 1 (1989): 1–14.

———. *Southerners: The Social Psychology of Sectionalism.* Chapel Hill: University of North Carolina Press, 1983.

Reed, T. V. "Toward an Environmental Justice Ecocriticism." In Adamson, Evans, and Stein, *Environmental Justice Reader,* 145–62.

Richards, Gary. *Lovers and Beloveds: Sexual Otherness in Southern Fiction, 1936–1961.* Baton Rouge: Louisiana State University Press, 2005.

Richardson, Riché. *Black Masculinity and the U.S. South: From Uncle Tom to Gangsta.* Athens: University of Georgia Press, 2007.

Rieger, Christopher. *Clear-Cutting Eden: Ecology and the Pastoral in Southern Literature.* Birmingham: University of Alabama Press, 2009.

Ring, Natalie J. *The Problem South: Region, Empire, and the New Liberal State, 1880–1930.* Athens: University of Georgia Press, 2012.

Roach, Joseph. *Cities of the Dead: Circum-Atlantic Performance.* New York: Columbia University Press, 1996.

Robin, Corey. "Conservatism and Counterrevolution." *Raritan* 30, no. 1 (Summer 2010): 1–17.

———. *The Reactionary Mind: Conservatism from Edmund Burke to Sarah Palin.* New York: Oxford University Press, 2011.

Robinson, Zandria F. "Crunk and Hip-Hop Culture." In *The New Encyclopedia of Southern Culture,* vol. 15, *Urbanization,* edited by Wanda Rushing, 41–44. Chapel Hill: University of North Carolina Press, 2010.

———. *This Ain't Chicago: Race, Class and Regional Identity in the Post-Soul South.* Chapel Hill: University of North Carolina Press, 2014.

Rodman, Selden. "All American." *New York Times,* July 10, 1966. Accessed June 5, 2006. NYT ProQuest.

Rodríguez, Clara E. Introduction to *Latin Looks: Images of Latinas and Latinos in the U.S. Media*, edited by Clara E. Rodríguez, 1–12. Boulder, Colo.: Westview Press, 1997.

Rodriguez, Richard. *Brown: The Last Discovery of America*. New York: Viking, 2002.

Romine, Scott. *The Narrative Forms of Southern Community*. Baton Rouge: Louisiana State University Press, 1999.

———. *The Real South: Southern Narrative in the Age of Cultural Reproduction*. Baton Rouge: Louisiana State University Press, 2008.

———. "Where Is Southern Literature? The Practice of Place in a Postsouthern Age." In Jones and Monteith, *South to a New Place*, 23–43.

Roscigno, Vincent J., and William F. Danaher. *The Voice of Southern Labor: Radio, Music, and Textile Strikes, 1929–1934*. Minneapolis: University of Minnesota Press, 2004.

Rose, Wickliffe. Letter to Frederick T. Gates, June 28, 1911. International Health Board, RG 5, series 200, subseries 252, box 19, folder 113, Rockefeller Archive Center, Sleepy Hollow, New York.

Rosen, Christine. *My Fundamentalist Education: A Memoir of a Divine Girlhood*. New York: PublicAffairs, 2005.

Ross, Charlotte. "Industrialization and the Attrition of Mountain Characteristics." In *Appalachia Inside Out*, vol. 1, edited by Robert J. Higgs, Ambrose N. Manning, and Jim Wayne Miller, 201–13. Knoxville: University of Tennessee Press, 1995.

Rothman, Adam. "Lafcadio Hearn in New Orleans and the Caribbean." *Atlantic Studies* 5 (August 2008): 265–83.

Rowe, John Carlos, ed. *Post-Nationalist American Studies*. Berkeley: University of California Press, 2000.

Rubin, Louis D., Jr. Introduction to Twelve Southerners, *I'll Take My Stand*, xxxi–xxxii.

———, ed. *The Literary South*. New York: John Wiley and Sons, 1979.

———. "Southern Literature and Southern Society: Notes on a Clouded Relationship." In Rubin and Holman, *Southern Literary Study*, 3–20.

Rubin, Louis D., Jr., and C. Hugh Holman. Appendix. In Rubin and Holman, *Southern Literary Study*, 227–35.

———. Preface to Rubin and Holman, *Southern Literary Study*, xi–xii.

———, eds. *Southern Literary Study: Problems and Possibilities*. Chapel Hill: University of North Carolina Press, 1975.

Rubin, Louis D. Jr., and Robert D. Jacobs, eds. *Southern Renascence: The Literature of the Modern South*. Baltimore: Johns Hopkins Press, 1953.

Rucker, Philip. "Romney Questions Obama's Commitment to 'American Exceptionalism.'" *Washington Post*, Post Politics blog, March 31, 2012. Accessed January 7, 2014. http ://www.washingtonpost.com/blogs/post-politics/post/romney-questions-obama-commit-ment-to-american-exceptionalism/2012/03/31/gIQA7xKUnS_blog.html.

Rudel, Tom, and Fu Chun. "A Requiem for the Southern Regionalists: Reforestation in the South and the Uses of Regional Social Science." *Social Science Quarterly* 77, no. 4 (1996): 804–20.

Rushing, Wanda. *Memphis and the Paradox of Place: Globalization in the American South*. Chapel Hill: University of North Carolina Press, 2009.

Russell, Heather. *Legba's Crossing: Narratology in the African Atlantic*. Athens: University of Georgia Press, 2009.

Sadowski-Smith, Claudia, and Claire Fox. "Theorizing the Hemisphere: Inter-Americas Work at the Intersection of American, Canadian, and Latin American Studies." *Comparative American Studies* 2, no. 1 (Spring 2004): 5–38.

391

Said, Edward. *Culture and Imperialism.* New York: Vintage, 1994.

——. *Nationalism, Colonialism, and Literature.* Minneapolis: University of Minnesota Press, 1990.

——. *Orientalism.* New York: Vintage, 1979.

Saldívar-Hull, Sonia. *Feminism on the Border: Chicana Gender Politics and Literature.* Berkeley: University of California Press, 2000.

Sally Hemings: An American Scandal. Directed by Charles Haid. CBS, 2000.

Saloy, Mona Lisa. *Red Beans and Ricely Yours.* Kirksville, Mo.: Truman State University Press, 2005.

Salvaggio, Ruth. *Hearing Sappho in New Orleans: The Call of Poetry from Congo Square to the Ninth Ward.* Baton Rouge: Louisiana State University Press, 2012.

Santner, Eric L. "History beyond the Pleasure Principle: Some Thoughts on the Representation of Trauma." In *Probing the Limits of Representation: Nazism and the "Final Solution,"* edited by Saul Friedlander, 143–54. Cambridge, Mass.: Harvard University Press, 1992.

——. *Stranded Objects: Mourning, Memory, and Film in Postwar Germany.* Ithaca, N.Y.: Cornell University Press, 1993.

Saporito, Salvatore, and Sohoni Deenesh. "Mapping Educational Inequality: Concentrations of Poverty among Poor and Minority Students in Public Schools." *Social Forces* 85, no. 3 (2007): 1227–53.

Schmidt, Peter. *Sitting in Darkness: New South Fiction, Education, and the Rise of Jim Crow Colonialism, 1865–1920.* Jackson: University of Mississippi Press, 2008.

Schulman, Bruce J. *From Cotton Belt to Sunbelt: Federal Policy, Economic Development, and the Transformation of the South, 1938–1980.* New York: Oxford University Press, 1991.

Schweiger, Beth Barton, and Donald G. Mathews, eds. *Religion in the American South: Protestants and Others in History and Culture.* Chapel Hill: University of North Carolina Press, 2004.

Sears, James T. *Lonely Hunters: An Oral History of Lesbian and Gay Southern Life, 1948–1969.* Boulder, Colo.: Westview Press, 1997.

Sedgwick, Eve Kosofsky. *Tendencies.* Durham, N.C.: Duke University Press, 1993.

Seed, Patricia. *Ceremonies of Possession in Europe's Conquest of the New World, 1492–1640.* Cambridge: Cambridge University Press, 1995.

Seigel, Micol. "Beyond Compare: Comparative Method after the Transnational Turn." *Radical History Review* 91 (2005): 62–90.

Sharky's Machine. Directed by Burt Reynolds. Orion Pictures, 1981. DVD.

Shearer, Cynthia. *The Celestial Jukebox: A Novel.* Washington, D.C.: Shoemaker and Hoard, 2005.

Sheller, Mimi. "Creolization in Discourses of Global Culture." In *Uprootings/Regroundings: Questions of Home and Migration,* edited by Sara Ahmed and Claudia Castañeda, 273–94. Oxford: Berg, 2004.

Sherman's March. Directed by Ross McElwee. Cinedigm, 1986. DVD.

Shewmaker, Kenneth E., ed. *Daniel Webster: "The Complete Man."* Hanover, N.H.: University Press of New England, 1990.

Shimakawa, Karen. *National Abjection: The Asian American Body Onstage.* Durham, N.C.: Duke University Press, 2002.

Shiva, Vandana. *Monocultures of the Mind: Perspectives on Biodiversity and Biotechnology.* London: Zed Books, 1993.

Shoemaker, Nancy. *A Strange Likeness: Becoming Red and White in Eighteenth-Century North America*. New York: Oxford University Press, 2004.

"Shrimp and Grits." Anson Mills. Accessed March 11, 2013. http://ansonmills.com/recipes/459?recipes_by=meal.

Sibley, David. *Geographies of Exclusion: Society and Difference in the West*. New York: Routledge, 1995.

Silko, Leslie Marmon. *Ceremony*. New York: Penguin Books, 1977.

Simmons, Philip E. "Toward the Postmodern Historical Imagination: Mass Culture in Walker Percy's *The Moviegoer* and Nicholson Baker's *The Mezzanine*." *Contemporary Literature* 33, no. 4 (1992): 601–24.

Simms, William Gilmore. *The Yemassee: A Romance of Carolina*. 1835. Boston: Houghton Mifflin, 1961.

Simpson, Lewis P. *The Brazen Face of History: Studies in the Literary Consciousness in America*. Baton Rouge: Louisiana State University Press, 1980.

Singal, Daniel Joseph. *The War Within: From Victorian to Modernist Thought in the South, 1919–1945*. Chapel Hill: University of North Carolina Press, 1982.

Skidmore, Thomas E., and Peter H. Smith, eds. *Modern Latin America*. 5th ed. New York: Oxford University Press, 2001.

Slacker. Directed by Richard Linklater. Orion Classics, 1991. DVD.

Smethurst, James. *The African American Roots of Modernism: From Reconstruction to the Harlem Renaissance*. Chapel Hill: University of North Carolina Press, 2011.

Smith, Caleb. *The Prison and the American Imagination*. New Haven, Conn.: Yale University Press, 2011.

Smith, Donna Jo. "Queering the South: Constructions of Southern/Queer Identity." In John Howard, *Carryin' On in the Lesbian and Gay South*, 370–86.

Smith, Jon. *Finding Purple America: The South and the Future of American Cultural Studies*. Athens: University of Georgia Press, 2013.

———. "Hot Bodies and 'Barbaric Tropics': The U.S. South and New World Natures." *Southern Literary Journal* 36 (Fall 2003): 104–20.

———. "Postcolonial, Black, and Nobody's Margin: The U.S. South and New World Studies." *American Literary History* 16, no. 1 (2004): 144–61.

———. Review of *The Postsouthern Sense of Place in Contemporary Fiction*, by Martyn Bone. *Mississippi Quarterly* 59, no. 2 (2006): 369–73.

———. "Toward a Post-Postpolitical Southern Studies: On the Limits of the 'Creating and Consuming' Paradigm." In Bone, Ward, and Link, *Creating and Consuming the American South*, 72–94.

Smith, Jon, and Deborah Cohn. "Introduction: Uncanny Hybridities." In Smith and Cohn, *Look Away!*, 1–19.

———, eds. *Look Away! The U.S. South in New World Studies*. Durham, N.C.: Duke University Press, 2004.

Smith, Linda Tuwahai. *Decolonizing Methodologies: Research and Indigenous Peoples*. London: Zed Books, 1999.

Soja, Edward. *Postmodern Geographies: The Reassertion of Space in Critical Social Theory*. London: Verso, 1989.

Speir, Jerry. "Of Novels and the Novelist: An Interview with Ellen Douglas." *University of Mississippi Studies in English* 5 (1984–87): 236.

Spillers, Hortense. "Changing the Letter: The Yokes, the Jokes of Discourse, or, Mrs. Stowe, Mr. Reed." In *Uncle Tom's Cabin*, by Harriet Beecher Stowe, edited by Elizabeth Ammons, 542–68. New York: W. W. Norton, 1994.

Stack, Carol. *Call to Home: African Americans Reclaim the Rural South*. New York: Basic Books, 1996.

Stampp, Kenneth M. *The Peculiar Institution: Slavery in the Antebellum South*. New York: Knopf, 1967.

Stanonis, Anthony J., ed. *Dixie Emporium: Tourism, Foodways, and Consumer Culture in the American South*. Athens: University of Georgia Press, 2008.

———. "Just Like Mammy Used to Make: Foodways in the Jim Crow South." In Stanonis, *Dixie Emporium*, 208–33.

Stecopoulos, Harilaos. *Reconstructing the World: Southern Fictions and U.S. Imperialisms, 1898–1976*. Ithaca, N.Y.: Cornell University Press, 2008.

Stepan, Nancy Leys. *Picturing Tropical Nature*. Ithaca, N.Y.: Cornell University Press, 2001.

Stewart, Charles, ed. *Creolization: History, Ethnography, Theory*. Walnut Creek, Calif.: Left Coast Press, 2007.

Stewart, Jacqueline Najuma. *Migrating to the Movies: Cinema and Black Urban Modernity*. Berkeley: University of California Press, 2005.

Still, James. *River of Earth*. 1940. Lexington: University of Kentucky Press, 1978.

Stockett, Kathryn. *The Help*. New York: Berkeley Books, 2009.

Stockton, Kathryn Bond. *The Queer Child, or, Growing Sideways in the Twentieth Century*. Durham, N.C.: Duke University Press, 2009.

Stoneback, H. R. "Rivers of Earth and Troublesome Creeks: The Agrarianism of James Still." In *James Still: Critical Essays on the Dean of Appalachian Literature*, edited by Ted Olson and Kathy Olson, 7–20. Jefferson, N.C.: McFarland, 2007.

Stowe, Harriet Beecher. *Uncle Tom's Cabin*. Edited by Elizabeth Ammons. New York: W. W. Norton: 2010.

Suarez, Ernest. "Writing Southern Literary History." *Southern Review* 36 (2000): 881–92.

Suleri, Sara. *The Rhetoric of English India*. Chicago: University of Chicago Press, 1992.

Sullivan, Andrew. *The Conservative Soul: Fundamentalism, Freedom, and the Future of the Right*. New York: HarperPerennial, 2007.

Sullivan, John Jeremiah. "Upon This Rock." *GQ*, February 2004. Accessed June 13, 2013. http://www.gq.com/entertainment/music/200401/rock-music-jesus.

Sullivan, M. Nell. "Persons in Pieces: Races and Aphanisis in *Light in August*." *Mississippi Quarterly* 49, no. 3 (1996): 497–517.

Sundquist, Eric J. *To Wake the Nations: Race in the Making of American Literature*. Cambridge, Mass.: Harvard University Press, 1993.

Sutter, Paul S., and Christopher J. Manganiello, eds. *Environmental History and the American South: A Reader*. Athens: University of Georgia Press, 2009.

Sutton, Matthew Avery. *Aimee Semple McPherson and the Resurrection of Christian America*. Cambridge, Mass.: Harvard University Press, 2007.

Swan, John D., MD. "Tropical Diseases and Health in the United States." *Southern Medical Journal* 4 (July 1911): 400.

Sweet, Timothy. *American Georgics: Economy and Environment in Early American Literature*. Philadelphia: University of Pennsylvania Press, 2002.

Szczesiul, Anthony. "Re-mapping Southern Hospitality: Discourse, Ethics, Politics." *European Journal of American Culture* 26, no. 2 (2007): 127–41.

394

Tarr, Rodger. "Eden Revisited: Florida and the American Literary Imagination." *Mississippi Quarterly* 46 (Fall 1993): 661–66.

Tarter, Michele Lise, and Richard Bell, eds. *Buried Lives: Incarcerated in Early America*. Athens: University of Georgia Press, 2012.

Taylor, Diana. *The Archive and the Repertoire: Performing Cultural Memory in the Americas*. Durham, N.C.: Duke University Press, 2003.

Taylor, Melanie Benson. *Reconstructing the Native South: American Indian Literature and the Lost Cause*. Athens: University of Georgia Press, 2011.

Taylor, William R. *Cavalier and Yankee: The Old South and American National Character*. 1961. New York: Oxford University Press, 1993.

Thompson, Brock. *The Un-Natural State: Arkansas and the Queer South*. Fayetteville: University of Arkansas Press, 2010.

Thompson, Edgar T. "The Climatic Theory of the Plantation." *Agricultural History* 15 (January 1941): 49–60.

Thompson, Robert Farris. *Flash of the Spirit: African and Afro-American Art and Philosophy*. New York: Vintage, 1983.

Tindall, George Brown. *The Emergence of the New South, 1913–1945*. Baton Rouge: Louisiana State University Press, 1967.

Titus, Mary. *The Ambivalent Art of Katherine Anne Porter*. Athens: University of Georgia Press, 2005.

Todorov, Tzvetan. "'Race,' Writing, and Culture." Translated by Loulou Mack. *Critical Inquiry* 13, no. 1 (1986): 171–81.

Toomer, Jean. "The *Cane* Years." In *The Wayward and the Seeking: A Collection of Writings by Jean Toomer*, edited by Darwin T. Turner, 116–27. Washington, D.C.: Howard University Press, 1980.

Tocqueville, Alexis de, and Gustave de Beaumont. *On the Penitentiary System in the United States and Its Application in France*. Carbondale: Southern Illinois University Press, 1979.

Tocqueville, Alexis de, and Charles Henri Maurice Clérel. *Democracy in America* [1835, 1840]. 2 vols. New York: Schocken Books, 1961.

Tourgée, Albion. *Bricks without Straw: A Novel*. New York: Fords, Howard, and Hulbert, 1880.

Trefzer, Annette. *Disturbing Indians: The Archaeology of Southern Fiction*. Tuscaloosa: University of Alabama Press, 2007.

Trinh T. Minh-ha. *Woman, Native, Other: Writing Postcoloniality and Feminism*. Bloomington: Indiana University Press, 1989.

Trouillot, Michel-Rolph. "Culture on the Edges: Caribbean Creolization in Historical Context." In *From the Margins: Historical Anthropology and Its Futures*, edited by Brian Keith Axel, 189–210. Durham, N.C.: Duke University Press, 2002.

———. *Silencing the Past: Power and the Production of History*. Boston: Beacon Press, 1995.

Tucker, Nathaniel Beverly. *A Key to the Disunion Conspiracy*. New York: Rudd and Carleton, 1861.

———. *The Partisan Leader*. Edited by Carl Bridenbaugh. New York: Knopf, 1933.

———. *The Partisan Leader: A Novel and an Apocalypse of the Origin and Struggles of the Southern Confederacy*. Edited by Thomas A. Ware. Richmond: West and Johnston, 1862.

———. *The Partisan Leader; a Key to the Disunion Conspiracy*. Upper Saddle River: Gregg Press, 1968.

———. *The Partisan Leader; a Tale of the Future*. [Washington, D.C.: Duff Green]: 1856 [1836].

———. *The Partisan Leader; a Tale of the Future.* Edited by C. Hugh Holman. Chapel Hill: University of North Carolina Press, 1971.

Turner, Frederick Jackson. "The Significance of the Frontier in American History" [1893]. In *History, Frontier, and Section: Three Essays by Frederick Jackson Turner*, edited by Martin Ridge, 59–91. Albuquerque: University of New Mexico Press, 1993.

Turner, Patricia A. "Dangerous White Stereotypes." *New York Times*, August 28, 2011. Accessed June 7, 2013. http://www.nytimes.com/2011/08/29/opinion/dangerous-white-stereotypes.html.

Twain, Mark. "The United States of Lyncherdom." In *Europe and Elsewhere*, vol. 20 of *The Complete Works of Mark Twain*, 239–49. New York: Harper and Brothers, 1923.

Twelve Southerners. *I'll Take My Stand: The South and the Agrarian Tradition.* 1930. Baton Rouge: Louisiana State University Press, 1977.

———. "Introduction: A Statement of Principles." In Twelve Southerners, *I'll Take My Stand*, xxxvii–xlviii.

Valente, Joseph. *Quare Joyce.* Ann Arbor: University of Michigan Press, 1998.

Vance, Rupert. *Human Geography of the South: A Study in Regional Resources and Human Adequacy.* Chapel Hill: University of North Carolina Press, 1932.

Von Eschen, Penny M. *Race against Empire: Black Americans and Anticolonialism, 1937–1957.* Ithaca, N.Y.: Cornell University Press, 1997.

———. *Satchmo Blows Up the World: Jazz Ambassadors Play the Cold War.* Cambridge, Mass.: Harvard University Press, 2004.

Wacker, Grant. *Heaven Below: Early Pentecostals and American Culture.* Cambridge, Mass.: Harvard University Press, 2003.

Walcott, Derek. *The Arkansas Testament.* New York: Farrar, Straus and Giroux, 1987.

Walker, David. *Walker's Appeal, in Four Articles.* Boston, 1830.

Walker, Jonathan. *Trial and Imprisonment of Jonathan Walker, at Pensacola, Florida, for Aiding Slaves to Escape from Bondage.* Boston, 1845.

Walker, Kara. *Kara Walker: Pictures from Another Time.* Edited by Annette Dixon. Ann Arbor: University of Michigan Museum of Art, 2002.

Wall, Cheryl. Afterword to *Representing Segregation: Toward an Aesthetics of Living Jim Crow, and Other Forms of Racial Division*, edited by Brian Norman and Piper Kendrix Williams, 256–68. Albany: State University of New York Press, 2010.

Wallerstein, Immanuel. *The Modern World-System.* Vol. 2, *Mercantilism and the Consolidation of the European World-Economy, 1600–1750.* Berkeley: University of California Press, 2011.

———. "What Can One Mean by Southern Culture?" In *The Evolution of Southern Culture*, edited by Numan V. Bartley, 1–13. Athens: University of Georgia Press, 1988.

Ward, Brian, Martyn Bone, and William A. Link, eds. *The American South and the Atlantic World.* Gainesville: University Press of Florida, 2013.

Ward, Jerry W., Jr. Preface to Killens and Ward, *Black Southern Voices*, 5–9.

Ward, Jesmyn. *Salvage the Bones.* New York: Bloomsbury, 2011.

Warner, Michael. *Letters of the Republic: Publication and the Public Sphere in Eighteenth-Century America.* Cambridge, Mass.: Harvard University Press, 1990.

———. "Tongues Untied: Memoirs of a Pentecostal Boyhood." *Curiouser* (2004): 215–24.

Warren, Kenneth W. *Black and White Strangers: Race and American Literary Realism.* Chicago: University of Chicago Press, 1995.

———. *What Was African American Literature?* Cambridge, Mass.: Harvard University Press, 2011.

Washington, Mary Helen. "'Disturbing the Peace': What Happens to American Studies If You Put African American Studies at the Center?" *American Quarterly* 50, no. 1 (1998): 1–23.

Watkins, Floyd C. *The Death of Art: Black and White in the Recent Southern Novel.* Athens: University of Georgia Press, 1970.

Watson, Jay. "Economics of a Cracker Landscape: Poverty as an Environmental Issue in Two Southern Writers." *Mississippi Quarterly* 55, no. 4 (Fall 2002): 497–513.

———. "Mapping Out a Postsouthern Cinema: Three Contemporary Films." In Barker and McKee, *American Cinema and the Southern Imaginary*, 219–52.

———. "Uncovering the Body, Discovering Ideology: Segregation and Sexual Anxiety in Lillian Smith's *Killers of the Dream.*" *American Quarterly* 49, no. 3 (1997): 470–503.

Watts, Trent A. *One Homogeneous People: Narratives of White Southern Identity 1890–1920.* Knoxville: University of Tennessee Press, 2010.

Weaver, Hilary N. "Indigenous Identity: What Is It, and Who *Really* Has It?" In Lobo, Talbot, and Morris, *Native American Voices*, 28–36.

Weaver, Jace. *The Red Atlantic: American Indigenes and the Making of the Modern World.* Chapel Hill: University of North Carolina Press, 2014.

Welch, Wilson H. "A People Who Would Not Be Driven." 1898. In Hobson, McAdams, and Walkiewicz, *People Who Stayed*, 77–78.

Wells, Ida B. *A Red Record: Tabulated Statistics and Alleged Causes of Lynchings in the United States, 1892–1893–1894.* Chicago: 1895.

Wells, Jeremy. *Romances of the White Man's Burden: Race, Empire, and the Plantation in American Literature, 1880–1936.* Nashville: Vanderbilt University Press, 2011.

Welty, Eudora. "Must the Novelist Crusade?" In *The Eye of the Story: Selected Essays and Reviews*, 146–58. New York: Vintage Books, 1979.

Wesling, Meg. *Empire's Proxy: American Literature and U.S. Imperialism in the Philippines.* New York: New York University Press, 2011.

Westerberg, Carl F. "Revolt of the Tropics." *North American Review* 231 (1931): 257–63.

"What We Do." Anson Mills. Accessed March 11, 2013. http://ansonmills.com /what_we_do_pages.

When We Were Kings. Directed by Leon Gast and Taylor Hackford. Polygram, 1996. DVD.

Whisnant, David E. *All That Is Native and Fine: The Politics of Culture in an American Region.* Chapel Hill: University of North Carolina Press, 1995.

White, Newman Ivey. *American Negro Folk-Songs.* Cambridge, Mass.: Harvard University Press, 1928.

———. "Racial Traits in the Negro Song." *Sewanee Review* 28, no. 3 (July 1920): 396–404.

Whitlock, Reta Ugena. *Queer South Rising: Voices of a Contested Place.* Charlotte, N.C.: Information Age, 2013.

Williams, Raymond. *The Country and the City.* New York: Oxford University Press, 1973.

———. *Keywords.* New ed. New York: Oxford University Press, 1983.

———. *Writing in Society.* London: Verso, 1983.

Williams, Robert F. *Negroes with Guns.* New York: Marzani and Munsell, 1962.

Williams, William Appleman. *Empire as a Way of Life.* New York: Ig Press, 2006.

Winders, Jamie. "Nashville's New 'Sonido': Latino Migration and the Changing Politics of Race." In *New Faces in New Places: The Changing Geography of American Immigration*, edited by Doug Massey, 249–73. New York: Russell Sage Foundation, 2008.

Winthrop, John. "A Model of Christian Charity" [1630]. In *The Journal of John Winthrop, 1630–1649*, edited by Richard S. Dunn and Laetitia Yeandle, 1–12. Cambridge, Mass.: Harvard University Press, 1996.

Wolfe, Tom. *A Man in Full*. London: Jonathan Cape, 1998.

Wood, Karenne. "Virginia Indians: Our Story." In *The Virginia Indian Heritage Trail*, 3rd ed., edited by Karenne Wood, 12–23. Charlottesville: Virginia Foundation for the Humanities, 2009.

Woodward, C. Vann. *The Burden of Southern History*. 1960. 3rd ed. Baton Rouge: Louisiana State University Press, 1993.

———. *Origins of the New South, 1877–1913*. Baton Rouge: Louisiana State University Press, 1972.

———. *The Strange Career of Jim Crow*. 1955. 3rd ed. New York: Oxford University Press, 1974.

Worster, Donald. *The Wealth of Nature: Environmental History and the Ecological Imagination*. Oxford: Oxford University Press, 1993.

Wright, Gavin. *Old South, New South: Revolutions in the Southern Economy since the Civil War*. Baton Rouge: Louisiana State University Press, 2006.

Wright, Richard. *Black Power: A Record of Reactions in a Land of Pathos*. New York: Harper and Brothers, 1954.

———. *The Colour Curtain*. London: D. Dobson, 1956.

———. *Uncle Tom's Children*. 1938. New York: Harper Perennial, 2008.

Wyatt-Brown, Bertram. *Southern Honor: Ethics and Behavior in the Old South*. London: Oxford University Press, 1983.

Yaeger, Patricia. *Dirt and Desire: Reconstructing Southern Women's Writing, 1930–1990*. Chicago: University of Chicago Press, 2000.

———. "Southern Orientalism: Flannery O'Connor's Cosmopolis." *Mississippi Quarterly* 56, no. 4 (2003): 491–510.

Young, Cynthia A. *Soul Power: Culture, Radicalism, and the Making of a U.S. Third World Left*. Durham, N.C.: Duke University Press, 2006.

Young, Stephen Flinn. "Post-Southernism: The Southern Sensibility in Postmodern Sculpture." *Southern Quarterly* 27, no. 1 (Fall 1989): 41–60.

Yuhl, Stephanie E. *A Golden Haze of Memory: The Making of Historic Charleston*. Chapel Hill: University of North Carolina Press, 2005.

Zibart, Eve. Review of "Jefferson in Paris." *Washington Post*, April 7, 1995. Accessed June 12, 2013. http://www.washingtonpost.com/wp-srv/style/longterm/movies/videos/jeffersonin parispg13zibart_c01065.htm.

Zimmerman, Andrew. *Alabama in Africa: Booker T. Washington, the German Empire, and the Globalization of the New South*. Princeton, N.J.: Princeton University Press, 2010.

Žižek, Slavoj. "Melancholy and the Act." In *Did Somebody Say Totalitarianism? Five Interventions in the (Mis)use of a Notion*, 141–89. New York: Verso, 2001.

———. *The Sublime Object of Ideology*. New York: Verso, 1997.

Contributors

ERIC GARY ANDERSON is an associate professor of English at George Mason University, where he teaches Native and southern studies. In addition to *American Indian Literature and the Southwest: Contexts and Dispositions* (Texas, 1999), he has published more than twenty essays in edited volumes and journals including *PMLA*, *American Literary History*, *Early American Literature*, *Southern Spaces*, *Mississippi Quarterly*, and *South to a New Place*. With Taylor Hagood and Daniel Cross Turner, he coedited the collection *Undead Souths: The Gothic and Beyond in Southern Literature and Culture* (LSU, 2015).

TED ATKINSON is an associate professor of English at Mississippi State University and editor of *Mississippi Quarterly*. Atkinson is the author of *Faulkner and the Great Depression: Aesthetics, Ideology, and Cultural Politics* (Georgia, 2006). He has published essays in *Southern Literary Journal*, *Faulkner Journal*, *Journal of American Studies*, *Mississippi Quarterly*, in addition to other journals and essay collections.

HOUSTON A. BAKER JR. is Distinguished University Professor and a professor of English and African American and African diaspora studies at Vanderbilt University. He has served as president of the Modern Language Association of America and is the author of articles, books, and essays devoted to African American literary criticism and theory. His book *Betrayal: How Black Intellectuals Have Abandoned the Ideals of the Civil Rights Era* received an American Book Award for 2009. His recent coedited collection of essays is titled *The Trouble with Post-Blackness* (Columbia, 2015).

MICHAEL P. BIBLER is an associate professor of southern studies at Louisiana State University. He is author of *Cotton's Queer Relations: Same-Sex Intimacy and the Literature of the Southern Plantation, 1936–1968* (Virginia, 2009) and coeditor of *Just below South: Intercultural Performance in the Caribbean and the U.S. South* (Virginia, 2007) and of the scholarly edition of Arna Bontemps's novel *Drums at Dusk* (LSU, 2009).

MARTYN BONE is an associate professor of American literature at the University of Copenhagen. He is the author of *The Postsouthern Sense of Place in Contemporary Fiction* (LSU, 2005), the editor of *Perspectives on Barry Hannah* (Mississippi, 2007), and a coeditor of *The American South in the Atlantic World* (Florida, 2013) and *Creating Citizenship in the Nineteenth-Century South* (Florida, 2013). His articles have appeared in *American Literature*, *CR: New Centennial Review*, *Journal of American Studies*, and elsewhere.

ANNA BRICKHOUSE is a professor of English at the University of Virginia and chair of the American Studies Program. She is the author of *Transamerican Literary Relations and the Nineteenth-Century Public Sphere* (Cambridge, 2005) and of *The Unsettlement of America: Translation, Interpretation, and the Story of Don Luis de Velasco, 1560–1945* (Oxford, 2014), which was awarded the James Russell Lowell Prize of the Modern Language Association.

JAYNA BROWN is an associate professor who teaches African American literature, culture, and performance in the English and ethnic studies departments at the University of California, Riverside. She is the author of the award-winning book *Babylon Girls: Black Women Performers and the Shaping of the Modern* (Duke, 2008). She has also published on black women, global pop, and postpunk music in Britain. Her work can be found in *Social Text, Journal for the Study of Popular Music*, and *Women and Performance*. Her current book project is titled "Black Utopias: Speculative Life and the Music of Other Worlds."

KEITH CARTWRIGHT is a professor of English at the University of North Florida. He is the author of *Reading Africa into American Literature: Epics, Fables, Gothic Tales* (Kentucky, 2002), and *Sacral Grooves, Limbo Gateways: Travels in Deep Southern Time, Circum-Caribbean Space, Afro-creole Authority* (Georgia, 2013).

SYLVIA SHIN HUEY CHONG is an associate professor of American studies and English and director of the Asian Pacific American Studies Minor at the University of Virginia. She is the author of *The Oriental Obscene: Violence and Racial Fantasies in the Vietnam Era* (Duke, 2011).

DEBORAH COHN is a professor of Spanish and American studies at Indiana University Bloomington, where her research focuses on inter-American literary relations and Cold War cultural diplomacy. She is the author of *The Latin American Literary Boom and U.S. Nationalism during the Cold War* (Vanderbilt, 2012) and *History and Memory in the Two Souths: Recent Southern and Spanish American Fiction* (Vanderbilt, 1999), as well as coeditor of *Look Away!: The U.S. South in New World Studies* (Duke, 2004). Her articles have appeared in journals such as *American Literature, Comparative Literature Studies, CR: The New Centennial Review, Global South, Latin American Literary Review, Latin American Research Review, Mississippi Quarterly*, and *Southern Quarterly*, as well as in several collections.

LEIGH ANNE DUCK is an associate professor of English at the University of Mississippi, where she edits the journal the *Global South*. She is the author of *The Nation's Region: Southern Modernism, Segregation, and U.S. Nationalism* (Georgia, 2006), as well as several essays on literary and visual representations of the U.S. South, often involving comparative or otherwise transnational methodologies. Her current book project is tentatively titled "Hollywood South: State, Cinema, and Societal Change."

JENNIFER RAE GREESON is an associate professor of English at the University of Virginia, where she also teaches in the American Studies Program. She is the author of *Our South: Geographic Fantasy and the Rise of National Literature* (Harvard, 2010) and editor, with Robert B. Stepto, of the Norton Critical Edition of Charles Chesnutt's *Conjure Stories* (2011). She is presently at work on a book called *American Enlightenment: The New World and Modern Western Thought.*

MATTHEW PRATT GUTERL is a professor of Africana studies and American studies at Brown University. He is the author of *Josephine Baker and the Rainbow Tribe* (Harvard, 2014), *Seeing Race in Modern America* (North Carolina, 2013), *American Mediterranean: Southern Slaveholders in the Age of Emancipation* (Harvard, 2009), and *The Color of Race in America, 1900–1940* (Harvard, 2001), which was named the best book of 2001 on race and ethnicity by the American Political Science Association. He is presently writing a biography of the queer, cosmopolitan, human rights activist Roger Casement and a book on class passing.

THOMAS F. HADDOX is a professor of English at the University of Tennessee. He is the author of *Hard Sayings: The Rhetoric of Christian Orthodoxy in Late Modern Fiction* (Ohio State, 2013) and *Fears and Fascinations: Representing Catholicism in the American South* (Fordham, 2005); and the coeditor, with Allen Dunn, of *The Limits of Literary Historicism* (Tennessee, 2011). His other publications include a guest-edited issue of the *Southern Quarterly* on "The South and the Sublime" (Spring 2011) and numerous articles and book reviews on southern literature.

BRIALLEN HOPPER is a lecturer in English at Yale and a Faculty Fellow at the University Church in Yale. Her writing on American literature and culture has appeared in the *Chronicle of Higher Education,* the *Huffington Post, Killing the Buddha, Los Angeles Review of Books,* the *New Inquiry,* the *New Republic, Religion & Politics,* and other scholarly and popular venues. She has contributed to the edited collections *American Cinema and the Southern Imaginary* and *James Baldwin: America and Beyond,* and she is working on a book on the afterlife of American Calvinism called *Total Depravity.*

COLEMAN HUTCHISON is an associate professor of English at the University of Texas at Austin, where he teaches courses in nineteenth-century U.S. literature and culture, bibliography and textual studies, and poetry and poetics. He is the author of *Apples and Ashes: Literature, Nationalism, and the Confederate States of America* (Georgia, 2012), the coauthor of *Writing about American Literature: A Guide for Students* (Norton, 2014), and the editor of *A History of American Civil War Literature* (Cambridge, 2015).

SUZANNE W. JONES is a professor of English and Tucker-Boatwright Professor of the Humanities at the University of Richmond. She is the author of *Race-Mixing: Southern Fiction since the Sixties* (Johns Hopkins, 2004) and the editor of two collections of stories, *Growing Up in the South* (Signet, 2003) and *Readings in Black and*

White (South Carolina, 2000), and three collections of essays, including *South to a New Place* with Sharon Monteith (LSU, 2002) and *Poverty and Progress in the U.S. South since 1920* with Mark Newman (VU, 2006). Her articles about southern literature have appeared in numerous journals and collections.

402 STEVEN E. KNEPPER is an assistant professor of English at the Virginia Military Institute. His essays have appeared in *Telos, Studies in American Culture,* the *Robert Frost Review* and the *Cormac McCarthy Journal.*

ERIC LOTT is a professor of English at the City University of New York Graduate Center, where he also teaches in the American Studies Program. He is the author of the multiple-award-winning book *Love and Theft: Blackface Minstrelsy and the American Working Class* (Oxford, 1993 and 2013) and *The Disappearing Liberal Intellectual* (Basic, 2006), as well as dozens of influential articles. His latest book, *Black Mirror: The Cultural Contradictions of American Racism,* will be published by Harvard University Press. He codirects the Dartmouth Futures of American Studies Institute.

JOHN T. MATTHEWS is a professor of English at Boston University, where his research concentrates on American literature, modernist studies, and literary theory. He has written several books on Faulkner, including *The Play of Faulkner's Language* (Cornell, 1982) and *William Faulkner: Seeing through the South* (Wiley-Blackwell, 2009). He has also edited *William Faulkner in Context* and *The New Cambridge Companion to William Faulkner* (both Cambridge, 2015).

CLAUDIA MILIAN is an associate professor of Spanish and Latin American studies in the Department of Romance Studies and serves as director of the Program in Latino/a Studies in the Global South at Duke University, where she works between and among the intellectual traditions of Latino/Latina studies, African American studies, southern studies, and hemispheric American studies. She is the author of *Latining America: Black-Brown Passages and the Coloring of Latino/a Studies* (Georgia, 2013).

ERICH NUNN is an associate professor of English at Auburn University, where he also teaches American studies. He is the author of *Sounding the Color Line: Music and Race in the Southern Imagination* (Georgia, 2015). His essays have appeared in *PMLA, Criticism,* the *Faulkner Journal,* the *Mark Twain Annual, Studies in American Culture,* and *Transatlantic Roots Music.*

RICHÉ RICHARDSON is an associate professor in the Africana Studies and Research Center at Cornell University. She is the author of *Black Masculinity and the U.S. South: From Uncle Tom to Gangsta* (Georgia, 2007), as well as numerous essays and reviews. Since 2005, she has served as coeditor of the New Southern Studies book series at the University of Georgia Press.

NATALIE J. RING is an associate professor of history at the University of Texas at Dallas. She is the author of *The Problem South: Region, Empire and the New Liberal State, 1880–1930* (Georgia, 2012), which was a finalist for the Best First Book Award from the Berkshire Conference on Women Historians and the TIL Award for the Most Significant Scholarly Book from the Texas Institute of Letters. She is also the coeditor of *The Folly of Jim Crow: Rethinking the Segregated South* (Texas A&M, 2012). She is currently working on a study of the Louisiana State Penitentiary (known as Angola Prison) in the twentieth century.

SCOTT ROMINE is a professor of English at the University of North Carolina at Greensboro. He is the author of *The Real South: Southern Narrative in the Age of Cultural Reproduction* (LSU, 2008) and *The Narrative Forms of Southern Community* (LSU, 1999) and is at work on a book about the literature of Reconstruction. He presently edits the Southern Literary Studies series at LSU Press, succeeding Fred Hobson and Louis D. Rubin Jr. in that role.

WANDA RUSHING is a professor of sociology at the University of Memphis. She is author of *Memphis and the Paradox of Place: Globalization in the American South* (North Carolina, 2009). She edited volume 15, *Urbanization*, of *The New Encyclopedia of Southern Culture* and has published articles on the Cold War and racial politics, empowerment zones and enterprise communities, gender and education, social capital, and educational reform.

JON SMITH is an associate professor of English at Simon Fraser University in Vancouver, British Columbia. He is the author of *Finding Purple America: The South and the Future of American Cultural Studies* (Georgia, 2013) and coeditor of *Look Away! The U.S. South in New World Studies* (Duke, 2004). His essays and essay-reviews have appeared in *American Literary History, American Literature, Modern Fiction Studies,* the *Global South,* and *Contemporary Literature,* among others, and in essay collections on topics ranging from William Faulkner to alt-country.

HARILAOS STECOPOULOS is an associate professor of English at the University of Iowa and the editor of the *Iowa Review.* He is the author of *Reconstructing the World: Southern Fictions and U.S. Imperialisms, 1898–1976* (Cornell, 2008) and the coeditor (with Michael Uebel) of *Race and the Subject of Masculinities* (Duke, 1997). A new book project, tentatively titled "Telling America's Story to the World: Literature, Internationalism, Propaganda," is nearing completion.

MELANIE BENSON TAYLOR is an associate professor of Native American studies at Dartmouth College. She is the author of *Disturbing Calculations: The Economics of Identity in Postcolonial Southern Literature, 1912–2002* (Georgia, 2008) and *Reconstructing the Native South: American Indian Literature and the Lost Cause* (Georgia, 2011). She is currently writing "Faulkner's Doom," an exploration of the Indian trope in Faulkner's fiction.

SHIRLEY ELIZABETH THOMPSON is an associate professor of American studies and African and African diaspora studies at the University of Texas at Austin. She is the author of *Exiles at Home: The Struggle to Become American in Creole New Orleans* (Harvard, 2009). She is presently researching a book titled "No More Auction Block for Me: African Americans and the Problem of Property," which traces legacies of slavery in African American encounters with property and ownership.

Index

The New Southern Studies